An Assessment of Coastal Water Resources and Watershed Conditions In and Adjacent to Canaveral National Seashore

Natural Resource Report NPS/CANA/NRR—2012/530

Kim A. Zarillo

Scientific Environmental Applications
Melbourne, FL 32934

Gary A. Zarillo, Dale I. McGinnis, Thomas V. Belanger

Department of Marine and Environmental Systems
Florida Institute of Technology
Melbourne, FL 32901

Doug H. Adams, Richard Paperno

Florida Fish and Wildlife Conservation Commission
Fish and Wildlife Research Institute
Melbourne, FL 32901

Anne C. Cox

Scientific Environmental Applications
Melbourne, FL 32934

Elizabeth A. Irlandi

Department of Marine and Environmental Systems
Florida Institute of Technology
Melbourne, FL 32901

June 2012

U.S. Department of the Interior
National Park Service
Natural Resource Stewardship and Science
Fort Collins, Colorado

The National Park Service, Natural Resource Stewardship and Science office in Fort Collins, Colorado publishes a range of reports that address natural resource topics of interest and applicability to a broad audience in the National Park Service and others in natural resource management, including scientists, conservation and environmental constituencies, and the public.

The Natural Resource Report Series is used to disseminate high-priority, current natural resource management information with managerial application. The series targets a general, diverse audience and may contain NPS policy considerations or address sensitive issues of management applicability.

All manuscripts in the series receive the appropriate level of peer review to ensure that the information is scientifically credible, technically accurate, appropriately written for the intended audience, and designed and published in a professional manner.

This report received formal peer review by subject-matter experts who were not directly involved in the collection, analysis, or reporting of the data, and whose background and expertise put them on par technically and scientifically with the authors of the information.

Views, statements, findings, conclusions, recommendations, and data in this report do not necessarily reflect views and policies of the National Park Service, U.S. Department of the Interior. Mention of trade names or commercial products does not constitute endorsement or recommendation for use by the U.S. Government.

This report is available from the Water Resources Division website (http://www.nature.nps.gov/water/nrca/coastalreports.cfm) and the Natural Resource Publications Management website (http://www.nature.nps.gov/publications/nrpm/).

Please cite this publication as:

Zarillo K. A., G. A. Zarillo, D. I. McGinnis, T. V. Belanger, D. H. Adams, R. Paperno, A. C. Cox and E. A. Irlandi. 2012. An assessment of coastal water resources and watershed conditions in and adjacent to Canaveral National Seashore Natural Resource Report NPS/CANA/NRR—2012/530. National Park Service, Fort Collins, Colorado.

NPS 639/114663, June 2012

Contents

	Page
List of Figures	vii
List of Tables	xiii
Executive Summary	xv
Resource Characterization	xv
Geological Setting and Resources	xv
Biological Resources	xvi
Assessment of Threats and Stressors	xxv
Conclusions and Recommendations	xxvii
Surface and Groundwater	xxvii
Biological Resources	xxvii
Acknowledgments	xxix
List of Abbreviations and Acronyms	xxxi
List of Abbreviations and Acronyms (continued)	xxxii
List of Abbreviations and Acronyms (continued)	xxxiii
Introduction	1
Description of Canaveral National Seashore	1
Location and Extent	1
Park History	3
Legislation and Management Objectives	4
Land Use and Land Cover	6
Public Use	7
Visitors	7
Camping	7

Contents (continued)

	Page
Fishing and Hunting	8
Boating	10
Resource Characterization	13
Climate	13
Wind and Storm Climatology	15
Physical Oceanography: Tidal Regime and Sea Levels	17
Climate Change	23
Geology	27
Geological Setting and Resources	27
Barrier Island Shoreline Changes	32
Groundwater and Aquifer Systems	34
Surficial Aquifer System	35
Soils	40
The Beach Dune and Ridge System	40
Saltwater Wetlands	40
Flatwoods, Grassy Sloughs, Isolated Freshwater Wetlands	40
Surface Water	41
Surface Water Data Sources	41
Trophic State of Surface Water	42
Physical and Chemical Properties of Mosquito Lagoon Surface Water	49
Contaminants and Pollutants	93
Trend Analysis	99
Mosquito Lagoon Hydrological and Water Quality Model	100

Contents (continued)

	Page
Biological Resources	104
Coastal Waters and Beach	104
Barrier Island Vegetation: Beach Dune Swale and Ridge System	109
Shorebirds	110
Mosquito Lagoon	112
Submerged Aquatic Vegetation	116
Animals of Mosquito Lagoon	121
Terrestrial Freshwater Systems	143
Animals of Terrestrial Freshwater Wetlands	144
Plant Communities	145
Vegetation of Wet Pine Flatwoods	146
Transitional and Embedded Wetlands	150
Forested Wetland or Hydric Hammocks	155
Prairie Hammocks – Cabbage Palm Hammocks	157
Disturbed Wetlands	161
Geographic Information System (GIS)	163
Organization of GIS Resources	163
Digital Imagery and Maps	163
Water	164
Landcover	164
Soils	165
Terrestrial Vegetation	165
Seagrasses	165

Contents (continued)

	Page
Digital Geological Map	166
Assessment of Threats and Stressors	167
Conclusions and Recommendations	199
Literature Cited	201
Appendix. Land Cover Class Descriptions and Soil Types	223

List of Figures

Page

Figure 1. Location of Canaveral National Seashore on the east coast of Florida 2

Figure 2. Population growth between 2000–2008 and expressed as percent change for Orange, Seminole, Volusia, and Brevard counties 6

Figure 3. Generalized land-use map (2004) 8

Figure 4. Number of annual visitors to Canaveral National Seashore from 1976 to 2009 9

Figure 5. Annual traffic counts to Apollo and Playalinda beaches from 1991 to 2009 9

Figure 6. Number of annual backcountry campers from 1982 to 2009 10

Figure 7. Annual number of boat registrations for Brevard, Volusia, Orange, Seminole and Indian River counties from 2005 to 2009 11

Figure 8. Boating destinations during peak season in Brevard County 12

Figure 9. Twenty-year record of precipitation for east Central Florida 14

Figure 10. Twenty-year record of air temperature for east Central Florida 14

Figure 11. Monthly mean wind speed (knots) at NOAA Buoy 41009 15

Figure 12. Monthly mean air temperature (degrees C) at NOAA Buoy 41009 16

Figure 13. Tropical cyclone tracks and number of cyclone occurrences over 103 years 17

Figure 14. Number of hurricane strikes in the South Atlantic Bight by county from 1900–2009 18

Figure 15. Predicted maximum water levels that could occur in the coastal area of Central Florida during a category 1 hurricane 19

Figure 16. Predicted maximum water levels that could occur in the coastal area of Central Florida during a category 4 hurricane 19

Figure 17. Comparison of 20-day water level records from Fernandina Beach (NOS Station 8720030) and Cape Canaveral 20

Figure 18. Non-tidal sea level records at four National Ocean Survey stations on the east Florida coast 21

vii

List of Figures (continued)

Page

Figure 19. Seasonal variation in mean sea level derived from water level records acquired between 1970–1985 at South Daytona Beach 21

Figure 20. Variation in mean seal level at Trident Pier NOS Station 8721604 in Port Canaveral in 2009. 22

Figure 21. Summary of hind cast wave heights and directions from 1980–1999 at WIS Station 431 23

Figure 22. Joint probability between significant wave height and peak direction at CHL Ponce Inlet Station DWG1INT1 from October to March 24

Figure 23. Significant wave height record at CHL gage DWG1INT1 located 2 mi (3.2 km) offshore of Ponce Inlet. 24

Figure 24. Mean sea level trends, Fernandina Beach, FL, at Station 8720030 26

Figure 25. Mean sea level trends, Mayport, FL, at Station 8720218 26

Figure 27. Exposure of the Anastasia Formation within Haulover Canal 28

Figure 28. Morphogenetic units within Canaveral National Seashore constructed from surficial sediment types in Figure 26 30

Figure 29. Relict tidal inlet flood shoal deposits included in the modern barrier island super structure in Canaveral National Seashore. 31

Figure 30. Idealized coarsening upward lithologic sequence associated with shoals situated offshore of Cape Canaveral 32

Figure 31. Historical shorelines from 1851–2000 are marked with a colored line. Black: 1999–2000, brown: 1967–1980, blue: 1923–1930, yellow: 1851–1884 34

Figure 32. Groundwater limits bounding Mosquito Lagoon 35

Figure 33. Contours of groundwater potentiometric survey and groundwater recharge/discharge areas near Canaveral National Seashore 37

Figure 34. Location of water quality stations in the Indian River Lagoon (IRL) system 43

Figure 35. Wet season mean salinity (ppt), 1990–2007, at IRLV17 and IRLML02 54

Figure 36. Dry season mean salinity (ppt), 1990–2007, at IRLV17 and IRLML02 55

viii

List of Figures (continued)

Page

Figure 37. Wet season mean water temperature (°C), 1990–2007, at IRLV17 and IRLML02 57

Figure 38. Dry season mean water temperature (°C), 1990–2007, at IRLV17 and IRLML02 58

Figure 39. Wet season mean pH from 1990–2007 at IRLV17 and IRLML02 65

Figure 40. Dry season mean pH from 1990–2007 at IRLV17 and IRLML02 66

Figure 41. Wet season mean total TKN (mg/L) from 1990–2007 at IRLV17 and IRLML02 68

Figure 42. Dry season mean TKN (mg/L) from 1990–2007 at IRLV17 and IRLML02 69

Figure 43. Wet season mean NO_x (mg/L) from 1996–2005 at IRLV17 and IRLML02 70

Figure 44. Dry season mean NO_x (mg/L) from 1996–2005 at IRLV17 and IRLML02 71

Figure 45. Trend in average annual atmospheric deposition of inorganic nitrogen in kg/ha from 1983–2008 at NADP monitoring site FL99 at KSC 74

Figure 46. Trend in average annual atmospheric deposition of ammonium (NH_4+) in kg/ha from 1983–2008 at NADP monitoring site FL99 at KSC. 74

Figure 47. Trend in average annual atmospheric deposition of nitrate (NO_3) in kg/ha from 1983–2008 at NADP monitoring site FL99 at KSC. 75

Figure 48. Wet season mean TP (mg/L) from 1990–2007 at IRLV17 and IRLML02 76

Figure 49. Dry season mean TP (mg/L) from 1990–2007 at IRLV17 and IRLML02 77

Figure 50. Wet season mean TOC (mg/L) from 1996–2007 at IRLV17 and IRLML02 79

Figure 51. Dry season mean total organic carbon (mg/L) from 1996–2007 at IRLV17 and IRLML02 80

Figure 52. Wet season mean Chlorophyll-a (μg/L) from 1990–2007 at IRLV17 and IRLML02 81

Figure 53. Dry season mean Chlorphyll-a (μg/L) from 1990–2007 at IRLV17 and IRLML02 82

Figure 54. Wet season color (pcu) from 1990–2001 at IRLV17 and IRLML02 85

List of Figures (continued)

Page

Figure 55. Dry season color (pcu) from 1990–2007 at IRLV17 and IRLML02 86

Figure 56. Wet season turbidity (NTU) from 1990–2007 at IRLV17 and IRLML02 87

Figure 57. Dry season turbidity (NTU) from 1990–2007 at IRLV17 and IRLML02 88

Figure 58. Wet season Secchi disk depth (m) from 1990–2007 at IRLV17 and IRLML02 90

Figure 59. Dry season Secchi disk depth (m) from 1990–2007 at IRLV17 and IRLML02 91

Figure 60. Wet season total suspended solids (mg/L) from 1990–2007 at IRLV17 and IRLML02 95

Figure 61. Dry season total suspended solids (mg/L) from 1990–2007 at IRLV17 and IRLML02 96

Figure 62. Model grid detail at Haulover Canal connecting the Mosquito Lagoon to the north end of the Indian River Lagoon 102

Figure 63. Comparison of measured and modeled water elevation data from the center of Haulover Canal for the 100-day calibration period 103

Figure 64. Comparison between predicted and measured dissolved oxygen values at station IRLV11 in the north section of the Mosquito Lagoon. 103

Figure 65. General features of the barrier island in Canaveral National Seashore 104

Figure 66. General features of the barrier island in Canaveral National Seashore noted are swale, back barrier, and Mosquito Lagoon 105

Figure 67. Comparison of loggerhead (*Caretta caretta*) and green (*Chelonia mydas*) sea turtle nest counts in Canaveral National Seashore from 1984–2010 106

Figure 68. Threats and stressors to sea turtle populations throughout the stages of their life cycle from nesting, hatchling, juveniles, and adults 107

Figure 69. Potential threats that can directly or indirectly affect the quantity and quality of beach and dune habitats in Canaveral National Seashore 111

Figure 70. Canaveral National Seashore (CANA) mangrove coverage in north Mosquito Lagoon 113

List of Figures (continued)

Page

Figure 71. Salt marsh coverage of Canaveral National Seashore (CANA) between Qh ridges as depicted in Figure 28 115

Figure 72. Saltwater wetland plant composition in Canaveral National Seashore 116

Figure 73. Percent coverage of seagrass in Canaveral National Seashore in 2009 (SJRWMD). 120

Figure 74. Threats and stressors to seagrasses. Blowout and scaring fragment habitat and often kill submerged vegetation 121

Figure 75. Threats and stressors to marine mammals 122

Figure 76. Blue crab landings in Brevard and Volusia counties for 2001–2010 126

Figure 77. Blue crab threats and stressors 128

Figure 78. Threats and stressors of horseshoe crabs 131

Figure 79. Threats and stressors to oyster reefs 132

Figure 80. Monthly indices of relative abundance for age-0 spot (*Leiostomus xanthurus*) and mean temperature from the Halifax River (1993–1997) and IRL (1991–1996) 136

Figure 81. Distribution and abundance of spot (*Leiostomus xanthurus*) in Mosquito Lagoon from FWC-FWRI's Fisheries-Independent Monitoring Program during 2007–2008 140

Figure 82. Number and timing of adult red drum (*Sciaenops ocellatus*) movements out of Mosquito Lagoon (ML) to Ponce Inlet or the northern Indian River Lagoon 141

Figure 83. Natural plant communites of Canaveral National Seashore north and south 148

Figure 84. Exposed coquina ledge south of Haulover Canal. Vegetation cover is disturbed cabbage palm (*Sabal palmetto*) 149

Figure 85. Overgrown pine flatwoods and scrubby flatwoods are a result of fire suppression 150

Figure 86. Swale margin (background) with a high density of pines and pine mortality from prescribed fire 151

List of Figures (continued)

Page

Figure 87. An example of a wet prairie embedded in a swale with adjacent pine flatwoods 152

Figure 88. Freshwater marsh embedded in swale 153

Figure 89. Expanse of sawgrass marsh bordered by pockets of mixed hardwoods in the northern portion of Canaveral National Seashore 154

Figure 90. Freshwater marsh in good condition located in the northern portion of Canaveral National Seashore embedded in swale 154

Figure 91. Freshwater marsh displacement by shrub and mixed hardwood succeession in a shallow swale in the northern portion of Canaveral National Seashore 155

Figure 92. Leopard frog (*Rana sphenocephala*). 156

Figure 93. Forested wetland or hydric hammock on north section of Canaveral National Seashore 156

Figure 94. Forested wetlands (hydric hammock) were dry 158

Figure 95. Forested wetland that previously grew citrus is now disturbed. Located in the north section of Canaveral National Seashore 158

Figure 96. Forested wetland (hydric hammock) was dry and being colonized by cabbage palms (*Sabal palmetto*) as the habitat becomes more mesic 159

Figure 97. Example of a prairie hammock with a small creek in center 160

Figure 98. Prairie hammock with fire scars on the cabbage palms (*Sabal palmetto*) 160

Figure 99. Soil disturbance on the perimeter of a freshwater marsh caused by rooting feral hogs and colonization by invasive species. 161

List of Tables

Page

Table 1. Change in land-use categories forNew Smyrna–Edgewater area (1994–2004). 7

Table 2. Drivers and effects of climate change 25

Table 3. Latitude, longitude, and general location of Mosquito Lagoon surface water monitoring stations in Canaveral National Seashore. 42

Table 4. Trophic State of Canaveral National Seashore (CANA) Surface Water (1990–2007) at IRLV17 44

Table 5. Trophic State of Canaveral National Seashore (CANA) Surface Water (1990–2007) at IRLML02 45

Table 6.Trophic State of Canaveral National Seashore (CANA) Surface Water, 1990–2007, based on the means of aggregate data from IRLML02 and IRLV17 46

Table 7. Depth classes in Mosquito Lagoon and corresponding areas and volumes 51

Table 8. Mean seasonal salinity at the Southeast Coast Network (SECN) monitoring station at Canaveral National Seashore 2005–2009 53

Table 9. Mean seasonal water temperature at the Southeast Coast Network (SECN) monitoring station at Canaveral National Seashore from 2005–2009. 56

Table 10. Mean seasonal dissolved oxygen concentrations at the Southeast Coast Network (SECN) monitoring station at Canaveral National Seashore from 2005–2009. 60

Table 11. Days with mean dissolved oxygen concentrations <5.0 mg/L (5 ppm) at the Southeast Coast Network (SECN) monitoring station, Canaveral National Seashore 61

Table 12. Minimum and maximum mean dissolved oxygen concentrations (mg/L) recorded for successive days at the Southeast Coast Network monitoring station 62

Table 13. Individual occurrences of DO concentrations <4.0 mg/L (4 ppm) at the Southeast Coast Network (SECN) monitoring station, Canaveral National Seashore 63

Table 14. Mean seasonal pH at the Southeast Coast Network (SECN) monitoring station at Canaveral National Seashore from 2005–2009. 64

Table 15. Average annual atmospheric deposition of NH_3, NO_3, and TIN in kg/ha from 1983–2008 at NADP monitoring site FL99 at KSC. 73

Table 16. Mean seasonal specific conductivity (mS/cm) at the SECN monitoring station at Canaveral National Seashore from 2005–2009. 83

List of Tables (continued)

                                                                                                                    Page

Table 17. Mean and median seasonal turbidity at the Southeast Coast Network (SECN) monitoring station at Canaveral National Seashore from 2005–2009. 89

Table 18. Mean and median turbidity by year and season at the Southeast coast Network (SECN) monitoring station at Canaveral National Seashore from 2005–2009. 92

Table 19. Total suspended solids (TSS) percent composition and origin description in the Canaveral National Seashore (CANA) region of Mosquito Lagoon. 93

Table 20. Trace metal concentrations in Mosquito Lagoon water from various agencies between 1979–2002 and Class II water quality criteria 97

Table 21. Significance of seasonal trends in 10 key surface water quality parameters from 1990–2007 at IRLML02 and IRLV17 in Mosquito Lagoon 100

Table 22. Water Quality variables calculated by the Hydrodynamic and Eutrophication Three-Dimensional Model. 102

Table 23. Land cover classes and size for saltwater wetlands 114

Table 24. Submerged aquatic vegetation coverage for Mosquito Lagoon for 1970–1974, 1986, and 1992 118

Table 25. Catch statistics for 10 dominant taxa in Mosquito Lagoon in 2007. 138

Table 26. Catch statistics for 10 dominant taxa in Mosquito Lagoon in 2008. 139

Table 27. Land-cover classes, descriptions, and size 146

Table 28. Land-cover classes and acreage of freshwater wetland communities estimated for 1943, 1990, 2003, and soils for 2003 146

Table 29. Thematic GIS coverages for the Canaveral National Seashore. 163

Table 30. Summaries of data and sources of significant threats and stressors of Canaveral National Seashore (CANA) resources. 169

Table 31. Canaveral National Seashore threats and stressors matrix. 193

Table A1. Land cover classes and descriptions from Duncan et al. (2004) 223

Table A2. Land cover classes and soil types associated with the habitat based on categories described by Duncan et al. (2004) and descriptions in soil surveys 224

Executive Summary

The conditions of terrestrial and estuarine resources within Canaveral National Seashore (CANA) were assessed and the threats and stresses to individual resources were identified and evaluated. With the exception of freshwater vegetation mapping, new data were not collected within CANA. Data and information derived from an intensive survey of the existing peer-reviewed and gray literature search were analyzed and synthesized to reveal the current state of each resource and to identify trends in resource quality and health.

Resource Characterization

The semidiurnal tidal range at CANA can be up to 3.28 ft (1 m) and seasonal fluctuations in mean sea level can exceed 1 ft (0.30 m). A review of predicted and measured directional wave data shows a strong seasonal signal in the wave regime that is punctuated by occasional storm-generated waves of up to 11.5 ft (3.5 m). The potential effects of climate change in the CANA area will be driven by increasing air temperature and ocean temperature, and increasing sea level. The most important effects of climate change at CANA are altered rainfall and storm patterns, harmful algal blooms, and sea level-induced changes in estuaries and tidal wetlands.

Geological Setting and Resources

The geological setting of CANA is sandy soils and wetland soils resting on a late Pleistocene coquina (Anastasia Formation), which dates from 100,000–130,000 yrs before present and represents shallow marine to shoreline high-energy deposits. Major morphological features constructed on the Anastasia Formation include the modern barrier island system of CANA as well as relict beach ridges from the early Holocene epoch. Relict inlet shoals that commonly form the west boundary of the barrier island indicate a history tidal inlet breaching. Sea level rise during the Holocene epoch, in combination with migrating tidal inlets, provided the overall transgressive process that formed and maintained the modern CANA barrier system and formed the system of discrete and compound shoals now situated on the inner continental shelf offshore of the park. Although subject to long-term barrier island migration with rising sea level during the Holocene epoch, analysis of CANA ocean shoreline position over the past 150 yrs indicates stability and some shoreline accretion.

Below the surface geology of CANA, the surface aquifer includes the Anastasia Formation and contains upper and lower permeable zones. Impermeable and semi-permeable clays, calcareous clays, and silty sands of the Hawthorn Formations underlie the surficial aquifer and provide an aquaclude above the Floridan aquifer. The aquifer is a system of limestone and dolomite beds that can be subdivided into two water-bearing aquifers – the Upper and Lower Floridan – that are separated by a less permeable, semi-confining unit. The top of the Floridan aquifer under the northern area of Mosquito Lagoon is found at -75 ft (-23 m) National Geodetic Vertical Datum (NGVD). Sampling indicates that groundwater discharge to the surface waters is important. Recent experiments using a numerical hydrodynamic and water quality models indicate that groundwater flux to the surface may be an important component of the Mosquito Lagoon's hydrological cycle and water quality regime.

Surface Waters

Trophic state indices (TSI) (Florida Department of Environmental Protection (FDEP), 1996; Winkler and Ceric, 2006; and Hand, 1988) and water quality parameters (chlorophyll-a, total nitrogen (TN), total phosphorus (TP), and Secchi depth) indicate the trophic state of CANA surface water is changing very little from year to year, achieving or remaining close to a good designation. The ratios of TN/TP generally indicated co-limitation by N and P (TN/TP 10–30) when data from the sampling stations were averaged, but data from southern stations often indicated P limitation (TN/TP >30). This is surprising as the vast majority of estuaries in the U.S. are limited by nitrogen rather than phosphorous.

Although most dissolved oxygen (DO) levels are above FDEP standards, Southeast Coast Network (SECN) data from one location indicate low dissolved oxygen levels in summer when temperatures peak and storm water runoff and decomposition rates are maximum. Dissolved oxygen at the SECN station was the only parameter that occasionally violated FDEP standards. Nitrogen levels (NOx, TKN, TN) suggest good water quality and have been fairly consistent with time, showing neither an upward or downward trend. Phosphorus levels have been acceptable also, but analyses indicated significantly higher concentrations of TP in the north CANA water region near Oak Hill as compared to the south CANA region of Mosquito Lagoon south of Haulover Canal. Chl-a concentrations in the CANA areas of Mosquito Lagoon were often lower in the southern area and during the dry season, but levels generally indicated mesotrophic and fair/good water quality conditions. Analyses identified a temporally decreasing Chl-a concentration trend in the northern and southern CANA regions of Mosquito Lagoon. Turbidity is a concern because it is a major factor affecting light attenuation and turbidity and total suspended solids (TSS) levels were usually higher in the wet season and near population centers in the northern area. SECN station data (2005–2009) exhibited an overall median turbidity of approximately 9 NTUs (n=1,205), but elevated levels (>25 NTUs) occurred 16% of the time. Particles (TSS) are responsible for 95% of the light attenuation in Mosquito Lagoon with aluminosilicates accounting for 67% (Trefry et al. 2007). Creek runoff containing aluminosilicates was identified as a major contributor to the light attenuation in Mosquito Lagoon (Trefry et al., 2005).

Biological Resources
CANA's natural resources are physically divided between the Atlantic Ocean and the Mosquito Lagoon by the barrier island system that is subjected to the harsh conditions of storms, limited freshwater water, and extreme temperatures. Habitats on either side of the barrier island are adapted to the different physical conditions. Although the barrier island physically separates the ocean and the lagoon, some of the plants and animals are found on both sides.

Natural disasters, such as northeasters and hurricanes, can modify the landscape. Climate change and the likelihood of sea level rise may diminish the total volume of the barrier shoreface, making the barrier island more vulnerable to breaching or overwash. Increased storm events as a result of global warming may increase rainfall and stormwater runoff, which can affect salinity levels. Pollution, marine debris, and some human activities threaten the health and well being of the natural resources in CANA. Exotic plants and animals can disrupt natural ecological systems.

Biological Resources of the Coastal Waters and Beach
The barrier island narrows to approximately 100 yds (91 m) and widens to about 1,100 yds (1,000 m) in other segments. The CANA coastline is within the northern right whale (*Eubalaena glacialis*) critical habitat (NMFS, 2009). Protected species, such as sea turtles, nest on the upper beach, and beach mice inhabit the dunes. Other species that inhabit or use the surf zone and

beach are reptiles, fishes, shore birds, mole crabs (*Emerita talpoida*), ghost crabs (*Ocypode quadrata*), and the coquina clam (*Donax variabilis*).

Two species of sea turtles frequently nest on the central Florida coast: loggerhead (*Caretta caretta*) and green (*Chelonia mydas*); leatherback (*Dermochelys coriacea*) and Kemp's Ridley (*Lepidochelys kempi*) nest occasionally. Nesting data from 1984–2010 revealed 85,489 loggerhead, 8,983 green, 172 leatherbacks, 47 Kemp's Ridley, and 44 unknown species nests in the park (Stiner, 2010a). Nesting data collected by counties is reported to the Florida Index Nesting Beach Survey Program (INBS). CANA loggerhead nest counts outnumber those of all other sea turtle species in Brevard and Volusia counties (Meylan et al., 1995; ACOE, 2007; Stiner, 2010a; FWC-FWRI, 2010a). The CANA nesting total in 2010 was 5,621, which was over 1,000 nests more than any previous year from 1984–2010 (Stiner, 2010a). Witherington et al. (2009) found a declining trend in the number of loggerhead nest counts in the INBS program from 1989–2006. An analysis that extended the data set to 2006–2010 suggests that the long-term downward trend of nest counts may be stabilizing (FWC-FWRI, 2010b).

Nest counts capture the status of the reproductive stage of adult females. Neither data from nesting count programs nor in-water samplings of sea turtles are used to estimate statewide population. Net studies in Mosquito Lagoon have documented numerous juvenile loggerhead and green turtles over the past 20 yrs (Provancha, 1998, 2006). The relative abundance of the two species has shifted dramatically; in the late 1970s, nearly 80% of the turtles captured were loggerheads and 20% were greens, while in the late 1990s, 15% were loggerheads and 85% were greens (Medonca and Ehrhart, 1982; Provancha et al., 1998).

Several common species of shellfish and crabs occupy the area between the dune and the swash zone. In the southeast and west coast of Florida, mole crab, ghost crab, and coquina clam are abundant and may serve as indicators of beach health (SCDNR, no date; Wolcott 1978). Scientists are concerned that mole crab activities are affected by hurricanes or events that upset the rhythm, timing of activity, and tide amplitude (Diaz, 1980; Forward et al., 2005). Studies of the abundance of mole crab, ghost crab, and coquina clam have not been conducted in CANA.

CANA's coastal-strand plant community is the natural plant association of the beach dune, swale, and ridge system and comprises grasses, herbs, woody shrubs, and scrub oaks. Soil conditions are poor; plants are normally <5 ft (1.5 m) tall and are salt pruned to nearly a 45° angle by wind-borne salt spray. Grasses sea oats (*Uniola paniculata*), beach grass (*Panicum amarum*), salt meadow cordgrass (*Spartina patens*), saltgrass (*Distichlis spicata*), and saw palmetto (*Serenoa repens*) dominate the dunes. Examples of listed species documented within coastal strand of NASA properties are East Coast lantana, (*Lantana depressa* var. *Floridana*), nakedwood (*Myrcianthes fragrans*), and shell mound prickly-pear (*Opuntia stricta*) (Schmalzer et al., 2002). Subtropical plants such as sea grape (*Coccoloba uvifera*) and snowberry (*Chiococca alba*) are also common.

Animals found in the beach dune swale and ridges system are gopher tortoise (*Gopherus polyphemus)*, southeastern beach mouse (*Peromyscus polionotus niveiventris*), six-lined racer (*Cnemidophorus sexlineatus*), southern hognose (*Heterodon* sp.), coachwhip (*Masticophis flagellum*), and eastern diamond rattlesnake (*Crotalus adamanteus*). Twelve reptiles and amphibians occurred at two stations on the barrier island in 2009 (Byrne et al., 2010).

Fairly healthy populations of the southeastern beach mouse were found in the early 1990s within CANA, Merritt Island National Wildlife Refuge (MINWR), and Cape Canaveral Air Force Station (Provancha and Oddy, 1992). A multi-agency survey is being conducted (2010–2011) to determine the presence/absence of the beach mouse throughout the area.

Since the 1950s, migratory and seasonal birds have been documented at MINWR during the annual Audubon Christmas Counts organized by the Space Coast Audubon Society (SCAS, 2010a). The Roseate Tern, a Florida threatened species observed in MINWR, nests in the lower Florida Keys, but travels during migration to all parts of the state (FWC, 2003; MINWR, 2008). White pelicans (*Pelecanus erythrorhynchos*), brown pelicans (*Pelecanus occidentalis*), osprey (*Pandion haliaetus*), sanderlings (*Calidris alba*), willets (*Tringa semipalmata*), red knots (*Calidris canutus*), ruddy turnstones (*Arenaria interpres*), black-bellied plovers (*Pluvialis squatarola*), piping plovers (rare) (*Charadrius melodus*), laughing gulls (*Leucophaeus atricilla*), ringbilled gulls (*Larus delawarensis*), herring gulls (*Larus smithsonianus*), great black-backed gulls (*Larus marinus*), Caspian terns (*Hydroprogne caspia*), royal terns (*Thalasseus maximus*), Sandwich terns (rare) (*Thalasseus sandvicensis*), common terns (rare) (*Sterna hirundo*), Forster's terns (*Sterna forsteri*), and least terns (*Sternula antillarum*) have been observed or are known to occur in the coastal areas of CANA-MINWR (SCAS, 2010b; MINWR, 2008; PIA, 2008). In the fall, migrating birds of prey, including merlins (*Falco columbarius*) and peregrine falcons (*Falco peregrinus*), are seen regularly and may winter at the seashore and the MINWR (SCA, 2010b).

Biological Resources of Mosquito Lagoon
Benthic macroinvertebrate samples collected in connection with Florida's Inshore Marine Monitoring and Assessment Program (IMAP) conducted from 2000–2004 provide the best information on benthic macroinvertebrates near CANA (McRae, 2002; McRae et al., 2003; McRae et al., 2005). Eight taxa (or taxa groups) of macroinvertebrates found an all sites in 2004, including Indian River Lagoon (IRL), were *Exogone rolani,* Rhynchocoela, Tubificidae, *Cirratulidae, Mediomastus* sp., Bivalvia, *Podarkeopsis levifuscina*, and *Scoloplos rubrar* (McRae et al., 2005). The most frequently sampled macroinvertebrates in IRL the Tubificidae, *Mediomastus* sp., and the gastropods, *Acteocina canaliculata* and *Mitrella lunata*.

Mangroves in CANA are adapted to the transition zone between subtropical and temperate climates and tend to dominate the interior wetlands in the southern portion of the IRL. Mangroves and salt marshes provide important habitat for birds, fish, manatees, amphibians, reptiles, and invertebrates. The total mangrove area in CANA dropped from 1,657 ac (671 ha) in 1943 to a low of 655 ac (265 ha) in 2003. Mangroves fringe Mosquito Lagoon, thrive in the interior, and are found on the edges of dikes or ridges within lagoon waters. Three species of mangroves—red mangrove (*Rhizophora mangle*), black mangrove (*Avicennia germinans*), and white mangrove (*Laguncularia racemosa*)—live in the salt marsh or tidal swamp. Buttonwood (*Conocarpus erectus*), sometimes called the fourth mangrove, occurs on higher ground adjacent to the back barrier or on the western edge of the lagoon. Following years of mild winters, the height, distribution, and abundance of mangroves may increase, however they do not tolerate prolonged freezing temperatures and periodically die back when freezes occur (Provancha et al., 1986; Stevens et al., 2006). Black mangroves are more tolerant of low temperatures and may persist when red and white mangroves perish (Markley et al., 1982; McMillan and Sherrod, 1986).

Saltwater wetlands in the northern portion of Mosquito Lagoon are dominated by herbaceous salt marsh plants and freeze-stunted mangroves (Schmalzer, 1995). Periodic freezes prevent mangroves from taking over saltwater wetlands in Mosquito Lagoon (Provancha et al., 1986). Salt marshes are composed of herbaceous, salt tolerant plants capable of living in low oxygen, muddy substrates. In Mosquito Lagoon, salt marsh communities are categorized by the vegetation association of sand cordgrass (*Spartina bakerii*), black needle rush (*Juncus romarianus*), glasswort (*Salicornia* spp.), saltwort (*Batis maritima*), salt grass, sea oxeye daisy (*Borrichia frutescens*), and seashore paspalum (*Paspalum vaginatum*) (Schmalzer, 1995). The total area of salt marsh within CANA dropped from 6,600 ac (2,671 ha) in 1943 to 6,998 ac (2,832 ha) in 2003.

Submerged aquatic vegetation (SAV) is a generic term for plants that live below the waterline, including seagrasses, macroalgae, and drift algae. Factors that influence SAV growth and distribution are water depth, water clarity, light availability, substrate type, nutrient levels, salinity, temperature, and anthropogenic influences (FWC-FWRI, 2003). SAV produces food and provides cover for many aquatic organisms, improves water clarity and quality, and helps stabilize sediments (FWC-FWRI, 2003). Four of seven seagrasses documented in the IRL system—shoal grass (*Halodule wrightii*), manatee grass (*Syringodium filiforme*), widgeon grass (*Ruppia maritima*), star grass (*Halophila englemanni*) —and macroalgae (*Caulerpa prolifera*)— occur in Mosquito Lagoon (Provancha et al., 1992; Woodward-Clyde Consultants 1994f; Virnstein, 1999). A recent study examining seagrass data in the IRL from 1943 to the 1990s calculated a 13% loss in seagrass cover, with some areas showing 90% loss (Virnstein et al., 2007). The greatest percent of seagrass area ranges from 4.3–50.8% is in the central and south portions of Mosquito Lagoon. *Caulerpa prolifera* is found throughout the IRL and reported to occur within the Mosquito Lagoon, but was not listed in a long-term study of SAV (Provancha and Scheidt, 2000).

Drift algae are a habitat comparable to seagrasses for some marine organisms within the IRL (Virnstein and Howard, 1987). A two-year survey of drift macrophytes in the Mosquito Lagoon identified 26 species (Abgrall and Walters, 2003). Red algae (*Gracilaria* spp.) accounted for 51.7%, followed by fragments of the seagrass *H. wrightii* (23.7%), *Cladophora* sp. (12.5%), *Dasya baillouviana* (7.7%), *Enteromorpha* spp. (1.5%), *Spyridia filamentosa* (1.4%), and 1.5% consisted of *Acanthophora spicifera, Hypnea spinella, Agardhiella subulata,* and *Chondria littoralis*. No correlations of drift algae abundance with respect to wind speed, flow, or temporal patterns were found by Abgrall and Walters (2003).

Drift algae coverage can be quite extensive in the IRL, but seasonal and spatial trends vary by location (Virnstein and Carbonara, 1985; Reigl et al., 2005). Nova Southeastern University Oceanographic Center (NSUOC) quantified the abundance and distribution of seasonal drift macroalgae in the IRL and found that drift macroalgae biomass per unit area (1654 lb/mi^2; 238.3 kg/km^2) was roughly 34% less than reported for the 2005 survey. The mean percent cover of drift macroalgae was significantly greater within the navigation channels (18.3%) than outside (12.2%) and significantly greater in the southern segments of the Indian River (12.9%) than in the Banana River (9.3%) (NSUOC, 2009). The study area did not include Mosquito Lagoon, yet a comparison of results from the Banana River and the southern IRL is useful since the northern IRL is more similar to Mosquito Lagoon than the other segments.

Marine mammals in the lagoon include the endangered Florida manatee (*Trichechus manatus latirostris*) and Atlantic bottlenose dolphin (*Tursiops truncatus*). Manatees are sensitive to cooler water temperature ($\leq 20°C$) and exhibit seasonal variation in their distribution (Shane, 1983; Reynolds and Odell, 1991). In the spring and summer, manatees are found throughout the IRL, although greater abundances tend to occur in the Banana River and in the IRL south of Titusville (Leatherman, 1979; Shane, 1983; Provancha and Provancha, 1988). Manatees loiter throughout the warmer months on the east side of Mosquito Lagoon along East Channel, Eldora, and North District ranger station (John Stiner, personal observation, January 7, 2010). The highest two-day statewide minimum count of manatees from winter synoptic aerial surveys and ground counts was 3,276 manatees in January 2001; the highest count on the east coast of Florida is 1,756, and the highest on the west coast is 1,520, both in 2001 (UFWS, 2002). Due to nearly ideal conditions in 2001, the results of the synoptic survey are the best available estimate of the current minimum population size of 3,276 (USFWS, 2002).

Atlantic bottlenose dolphins are seen throughout the IRL system and are long-term residents (Provancha et al., 1982; Odell and Asper, 1990; Fick, 1995) that exhibit a high degree of site fidelity (Mazzoil et al., 2008; Murdoch et al., 2008). Nearly 2,000 dolphins were sighted in the Mosquito Lagoon from 2002–2005, with the highest repeated sighting rate, the strongest site fidelity, and a mean range of 22 km (Mazzoil et al., 2008).

The number of birds and bird species are not identified separately for CANA and Merritt Island National Wildlife Refuge (MINWR), which is a joint management area. Bird studies occasionally include property within NASA ownership. The diversity of birds that frequent NASA lands, including CANA, is legendary. Species of particular concern are the wood stork (*Mycteria americana*), the northern pintail (*Anas acuta*), and the lesser scaup (*Aythya affinis*). Populations of the federally endangered wood stork in Florida have declined from 60,000 in the 1930s to 5,000 pairs. No successful nesting has occurred in MINWR since 1986, although approximately 250 wood storks currently use the refuge for feeding and roosting.

Pintail populations declined by 93% from 1978–2003 and may no longer winter at the refuge. A similar decline was witnessed for the continental lesser scaup since the mid-1980s. The estuarine areas of Banana River, IRL, and Mosquito Lagoon are the most valuable wintering habitat for scaup on the Atlantic Flyway, harboring up to 62% of the flyway's scaup and 15% of the continental scaup population (MINWR, 2003).

Probably due to the importance of blue crabs (*Callinectes sapidus*) to commercial and recreational fisheries, landings data have been collected for the east and west coasts of Florida since 1950 (Murphy et al., 2007). Statewide, blue crabs are believed to be resilient to overfishing, have increased in stock size, and the cycles of dry and wet weather associated with storms during 2002–2005 seems to have caused fluctuations observed in biomass (Murphy et al., 2007). Blue crab data are not available for Mosquito Lagoon.

Population estimates for horseshoe crabs (*Limulus polyphemus*) in Florida are not available; most research has focused in northeastern states, particularly Delaware Bay. During 1978–1979, large numbers of horseshoe crabs were caught as bycatch in nets set to assess juvenile sea turtle populations in Mosquito Lagoon; in 1994, smaller numbers were netted (Provancha, 1998). More than 22,000 horseshoe crabs were harvested in Florida in 2005 for resale to aquaria and as research specimens (Gerhart, 2007). The extent of harvest within Mosquito Lagoon is unknown, but truckloads of adult horseshoe crabs have been observed leaving the IRL (EPA, 2003).

Numerous oyster reefs occur in the northern end of Mosquito Lagoon; however, over the past 50 yrs, a declining trend in the distribution of oyster reefs within CANA has been observed, with a significant increase in the mortality of oysters along the reef margins adjacent to boat channels (Grizzle et al., 2002). Grizzle et al. found that 60 of 400 reefs had dead margins from aerial images. Data show some variability in the trend, but there was a decrease of overall live reef area from 16.2 ac to 10 ac (6.6 to 4.0 ha) and an increase in dead margin area from 0.5 to 2.8 ac (0.2 to 1.1 ha). In a biannual sampling of oyster reefs during a three-year study in Mosquito Lagoon, live oysters were more abundant than dead oysters in most sampling periods, with shell heights varying from 36.2 mm (±11.6 SD) to 61.0 mm (±22.3 SD) (Arnold et al., 2008).

Netting studies in Mosquito Lagoon have documented numerous juvenile loggerhead and green turtles over the past 20 yrs (Provancha, 1998; 2006). The relative abundance of the two species has shifted dramatically; in the late 1970s, nearly 80% of the turtles captured were loggerheads and 20% were greens, while in the late 1990s, 15% were loggerheads and 85% were greens (Medonca and Ehrhart, 1982; Provancha et al., 1998).

Compared to other regions in Florida, waters near CANA marine and estuarine fishes have not been well-studied. Although there are differences in sampling techniques and experimental designs between past and present fishery studies, historical results can provide important broad-scale benchmark information regarding fishes in CANA waters.

1976–1990s
Early survey work provided detailed life history information on several elasmobranchs with comments on factors that affect their distribution and abundance in the system (Mulligan and Snelson, 1983; Snelson and Williams, 1981; Snelson et al., 1988). Studies of estuarine fishes in the CANA region of Mosquito Lagoon used gigs, dip nets, seines, gill nets, and fixed station trawl sampling (Snelson 1976, 1980, 1983) that collected 141 species. Bay anchovy (*Anchoa mitchilli*) was numerically dominant, accounting for about 85–90% of the total catches in the mid 1970s to 1990s (Snelson 1976, 1980, 1983; Snelson and Johnson, 1995). Other numerical dominants included silver perch (*Bairdiella chrysoura*), pinfish (*Lagodon rhomboids*), spot (*Leiostomus xanthurus*), croaker (*Micropogonias undulates*), Gulf pipefish (*Syngnathus scovelli*), silver jenny (*Eucinostomus harengulus*), and code goby (*Gobiosoma robustum*).

1998
Mosquito impoundments in the IRL have long been recognized as valuable habitats for fish populations (Stevens et al., 2006). Concomitant with the FWC-FWRI's early survey, Klassen (1998) sampled the fish community within an unmanaged impoundment on the eastern shore of Mosquito Lagoon documenting the spatial and temporal use of the impoundment by resident and important transient fish species (i.e., spot, ladyfish [*Elops saurus*], and striped mullet [*Mugil cephalus*]), which proved useful planning future restoration efforts for the area.

2001–2002
Paperno et al. (2001) sampled fishes at 11 year-round fixed stations in Mosquito Lagoon (1993–1997) and found the fish assemblage was dominated by seagrass-associated species rainwater

killifish (*Lucania parva*) and pinfish, both common in seagrass habitats of the lagoon. Paperno (2002) also provided a detailed comparison of spot recruitment and growth in Mosquito Lagoon/Halifax River and the greater IRL system.

2004

Twenty-two freshwater, estuarine, and marine sites within CANA were sampled by the NPS SECN in July 2004 (C. Wright, NPS, Southeast Coast Network, 2010, personal communication) and recorded 65 estuarine and freshwater fish species (Johnston et al., 2006).

2007–2008

The FWC-FWRI's Fisheries-Independent Monitoring Program recently expaned into Mosquito Lagoon (Adams and Paperno, 2008; 2009) and collected more than 148,200 fish and macroinvertebrates in 2007–2008. A total of 140 fish species/taxa was collected; the numerically dominate species were rainwater killifish, bay anchovy, and silversides (*Menidia* spp.). Spot were abundant throughout the Mosquito Lagoon during key recruitment periods; large concentrations of young-of-the-year were found in distinct habitats.

The recreational fishery in Mosquito Lagoon, especially for red drum (*Sciaenops ocellatus*), has attained national recognition (FWC-FWRI, unpublished data; Florida Department of Environmental Protection, 2009). Some adult red drum reside and spawn within Mosquito Lagoon as evidenced by the collection of ripe/gravid individuals and red drum eggs (Johnson and Funicelli, 1991; Murphy and Taylor, 1991). An intensive two-year ichthyoplankton survey consistently collected red drum larvae up to 90 km away from the nearest ocean inlet from June to October, with average nightly larval densities as high as 5/10,000 gal (15/100 m^3) of water (Reyier and Shenker, 2007). Conventional mark–recapture tagging efforts also suggest that some mature fish are year-round estuarine residents (Stevens and Sulak, 2001; Tremain et al., 2004) as opposed to transient seasonal migrants from offshore waters.

Autonomous acoustic telemetry showed the majority of tagged red drum exhibited strong site fidelity from winter through early summer, with movement rates increasing significantly during fall spawning months (Reyier et al., 2010). While some fish migrated to the nearest ocean inlet during the spawning period, the majority remained in the lagoon year-round, suggesting that estuarine reproduction, an activity uncommon or poorly documented elsewhere, is the dominant life history strategy in the Mosquito Lagoon basin (Reyier et al., 2010). Tag recaptures suggest high fishing pressure on large breeding adult red drum data in Mosquito Lagoon, with a 41% recapture rate in a 50-month period.

Information on marine fish populations adjacent to CANA area in the Cape Canaveral region is limited (Collins et al., 1989; SEAMAP-SCDNR, 2000; and others). Few data are available on the recent discoveries of critical nursery habitats for several sharks in nearshore waters adjacent to CANA and the Cape Canaveral region (Adams and Paperno, 2007; Aubrey and Snelson, 2007; Reyier et. al., 2008).

Biological Resources of Terrestrial Freshwater Wetlands

Freshwater wetland communities, forested wetlands, and freshwater marshes occupy approximately 1,355 ac (508 ha) or 7%, of the approximately 20,000 ac (8,094 ha) of the terrestrial communities on CANA. The diversity and composition of the natural plant communities of terrestrial freshwater systems reflect the soils and the underlying geologic structure of the Anastasia Formation, which are topographically expressed in dune and swale or ridge features. Surface water and groundwater movement in and among these geologic features affects plant species composition and viability. Freshwater is limited by rainfall, groundwater withdrawal from the system for potable water, and changes to natural hydrology (i.e., Haulover Canal, mosquito ditching, and stormwater canals). Wildfires induced by lightning, and historically by Native Americans, helped maintain healthy natural communities in Florida.

An estimated 530 ac (215 ha) of wet flatwoods occur on the lower elevations of the ridges in the transition areas bordering the wetlands (Duncan et al., 2004). Wet flatwoods are referred to as low pine flatwoods, pond pine flatwoods, cabbage palm/pine savannah, and flatwoods based on the canopy species. Typical canopy plants include south Florida slash pine (*Pinus elliottii* var. *densa*), long-leaf pine (*Pinus palustris*), pond pine (*Pinus serotina*), and cabbage palms (*Sabal palmetto*), and may include sweet bay magnolia (*Magnolia virginiana*) or other hardwoods. Understory woody vegetation includes wax myrtle (*Myrica cerifera*), gallberry (*Ilex glabra*), titi (*Cyrilla racemosa*), saw palmetto, Carolina willow (*Salix caroliniana*), and other wetland shrubs. Groundcover includes spike rush (*Eleocharis* spp.), beak rush (*Rhynchospora* spp.), sedges (*Carex* spp. *Cyperus* spp. and other sedges), grasses (*Andropogon* spp., *Aristida* spp., and other grasses), and pitcher plants (*Saracinia* spp.).

The canopy structure ranges from scattered pines to a mixture of pine and cabbage palms to cabbage palm prairies that border the intermittent ponds, with cabbage palms sometimes growing in the wet sloughs (USDA, 1974). Soils are poorly drained, weakly cemented, sandy layers underlain by sand or loam. Wet pine woods are interspersed with grassy sloughs, ponds, and swamps. Water movement is gradual and pine-dominated flatwoods may be flooded for several days following heavy rains.

In recent years, prescribed burns and mechanical reduction of plant material have been used to manage the habitats in CANA; however, more fire is needed to maintain wet flatwoods and their associated species. Further reduction of the fuel and a decrease in the growth of woody understory species is necessary at the appropriate season and frequency to maintain wet habitats.

The 910 ac (368 ha) of freshwater marsh include wet prairie, inland ponds and sloughs, and emergent aquatic vegetation. The marshes are characterized as herbaceous or shrubby wetland in a relatively large or irregular basin (FNAI-FDNR, 1990). The majority of marshes at CANA are more similar in shape to broad shallow channels of freshwater sloughs without flowing water. The vegetation is composed of herbaceous reeds, grasses, broad-leaved species, and wetland woody shrubs. Vegetation of freshwater marsh includes marsh pink (*Sebatia stellaris*), cordgrass (*Spartina bakerii*), sawgrass (*Cladium jamaicense*), broom sedge (*Andropogon* spp.), and other species of grasses, sedges, and rushes. Plants in the deeper areas with open water may include fragrant water lily (*Nymphaea odorata*), large emergent herbs, and floating aquatic plants. Wet prairie species include spikerush (*Eleocharis* spp.), maidencane (*Panicum hemitomon*), and spike rush (*Rhynchospora* spp.). Shrubs that colonize the perimeters include coastal plain willow (*Salix caroliniana*), buttonbush (*Cephalanthus occidentalis*), and elderberry (*Sambucus caroliniana*).

The largest areas of freshwater marsh in CANA occur north of Haulover Canal and are in good condition. Some marshes are invaded by willow and red maple (*Acer rubrum*) along the extensive edges due to a prolonged absence of fire (NPS, 2010b). Many of the smaller, shallow marshes have converted to willow thickets, as observed along the roadsides that cross from east to west through the linear marshes. Feral hogs are a serious threat to marsh wetlands and amphibian habitat. They destroy the vegetation of freshwater marshes as they root in the moist organic soil horizon for food. Their activity increases during droughts (Seigel and Pike, 2003; MINWR, 2008).

The freshwater forested wetlands, or hydric hammocks, occupy 445 ac (180 ha) at CANA. The term hammock generally refers to a closed canopy forest surrounded or embedded in another vegetation type (Davis, 1943) and may be misleading unless the hydric term is applied. Wetland forests occur on loamy subsoil over hard limestone of low marine terraces and have very poorly drained sandy soils with loam below (USDA, 1974). The canopy may include live oak (*Quercus virginiana*), laurel oak (*Q. laurifolia*), red maple, other hardwoods, and cabbage palm. The mid-story or sub-canopy trees include southern red cedar (*Juniperus silicicola*), redbay (*Persea borbonia*), southern magnolia (*Magnolia grandiflora* and *M. virginiana*), hackberry (*Celtis laevigata*), and pignut hickory (*Carya glabra*). Understory small trees and shrubs may include tropical species such as nakedwood (*Myrsianthes fragrans*), marlberry (*Ardisia escallonioides*), stoppers (*Eugenia* spp.), and yaupon holly (*Ilex vomitoria*) (FNAI-FDNR, 1990; Schmalzer et al., 2002). The sparse groundcover is typically ferns, vines, a few grasses, and shade-tolerant wetland herbs (FNAI-FDNR, 1990). Several species of rare orchids, bromeliads (*Tillandsia* spp.), and epiphytic ferns may be observed growing on the limbs of the canopy trees, particularly on large live oaks.

Roads and drainage in the vicinity of large hydric hammocks have impacted this smaller habitat at CANA. Excavation of adjacent flatwoods between two linear hydric hammocks and a former citrus grove, along with associated roads and ditches, have affected the hydrology. Ditches along the edge of the road contain some water, but as the habitat has become more mesic, other portions of the hydric hammocks were dry and are being colonized by cabbage palms.

Hammocks, also known as prairie hammocks or cabbage palm hammocks, occupy 128 ac (52 ha) at CANA. Prairie hammocks occur on slight elevation changes in flat terrain. They comprise a cluster of tall cabbage palms and live oaks in the middle of, and on, the borders of wet prairie or marsh communities. Saw palmettos may ring the perimeter of the rounded clusters of hammocks in very wet areas. Generally, the understory is open, although tropical species may be present. Prairie hammocks are normally on flat substrates with sand over marl or limestone (FNAI-FDNR 1990). During high water, they may flood, but are rarely under water more than several weeks. The canopy is dominated by cabbage palms and live oak, laurel oak, and magnolia; water oak may occur in the canopy or understory. Shrubs found in prairie hammocks are wax myrtle (*Myrica cerifera*), coastal plain willow, and elderberry (*Sambucus canadensis*). Tropical species that may occur include stoppers, marlberry, and pigeon plum (*Cocoloba diversifolia*). Herbaceous species include grape vine (*Vitis* spp.), poison ivy (*Toxicodendron radicans*), orchids, and wildflowers.

Prairie hammocks have been affected by hydrological alterations and invasive exotic pest plants. In some locations, hogs have damaged the soil surface. As a result, the management of feral hogs and the removal of pest plants is an ongoing endeavor by CANA and MINWR. In the 2008 management plan, MINWR's landscape approach to land management established goals and objectives for exotic plant and feral hog removal. Removal and eradication of exotics were prioritized for Melaleuca (*Melaleuca quinquenervia*); treatment of Brazilian pepper-tree (*Schinus terebinthifolius*) has begun in disturbed locations (MINWR, 2008; John Stiner, personal communication, January 7, 2011).

Disturbed wetlands occupy 596 ac (241 ha) of CANA and include freshwater marshes and forested wetlands, as well as prairie hammocks and wet flatwoods. The primary causes of disturbance are drainage, soil disturbance, and invasion by non-native plants and animals.

Assessment of Threats and Stressors

Threats and stressors of the diverse natural systems and inhabitants of the coastal ocean, beach, and lagoon in CANA are loss of habitat, degradation of habitat, disease and parasites that may be accelerated by degradation of the environment, and the impaired health of target species. The introduction of non-native plants and animals has furthered the damage to the habitat. The potential threat of climate change may accentuate the threats to habitats and species.

Geological Features

The greatest threats and stressors to the physical and geological resources of CANA are the potential impacts of climate change and natural variability. Predicted increase in water and air temperature, sea level, and storm intensity due to climate change have the potential to alter the physical setting that supports existing habitats to the degree that major shifts in the ecosystem may occur. The potential for acceleration in the rate of sea level rise may alter the stability and morphology of the CANA barrier island system and increase storm surge and flooding in the back barrier areas. An increase in the frequency of barrier island breaching by new tidal inlets has the potential to cause major changes in the salinity and tidal regime of the Mosquito Lagoon.

Surface and Groundwater

Although the water quality of the CANA section of Mosquito Lagoon has remained good, threats from sources such as stormwater runoff, On-Site Treatment and Detention Systems (OSTDS) and Publicly Owned Treatment Works (POTW) still need to be recognized and minimized when possible.

Biological Resources of the Coastal Waters and Beach, and Mosquito Lagoon

Boating Activity: Sea turtles, marine mammals, fish, oyster reefs and SAV are negatively affected directly or indirectly by boat activity. From 1998–2003, there was a 42.8% increase in the number of recreational vessels registered in Florida; although the number of registered vessels decreased in years 2007–2009 (see Public Use, subsection Boating in this report). Mosquito Lagoon is among one of the "hot spot" destinations with three seasons: a peak season from May to July, a shoulder season (March, April, August, September, and October), and an off-season (November, December, January, and February).

Loggerhead sea turtles are known to suffer injury from encounters with the propellers of boats and from direct boat strikes. Since the 1990s, Brevard County has the highest rate of manatee boat-related mortality, and boater noncompliance of speed zones is greater on weekends in the Banana River region of the IRL. Much of the recent decline in oyster reefs in CANA has been attributed to boating activity.

Increase in watercraft use within CANA, predominately related to fishing, suggest greater fishing pressure or fishing effort within the area in recent years (Scheidt and Garreau, 2007; Reyier et al., 2011). Recreational anglers, the largest user group encountered during the boat ramp survey, primarily targeted red drum and spotted sea trout (*Cynoscion nebulosus*) within CANA waters (Scheidt and Garreau, 2007: Reyier et al., 2011). These authors concluded that the increase in watercraft use will have a direct negative influence on the natural resources in Mosquito Lagoon managed by CANA and MINWR.

Damage to SAV in the Indian River Lagoon from propeller scars was well documented by aerial photos taken at locations within Florida in the early 1990s (Sargent et al., 1995). In CANA seagrass scarring and blowouts from boats powering off have occurred.

Harmful Algal Blooms
Harmful algal blooms (HABs) have occurred in nearshore coastal waters near CANA, resulting in fish kills. Statewide HABs have caused illness and death in sea turtles, manatees, and dolphins. Public health restrictions have been issued for shellfish harvesting due to toxins associated with HABs. Whereas the long-term impacts of these HABs are unknown, recent research in the surf zone off Cape Canaveral suggests brevetoxins produced by HABs can cause sub-lethal effects in sharks and potentially other marine biota.

Pollution
Periodic testing of contaminants in spot, Atlantic croaker, blue crab, and penaeid shrimp in the southeastern U.S. found that measured analytes were below U.S. Food and Drug Administration action levels (EPA, 2001). The action levels are related to human consumption. Limited information exists for contaminants in tissue of estuarine fishes from Mosquito Lagoon. Total mercury was analyzed in marine fishes (e.g., tunas, mackerels, grouper–snapper complex, dolphinfish) from waters offshore of Volusia County and Brevard County, FL, adjacent to CANA (Adams et al., 2003; Adams and McMichael, 2007; Adams 2004; 2010). Given the sampling designs and highly migratory nature of the species, it was not possible to determine spatial variation in total mercury around CANA. Limited results for juvenile bull sharks (*Carcharhinus leucas*) from the IRL system (Adams and McMichael, 1999) show mean total mercury concentration in dorsal muscle was 0.77 ppm, which was similar to concentrations of total mercury found in juveniles bull sharks from sampling elsewhere in Florida (Adams et al., 2003).

Loss and Fragmentation of Habitat
Loss of habitat in CANA can harm the animals dependent on barrier island, lagoon, and dune and ridge systems of the uplands. Sea level rise could alter the salinity regime in CANA and affect organisms sensitive to salinity changes. Increased storms and the associated increased runoff anticipated from climate change could raise water elevations and drown the saltwater wetlands. Invasive exotic plants have contributed to the disruption of freshwater wetlands in some areas. Invasive exotic plants in saltwater wetlands are most numerous along the perimeter of public infrastructure right-of-ways; while they do not seem to have drastically altered habitat in CANA, the potential for continued invasion and disturbance of saltwater wetlands exists. Exotic animals, such as green mussels and brown anoles, occupy the niches of native species and compete for resources. Feral hogs dig up and kill fragile freshwater wetlands and in the process remove the habitat of the amphibians. Historical habitat and water quality changes (e.g., loss of

oyster habitat, seagrass degradation, and presence of HABs) influence overall community structure.

Conclusions and Recommendations

The majority of factors that threaten to impair CANA waters and terrestrial ecosystems are due to the pressures exerted by an increasing population near CANA and the associated increase in development. Climate change may alter weather patterns, water and air temperature, and the rate of sea level rise. Climate change and natural variability are the greatest threats and stressors to the physical and geological setting. Since the magnitude of climate change is uncertain, it is recommended that the NPS establish well-defined baselines from which to evaluate this threat. The NPS should re-evaluate trends and variability of water levels and shoreline position on an annual basis in a convenient format so that the analysis can be extended year by year with limited effort.

Surface and Groundwater

Analyses of CANA surface waters using 1990-2007 data indicate that the trophic state is stable and water quality has remained in the fair/good range, with the last two years of data (2006, 2007) falling well within the allowable limit for a good designation. Nitrogen and phosphorous were generally co-limiting; however phosphorous limitation occurred many times in the southern Mosquito Lagoon. This is in contrast to most of the IRL and the majority of estuaries in the U.S. Although the water quality of the CANA section of Mosquito Lagoon has remained good, threats from sources such as stormwater runoff, OSTDS, and POTWs need to be recognized and minimized when possible. The surface water hydrology in Mosquito Lagoon is fairly well understood, but the role of submarine groundwater discharge to the lagoon has been largely ignored. Groundwater seepage can affect the receiving water quality. Advective sediment water exchange processes, induced by submarine groundwater discharge, are often critical components of coastal nutrient. However, very little groundwater quantity or quality data have been collected in Mosquito Lagoon.

Biological Resources

Increasing development in the Mosquito Lagoon watershed, particularly north of CANA negatively impacts water quality by increasing pollution from point and nonpoint sources. Water quality of the Mosquito Lagoon is generally regarded as good and, by comparison to other parts of the Indian River Lagoon System, Mosquito Lagoon is in better condition. However, an unexpected increase in nutrient enrichment could affect healthy SAV, primarily the areas of seagrass in the central and southern parts of the Mosquito Lagoon and saltwater wetlands. The SAV and saltwater wetlands in CANA are in good condition. Freshwater wetlands have been disturbed by road cuts, invasive exotic plants, and alterations to the local hydrology. Park staff is cooperating with MINWR to remedy the impacts to wetlands in CANA. Results of monitoring amphibians and reptiles in CANA have demonstrated the diversity of species that inhabit the swales of freshwater wetlands and their susceptibility to changes in habitat.

Boating and fishing have been a part of the Mosquito Lagoon's history, but have intensified in recent years. Boating impacts populations of fish, shellfish, marine mammals, and SAV. Watercraft activities are probably one of the greatest sources of negative impacts to the park's natural resources.

Ongoing biological monitoring programs conducted by CANA, MINWR, CAFS, FWC-FWRI and NASA in the park and local environs have established baseline knowledge for the salt water wetlands, the terrestrial ecology, and several species. The in-water sea turtle monitoring and nest counts, amphibian and reptile monitoring, fish sampling, horseshoe crab, oyster reef research, and the MINWR land management plan should continue. Additional research in the park to establish a baseline status for other key species (e.g., blue crabs and clams should be considered). Plant community field surveys in CANA should be considered to inventory freshwater wetlands, saltwater wetlands, and ground truth aerial imagery.

Comparisons of current measures of community structure (Adams and Paperno, 2008; 2009) to historical fisheries studies within Mosquito Lagoon (Snelson and Johnson, 1995; Paperno et al., 2001) and in adjacent IRL basins (Tremain and Adams, 1995) suggest relatively stable fish communities within recent time. Recent management measures within Mosquito Lagoon (e.g., reconnection of salt marsh systems to lagoon waters, pole-and-troll zones/no-motor zones, and continued control of shoreline development) will likely have direct positive effects on CANA fish communities. Research on these potential effects is ongoing.

An extensive review of natural resources data were conducted for this assessment. However, the knowledge base is incomplete in many areas. For example, some of the knowledge gaps that cut across biotic categories include the potential effects of climate change, storms, pollution loading, and invasion of non-native species. It is recommended that the NPS consider expanding their ongoing monitoring and modeling efforts to account for these gaps. A useful tool would be an annual state-of-the-park update based on this report that addresses key issues of concern. It is recommended that CANA establish a central digital database that includes raw data files, GIS thematic coverages, and a digital reference library. The database should be updated on a continuing basis. This process can begin with the GIS files assembled for this study.

Acknowledgments

We thank John Stiner, Candace Carter, and Christopher Barrow of Canaveral National Seashore for graciously providing assistance on field site visits and making GIS and other data available to us. We also thank Dr. Brean Duncan, Dr. Paul Schmalzer, and Vickie Larson for sharing GIS data files from their 2004 study. We appreciate Dr. Schmalzer sending copies of papers to us and being available for questions. Finally, we thank Eva DiDonato from the National Park Service Water Resources Division and the CANA Assessment Project Coordinator for her valuable guidance during all phases of this assessment.

List of Abbreviations and Acronyms

ACOE	U.S. Army Corps of Engineers
AIWW	Atlantic Intracoastal Waterway
ASMFC	Atlantic States Marine Fishery Commission
BMP	Best Management Practices
BOD	Biological Oxygen Demand
CANA	Canaveral National Seashore
CCAFS	Cape Canaveral Air Force Station
CFU	Colony Forming Units
CHL	Coastal and Hydraulics Laboratory
Chl-a	Chlorophyll-a
Chl-b	Chlorophyll-b
COD	Chemical Oxygen Demand
DO	Dissolved Oxygen
DOQQ	Digital Orthographic Quarter Quadrangle
EFDC/HEM3D	Environmental Fluid Dynamics Code/Hydrodynamic and Eutrophication Three-Dimensional Model
EPA	U.S. Environmental Protection Agency
FAC	Florida Administrative Code
FDACS	Florida Department of Agriculture and Consumer Services
FDEP	Florida Department of Environmental Protection
FDNR	Florida Department of Natural Resources
FGS	Florida Geological Survey
FIND	Florida Inland Navigation District
FLDMV	Florida Department of Motor Vehicles
FLUCFCS	Florida Land Use, Cover and Forms Classification System
FNAI	Florida Natural Areas Inventory
FOCC	Florida Oceans and Coastal Council
FP	Fibropapillomatosis
FWC	Fish and Wildlife Conservation Commission
FWRI	Fish and Wildlife Research Institute
FWS	U.S. Fish and Wildlife Service
GIS	Geographic Information System
HAB	Harmful Algal Bloom
IMAP	Inshore Marine Monitoring and Assessment Program
IRL	Indian River Lagoon
IRLNEP	Indian River Lagoon National Estuary Program
IRN	Northern Indian River Lagoon
IWW	Intracoastal Waterway
KSC	Kennedy Space Center
LiDAR	Light Detection and Ranging
MGD	Millions of gallons per day
MGWD	Meteoric groundwater discharge

List of Abbreviations and Acronyms (continued)

MINWR	Merritt Island National Wildlife Refuge
MLAP	Mosquito Lagoon Aquatic Preserve
MPN	Most Probable Number
MRC	Indian River Lagoon Marine Resources Council
mS/cm	milli Siemens/cm
NADP	National Atmospheric Deposition Program
NASA	National Aeronautics and Space Administration
NEP	National Estuary Program
NGVD	National Geodetic Vertical Datum
NH_4+	Ammonium
NH_3-N	Ammonia Nitrogen
NM	Nautical Miles
NMFS	National Marine Fisheries Service
NO_3-N	Nitrate Nitrogen
NO_2-N	Nitrite Nitrogen
NOx	Nitrate and Nitrite Nitrogen
NOS	National Ocean Survey
NPS	National Park Service
NRCS	National Resources Conservation Service
NSUOC	Nova Southeastern University Oceanographic Center
NTN	National Trends Network
NTU	Nephelometric Turbidity Units
OSTDS	On-Site Treatment and Detention Systems
PCB	Polychlorinated Biphenyl
PCU	Platinum-Cobalt Units
PO_4	Ortho-Phosphate
POTW	Publicly Owned Treatment Works
Ra	Radium
Rn	Radon
RIM	Rotational Impoundment Management
SAB	South Atlantic Bight
SAV	Submerged Aquatic Vegetation
SAVI	Submerged Aquatic Vegetative Initiative
SCAS	Space Coast Audubon Society
SCS	Soil Conservation Service
SDD	Secchi Disk Depth
SECN	Southeast Coast Network
SGD	Submarine Groundwater Discharge
SJRWMD	St. Johns River Water Management District
SO_4	Sulfate
SRP	Soluble Reactive Phosphorus
STORET	U.S. EPA's STOrage and RETrieval Data Warehouse

List of Abbreviations and Acronyms (continued)

SWIM	Surface Water Improvement and Management
TAN	Total Ammonia Nitrogen
TDS	Total Dissolved Solids
TIN	Total Inorganic Nitrogen
TKN	Total Kjeldahl Nitrogen
TMDLS	Total Maximum Daily Load
TN	Total Nitrogen
TOC	Total Organic Carbon
TP	Total Phosphorus
TSI	Trophic State Indices
TSS	Total Suspended Solids
USGS	U.S. Geological Survey
UTM	Universal Transverse Mercator Projection
VCEHL	Volusia County Environmental Health Laboratory
WBID	Water Body Identifier
WIS	Wave Information Study
WWTP	Wastewater Treatment Plants

Introduction

This study assesses the coastal water resources and watershed conditions at Canaveral National Seashore (CANA), Canaveral, Florida. The literature was reviewed to evaluate information about the abotic and biotic conditions of the terrestrial and aquatic ecosystems of the park and its surroundings. This assessment focuses on the condition of natural resources found in the coastal Atlantic Ocean, Mosquito Lagoon, and select inland freshwater wetlands. A description is provided on the geologic processes and hydrodynamics of the coastline, the lagoon, and the aquifer structure to identify stressors for different scenarios that can occur from interactions between the ecosystems and the natural physical processes. Information was collected from existing scientific publications, technical materials, and site visits made during 2010. Data are summarized and analyzed to identify the existing and potential threats and stressors to the natural resources of CANA coastal waters and watersheds. Threats and stressors are categorized qualitatively to estimate the level of threat. Information and data used in the assessment of the natural resources of CANA are evaluated and ranked for availability and depth.

The ecological systems are grouped by geographical context and function into 1) aquatic: marine and estuary and 2) terrestrial: marine and freshwater. The inhabitants of the coastal waters and the lagoon include fish, marine mammals, sea turtles, and invertebrates. Seagrass beds, oyster reefs, tidal swamps, and salt marshes are considered part of the lagoon system. Terrestrial marine and freshwater pine flatwoods systems were evaluated for flora and fauna.

Description of Canaveral National Seashore

Canaveral National Seashore, formed in 1975, is 57,662 ac (23,330 ha) situated on the east coast of Florida (Figure 1). It lies north of Kennedy Space Center in Brevard County and south of New Smyrna Beach in Volusia County. The Atlantic Ocean is the eastern boundary, and the park's western border is the Indian River Lagoon (IRL). A discussion follows of the park's history, legislative intent and objectives, location and property boundaries, buildings, utilization by visitors and others, and climate.

Location and Extent

Cohenour (1974) geographically defines the northern and southern extents of Mosquito Lagoon between 28°52'N and 28°40'N latitude (Figure 1). CANA is situated between the latitudes of 28°38'N and 28°58'N on the east coast of Florida. The park lies south of New Smyrna Beach and north of Cape Canaveral and encompasses approximately 58,000 ac (23,470 ha) of lagoon and barrier islands (Walters et al., 2001). The largest surface area, about 38,000 ac (15,380 ha) is the Mosquito Lagoon. The park boundaries, as set forth by Congress in 1975 (16 U.S.C. Sec.459j (c) at www.gpoaccess.gov) are as follows:

> ...approximately sixty-seven thousand five hundred acres within the area more particularly described by a line beginning at the intersection of State Highway 3 and State Road 402, thence generally easterly following State Road 402 to a point one-half mile offshore in the Atlantic Ocean, thence northwesterly along a line which is at each point one-half mile distant from the high water mark to Bethune Beach, thence inland in a generally westerly direction through Turner Flats and Shipyard Canal, thence northwesterly to the Intracoastal Waterway, thence southerly along the Intracoastal Waterway to the boundary of the Kennedy Space Center, thence southwesterly to United States Highway 1, thence southerly along State Highway 3 to the point of beginning.

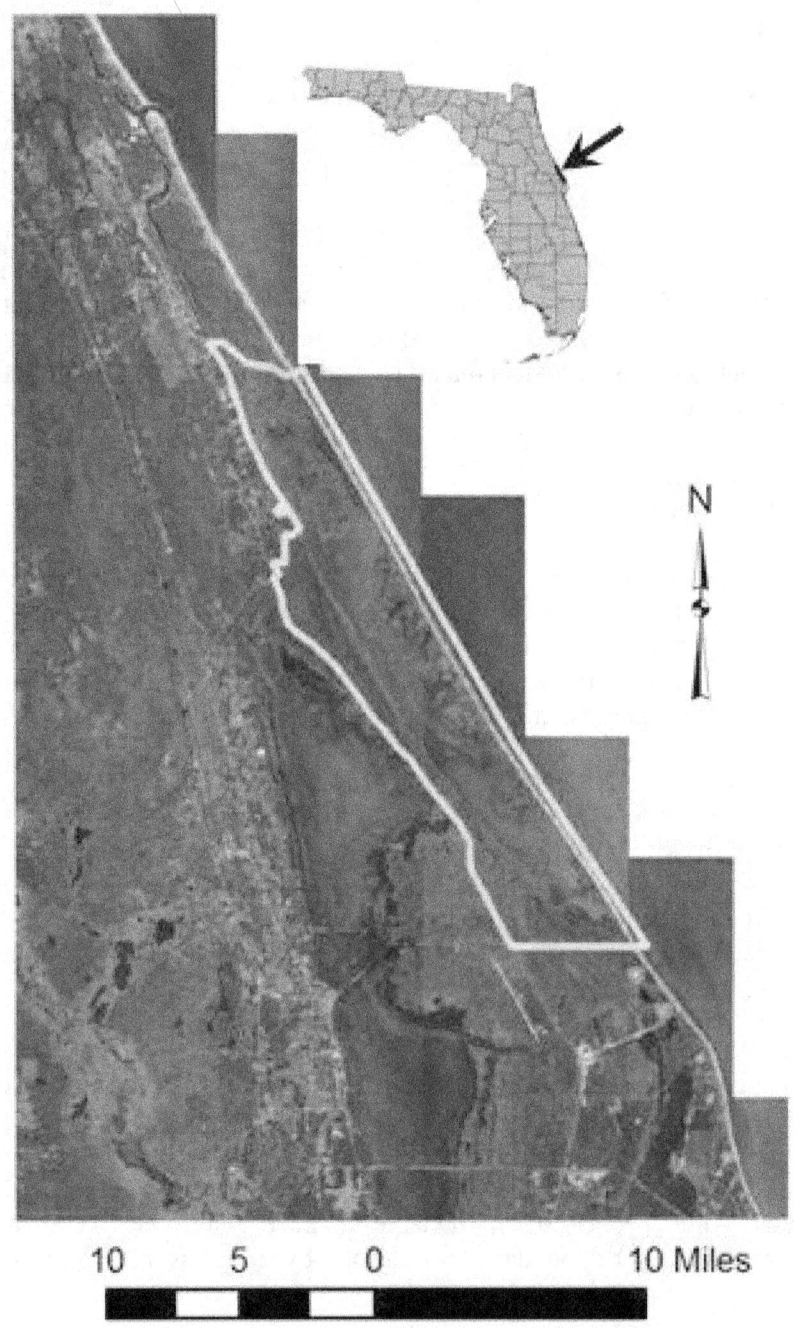

Figure 1. Location of Canaveral National Seashore on the east coast of Florida. The park boundary is marked in yellow.

Changes to the property within CANA since 1975 have been place names and land transfers. Shipyard Canal was modified; Government Cut now provides the connection to the Atlantic Intracoastal Waterway (AIWW) (FDEP, 2009). In 1988, The Nature Conservancy acquired Seminole Rest, also known as Snyder Mound, and transferred ownership to CANA in 1990, thus expanding the park boundary to the west bank of Mosquito Lagoon at Oak Hill (Parker, 2008). The 1975 extent of CANA property was amended to add several tracts of adjacent land that were donated or purchased on various occasions. Approximately 16,000 ac (6,475 ha) were donated to CANA by Brevard County and the state of Florida and included the former 730-ac (295 ha) Apollo State Park, where Turtle Mound and Castle Windy Midden are located. Another 813 ac (329 ha) of purchased private land was donated by citizens.

Park History

Over 40 yrs, an unconventional alliance of military, the state of Florida, local groups and agencies, the National Aeronautics and Space Administration (NASA), the U. S. Fish and Wildlife Service (USFWS), and the National Park Service (NPS) converged to acquire and manage land that would provide protective buffer for the space program and support access and management of natural areas for wildlife and recreation. Beginning in the 1930s, NPS envisioned expanding the country's park system to add undeveloped coastal landscapes. After World War II, the park service selected 16 properties from a list of 126 candidates to be considered as the next national park on the east coast (Parker, 2008). Meanwhile in Florida, Banana River Naval Air Station, established at Cape Canaveral during World War II, became "The Joint Long Range Proving Ground" and the new home of the U. S. rocket program that was relocated from White Sands, New Mexico (Hannah, 1965; Parker, 2008). Between 1961 and 1964, during the Kennedy administration, the Army Corp of Engineers (ACOE) acquired 84,015 ac (34,000 ha) north and west by fee simple or condemnation. ACOE also negotiated with Florida to use another 55,599 ac (22,500 ha) of submerged land—mostly the Mosquito Lagoon and adjacent land—to create a secure buffer zone for rocket launch operations (Parker, 2008).

In 1963, the USFWS entered into an interagency agreement with NASA to form the Merritt Island National Wildlife Refuge (MINWR) in 1963 (USDOI, 2008). The initial agreement authorized MINWR to manage portions of the land and waters associated with Kennedy Space Center (KSC). During the 1960s and early 1970s, their authority was expanded to cover the entire property. Brevard County also cooperated with MINWR in oversight of activities near the lagoon and Playalinda Beach (Parker, 2008).

Florida legislation during the 1960s and 1970s increased protection of the resources of Mosquito Lagoon. In 1970, approximately 39,000 ac (15,780 ha) of Mosquito Lagoon and the land surrounding the lagoon basin were designated as the Mosquito Lagoon Aquatic Preserve (MLAP) by a resolution of the Florida governor and his cabinet (FDEP, 2009). The Florida Aquatic Preserve Act of 1975 codified protection for state-owned submerged lands in areas with exceptional biological, aesthetic, and scientific value to be set aside forever as aquatic preserves or sanctuaries for the benefit of future generations (FL Legislature, 2010). In 1979, Mosquito Lagoon was also designated as an Outstanding Florida Water (FDEP, 2009). Florida Department of Natural Resources (FDNR), now the Florida Department of Environmental Protection (FDEP), managed the original 28,000-acre MLAP until control of the bottomland was transferred to NASA to be managed by MINWR; at that point, the state-managed area was limited to 4,740 ac (1918 ha) bound on the north by the city of New Smyrna Beach in Volusia County (FDEP, 2009). Since the largest area of the lagoon is in federal hands, the 2009–2019 MLAP management plan pertains to the smaller acreage in Volusia County (FDEP, 2009).

On January 3, 1975, the 93rd Congress of the United States passed Public Law 93-626, establishing the Canaveral National Seashore. The enabling legislation decreed the purpose of the park was to:

> preserve and protect the outstanding natural, scenic, scientific, ecologic, and historic values of certain lands, shorelines, and waters of the State of Florida and to provide for public outdoor recreation use and enjoyment of the same.

The act transferred management responsibilities for land and water within the Mosquito Lagoon and the barrier island, while land ownership remained with NASA. A joint management responsibility of approximately 34,345 ac (13,900 ha) in and around the central and southern sections of Mosquito Lagoon was delegated to the USFWS and NPS (MINWR, 2008). Other parcels under CANA management are 6,655 ac (2,693 ha) of land and wetlands owned by NASA in the north section of Mosquito Lagoon, Playalinda Beach, and 1,000 ac (405 ha) north of the Gomez Grant line (MINWR, 2008; Parker, 2008).

Legislation and Management Objectives

In addition to legislation that governs CANA, several agencies with different missions have jurisdiction or own land within and adjacent to the park. NPS cooperates with these agencies where overlaps of common program objectives exist, e.g., to plan and implement initiatives to restore and maintain water quality, monitor wildlife, and provide land management operations. These agencies are USFWS, U.S. Army Corps of Engineers (ACOE), St. Johns River Water Management District (SJRWMD), Florida Game and Fresh Water Fish Commission (FWC), Florida Inland Navigation District (FIND), and Brevard and Volusia counties. A brief description of the most important operations and/or programs by these agencies follows.

Merritt Island National Wildlife Refuge

A large section of the park, 34,435 ac (13,940 ha), was overlaid on land designated by NASA as Merritt Island National Wildlife Refuge (MINWR) in 1963. After the formation of CANA, responsibility for land management and services was divided. MINWR, under USFWS, performs management of the park's natural resources (MINWR, 2008), while NPS manages the cultural resources and provides visitor services within the present boundaries of CANA (Parker, 2009). In addition, CANA provides visitor services and management for the natural resources on about 16,000 ac (6,475 ha) of lagoon and the barrier island. Although the missions of MINWR and CANA differ, they are compatible. The NPS mission places protection of natural resources equal to cultural resources and public recreation. MINWR ranks protection of biodiversity first, while public recreation activities must be complimentary to the protection of species. The MINWR mission statement is:

> To protect, enhance, and manage wetlands and uplands for biodiversity and for the benefit of all species native to MINWR; provide feeding, resting, and wintering habitat for waterfowl and other migratory birds; protect and manage threatened and endangered species and their habitats; and provide opportunities for compatible public recreation and environmental education.

CANA and MINWR work together and with outside agencies to protect natural resources and to use funds efficiently by coordinating prescribed fire treatment, treatment of invasive species, infrastructure improvements, and NASA closures to enhance the shared oversight of public land.

Mosquito Lagoon Aquatic Preserve
North of the CANA, the present area of Mosquito Lagoon Aquatic Preserve (MLAP) in Volusia County as managed by the FDEP's Office of Coastal and Aquatic Managed Areas (FDEP, 2009), is an artificial—not a physical— boundary of the Mosquito Lagoon. The status and issues of the natural resources are very similar for the entire water body: exotic pest species, water quality, damage from improper use of boats, species protection, and the ability to scientifically monitor the status of the lagoon. In the FDEP (2009) MLAP management plan, a description of the natural resources and the efforts that are planned and/or underway to improve and maintain the lagoon for the next decade are discussed. CANA and other entities participate in activities designed to meet the goals set in MLAP Management Plan that affect the lagoon. The ongoing program between CANA and the University of Central Florida to restore oyster reefs is one example (FDEP, 2009).

Haulover Canal
Haulover Canal has been a portage connection between the IRL and Mosquito Lagoon since prehistoric times (Parker, 2008). It is jointly managed by the U.S. ACOE, with FIND acting as the local sponsor (FDEP, 2009). Construction of an east coast water route, known as the AIWW (Atlantic Intracoastal Waterway) was completed in the 1930s (ACOE, 2006). The 125-ft (38 m) wide and 12-ft (3.7 m) deep canal connects the AIWW from the north basin of the IRL to Mosquito Lagoon. Maintenance of the canal, drawbridge, boat ramp, and boat safety and manatee observation deck are managed by ACOE, FIND, and Brevard County (ACOE, 2006; Brevard County, 2010).

Special Designation and Recognition
In 1990, the IRL, which included Mosquito Lagoon, was designated Estuary of National (NEP) Significance by the U.S. Environmental Protection Agency (SJRWMD, 2008). Florida provides special protection to Mosquito Lagoon as an Outstanding Florida Waterway (FDEP, 2009) for the worthiness of its natural attributes (Rule 62-302.700 (9), F.A.C.) (https://www.flrules.org/gateway/ruleNo.asp?id=62-302.700). The state of Florida also designated the Mosquito Lagoon as Class II water (shellfish harvesting); classes I, II, and III surface waters share water quality criteria established to protect recreation and the propagation and maintenance of a healthy, well-balanced population of fish and wildlife (Rule 62-302.400 F.A.C.).

The biological diversity and water quality of the CANA environs has been identified internationally and has been recognized by federal and state authorities. The International Union for the Conservation of Nature identifies CANA a Category V protected landscape/seascape (http://www.protectedplanet.net/sites/Canaveral_National_Seashore_Nps).

CANA is rich with cultural and historical resources as well. There are over 150 historic and archeological sites, including Native American grave sites whose location and integrity are protected under Public Law 101-601 (John Stiner, NPS, personal communication, January 7, 2011).

Critical Habitat: Northern Right Whale and Manatee Protection Zone
In 1994, the National Marine Fisheries Service (NMFS) delineated the critical habitat boundary for northern right whale (*Eubalaena glacialis*) to extend from Georgia to slightly south of Cape

Canaveral along the Atlantic Ocean (http://www.nmfs.noaa.gov/pr/species/criticalhabitat.htm, Federal Register, 1994; NMFS, 2010a).

In 2002, a final rule was issued by USFWS demarcating 13 manatee protection zones with year-round slow speed zones in Florida, including Haulover Canal. Florida-designated manatee protection zones shoulder either side of the canal. West of the canal, year-round slow speed zones extend landward to slightly beyond the AIWW from the southern portion of Turnbull Basin and east a short distance north along the AIWW in the lagoon (FWC, 2002).

Oyster Bed Leases

In 1975, there were approximately 30 oyster lease plots within the park that could not be sold or transferred and had to be renewed annually to avoid expiration (Barber, 2007). In 2001, only 14 leases remained. Commercial and recreational harvesting of the eastern oyster still occurs within park boundaries (Walters et al., 2001). Today, seven commercial oyster bed leases within CANA are retained by individual lessees (FDEP, 2009).

Land Use and Land Cover

Canaveral National Seashore is the longest natural coastline in central Florida within 60 miles of four urban counties: Orange, Seminole, Volusia, and Brevard. Population estimates for 2008 (http://www.bebr.ufl.edu/system/files/2008_Estimates_Table01_0.pdf) by the Bureau of Economic and Business Research (BEBR, 2008) for these counties are Orange (1.8 million), Seminole (426,413), Volusia (510,000) and Brevard (556,213). Population estimates for counties do not account for the number of tourists. Population growth from 2000 to 2008 of four counties that are within one to two hours driving distance to CANA is shown Figure 2.

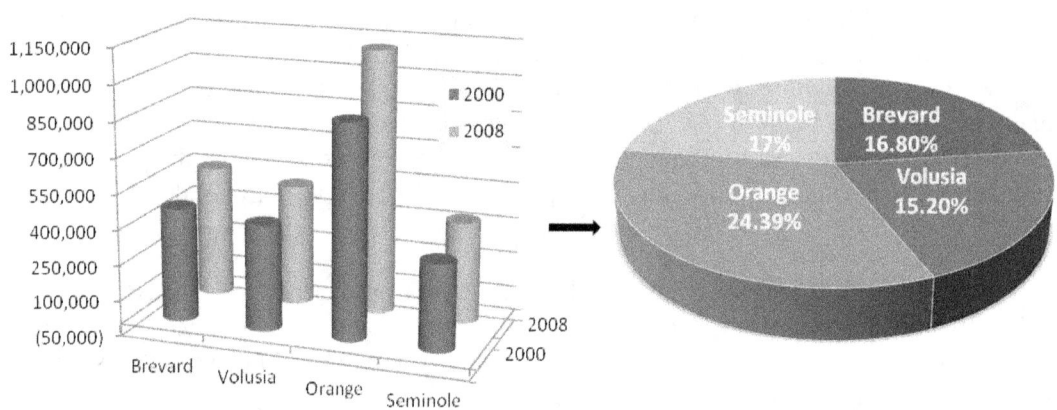

Figure 2. Population growth between 2000–2008 (left) and expressed as percent change (right) for Orange, Seminole, Volusia, and Brevard counties. All four counties are within a 1-2-hr travel time to Canaveral National Seashore.

Figure 3 shows generalized land-use codes (LUCODE) for Brevard and Volusia counties provided by the SJRWMD. Land-use categories follow a modified Florida Land Use/Land Cover and Forms Classification System (FLUCCS). A detailed listing of land-use codes can be found in the Appendix. The percent change in selected land-use categories for the New Smyrna–Edgewater area was tabulated for 1973 and 2004 and are listed by land-use code in Table 1. The greatest percent increase in land-use categories were residential medium and high density locations, commercial and services, and pine flatwoods for a total increase of 48.1%. Losses occurred in low-density residential, golf courses, and citrus groves, with the greatest losses in shrub and brushland, open land, and upland hardwood forests, totaling -240.46%. Categories with large negative percentages were likely reassigned into the gaining categories and/or may have been shifted into other uses in county comprehensive plan amendments.

Table 1. Change in land-use (LU) categories for New Smyrna–Edgewater area (1994–2004).

LU Code	Land-use Category	1995 area (acres)	2004 area (acres)	Percent Change
1100	Residential, low density	2,875	2,459	-14.5%
1200	Residential, medium density	4,969	5,004	0.7%
1300	Residential, high density	481	620	28.9%
1400	Commercial and services	681	739	8.5%
1820	Golf courses	594	513	-13.6%
1900	Open land	81	16	-80.0%
2210	Citrus groves	155	126	-18.7%
3200	Shrub and brushland	1,626	265	-83.7%
4110	Pine flatwoods	1,029	1,133	10.0%
4200	Upland hardwood forests	171	110	-35.8%

Public Use
Visitors
Park visitor data obtained from the Social Science Division of NPS (NPS-SSD, 2010a) (http://www.nature.nps.gov/stats) show an average of 1,052,554 annual visitors from 1976–2009 and a total of 35,786,850 over the 33-year history. Annual visitor numbers peaked between 1994 and 1997 and seems to have stabilized around one million (Figure 4). Specific types of visitor use are recorded for traffic counts to Playalinda Beach and Apollo Beach, backcountry campers, and non-recreational visitors. Information for hunting, fishing, and boating activities, as provided below, was obtained from sources outside NPS. A comparison of traffic counts for two very popular tourist destinations—Playalinda Beach and Apollo Beach—from the early 1990s to 2009 is shown in Figure 5. At Apollo Beach, the average annual traffic count from 1991–2009 was 166,433 and the average count was 183,879 at Playalinda Beach for the same period (NPS-SSD, 2010b). NPS projects a small increase of 0.1% growth in the number of visitors to CANA for 2011 (NPS-SSD, 2010c).

Camping
Records for backcountry campers are available for 1982–2009 (http://www.nature.nps.gov/stats). The number of backcountry campers grew from 80 campers in 1982, peaked at 5,185 in 1997, and since 1998 has varied between 2,000–4,300 campers (Figure 6).

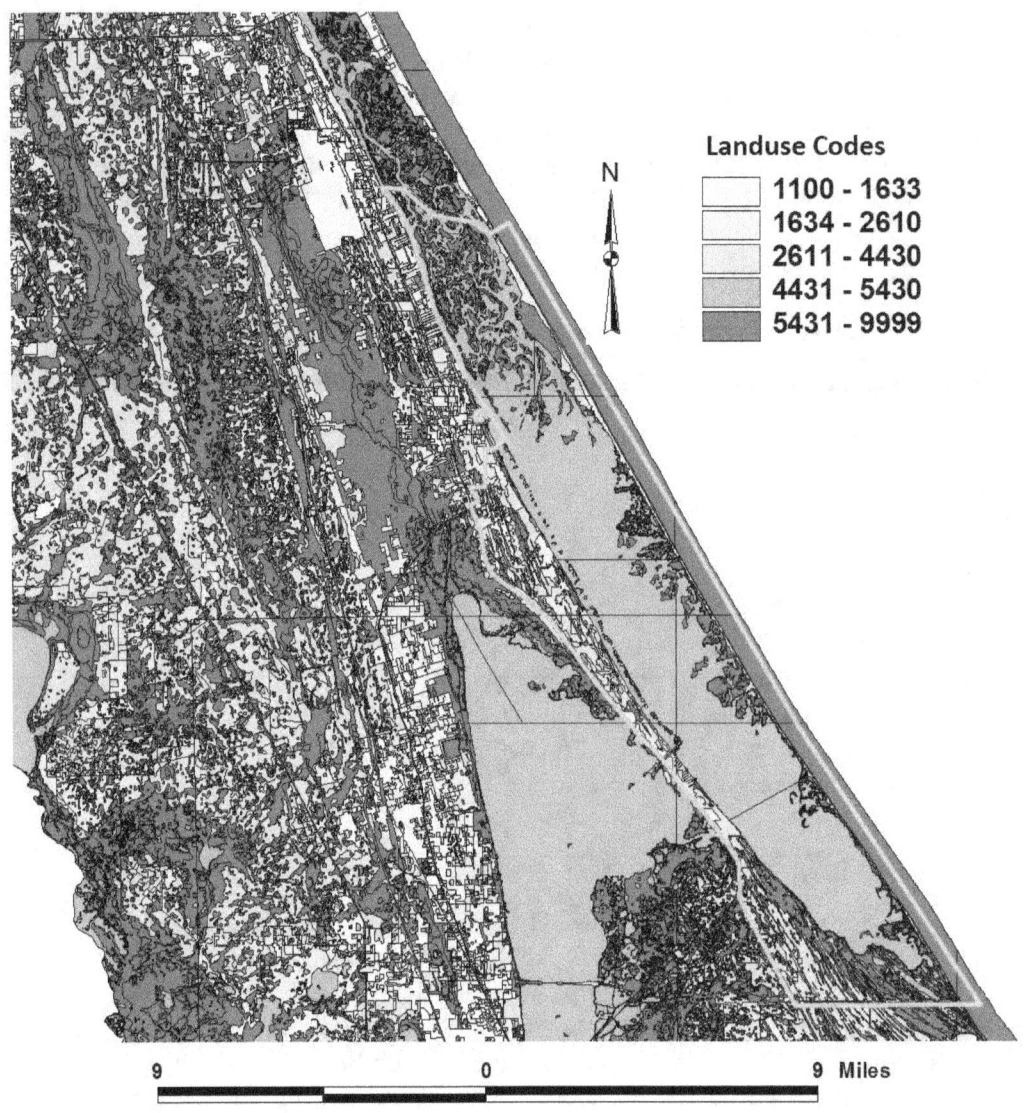

Figure 3. Generalized land-use map (2004). Land-use codes are described in Table 1 (St. Johns River Water Management District).

Fishing and Hunting

Permits and regulations for fishing and hunting in the Mosquito Lagoon require compliance with Florida FWC licensing (www.MyFWC.com) and MINWR. A self-signed MINWR permit (http://www.fws.gov/merrittisland/FishingRegs.html) is required for fishing crab, fish, clam, oyster, and shrimp in IRL, Mosquito Lagoon, mosquito control impoundments, and interior freshwater lakes. Seasonal hunting of migratory water fowl is allowed in the seashore and refuge and is part of the refuge's waterfowl management program. A self-sign MINWR hunt permit is required and additional Florida legal requirements must be met(http://www.fws.gov/merrittisland/Hunting%202010-11.pdf). Special hunting permits may apply to limited locations or for waterfowl hunting. Both activities are subject to closure by

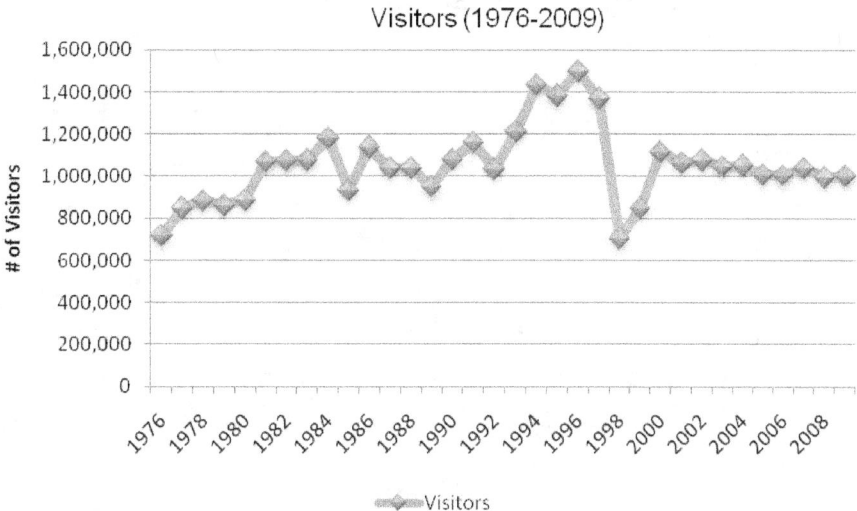

Figure 4. Number of annual visitors to Canaveral National Seashore from 1976–2009 (http://www.nature.nps.gov/stats).

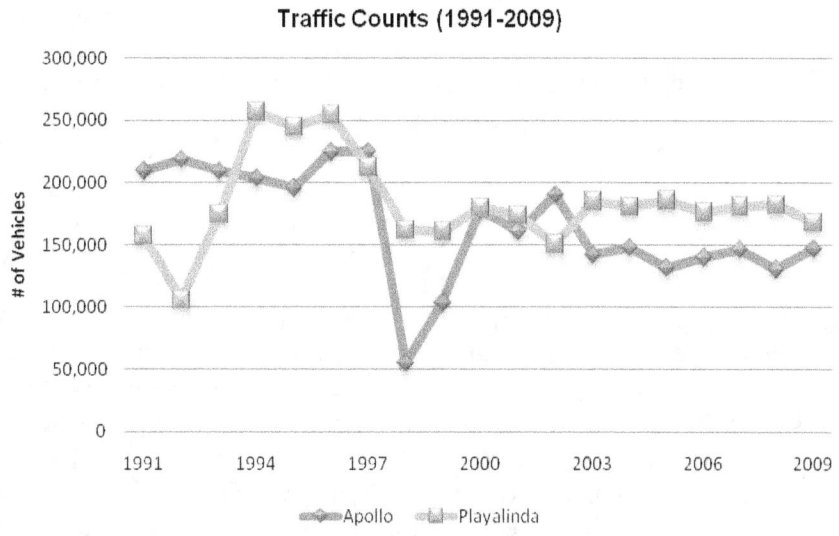

Figure 5. Annual traffic counts to Apollo and Playalinda beaches from 1991–2009 (http://www.nature.nps.gov/stats).

Kennedy Space Center during space shuttle launches. NPS does not maintain data on these activities; hence sources of information are MINWR and the U.S. Census Bureau. The number of fishermen (163,670) and hunters (958), estimated in 2003 by MINWR, applies to all areas under refuge management and may be slightly higher than actual for inside CANA proper (MINWR, 2008).

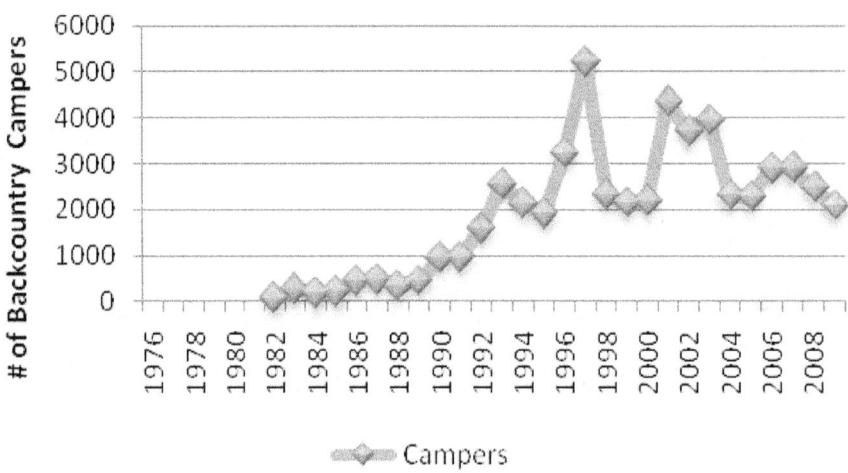

Figure 6. Number of annual backcountry campers from 1982–2009 (http://www.nature.nps.gov/stats).

Boating

Boats and mechanical marine vessels used for commerce or recreation are part of Florida's history and a draw for tourists, including those in the region of CANA (Sidman et al., 2007). Recreational and commercial boating activities impact water quality and harm wildlife and habitat in the park and surrounding areas (Morris, J. and B. Nodine, 1995; USFWS, 2001; Walters et al., 2003; Walters, et al., 2007; Scheidt and Garreau, 2007; MINWR, 2008: Schaub et al., 2009). Understanding boaters and their behavior is useful for minimizing the potential impacts of boating and related activities. Boating activity was examined to identify programs that improve boating-related recreation and reduce the impact to natural resources.

In a year-long study of recreational boating for Brevard County (Sidman et al., 2007) researchers characterized attributes associated with boating, such as destinations in Brevard County, vessel registration location, and boaters' perceptions of constraints and opportunities for boating activities. The Florida Department of Highway Safety and Motor Vehicles (FLDMV) issues annual vessel registrations and maintains a database of boat registrations by size class and whether the vessel is usd for commerce or pleasure (http://www.flhsmv.gov). The total number of vessels registered in Brevard, Indian River, Orange, Seminole, and Volusia counties from 2005–2009 peaked between 2005–2007 (Figure 7); the largest category was recreational vessels. These statistics mirror the pattern of registration numbers across Florida where licensed vessels decreased from 799,496 during the fiscal year 2007–2008 to 746,862 during the fiscal year 2008–2009 (FLDMV, 2010). It is unknown whether the most recent decline in vessel registration is caused by the economic downturn or increased fuel prices, or if the decline is short term or long term.

Mosquito Lagoon is one of the "hot spot" destinations with three seasons: a peak season from May–July, two shoulder seasons (March–April, August–October), and an off season (November–February) (Sidman et al., 2007). The study tracked vessel origination by county: Brevard (66.2%), Orange (12.9%), Seminole (7.1%), Indian River (3.6%), and Volusia (2.2%).

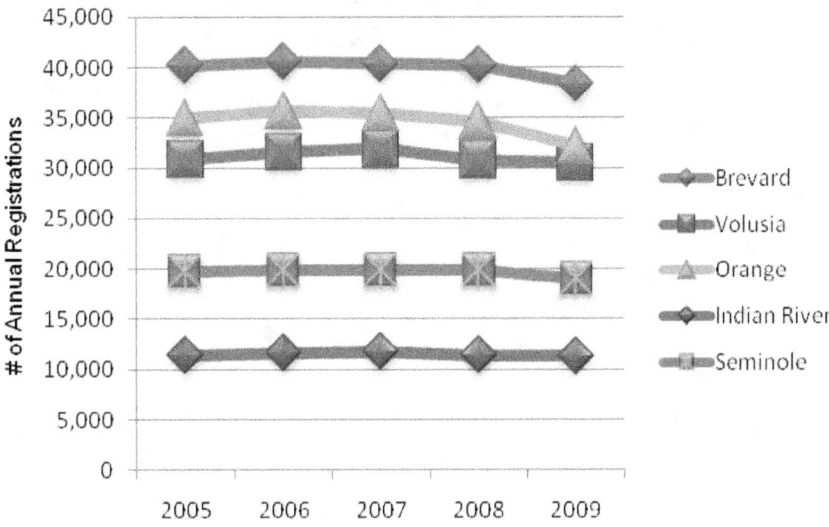

Figure 7. Annual number of boat registrations for Brevard, Volusia, Orange, Seminole and Indian River counties from 2005–2009 (http://www.flhsmv.gov).

Countywide, the top three activities ranked from highest to lowest were fishing, nature viewing, and sightseeing. Figure 8 shows boater destinations in Brevard County during peak season projected. Boater destinations are concentrated along the AIWW near Haulover Canal transiting north to Volusia County and in the southern end of the Mosquito Lagoon. A study by Sidman et al. (2007) provides new information for the NPS estimate of 20 boats per day in Mosquito Lagoon (NPS, 2005; http://www.nature.nps.gov/stats/CountingInstructions/CANACI2005.pdf).

Attempts to quantify the use of boats and resource use by boaters in Mosquito Lagoon have been ongoing since 1987 (Scheidt et al., 2002a). Aerial boat surveys flown in 2002 over portions of Mosquito Lagoon under MINWR and KSC jurisdiction identified more than 3,400 boaters during 43 flights. Use was greatest on Saturdays and the highest density of users was in Haulover Canal and the areas around Georges Bar (Scheidt et al., 2002b). Between June 2006 and May 2007, Scheidt and Garreau (2007) flew bi-weekly aerial surveys over Mosquito Lagoon, and they estimated more than 46,000 boats in the lagoon over the 12-months.

Programs administered by government agencies, cities, and counties that involve boating, such as law enforcement of fishing and hunting, species protection, boater safety, and marine sanitation devices, are shared by FWC, USWFS, and county sheriff departments. Special programs such as collection and recycling of monofilament line and derelict boats and promoting properly operating pump-out stations are often managed at the county level.

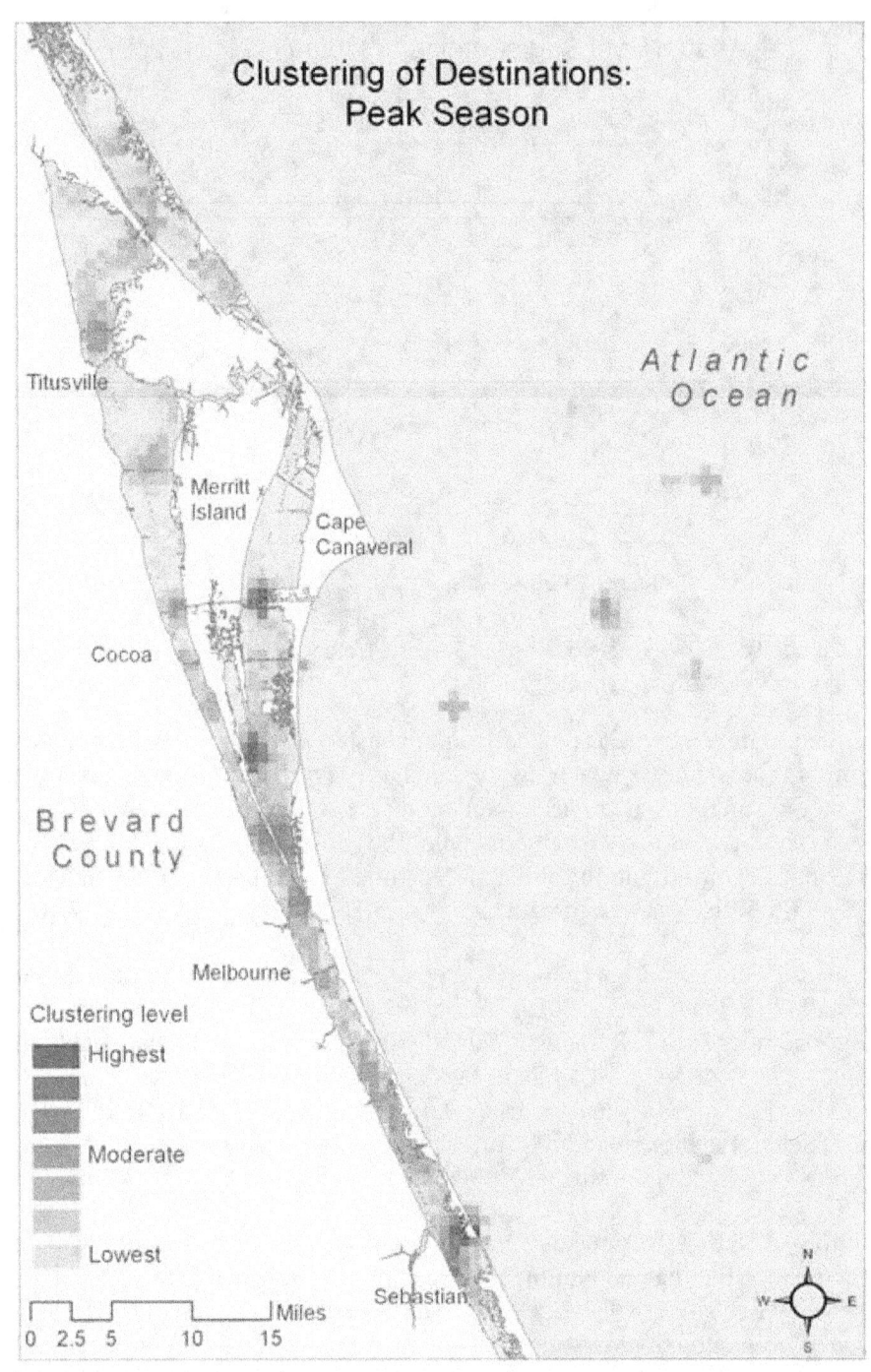

Figure 8. Boating destinations during peak season in Brevard County. Density clusters are greatest near Haulover Canal in north Mosquito Lagoon and in the southern end of the lagoon (Sidman et al., 2007).

Resource Characterization

CANA resources span the Atlantic Ocean coastal waters, barrier island, and estuarine lagoon with unparalleled diversity in the United States (FDEP, 2009). The microtidal environment of the Atlantic Ocean on Florida's central east coast is punctuated with northeasters and hurricanes. These natural events cause relatively little impact to the undeveloped beach due to the beach's ability to withstand the cycles of shifting coastline, unlike hardened coastal shorelines to the north and south of the park. The northern portion of the beach gradually widens to a flat, hard-packed, fine-grained sandy surface, whereas at the southern end of CANA near the Kennedy Space Center (KSC), the beach narrows and is a steeply sloped surface of shell-rich sand.

The beach, the shoreface, and the coastal waters of the Atlantic Ocean offer habitat to benthic organisms, fish, birds, mammals, and reptiles. Northern right whales and West Indian manatee (*Trichechus manatus*) also utilize the coastal ocean (USFWS, 2002; 2009). Commercial and recreational fishing contribute to state and local economies. Canaveral National Seashore is in the eastern North American migratory bird path known as the Atlantic Flyway; as birds migrate, they stop for food, cover, and resting areas (USFWS, 2008). The beach is an important nesting area for five species of sea turtles (USFWS, 2008; FWC-FWRI, 2006a). The beach is also a place for resident birds to nest, feed, and rest. From east to west, native plant communities on the dune and associated swales west of the dune are coastal strand, palmetto scrub, and oak scrub. There are no distinctive lines between the plant communities, as they often blend depending on soils, topography, and available water.

The plant communities of Mosquito Lagoon from back barrier to the western shoreline are composed of cabbage palm (palm hammock), saltwater wetland shrub-scrub, mangroves, salt marsh, and seagrasses (USFWS, 2008), which are all vital habitat for many species of fish, reptiles, birds (wading, waterfowl, raptors), and mammals. Protected species, such as the wood stork (*Mycteria americana*), Atlantic water snake (*Nerodia clarkii taeniata)*, manatee, and juvenile sea turtles, use the lagoon during at least one stage of their life cycle (USFWS, 2008; FDEP, 2009).

Mosquito Lagoon is in 15 watersheds, as defined by SJRWMD, which extend well beyond the park boundaries; it contains the populated municipal areas of New Smyrna Beach and industrialized areas of KSC at Cape Canaveral. Inputs to watersheds within and outside of CANA that may affect the park resources were included where appropriate.

Climate

The climate of Central Florida, including the Mosquito Lagoon area, is humid subtropical. There is a defined rainy season from approximately June through September, which are the months most likely to include landfall of tropical cyclones. Figure 9 shows a plot of monthly precipitation data and the annual average derived from the U.S. National Climatic Data Center database for north Central Florida. The interannual variability and correspondence of high rainfall rates with the wet season are apparent. Figure 10 shows a 20-year record of air temperature in Central Florida that demonstrates year-to-year variation and seasonal changes.

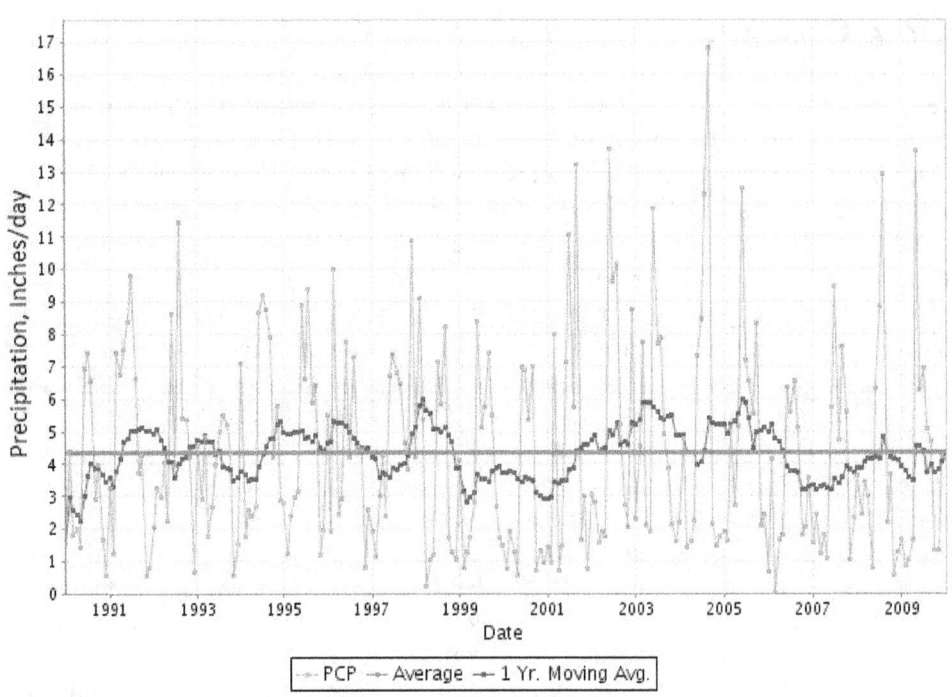

Figure 9. Twenty-year record of precipitation for east Central Florida (U.S. National Climatic Data Center).

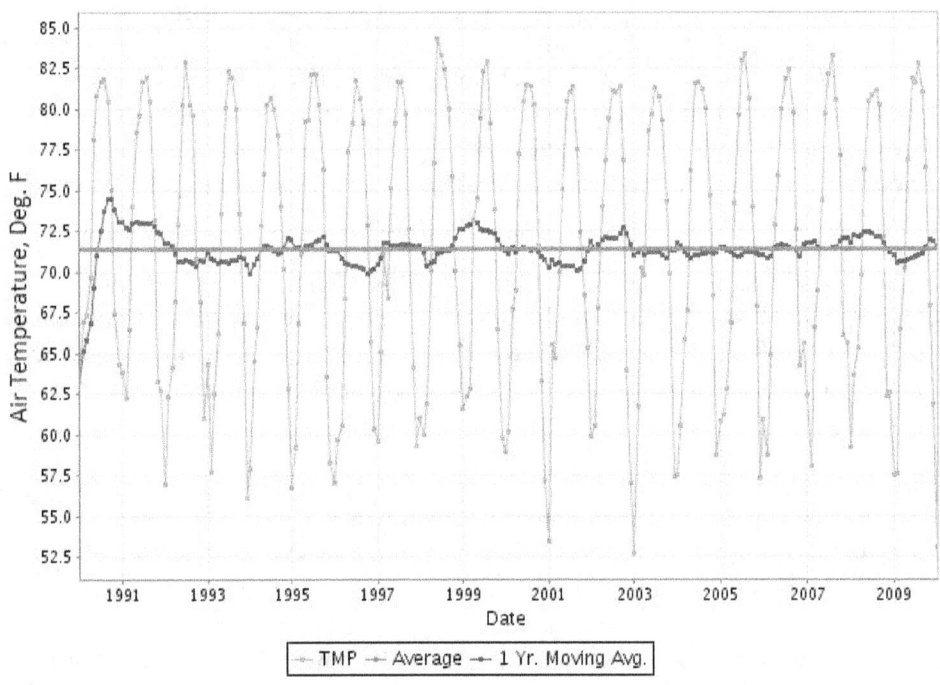

Figure 10. Twenty-year record of air temperature for east Central Florida (U.S. National Climatic Data Center).

The wet season is characterized by thunder storms, lightning, and occasional tornado activity. Another summer phenomenon not widely recognized by the general public is increased atmospheric dust emanating from Africa that affects air quality. Between October and May, fronts regularly cross through the state, which keep conditions dry. Occasional tropical storms affect the area and influence current and wave action in the coastal ocean. Both tropical cyclones and extra tropical northeastern events can strongly influence circulation and wave action in the coastal ocean and may cause storm surge at the coastline. During winters when an El Niño climate cycle occurs, rainfall increases and temperatures are cooler statewide.

Seasonal variations in air temperature and wind velocity over the coastal ocean are conveniently summarized from long-term records (1988–2008) of NOAA NBDC Buoy 41009. Figure 11 shows the average monthly wind speed in knots (about 0.5 m/s) at Buoy 41009 between 1988 and 2008. Similarly, Figure 12 shows the mean and standard deviation of air temperatures recorded during the 20-year period at the buoy between 1988 and 2008. In both plots, the seasonal signals are apparent, including increases in monthly average wind speeds and lower temperatures during the winter months and decreased wind speed and an increase in air temperature during the summer months.

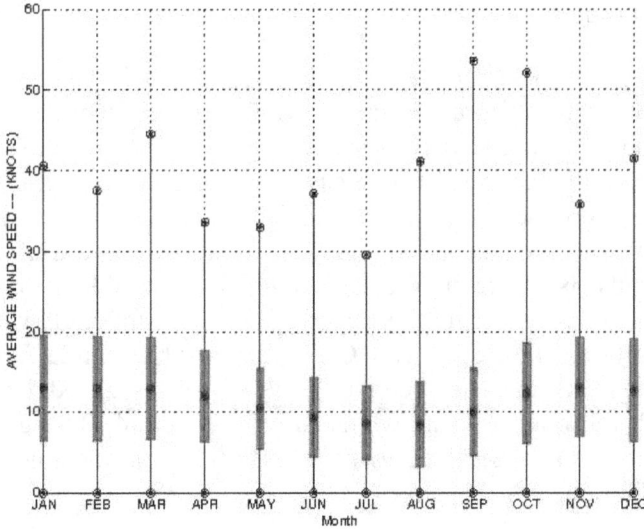

Figure 11. Monthly mean wind speed (knots) at NOAA Buoy 41009. The red bar is 1 standard deviation about the mean; the line above the bar is the maximum wind speed; and the line below the bar is the minimum wind speed.

Wind and Storm Climatology

The climatic regime and episodic occurrence of storms in the South Atlantic Bight (SAB) region of the U.S. has an important influence on continental shelf dynamics. Climatic and storm signals are particularly apparent over the inner continental shelf and at the shoreline where tides, waves, and storm surge are amplified by the shallow depths. Many of these signals, although filtered by constricted tidal inlets, can propagate into shallow coastal waters such as the Mosquito Lagoon.

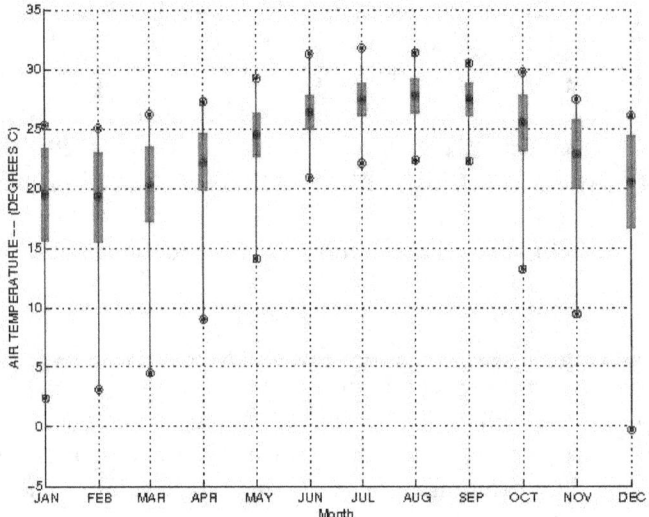

Figure 12. Monthly mean air temperature (degrees C) at NOAA Buoy 41009. The red bar is 1 standard deviation about the mean; the line above the bar is the maximum air temperature; and the line below the bar is the minimum air temperature.

Five seasonal wind regimes are associated with East Florida Shelf regions (Weber and Blanton, 1980). In winter (November to February/March), winds are persistently southeastward in North Carolina and turn more southward over Florida. During the winter months, frequent extra-tropical cyclones can develop across the southeastern states and out over the Atlantic Ocean. These storms frequently produce gale force winds that can cause property damage and beach erosion. During spring transition (March to May) winds shift westward from Florida to South Carolina, with the winds elsewhere in the region being more variable. In summer (June and July) westward winds dominate the southern reaches of the domain, and northward flow sets in for the central to northern portions of the SAB from Georgia to North Carolina. During August, the summer wind pattern breaks down and becomes generally disorganized. However, Florida can experience westward and southwestward winds during this period. During the "Mariner's fall" (September and October) strong southwestward winds occur over the domain, with westward winds at times over Florida.

The southeast U.S. region typically experiences weekly easterly tropical waves and several tropical cyclones and hurricanes each year. Neumann et al. (1993) quantified the mean direction of the tropical cyclone tracks from 1886 to 1989 (Figure 13). Generally, if storms do not recurve east of 60° W, they will make landfall along the U.S. coast. The official Atlantic hurricane season runs from June 1 through November 30, with a peak from mid-August through mid-October. For 2010, NOAA estimated that 12 to 15 tropical storms would form, including 6–8 becoming major hurricanes of category 3 or higher on the Saffir–Simpson Hurricane Scale. Figure 14 shows the total hurricane strikes by county between 1900 and 2009 in the SAB. From Figure 14, it can be seen that the Brevard–Volusia area has been impacted by 7–10 hurricanes over the past 109 years.

The NOAA Sea, Lake, and Overland Surges from Hurricanes model, among others, has been used to predict maximum levels of a storm's surge that can occur due to storms of varying intensity. Figure 15 shows predicted maximum water levels that could occur in the coastal area of Central Florida from a category 1 hurricane, which can be compared to Figure 16 showing predicted water levels from a category 4 hurricane. For the minimal hurricane, water levels along the open coast could reach about 6 ft (1.8 m) above normal and 2–3 (0.61-0.91 m) feet above normal in the Mosquito Lagoon. For a category 4 storm, coastal water levels could reach up to 14 ft (4.3 m) above normal and 7–10 ft (2.1-3.0 m) above normal in the Mosquito Lagoon. Breaching of the barrier system could result in more inland flooding.

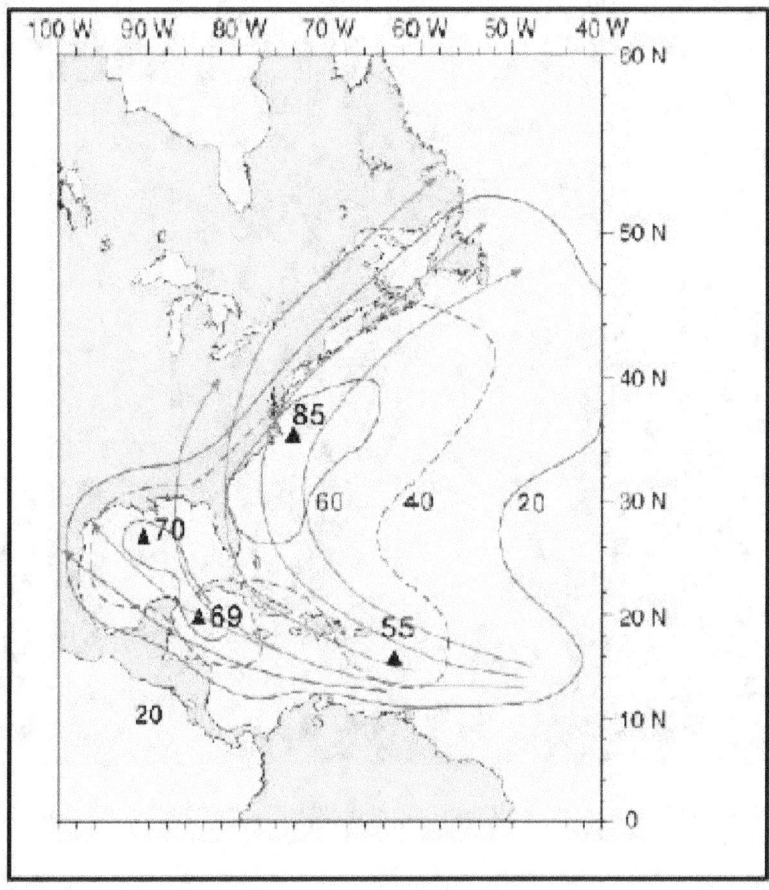

Figure 13. Tropical cyclone tracks (red) and number of cyclone occurrences (blue contours) over 103 years (Neumann et al., 1993).

Physical Oceanography: Tidal Regime and Sea Levels

The tides of the Florida inner continental shelf are strongly dominated by the semidiurnal forcing of the M2 (lunar) and S2 (solar) constituents. In the CANA project area, ocean tides are monitored continuously by only one National Ocean Survey (NOS) station (#8721604) that is in the somewhat protected Trident basin area of Port Canaveral. Real-time and historical water level data from this station can be obtained from the NOAA Center for Operational Oceanographic Products and Services. The next operational NOS station to the north is at Fernandina Beach in Duval County. Between Brevard and Duval County, there is a major shift from a microtidal regime, where the mean tidal range is approximately 3.3 ft (1 m), to a near

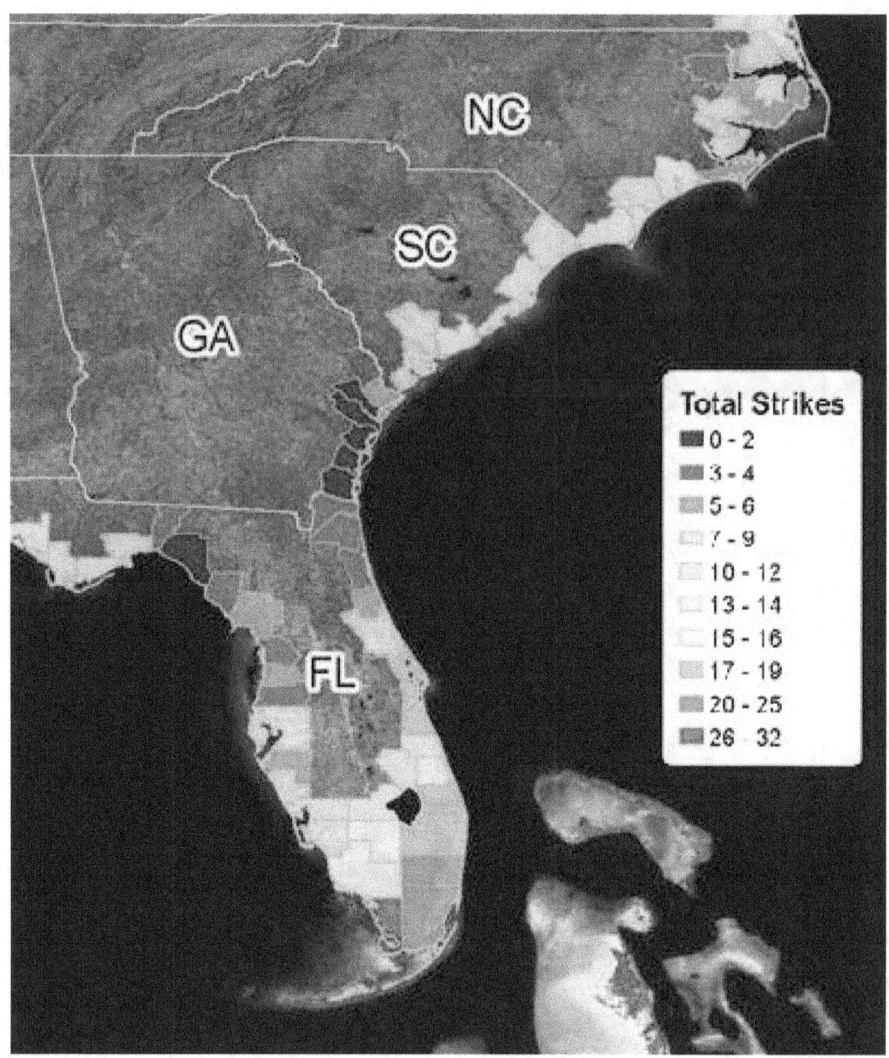

Figure 14. Number of hurricane strikes in the South Atlantic Bight by county from 1900–2009 (NOAA National Hurricane Center).

mesotidal regime at the Florida–Georgia border, where the mean tidal range is above 3.3 ft (1 m) m and approaches 6.6 ft (2 m) during spring tide conditions. The increase in tidal range corresponds with tidal amplification over the widening continental shelf north of Cape Canaveral to a maximum offshore of Savannah, Georgia, at the apex of the Georgia Bight. Some of this transition takes place along the length of the Mosquito Lagoon. Figure 17 compares recorded water levels from the Fernandina Beach and Trident Pier gages for a two-week period in late 2005. The tides at both stations are very close in phase, but the tidal range at the Fernandina Beach station is distinctly larger. A relatively weak diurnal inequality is apparent in both records. McBride (1987) noted the inverse relationship between tide and wave regime along the Florida coast, classifying the northeast Florida coast as mostly tide-dominated, which is similar to the conceptual model described by Hayes (1979).

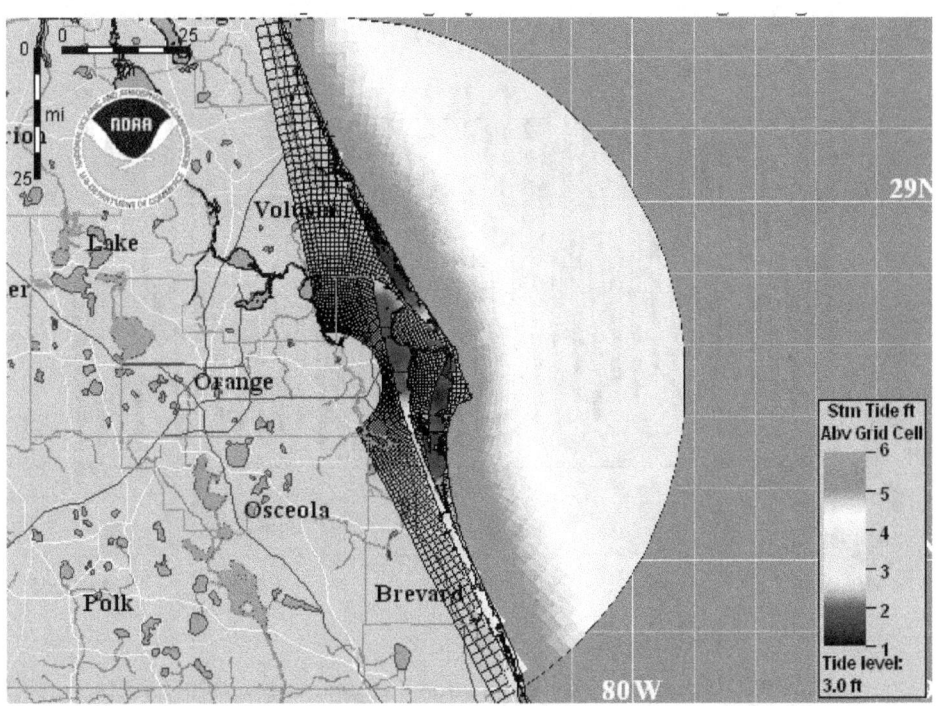

Figure 15. Predicted maximum water levels that could occur in the coastal area of Central Florida during a category 1 hurricane (NOAA National Hurricane Center).

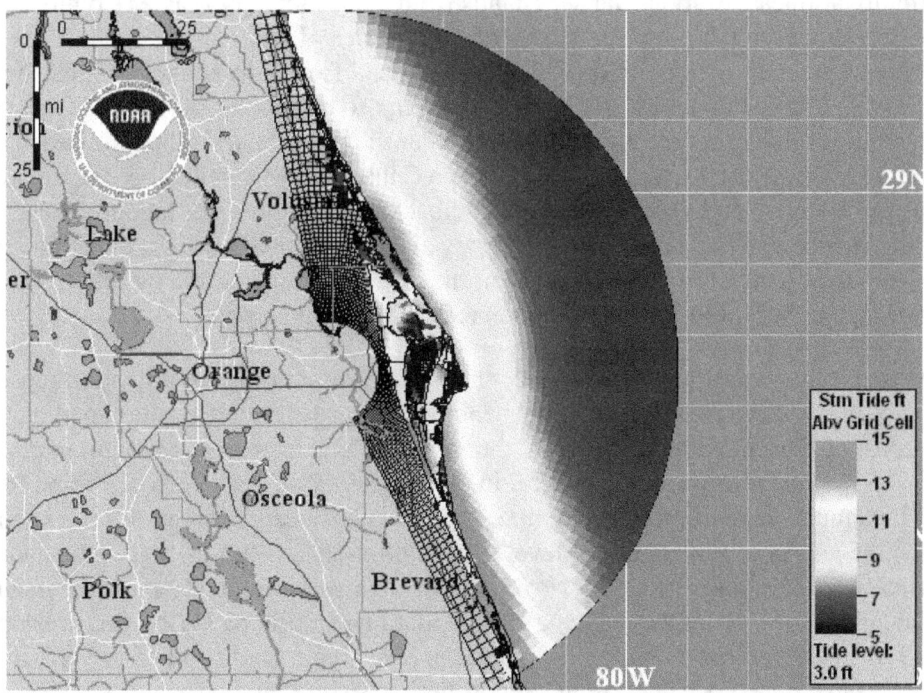

Figure 16. Predicted maximum water levels that could occur in the coastal area of Central Florida during a category 4 hurricane (NOAA National Hurricane Center).

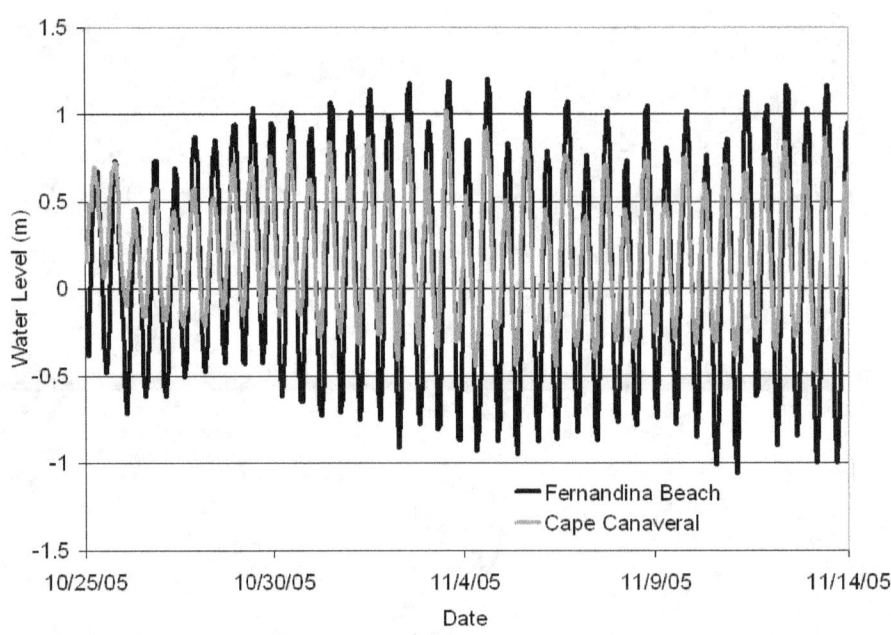

Figure 17. Comparison of 20-day water level records from Fernandina Beach (NOS Station 8720030) and Cape Canaveral (NOS Station 8721604).

Barrier island morphology reflects the transition from the microtidal to mesotidal regime from East Central to Northeast Florida. Barrier islands from approximately Flagler County and north are predominantly beach ridge barriers composed of a series of coalescing beach ridges added progressively to the seaward side of these features by sand from tide-generated inlet shoal deposits (Hayes, 1979). In contrast, the barrier along the southern half of Volusia County is a single-ridge barrier bordering the Mosquito Lagoon until it merges with the relic beach ridge system that forms the False Cape just north of Cape Canaveral. Microtidal barrier islands are more likely to be storm- and wave-dominated and backed by open-water lagoons rather than the marshy back-barrier areas of a mesotidal barrier system. The transition from a marsh- and mangrove-dominated back-barrier area in the north part of the lagoon to a largely open-water, back-barrier area in the south Mosquito lagoon reflects this transition.

In addition to strong tidal influence, the inner shelf of Northeast Florida is also influenced by large changes in sea level at the subtidal frequency. Figure 18 compares water level records along the coast of Florida with the tidal signal removed. The records are coherent in phase along the entire coast of east Florida, but can differ in the magnitude of sea level oscillation from place to place. The annual range of sea level along east Florida has been as great as 9.9 ft (3 m) in some years; the annual low stand of sea level is most often in late July, whereas the annual high stand is usually in late October to early November of each year. Figure 19 plots the mean annual nontidal range of sea level for the Daytona Shores Station (Station 8721120) that was operated between 1970–1985. It clearly shows the annual sea level cycle that is linked to variations in wind, water temperatures, ocean currents, atmospheric pressure, and passing storms.

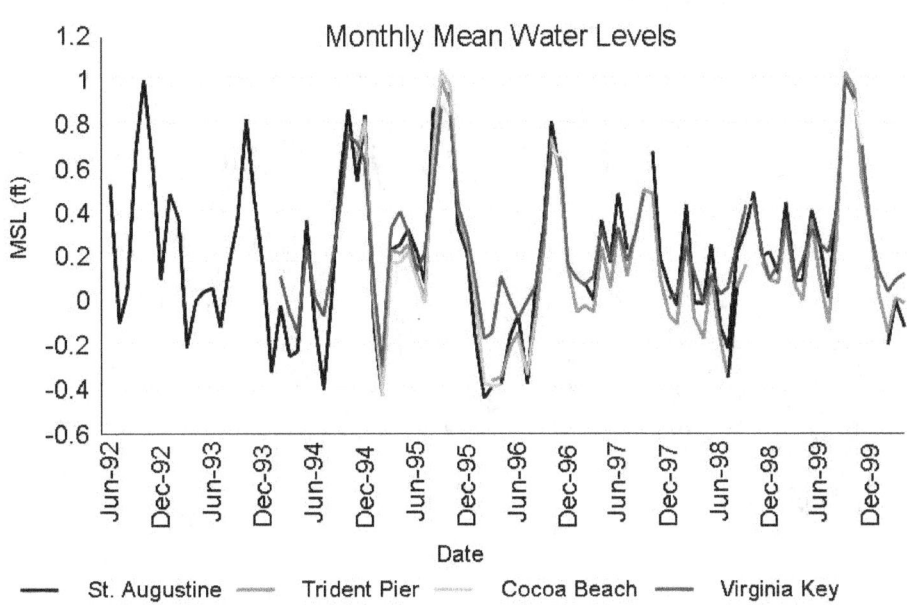

Figure 18. Non-tidal sea level records at four National Ocean Survey stations on the east Florida coast.

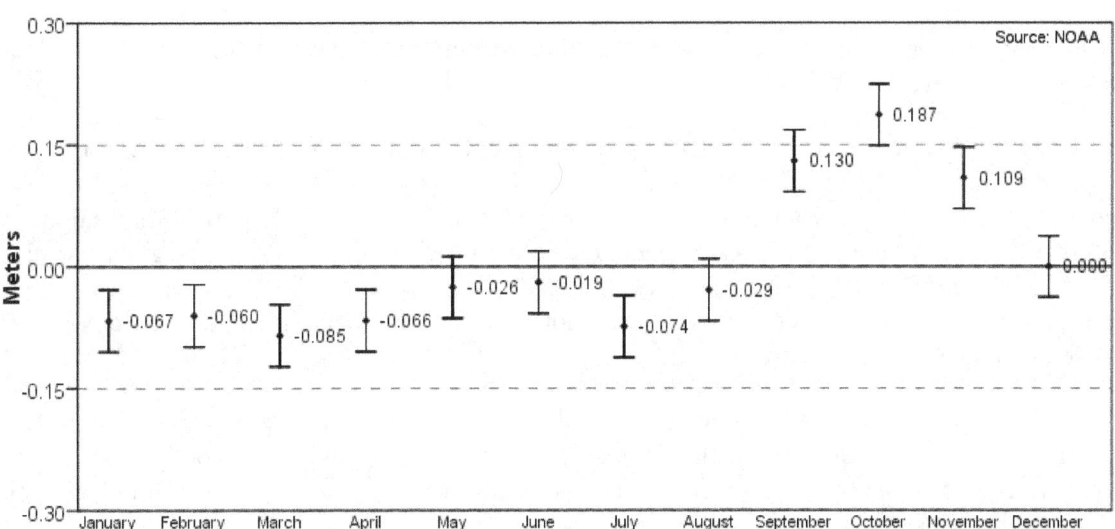

Figure 19. Seasonal variation in mean sea level derived from water level records acquired between 1970–1985 at South Daytona Beach (NOAA Center for Operational Oceanographic Products and Services).

The period of record for the Trident Pier NOS station is shorter than other NOS stations in Florida. However, the 2009 record of sea level at Port Canaveral has a similar seasonal record, as shown in Figure 20. Mean sea level varied over a range of about 2.3 ft (0.7 m). Similar to

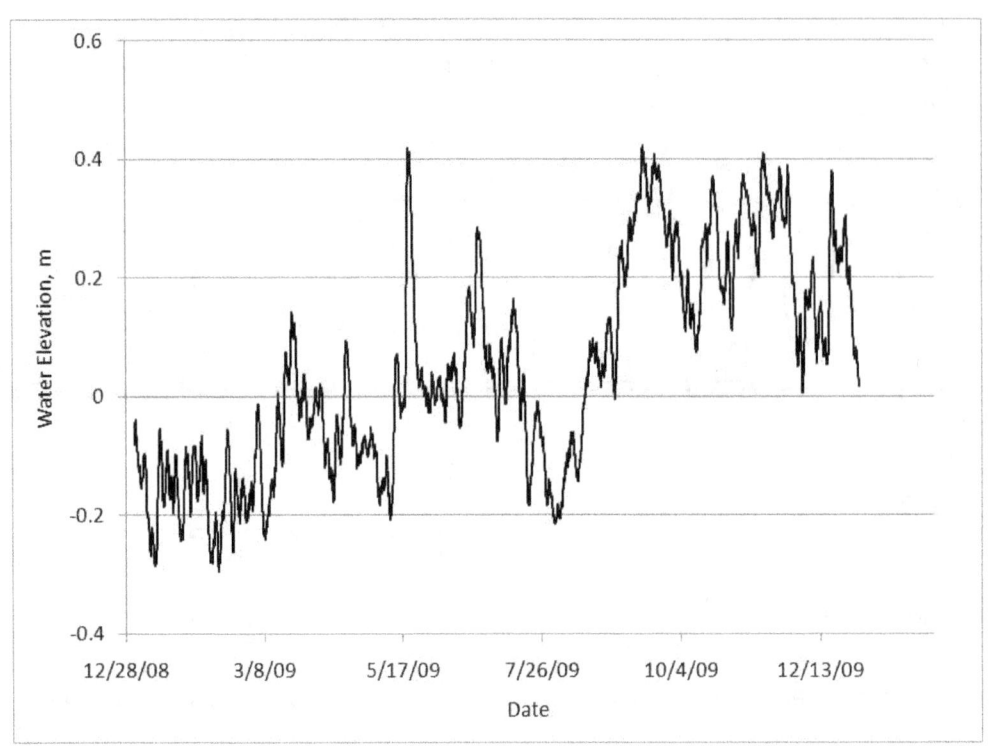

Figure 20. Variation in mean seal level at Trident Pier NOS Station 8721604 in Port Canaveral in 2009.

other stations along the east coast of Florida, minimum sea level occurred in late July followed by higher sea level in the fall months.

Long-term observations of the spectral wave field in either shallow or deep water are very limited in the coastal ocean offshore of CANA. Long-term hind casts of swell and wind wave conditions across the continental shelf are available from the U.S. ACOE Wave Information Study (WIS). WIS hind cast data are generated from numerical models driven by global wind field predictions placed on model grids containing bathymetric data. The WIS numerical hind casts provide long-term wave climate information at near-shore locations (numerical recording stations) of U.S. coastal oceans.

WIS hind cast wave information indicates that the dominant or most energetic waves approach from the easterly direction, although distinctive seasonal differences occur in both direction and energy. Figure 21 shows a summary of hind cast significant wave height by direction from WIS numerical Station 431, just offshore of the Mosquito Lagoon.

Few long-term directional wave gages have been deployed in shallow water along the northeast Florida coast. Several directional wave gages were deployed at Ponce Inlet from October 1995 through March 1997. The deployment was part of the Coastal Inlets Research program of the U.S. ACOE Coastal and Hydraulics Laboratory (CHL). The CHL directional wave gage was located about 1.2 mi (2 km) offshore to the northeast of Ponce Inlet in a water depth of about 46 ft (14 m). Figure 22 shows the joint probability between significant wave height and direction of

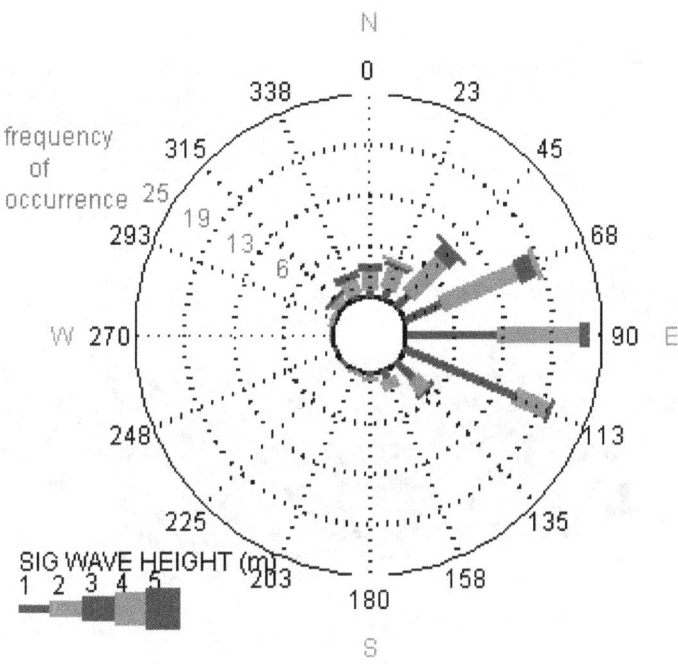

Figure 21. Summary of hind cast wave heights and directions from 1980–1999 at WIS Station 431 (Coastal and Hydraulics Laboratory Wave Information Study).

data collected at this station for the fall and winter months from 1995 to 1997. The nearshore wave spectrum has a joint probability maximum from the east–northeast at an approach of 75° and significant wave height of about 1.6 ft (0.5 m) for data recorded during the October to March period. For spring and summer, energy peak at this station shifted to approximately 80° at a significant wave height of about 1 ft (0.3 m).

The period of record at the Ponce Inlet gage is not long enough to distinctly resolve seasonal variations in wave energy. The wave records show distinct variations in the mean wave height over several months as well as maximum significant wave heights of 8.9 ft (2.7 m) and 12.1 ft (3.7) m during the period of record (Figure 23).

Climate Change

Global climate change is a complex and controversial subject that has direct implications for the management of CANA resources. A comprehensive review of the scientific basis for climate change and forecasts of climate change can be found in the multi-volume report of the Intergovernmental Panel on Climate Change (Soloman et al., 2007).

The four major aspects of climate change are: 1) increasing greenhouse gases, 2) increasing air temperature and water vapor, 3) increasing ocean temperature, and 4) and increasing sea level. In a 2009 report by the Florida Oceans and Coastal Council (FOCC, 2009), these components of climate are called "drivers," and for each driver, the effects on Florida's ocean and coastal resources are described in terms of probable and possible effects. The FOCC document provides a reference list of publications and government reports that describe the science behind the FOCC analysis. The FOCC report states that none of the effects of climate change are expected

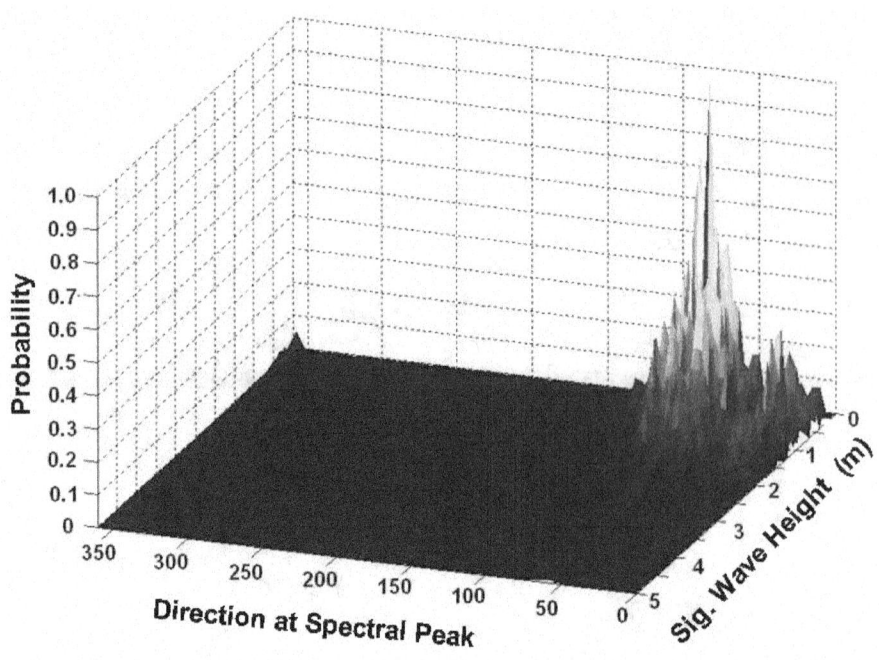

Figure 22. Joint probability between significant wave height and peak direction at CHL Ponce Inlet Station DWG1INT1 from October to March. Monitoring period is 1995–1997.

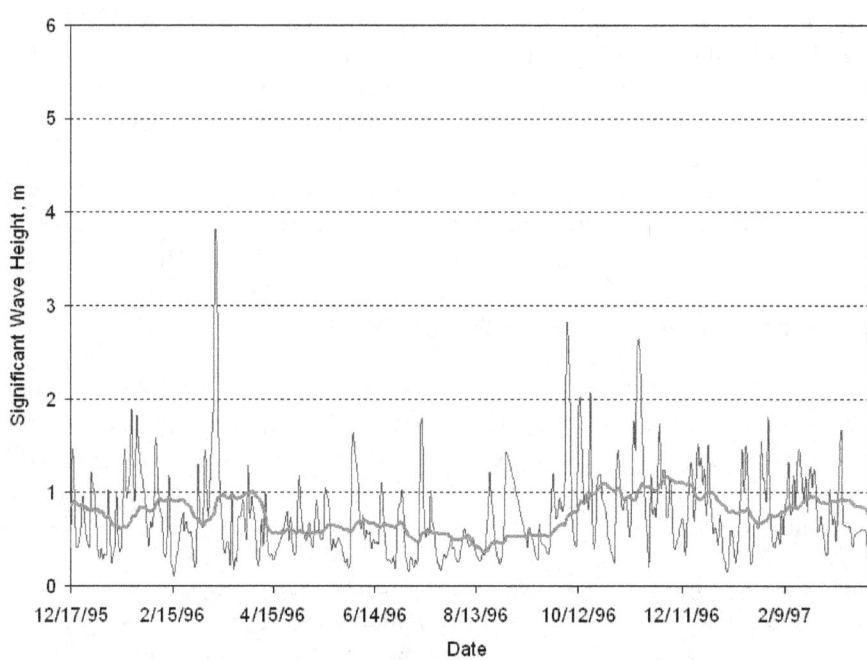

Figure 23. Significant wave height record at CHL gage DWG1INT1 located 2 mi (3.2 km) offshore of Ponce Inlet.

to be beneficial to Florida. Coastal Florida, including the CANA area, is particularly vulnerable to climate change due to its low elevation and sensitive coastal ecosystems that are formed largely by emergent wetlands and submerged aquatic vegetation (SAV) separated from the coastal ocean by a dynamic barrier island system.

Table 2 lists the drivers of climate change and the potential effects on Florida's coastal and ocean resources discussed in the FOCC report. Virtually all of the drivers and associated effects may impact CANA resources. Of particular importance, however, are effects that are related directly to rising sea level. Wetlands that are unable to keep pace with rising sea level through sedimentation can fragment and eventually drown. The CANA barrier island system responds to rising sea level at the millennia time scale by migrating landward and upward over its own back barrier sediments. However, any acceleration in the rate of sea level rise linked to global warming may limit the ability of the barrier to remain fully integrated. The predicted increase in the intensity of storms linked to global climate change may increase episodes of barrier island breaching and accelerate the transgression rate of the coastal barrier and associated sedimentary environment. To help recognize impacts of climate change on the CANA barrier island and back barrier shorelines, the NPS Southeast Coast Network (SECN) will implement ocean shoreline change measurements in CANA using GPS method from amphibious all-terrain vehicle ATV supplemented by remote sensing (DeVivo et al., 2008).

Table 2. Drivers and effects of climate change. Adapted from Florida Oceans and Coastal Council (2009).

Driver	Effect/Change
Increasing Greenhouse Gasses	Increases in Ocean Acidification
Increasing Air Temperature and Water Vapor	Altered Rainfall and Runoff Patterns
	Altered Frequency and Intensity of Tropical Storms and Hurricanes
Increasing Ocean Temperature	Changes in Nutrient Supply, Recycling, and Food Webs
	Increases in Fish Diseases, Sponge Die-offs, Loss of Marine Life
	Harmful Algal Blooms and Hypoxia
	Changes in the Distribution of Native and Exotic Species
	Increases in Coral Bleaching and Disease
Increasing Sea Level	Changes in Estuaries, Tidal Wetlands, and Tidal Rivers
	Changes in Beaches, Barrier Islands, and Inlets
	Reduced Coastal Water Supplies

To date, the long-term records of sea level from several NOS water level gages indicate linear trends of sea level rise over the past 50–100 yrs without measurable acceleration in the rate of sea level rise. Figure 24 shows the analysis of sea level trends from the NOS gage at Fernandina Beach (NOS Station 8720030). The mean sea level trend is 0.08 in/yr (2.02 mm/yr) with a 95% confidence interval of ±0.008 in/yr (±0.20 mm/yr) based on monthly mean sea level data from 1897–2006, which is equivalent to a change of 0.66 ft (0.2 m) in 100 yrs. A similar trend can be found in data from NOS Station 8720218 where the trend is 0.094 in/yr (2.39 mm/yr), which is equivalent to a change of 0.79 ft (0.24 m) in 100 yrs (Figure 25).

The predictions of future sea levels based on global climate models are uncertain. The longest sea level records in Florida, and elsewhere on the North American continent, do not show noticeable acceleration over the past 50–100 yrs. A discussion of sea level predictions, along

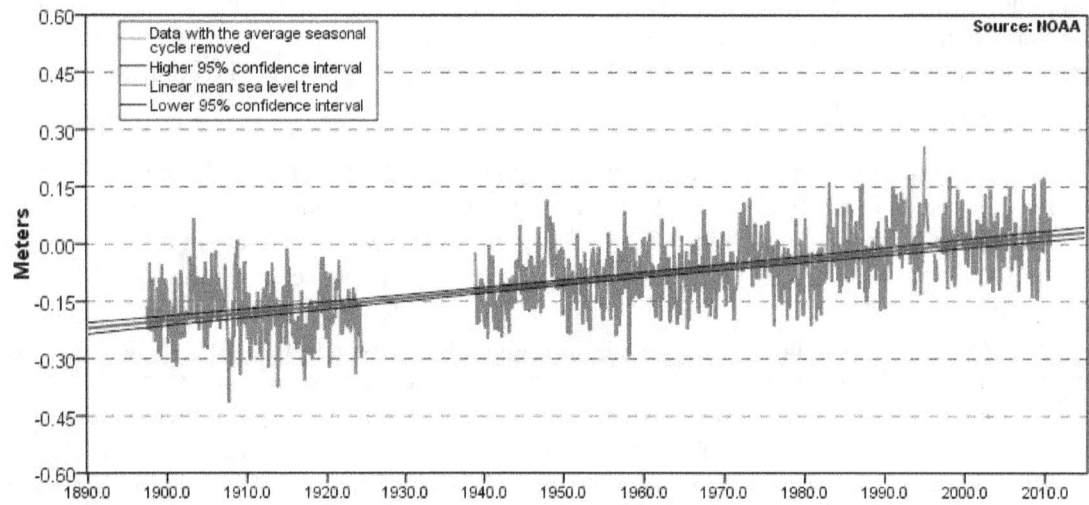

Figure 24. Mean sea level trends, Fernandina Beach, FL, at Station 8720030 (NOAA Center for Operational Oceanographic Products and Services).

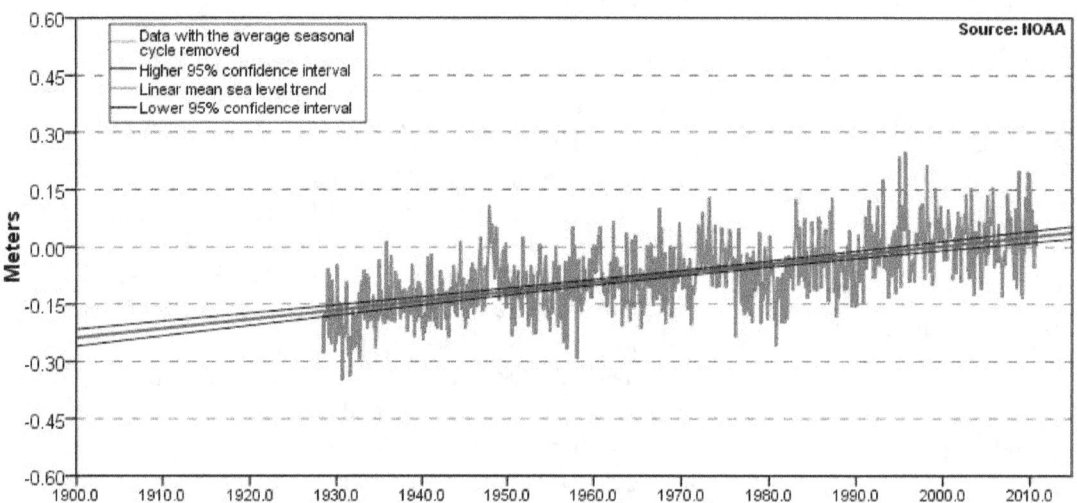

Figure 25. Mean sea level trends, Mayport, FL, at Station 8720218 (NOAA Center for Operational Oceanographic Products and Services).

with many other aspects on climate change, can be found in the 2007 assessment report on global climate change by the Intergovernmental Panel on Climate Change (Soloman et al., 2007).

Overall, the global or eustatic sea level is predicted to rise between about 2.3 ft (0.7 m) to more than 6.6 ft (2 m) over the next 100 yrs. The uncertainty in these predictions is great. Any acceleration in the rate of sea level rise is likely to trigger a broad range of issues for the management of CANA, beginning with the simple submergence and disintegration of wetlands, increased coastal flooding, and accelerated migration and evolution transgression of the CANA barrier system.

Geology
Geological Setting and Resources

The major components of surficial and near surface geology are summarized in the State Geological Map (Scott et al., 2001). CANA is largely within near surface units of the late Pleistocene to early Holocene fine grain sands overlying the Anastasia Formation (Figure 26).The modern surficial geology of the park has been shaped by the late Pleistocene epoch to early Holocene sea level cycle. At low stands of sea level, the carbonate-rich shoreline and

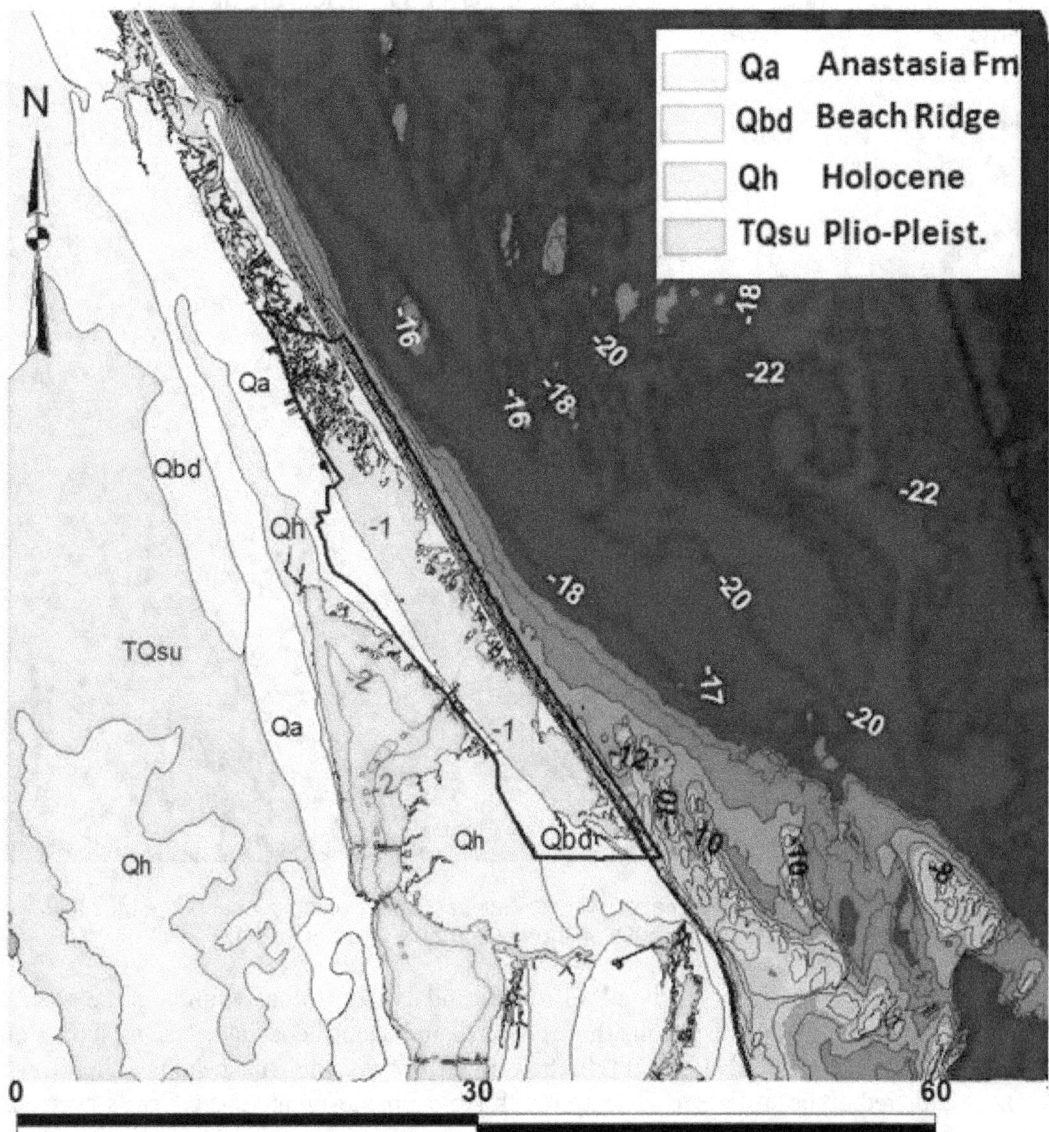

Figure 26. Surficial geology of the Canaveral National Seashore area. Qh indicates modern Holocene sediment types (beach, tidal inlet, storm washover, and undifferentiated shallow marine sands). Sediments Qbd include beach ridge sands of late Pleistocene and early Holocene epoch. Qa is shell-rich sediments of the late Pleistocene Anastasia Formation that are generally lithified in near-surface and surface exposures. TQsu is shelly sediments of late Pliocene and early Pleistocene age (Scott et al., 2001).

nearshore carbonate-rich sand are partially lithified to a coquina limestone by groundwater action. Figure 27 is an example of an exposure of the Anastasia Formation within Haulover Canal, connecting the Mosquito Lagoon with the northern compartment of the IRL. The tabular stratification consisting of coarse shell fragments is typical of the Anastasia coquina rock in the area and indicates deposition in a shallow marine, high-energy environment. The coquina of the Anastasia Formation and unconsolidated sands are the surface on which the modern barrier island has been constructed. It is likely that the erosion of the Anastasia by migrating tidal inlets contributed to the long-term sediment budget of the Canaveral area, leaving the relatively coarse carbonate-rich sands of the modern beach and shoreface.

Figure 27. Exposure of the Anastasia Formation within Haulover Canal, which connects the Mosquito Lagoon with the northern compartment of the IRL. (Photo: G. Zarillo, October 2010)

Figure 26 shows the major exposures of late Pleistocene and earlier Holocene units in the area. The Anastasia Formation (Qa) is ubiquitous through north and central coastal areas, as shown on the State Geological Map (Scott et al., 2001). In the Canaveral area, the Anastasia is either exposed and weathered at the surface or veneered with Holocene designated as Qh or is overlain by beach ridge sands of late Pleistocene or early Holocene age, designated as Qb in Figure 26. Qh sediment includes a range of textures that are typical of beach, shoreface, tidal inlet, storm washover, and undifferentiated shallow marine sands. Beach and upper shoreface sands include fine quartz-rich sand mixed with a carbonate fraction of shell fragments and whole shells that can extend into the fine gravel range coarser than 0.158 in (4 mm). Shell-rich modern sands can lithologically resemble sediments of the Anastasia Formations, indicating that the deposition of both occurred in beach and nearshore environments characterized by high energy. Tidal inlet sediment and washover sediment incorporated into the modern barrier island system of the park provide evidence of storms in shaping and maintaining the barrier island. The components of Qh sediments range in texture from medium to very fine sand and may include layers of coarse shells fragments indicative of storm deposition.

The storm washover and relict flood shoal deposits of Qh in Figure 26 can be stabilized by wetland and dune vegetation labeled as "BPw-Barrier Island, Platform, wetland" in Figure 28 (Parkinson and Schaub, 2007). Subtidal areas are likely to be silty sands and well-sorted, very fine sands deposited on the distal portion of a storm overwash terrace or distal flood shoal. The subtidal area is subject to seagrass colonization. The so-called barren areas "LSb-Lagoon Subtidal Barren" morphogenetic unit shown in Figure 28 (Parkinson and Schaub, 2007) of the shallow Mosquito Lagoon most likely consist of the typical fine-grained silty clays and silty sands of the back barrier lagoon. Relict beach ridges on the west side of the lagoon shown in Figure 26 and within Cape Canaveral proper are of uncertain data but may be late Pleistocene ridges related to an earlier high stand of sea level. These morphogenetic units are within the Qbd classification on the State Geologic Map.

The build-out of Cape Canaveral south of the Canaveral barrier island system has resulted from sand supplied by converging littoral drifts. Judging from the relict flood shoal features that are now incorporated into the superstructure of the Canaveral barrier island system (Figure 29), it is likely that a portion of the sand supply came from subtidal erosion of the older Pleistocene sediments by migrating tidal inlets. Sea level rise during the Holocene epoch, in combination with migrating tidal inlets, provided the overall transgressive process that formed and maintained the modern CANA barrier system and formed the system of discrete and compound shoals now situated on the inner continental shelf. During this process, the barrier island system migrated, overriding back barrier lagoon sediments. It left a shoal platform of sands like those situated offshore of Cape Canaveral, as well as discrete shoals that evolved from the ebb shoals and littoral sands processed by tidal inlets (McBride and Moslow, 1991).

Geological resources seaward of CANA have been documented to a limited degree by studies conducted for beach nourishment projects. Some detailed studies are available from the Canaveral Shoal system seaward of the Cape. Here, core borings through selected shoals show the typical coarsening sequence beginning with back barrier clays and silts common in the estuarine environment followed by coarse-grained transgressive units of sand along the crest of the shoals (Zarillo and Bacchus, 1992). Figure 30 illustrates the sequence that includes all possible units. In some areas, a layer of salt marsh peat or peat/organic-rich mud resting on top of the Pleistocene carbonate surface marks the first occurrence of near-marine conditions due to sea level rise in the early Holocene.

Sand resource investigations by Brevard, St. Johns, and Volusia counties, U.S. ACOE, the Florida Geological Survey (FGS), and the U.S. Bureau of Ocean Energy Management and Regulation (formerly the Minerals Management Service) were conducted for beach nourishment projects near the vicinity of CANA. Nearshore sand resources within state waters and in federal waters offshore of CANA have not been as thoroughly investigated as the Canaveral Shoals, south of the park, or the inner continental shelf shoal features north of Ponce Inlet. Approximately 3 million yds^3 (2.3 million m^3) of sand have been excavated from Canaveral Shoals for Brevard County beach fill projects. Investigations of inner shelf sand deposits were

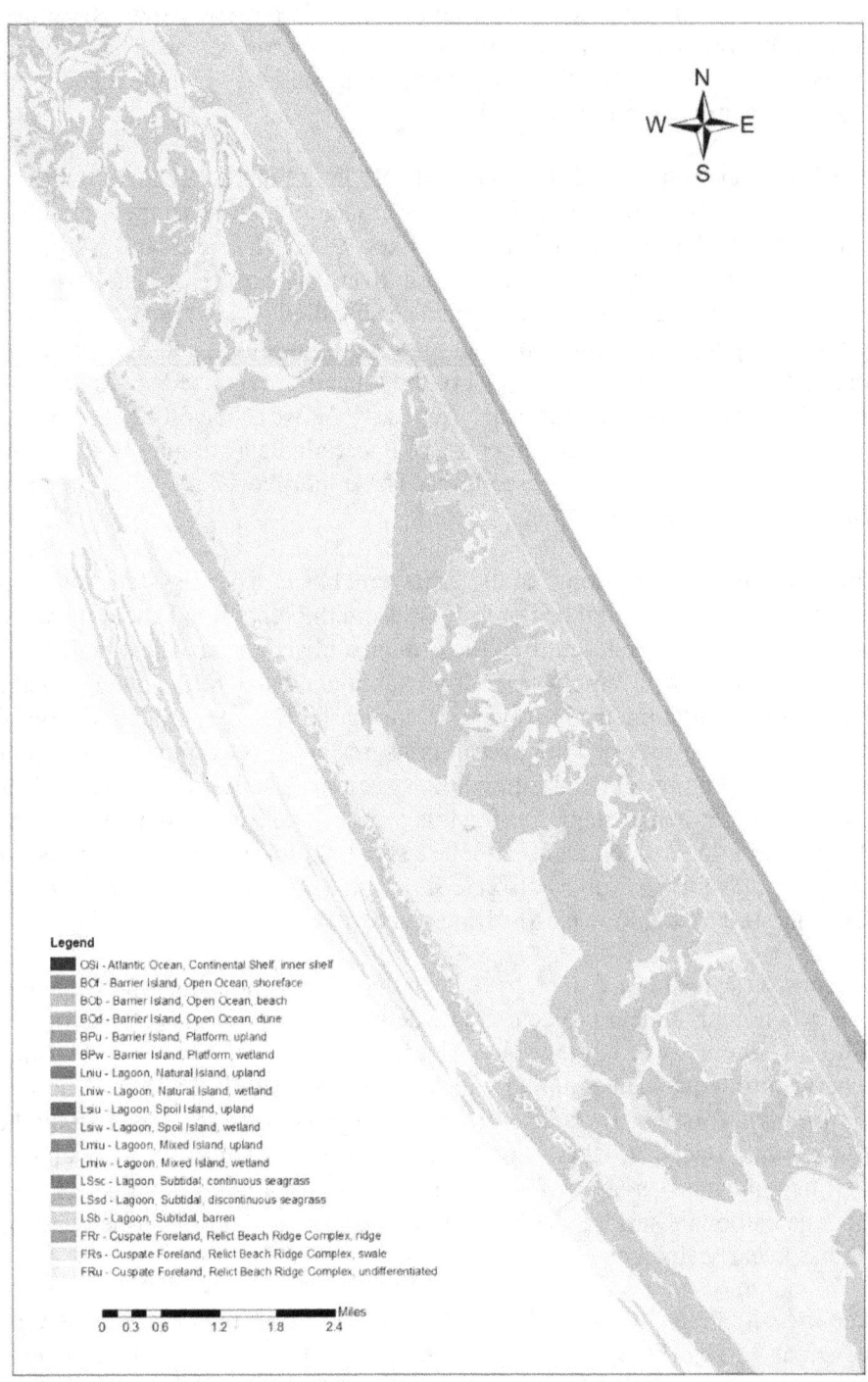

Figure 28. Morphogenetic units within Canaveral National Seashore constructed from surficial sediment types in Figure 26. BPw-Barrier Island, Platform, wetland is equivalent to Qh storm washover sediments. LSb-Lagoon Subtidal Barren likely consists of typical fine-grained silty clays and silty sands of the back barrier lagoon. Morphogenetic units FRr, FRs, Fru are within the Qbd (from Scott et al., 2001) and morphogenetic units (Parkinson and Schaub, 2007).

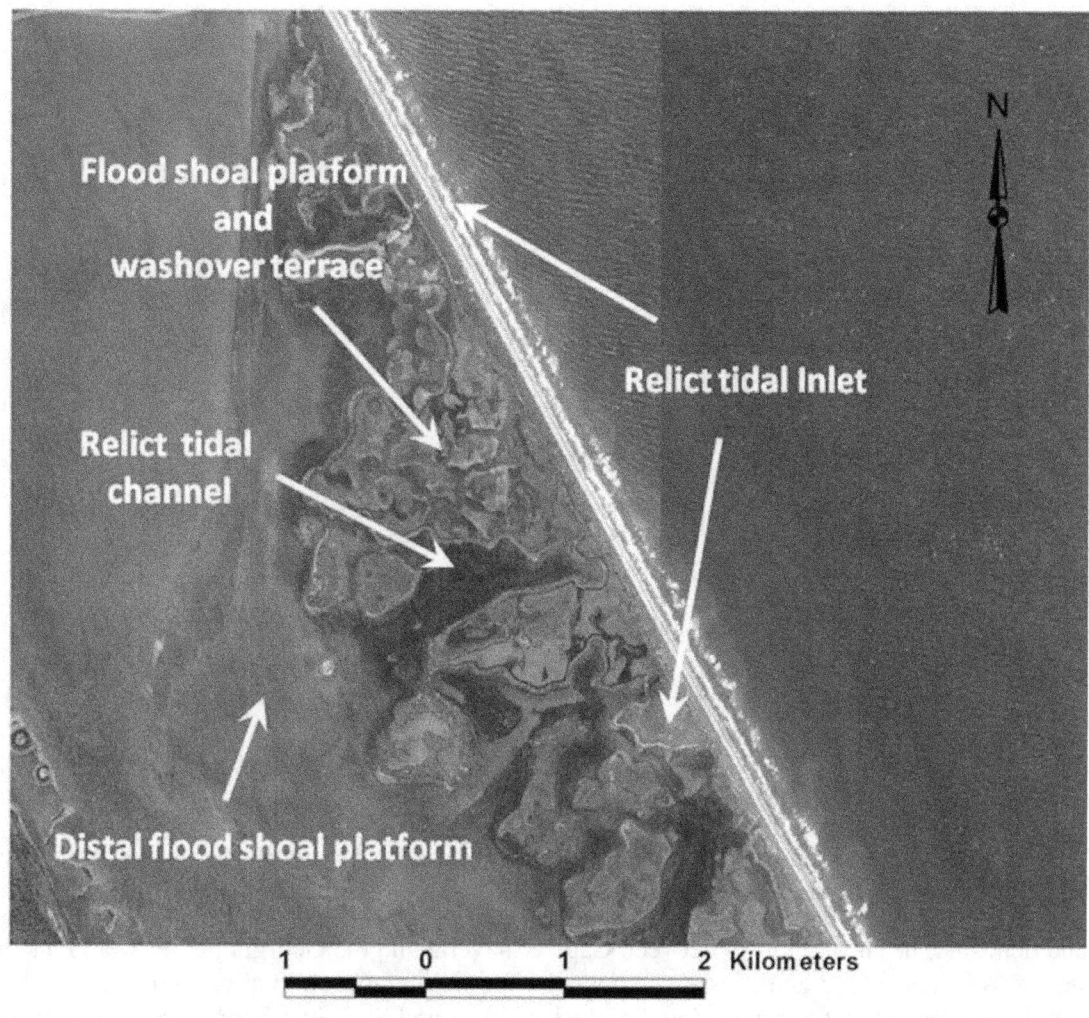

Figure 29. Relict tidal inlet flood shoal deposits included in the modern barrier island super structure in Canaveral National Seashore.

conducted north of Ponce Inlet for beach replenishment of Northeast Florida beaches. These studies conducted by the U.S. ACOE (1975; 1990a; 1990b; 1998) provide local knowledge of topography and shallow structures. The most comprehensive regional investigations of inner shelf sediments include a wide-ranging federal study conducted in the late 1960s to mid-1970s by Meisburger and Field (1975;1976) and a more recent series of field studies conducted by the FGS beginning in the early 1990s (Nocita et al., 1991). Publications by Meisburger and Field (1975; 1976) summarize the findings of the federal study of the Florida inner continental shelf from Cape Canaveral to the Georgia border, including the areas offshore of CANA. During this study, more than 1,327 mi (1,153 nm) of seismic-reflection profiles were collected along with 197 cores borings. The project was part of the Inner Continental Shelf Sediment and Structure (ICONS) study. The ICONS studies by Meisburger and Field (1975, 1976) address the sub-bottom structure of the inner continental shelf as well as the surficial sediments in the study area. This work emphasized shallow lithologic units in an effort to define areas of beach-quality

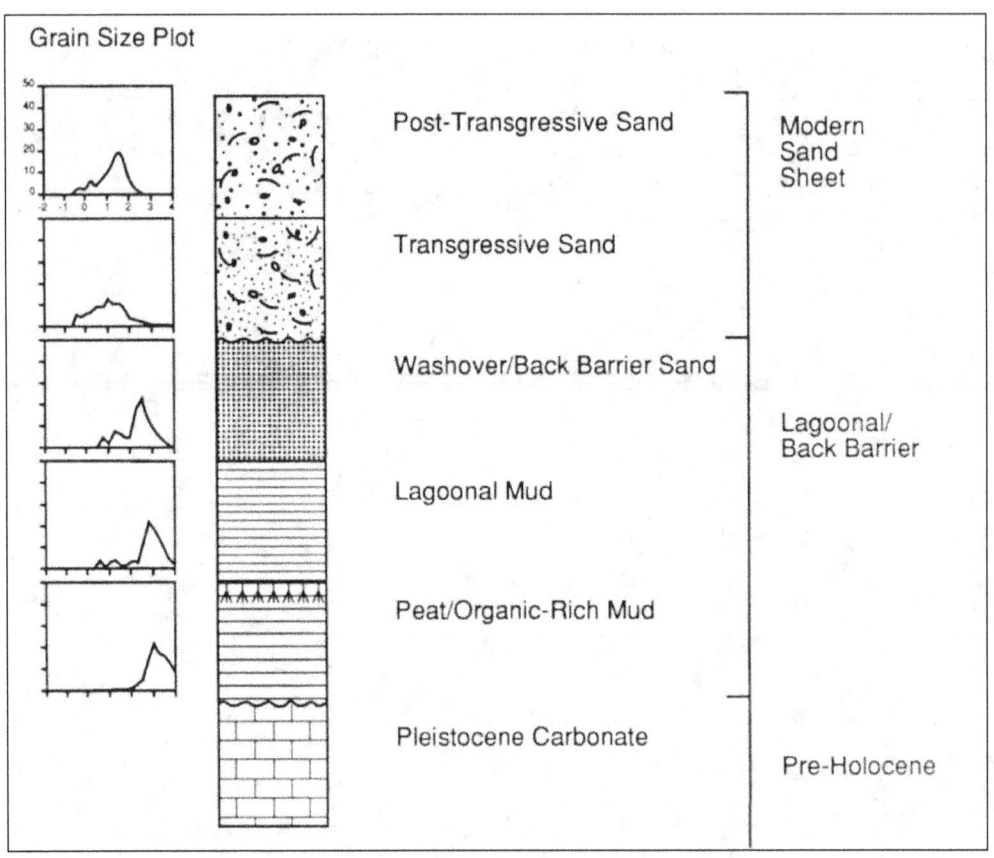

Figure 30. Idealized coarsening upward lithologic sequence associated with shoals situated offshore of Cape Canaveral (Zarillo and Bacchus, 1992).

sand deposits. The shoal features between Cape Canaveral and the Georgia border were ranked either A or B depending on the assessed potential for yielding beach-quality sand. More recently, several of the shoal features offshore of Volusia County and St. Johns County were subject to more detailed surveys consisting of sub-bottom acoustic profiles and core borings for direct sampling of lithology (Zarillo and Bishop, 2009). Results of these studies showed that stratigraphy of the shoal included the upward coarsening sequence found in the Canaveral Shoals and other similar features along the eastern U.S. inner continental shelf (Figure 30). None of the five major shoals situated in federal waters offshore of CANA shoals, termed B13 to B18, by Meisburger and Field (1975) has been surveyed. It is likely that these shoals will include sand resources similar to those to the north and south, offshore of Cape Canaveral. In the event of a major storm surge and breaching of the CANA barrier island system, these five shoals would be good candidates for sand resources for reconstructing the barrier system. Local governments to the north and south may also consider the sand sources for future beach protection projects.

Barrier Island Shoreline Changes
Shoreline changes within CANA have been mapped under three distinct efforts by the U.S. Geological Survey (USGS, 2005), the Beaches and Shores Division of the Florida Department of Environmental Protection (FDEP) and Schaub (2002). The USGS (2005) published an open file report of historical shoreline changes for the southeast Atlantic coast, including the Canaveral

area. The study of the U.S. southeast shoreline positions was part of a comprehensive analysis of shoreline movement that is intended to be consistent from one coastal region to another. One purpose of this work was to develop a standard, repeatable set of methods that is systematic and internally consistent for mapping and analyzing shoreline movement so that periodic updates regarding coastal erosion and land loss can be made nationally (Morton and Miller, 2005). The USGS (2005) analysis covers the southeastern Atlantic coast from east Florida through Georgia, South Carolina, and North Carolina.

The historical shorelines presented in the USGS analysis generally represent the following periods: 1800s, 1920s–1930s, and 1970s, whereas shorelines established from Light Detection and Ranging (LiDAR) methods and aerial image data are from 1998 through 2002. Long-term rates of change were calculated using four shorelines (1800s to LiDAR shoreline), whereas short-term rates of change were calculated for the most recent period (1970s to LiDAR shoreline). For each time period covered by the analysis, the USGS project provides thematic shorelines in the form of GIS-compatible files with established transects from a common baseline to each of the shorelines. The attribute tables for the transects provide data for calculating the net change in shoreline position between each shoreline map and for calculating rates of shoreline change. A very similar project was conducted by the Beaches and Shores Division of the FDEP. The FDEP shoreline analysis is based on essentially the same historical maps used by the USGS, but shorelines since the 1970s were extracted from beach profile data. The FDEP shoreline data are provided in the DXF or DWG file formats compatible with CAD software. Most common GIS platforms are able to import CAD files and convert them to GIS shape files. In addition to the efforts at the federal and state levels, the NPS also has made an inventory of CANA shoreline positions (Schaub, 2002). Schaub added shorelines to the FDEP analysis by digitizing shorelines and dune positions using rectified aerial photography from 1969, 1994, 1999, and 2000.

The historical rates of change presented in the USGS analysis represent past conditions and therefore are not intended for predicting future shoreline positions or rates of change. The largest rates of erosion in Florida were generally localized around tidal inlets. The most stable southeast Atlantic beaches were along the east coast of Florida where low wave energy and frequent beach nourishment minimized erosion. Some beach segments in Florida have accreted in the long term as a result of net longshore drift convergence around Cape Canaveral. The accretion can be clearly seen in Figure 31, which compares shorelines within a section of CANA from the years 1851–2000, or all four time periods examined in the USGS study. Although the CANA shoreline has been stable or has accreted in the long term, the beaches of the CANA undergo seasonal and storm cycles during which the width of the intertidal and super tidal beach may significantly change. There have been no detailed studies of storm/fair-weather beach cycles of the CANA beaches. The results of many other beach studies show that the shoreline position can dramatically change with the state of the beach and associated shore face. The beach/shoreface system oscillates between a fully accreted reflective state and a fully dissipative state, possibly from the impacts of storms. Most beaches have a model of most frequent conditions that are a function of wave clime, storm frequency, and available sediment texture. More information of beach states can be found in Wright and Short (1984) among others. The modal state or condition of the beaches and shoreface along CANA has not been quantified through repeated profile or image surveys on a seasonal basis.

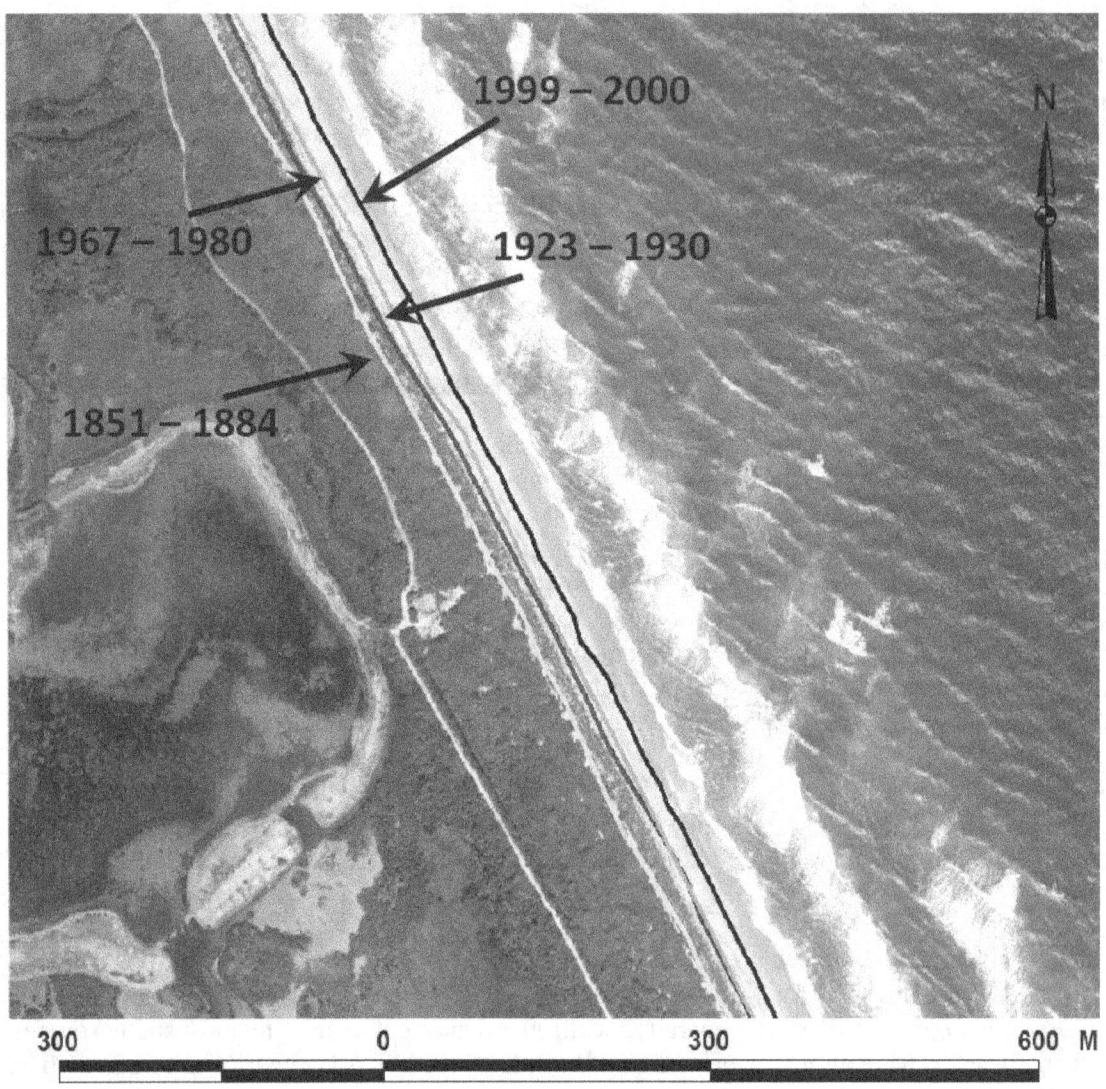

Figure 31. Historical shorelines from 1851–2000 are marked with a colored line. Black: 1999–2000, brown: 1967–1980, blue: 1923–1930, yellow: 1851–1884 (Morton and Miller, 2005).

Groundwater and Aquifer Systems

The subsurface system in central coastal Florida consists of a surficial aquifer system and a confined aquifer known as the Floridian aquifer. The two aquifers are separated by a relatively impermeable formation known as the intermediate confining unit or Hawthorn Formation. Very little groundwater quality data are available from the CANA area, although data were compiled from 1954–2004 by Kroening (2008). His study found that the groundwater quality varied over Mosquito Lagoon, ranging from water dominated by calcium carbonate and sodium chloride to a mixture of both constituents. According to Kroening, groundwater containing more than 5,000 mg/L (5,000 ppm) of chloride may be located at depths of 200-600 ft (61-183 m), although no wells that deep were sampled. Figure 32 shows the major groundwater basins defined by the SJRWMD, along with the location of wells to monitor groundwater water level and groundwater

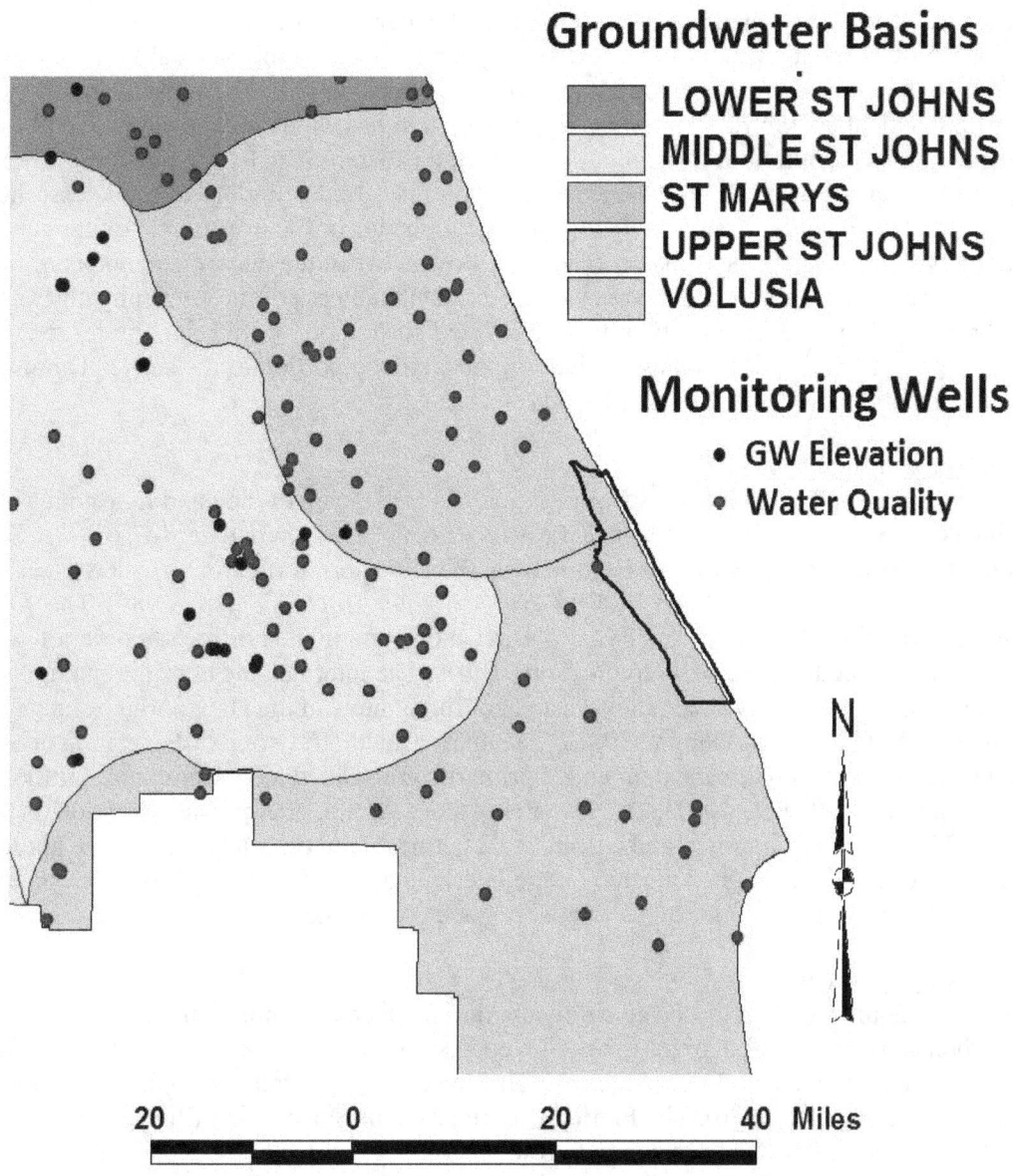

Figure 32. Groundwater limits bounding Mosquito Lagoon (SJRWMD GIS data).

water quality. As seen in Figure 32, only two monitoring wells are located near the northwest boundary of CANA.

Surficial Aquifer System

Toth (1987) described the lithology of the surficial aquifer system in the CANA area in great detail and noted that the aquifer includes the Anastasia Formation and contains upper and lower permeable zones. The surficial aquifer system is approximately 131 ft (40 m) thick in northern IRL and Mosquito Lagoon and is located approximately 16–66 ft (5–20 m) below land surface, varying from about 56–112 ft (17–34 m) in thickness. It is primarily comprised of unconsolidated to poorly indurated sand and clastic deposits, but contains beds or lenses of limestone, sandstone, and shell and is unconfined and under non-artesian or water table conditions (SEGs Ad Hoc Commission, 1986). Impermeable and semi-permeable clays, calcareous clays, and silty sands of the Hawthorn Formations underlie the surficial aquifer and form its base (Lichtler, 1960). The surficial aquifer system has variable chloride and total dissolved solids concentrations throughout the year and is determined by the amount of precipitation, tidal influences, and distance to the shoreline. Depending on the thickness, shell content, and clay content, transmissivity and storage in the unconfined surficial aquifer can vary considerably. Leakance, or the measure of vertical flow between the unconfined and confined portions of the surficial aquifer, also varies depending on thickness of the confining unit and its vertical permeability. Transmissivity of the unconfined portion of the surficial aquifer in the region averages 12,500 gpd/ft. Transmissivity in the confined portion of the surficial aquifer ranges from 8,400−7,000 gpd/ft (Szell, 1993).

Intermediate Confining Unit
The intermediate confining unit (Hawthorn Formation) is made up of clay and limestone with some interspersed layers of sand and shell (Provancha et al., 1992; Woodward-Clyde Consultants, 1994c). In the Mosquito Lagoon area, the Hawthorn formation is called a leaky confining layer because it is only 49−108 ft (15−33 m) thick (McGurk et al., 1989). The Hawthorn Formation is absent in much of Volusia County and in the northwest corner of Brevard County, but thickens to the south (Toth, 1987). The intermediate confining unit in the CANA area consists of many small aquifers and confining units in the Hawthorn Group of Miocene age (SEGS Ad Hoc Comm., 1986). The upper Hawthorn Group or Formation does not contain suitable aquifers of areal extent and is primarily considered a confining unit for the Floridan aquifer (Scott et al., 2001). The lower Hawthorn Group, or Arcadia Formation, is the top of the Floridan aquifer system and is somewhat permeable in the study area. Little hydraulic parameter information has been collected on the intermediate confining unit; however, the Hawthorn Group is believed to provide relatively good confinement for the Floridan aquifer.

Floridan Aquifer System
The Floridan aquifer system is located below the intermediate confining unit and consists of a thick carbonate sequence of all or part of the Paleocene to early Miocene series. The Floridan aquifer includes carbonate units from the early Eocene Oldsmar Formation to the early Miocene Hawthorn Group (Miller, 1986). The Floridan aquifer system is a system of limestone and dolomite beds and can be subdivided into two water bearing aquifers—the Upper and Lower Floridan—that is separated by a less permeable semi-confining unit. The top of the Floridan aquifer under the northern area of Mosquito Lagoon is found at -75 ft (-23 m) NGVD. Potentiometric surface maps of the Upper Floridan aquifer indicate elevations that are above sea level for the entire length of the lagoon and increase in height from north to south as the Hawthorn Formation increases in thickness (Figure 33). The thinness and possible absence of the confining layer in the northern Indian River and Mosquito Lagoon areas indicates that there is a possibility of seepage from the Floridan aquifer into the surficial aquifer via the Hawthorn Formation. In the northern IRL, Toth (1987) believes the Floridan aquifer probably discharges directly to the surficial aquifer in the dry season due the significant upward flow potential during that time. He defines the Mosquito Lagoon subbasin of the IRL as an area of active discharge from the Floridan aquifer. Discharge may occur through springs, artesian wells, or leakage into the surficial aquifer through the thin or discontinuous confining bed (Provancha et al., 1992).

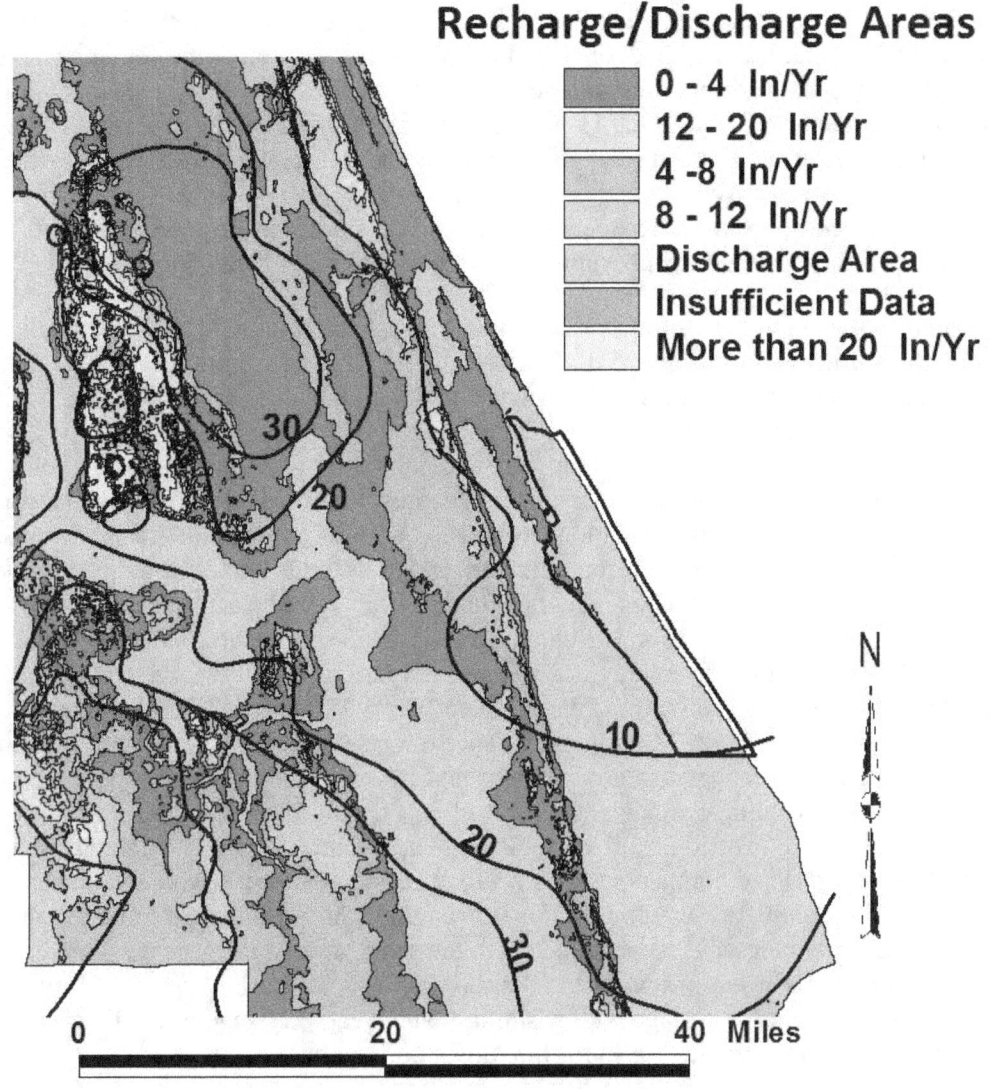

Figure 33. Contours of groundwater potentiometric survey and groundwater recharge/discharge areas near Canaveral National Seashore (SJRWMD GIS data).

Groundwater/Surface Water Interaction Data
Although the surface water hydrology in Mosquito Lagoon is fairly well understood, the role of submarine groundwater discharge to the lagoon has been largely ignored. In addition, groundwater seepage can affect the receiving water quality, as it can be enriched from many sources such as septic tank and landfill leachate, inputs from leaky sewer pipes, agriculture, natural geology, etc. Advective sediment water exchange processes, induced by submarine groundwater discharge, are often critical components of coastal nutrient budgets (Johannes, 1980; Krest et al., 2000); however, very little groundwater quantity or quality data have been collected in Mosquito Lagoon.

In a study for the NPS by Belanger et al. (1997), 46 seepage meters were placed in the Mosquito Lagoon area in nine transects extending from the mainland (west) and barrier island (east shore areas toward the central lagoon), with one 13-ft (4-m) transect located in the center of the lagoon. Areal weighting techniques were used to determine transect seepage rate averages for Mosquito Lagoon. One transect was located near Haulover Canal in northern Brevard County, while others were located between Oak Hill and Edgewater in southern Volusia County. Measurements were made over 2 yrs between July 1995 and July 1997 under a variety of tidal and environmental conditions. The average groundwater seepage rate over the study period was 0.025 gal/ft^2/hr (1.25 L/m^2/hr), indicating significant groundwater seepage to the lagoon.

Cable et al. (2004) completed a study to determine the importance of submarine groundwater seepage to the northern IRL during the dry (May) and wet (August) seasons in 1999 and in the central Banana River Lagoon area in May, August, and December of 2000. Fifty-two field stations were established, with 28 located in the northern study area and 24 in the central Banana River Lagoon study area. At each station, lagoon and interstitial water samples were collected, and groundwater seepage was measured using conventional seepage meters. Interstitial water samples were obtained from several stations using custom-built multi-samplers. Six groundwater samples were collected from wells surrounding the lagoon. Benthic fluxes of radium (Ra) to the IRL were calculated using three independent methods that rely on the activities of the short-lived isotopes: (1) lagoon budget, (2) benthic flux chambers, and (3) pore water modeling. Rn-222 (Radon) and Ra-226 isotopes from previous studies provided regionally integrated estimates of seepage flux in varied coastal environments (Cable et al., 1997; Moore, 1996; Swarzenski et al., 2001). By using Rn-222 and Ra-226 as mass balance tracers of seepage flux, it is possible to obtain measurements of seepage that are independent of the short-lived Ra isotopes. Assumptions for this technique are that negligible effects occurred from surface water exchange to the lagoon, tides, and diffusion from the sediments. In the northern most 6.2 mi (10 km) of the IRL, the USGS and other researchers, using Ra 226 pore water activities, calculated maximum upward surface flows of 0.16–0.56 ft/d (0.050–0.170 m/d). These values are similar to the rates recorded with directly measured seepage meters in the same area. Mean seepage meter rate values for the dry and wet seasons were 0.190 ft/d (0.058 m/d) and 0.171 ft/d (0.052 m/d), respectively. The dry season average is very similar to the yearly average of 0.299 ft/d (0.091 m/d) recorded by Belanger et al. (1997) for the Mosquito Lagoon.

The majority of data imply that groundwater discharge to Mosquito Lagoon is very important, and a review of the available hydrogeological data suggests that measurable seepage rates are possible. Although studies on flow and wave effects (water motion) on seepage meter results indicate negligible effects (Cable et al., 1997; Semmler, 2003), others believe these effects may be significant (Libelo and McIntyre, 1999; Shinn et al., 2002), or that shallow recirculating pore water derived from the overlying surface water column may represent a significant fraction of the measured groundwater input in the seepage meters (Cable et al., 2004). Possible mechanisms driving pore water advection include tides, waves, and bioturbation; bioirrigating organisms are the leading candidates (Martin et al., 2006). Further tests are needed to prove or disprove the previous test results and to determine the importance of groundwater inputs to the lagoon. Accurate groundwater data are needed for the coupled hydrodynamic water quality model to be used as a management tool for tracking and quantifying pollution inputs to the lagoon. The hydrodynamic water quality model is the result of a three-year study by Zarillo et al. (2010).

Although not measured in the Mosquito Lagoon, perhaps the best and most accurate groundwater–surface water interaction data set for the northern IRL was collected by Pandit et al. (2010) for a transect located near Titusville, FL. Pandit's study represents the most comprehensive and detailed study on meteoric groundwater discharge (MGWD) in the IRL, and his 2007 and 2008 Titusville transect results may be applicable to the CANA section of Mosquito Lagoon. Whereas Pandit et al. (2010) focused on MGWD, other previously discussed studies on the IRL and Mosquito Lagoon measured submarine groundwater discharge (SGD). The difference in the two terms is that MGDW discharge results from rain and infiltration, while SGD is the sum of the net groundwater discharge plus any groundwater flow that might result from wave formation and tidal influence.

The main objective of Pandit et al. (2010) was to measure MGWD flow rates as well as the dissolved nitrogen and phosphorus loads into the IRL at three transverse transects (Titusville, Palm Bay, and Vero Beach). The estimate was done with appropriate, calibrated, single and/or multi-layer cross-sectional groundwater flow models, coupled with numerous shallow and deep groundwater field samples and head measurements. Another project goal was to determine the salinity of the groundwater at several locations below the lagoon bed. The results of the study indicate a wide variation in the MGWD at the three different transect locations. The MGWD rate at the Titusville transect ranged 4.01–4.57 ft^3/day/ft of lagoon shoreline for the time period from October 2007 to October 2008, averaging 4.35 ft^3/day/ft of lagoon shoreline. The estimated annual MGWD was found to be 1.6% of the annual rainfall at this location. The Modfow Finite Difference Model predicted directions and spatial distributions of MGWD and showed that MGWD can occur across the IRL and is not constrained to nearshore sites, as MGWD occurred up to a distance of approximately 3,500 ft (1,067 m) from the west shore of the IRL. The bulk of the MGWD occurs near the west shore of the lagoon, which is to be expected and would occur in Mosquito Lagoon, as well, since the west shore receives groundwater from a much larger watershed than the east shore. This fact emphasizes the importance minimizing nutrient inputs to groundwater in the western watershed area as much as possible.

At the Titusville transect the total nitrogen (TN) loads ranged from 620–703 mg/day/ft of lagoon shoreline while the total phosphorus (TP) high load was 50 mg/day/ft of lagoon shoreline. TP loads, however, were not measureable during the dry season. Assuming this transect represents a typical urban area, the average daily TN and TP load, via MGWD, would be 567 mg/day and 140 mg/day per ft of lagoon shoreline, respectively. These may be reasonable estimates for Mosquito Lagoon and CANA water in the urbanized Oak Hill and Edgewater areas but are likely high for the area south of Haulover Canal. The results of groundwater discharge/recharge data from Pandit (2010), if applied to the 3-D hydrological model (Zarillo et al., 2010), may improve predictions of water quality for portions of the Mosquito Lagoon where groundwater/surface water interaction is important.

Other than Pandit's (2010) data, very little additional groundwater nutrient loading data are available. A 1985 report described soluble reactive phosphorus (SRP) flux in Mosquito Lagoon of 29–50 x 10^6 $g/m^2/d$ from submarine groundwater discharge (Zimmerman et al., 1985). Crude estimates of groundwater nutrient loading to CANA by FDEP (2010) indicate the TN and TP loading is approximately 20% (TN) and 35% (TP) of the estimated total external loading for ML 3-4 (southern CANA region) and 15.3% (TN) and 14.3% (TP) for ML 2 (northern CANA region).

Soils

Data used in this report to identify soils, soil properties, and natural plant communities affiliated with soils are from the U.S. Soil Conservation Service (SCS) and the NPS GIS thematic soil layer. Soil surveys completed in the 1970s and 1980s by the SCS match soil associations with plant communities found in the landscape. Data and maps from these soil surveys conducted by the SCS in Brevard and Volusia counties provide the most detailed aerial maps and descriptions of soils and soil properties in the CANA area (USDA, 1974; USDA, 1980). The soil associations described and assigned by the SCS to the same geographic features in Brevard and Volusia counties differ slightly in nomenclature. For example, soils of barrier island features (beach, dune, and ridges) in Brevard are labeled as the Canaveral–Palm Beach–Welaka soil association and in Volusia, the same features are labeled Palm Beach–Paola–Canaveral Association. The vegetation for both soil associations are the much the same. The soil associations assigned to geographical features and the plant communities are described below.

The Beach Dune and Ridge System
Canaveral–Palm Beach–Welaka Association
These soils are nearly level to gently sloping sands that drain moderately well to excessively. They are found on narrow ridges and sloughs parallel to the Atlantic Ocean. In Volusia County, the Palm Beach–Paola–Canaveral Association is the counterpart soil association. The soils of these associations consist of excessively drained to poorly drained, shelly, and sandy soils. The natural vegetation for the soil associations of beach, dune, and ridge features are scrub oaks, saw palmetto, cactus, sea grape, and grasses.

Saltwater Wetlands
Tidal Marsh–Tidal Swamp Association
In Volusia County, it is known as Hydraquents–Turnbull Association. Soils are variable, nearly level, poorly drained, and frequently covered in saline to brackish water. Soils vary from mucky sands that may overlay marl or limestone or mixed sands that are not uniformly stratified with shell and/or organic matter. Salt marsh halophytic grasses and herbs dominate the tidal marsh, and mangrove trees dominate the tidal swamp. Shrub wetland species, such as coastal willow, grows in brackish pockets along the edges behind the barrier island. Shrub wetlands and freshwater trees like sugar berry and tropical shrubs are also observed on dikes and intermittently along the western edge of Mosquito Lagoon.

Flatwoods, Grassy Sloughs, Isolated Freshwater Wetlands
Associations Paola–Pomello–Astatula (Brevard) and Daytona–Paola–Astatula (Volusia)
These soils are found in Brevard and Volusia counties on narrow undulating sand ridges between the IRL and Mosquito Lagoon. The associations consist of sands that drain excessively to moderately well. Coquina rock may be 50 in (127 cm) from the surface. In wet weather, the water table is generally below 3–5 ft (0.9–1.5 m). Slopes range from nearly level to strongly sloping. On the ridges, sand pine trees, wire grasses, scrub oaks, and palmettos live. Slash pine, long leaf pine, and palmettos grow in the flat areas between ridges. In wetland depressions, freshwater grasses and herbs are the natural vegetation.

Myakka–Eau Gallia–Immokalee (Brevard) and Myakka–Smyrna–Immokalee (Volusia) Associations: Soils of these associations are nearly level, poorly drained, acidic soils. The sandy soils reach a depth of 40 in (102 cm) and are loamy below. These soils are found between the ridges on the west side of Mosquito Lagoon. Water tables are usually within 30 in (76 cm) of the surface. Standing water may be present for short periods of time after heavy rainfall. Native dominant plants are scrub oak, saw palmetto, and scattered pines on the low ridges. On edges of sloughs or ponds, cabbage palms (*Sabal palmetto*) and mixed hardwood swamps are found. Herbaceous freshwater wetlands occur in low-lying areas of sloughs and pond edges.

Copeland–Wabash (Brevard) and Tuscawilla–Chobee (Volusia) Associations
These soils are nearly level and poorly/very poorly drained. Associations have a higher pH than most flatwoods soils due to the presence of underlying limestone or coquina. Cabbage palms, mesic hardwoods, and pines are commonly found.

The NPS GIS soil layer was created by National Resources Conservation Service (NRCS) in 2008. A comparison was made of Soil Conservation Survey (SCS) soil surveys (1974 and 1980), NPS soils maps (2010a), and GIS vegetation maps available from Duncan et al. (2004) to verify vegetation coverage and change over time. The GIS soil layer and soil associations as defined in earlier SCS surveys also were used to ground-truth plant coverage in limited spots within CANA.

Surface Water

The water quality of Mosquito Lagoon within CANA boundaries is considered in the following section; the Atlantic Ocean is discussed only in context of the fishery and biotic resources. Information on historical water quality studies and current monitoring programs was collected from government agencies, in-house data sets, and consultant reports. Data compiled from two SJRWMD stations in the Mosquito Lagoon that were located within CANA boundaries are summarized and presented. A discussion and summary of the Mosquito Lagoon's trophic state and the physical and chemical properties depicts the condition of the lagoon over the last 10 yrs.

Surface Water Data Sources

Monitoring of surface water in the Mosquito Lagoon basin has been conducted by many agencies, and the water has been analyzed for a considerable number of parameters. The Volusia County Environmental Health Laboratory (VCEHL), the SJRWMD, as well as the NPS and FDEP, all have had surface water monitoring programs committed to identifying and documenting water conditions and trends near the CANA region of Mosquito Lagoon. However, data for the region of Mosquito Lagoon lying strictly within CANA boundaries have been collected from only a few different locations, and these data are often unreliable due to various issues with the collection and analysis. Furthermore, many gaps within the data record exist for extended periods of time. This is more often the case for parameters requiring specialized handling and preservation (e.g., nutrients) and less often the case with more easily obtained data (salinity or Secchi depth).

The USGS compiled a complete listing of surface water sites in the Mosquito Lagoon basin that were regularly monitored by various federal, state, and local agencies, including one private agency, from 1999–2003. Monitoring times, site locations, and parameters sampled or measured are all identified for the following agencies active in the Mosquito Lagoon basin: VCEHL, SJRWMD, Brevard County, NASA, Marine Resources Council (MRC), and Florida Department of Agriculture and Consumer Services (FDACS) (Kroening, 2008). FDACS's involvement in the Mosquito Lagoon is primarily in determining and evaluating Best Management Practices (BMP) for agriculture since state law requires that farmers reduce impacts to surface water quality by adopting these BMPs (USEPA, 2010).

CANA surface water has been assessed herein using data gathered from two primary sources: the NPS's Southeast Coast Network (SECN) and the SJRWMD. The SECN station, where the data were collected, is located on the northeast side of Mosquito Lagoon on the dock behind the visitor center. Measurements of dissolved oxygen (DO), pH, turbidity, salinity, depth, temperature, and conductivity were recorded with a YSI 6600 EDS datasonde every half hour for much of the period between July 21, 2005 and February 10, 2009. These are the most current water quality data published for the CANA region of the Mosquito Lagoon and are the most complete set of continuous DO data available, although there are gaps in the data due to occasional equipment malfunctions and calibration errors. Data marked suspect by SECN staff were not included in the assessment. Because of data omissions due to instrument and quality assurance problems, the data are discontinuous for each parameter with many gaps, some extending as long as an entire season. The remaining data were separated and organized by year and season. Temperature and DO were sepatated by time of day.

Data obtained from a SJRWMD data set primarily consists of data archived in FDEP's STORET database, mostly from the IRL monitoring program conducted by the SJRWMD between 1997 and 2004. To ensure that this assessment is truly representative of CANA surface water, only data collected at stations within the CANA park boundary were used. Two data collection stations, IRLML02 located in southern CANA and IRLV17 located in northern CANA, have data sets for a wide range of parameters spanning more than 10 yrs. The specific locations of these stations are described in Table 3, and a map of their locations is shown in Figure 34.

Table 3. Latitude, longitude, and general location of Mosquito Lagoon surface water monitoring stations in Canaveral National Seashore.

Station	Latitude	Longitude	General Location Description
IRLML02	28 43' 35" N	80 43' 05" W	Mosquito Lagoon, open water, approximately two miles south of Haulover Canal and one mile east of western shore
IRLV17	28 52' 41" N	80 50' 22" W	A dock on the western shore of Mosquito Lagoon located near the Lopez RV Park & Marina in Oak Hill

Trophic State of Surface Water
A chief concern in an estuary surrounded by an increasing human population, such as CANA, is the potential for a system-wide shift from a macrophyte-based system to an algal-based system. Such a change in trophic state would have disastrous consequences for the endemic community structure. To assess the present trophic state in CANA surface water, several Trophic State Indices (TSI) were used as metrics, and these data are presented in Tables 4, 5, and 6.

The TSI used in this assessment is derived from Carlson (1977). However, it has been modified based on the work of Winkler and Ceric (2006) who conducted a district-wide study of water quality for the SJRWMD, including the Mosquito Lagoon. Their method of calculating the TSI is similar to the method used by FDEP when meeting the federal reporting requirements mandated by Section 305(b) of the Clean Water Act (FDEP, 1996). For the sake of making uniform comparisons across district waters, Winkler and Ceric (2006) omitted Secchi dish depth

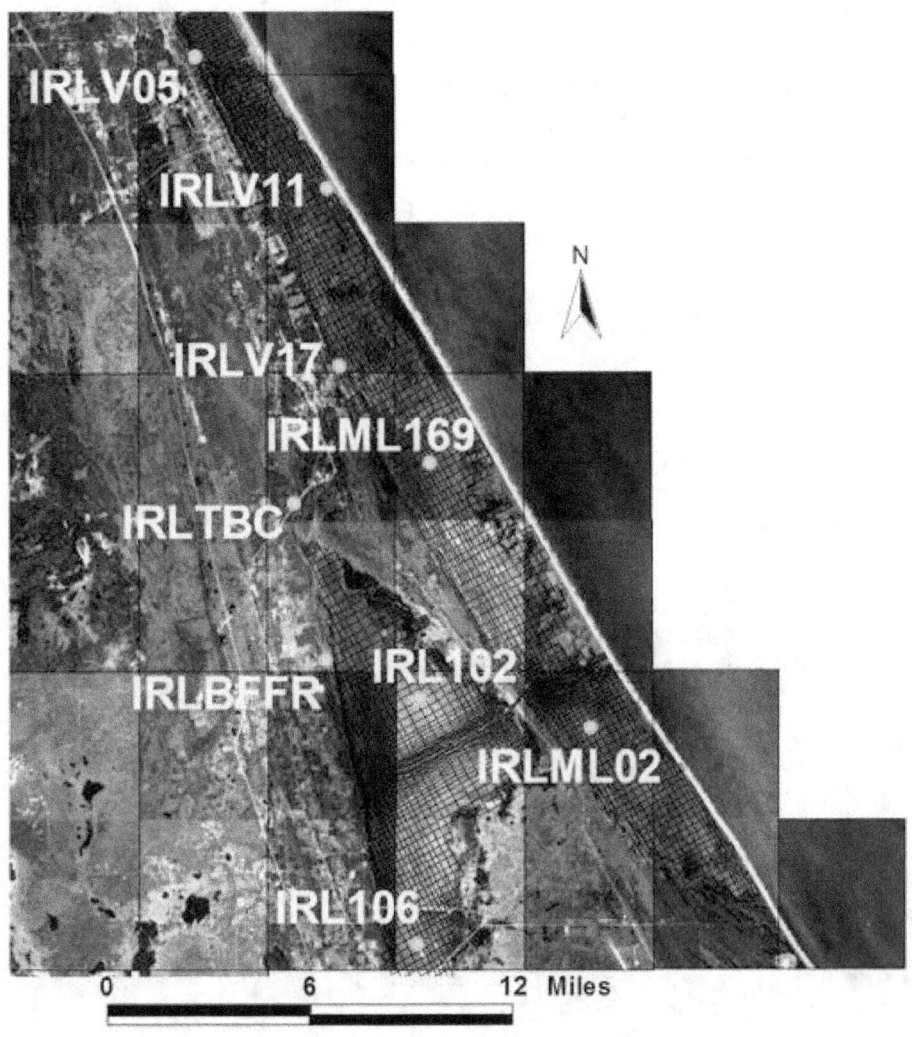

Figure 34. Location of water quality stations in the Indian River Lagoon (IRL) system. Stations IRLV17 and IRLML02, located in Mosquito Lagoon, are labeled and marked with a green circle (SJRWMD).

(SDD) from the TSI calculation, as did FDEP (1996), since many Florida waters are naturally dark from stream inputs containing humic acids. As such, TSIs reported by Winkler and Ceric (2006) and FDEP (1996) utilize only chlorophyll-a (Chl-a) (ug/L), TN (mg/L), and TP (mg/L) in the computation of the TSI. As CANA waters are not naturally colored, the example of Hand (1988) was followed and so was an additional parameter. Results for computations both with and without SDD are presented.

The data used in these computations were collected between 1990–2007. Much of the data obtained from SJRWMD was marked with various STORET qualifier codes indicating irregularities in collection, handling, and analysis procedures. The most common was STORET

Table 4. Trophic State of Canaveral National Seashore (CANA) Surface Water (1990–2007) at IRLV17 (Figure 34). 1 mg/L = 1 ppm; 1 μg/l = 1 ppb.

		1990	1991	1992	1993	1994	1995	1996	1997	1998	1999	2000	2001	2002	2003	2004	2005	2006	2007
Parameter Mean	Chlorophyll-a (μg/L)	7.0	5.7	7.5	6.3	5.0	4.5	8.3	5.6	6.4	6.1	4.6	5.3	3.6	3.0	4.5	4.4	2.7	1.8
	Secchi Depth (m)	0.7	0.8	0.8	0.8	0.7	0.9	1.1	1.0	1.1	1.2	1.2	1.0	1.0	1.1	0.9	0.9	1.0	1.0
	Total Kjeldahl Nitrogen (mg/L)	1.323	1.092	1.198	0.732	0.867	0.919	0.973	1.025	1.157	0.820	0.718	0.900	1.050	0.851	0.714	0.651	0.594	0.497
	NOx (mg/L)	-	-	-	-	-	-	0.009	0.005	0.050	0.011	0.011	0.010	0.050	0.026	0.031	0.018	-	-
	Estimated Total Nitrogen (mg/L)	1.323	1.092	1.198	0.732	0.867	0.919	0.982	1.030	1.207	0.831	0.729	0.910	1.100	0.876	0.745	0.670	0.594	0.497
	Total Phosphorus (mg/L)	0.054	0.054	0.075	0.048	0.119	0.047	0.069	0.060	0.055	0.056	0.037	0.045	0.042	0.068	0.050	0.060	0.050	0.040
Total Number of Observations Used to Calculate Parameter Means (= n)	Chlorophyll-a	13	14	14	10	13	16	47	51	49	36	24	24	24	16	12	14	25	15
	Secchi Depth	13	13	13	5	13	16	42	34	49	36	23	24	24	16	12	14	25	15
	Total Kjeldahl Nitrogen	13	13	13	5	13	15	33	45	48	36	24	24	24	16	12	14	25	15
	NOx	0	0	0	0	0	0	40	51	49	36	24	24	23	16	12	9	0	0
	Estimated Total Nitrogen	13	13	13	5	13	15	73	96	97	72	48	48	47	32	24	23	25	15
	Total Phosphorus	13	14	13	5	13	15	32	41	48	36	24	24	24	16	12	14	25	15
Parameter Index	Total Nitrogen : Total Phosphorus Ratio	24.6	20.1	16.1	15.1	7.3	19.5	14.2	17.2	21.9	14.7	19.6	20.2	26.2	12.9	14.8	11.2	12.0	12.6
	Chl-a TSI	44.8	41.8	45.8	43.4	40.1	38.6	47.3	41.6	43.6	42.8	38.7	40.8	35.4	32.4	38.3	38.2	31.1	25.6
	SD TSI	69.4	67.6	68.5	68.2	68.9	64.4	56.9	61.3	58.5	55.1	55.5	60.8	60.0	58.5	62.6	61.8	61.0	59.2
	TN TSI	61.5	57.7	59.6	49.8	53.2	54.3	55.6	56.6	59.7	52.3	49.7	54.1	57.9	53.4	50.2	48.1	45.7	42.2
	TN TSI-2	65.6	61.5	63.5	52.9	56.6	57.8	59.2	60.2	63.7	55.6	52.8	57.6	61.7	56.8	53.3	51.0	48.5	44.6
	TP	55.7	55.9	61.8	53.8	70.5	53.2	60.4	57.7	56.2	56.6	48.8	52.4	51.1	60.1	54.5	57.6	54.2	50.0
	TP TSI-2	70.3	70.5	77.9	67.8	89.0	67.1	76.1	72.8	70.8	71.4	61.5	66.0	64.4	75.8	68.7	72.7	68.3	63.0
	(TN TSI + TP TSI) / 2	61.0	58.4	61.6	52.2	60.1	55.1	58.4	58.2	59.8	54.9	50.5	54.7	56.9	56.8	52.7	52.2	49.5	45.6
	Trophic State Index Value	58	56	59	55	55	53	54	54	54	51	48	52	52	49	51	51	47	43
	Condition Assessment	Fair	Fair	Fair	Fair	Fair	Fair	Fair	Fair	Fair	Fair	Fair	Fair	Fair	Fair	Fair	Fair	Fair	Good
	Trophic State Index Value Without SD	53	50	54	48	48	47	53	50	52	49	45	48	46	45	45	45	40	36
	Condition Assessment	Fair	Fair	Fair	Good	Good	Good	Fair	Fair	Fair	Good	Good	Good	Good	Good	Good	Good	Good	Good

Table 5. Trophic State of Canaveral National Seashore (CANA) Surface Water (1990–2007) at IRLML02 (Figure 34). 1 mg/L = 1 ppm; 1 µg/l = 1 ppb.

TROPHIC STATE OF CANA SURFACE WATER AT IRLML02 (1990 - 2007)
(0 - 49 = Good, 50 - 59 = Fair, 60 - 100 = Poor)

	Year	1990	1991	1992	1993	1994	1995	1996	1997	1998	1999	2000	2001	2002	2003	2004	2005	2006	2007
Parameter Mean	Chlorophyll-a (µg/L)							6.2	5.2	6.8	8.0	4.2	4.9	6.3	2.0	4.1	4.1	2.0	2.6
	Secchi Depth (m)	1.2	1.4	1.1	0.9	0.8	1.2	1.0	1.1	0.9	0.7	1.3	1.5	1.1	1.3	1.0	1.3	1.0	1.4
	Total Kjeldahl Nitrogen (mg/L)	1.153	1.223	0.845	0.708	1.380	1.137	1.294	1.497	1.948	1.529	1.156	1.117	1.523	1.214	1.012	1.166	1.110	1.022
	NOx (mg/L)					0.025	0.020	0.022	0.021	0.010	0.024	0.007	0.010	0.022	0.037	0.022	0.017		
	Estimated Total Nitrogen (mg/L)	1.153	1.223	0.845	0.708	1.405	1.157	1.317	1.518	1.958	1.553	1.164	1.127	1.545	1.251	1.034	1.183	1.110	1.022
	Total Phosphorus (mg/L)	0.043	0.041	0.021	0.029	0.054	0.027	0.044	0.053	0.087	0.063	0.034	0.023	0.016	0.023	0.035	0.040	0.034	0.034
(n =)	Chlorophyll-a	0	0	0	0	0	0	47	58	58	48	35	33	35	35	31	27	33	26
	Secchi Depth	12	12	11	12	12	10	49	53	58	48	35	33	32	36	32	27	33	26
	Total Kjeldahl Nitrogen	4	4	4	4	4	3	37	56	58	48	35	33	35	36	32	27	33	26
	NOx	0	0	0	0	2	3	39	57	58	48	35	33	35	36	32	21	0	0
	Estimated Total Nitrogen	4	4	4	4	6	6	76	113	116	96	70	66	70	72	64	48	33	26
	Total Phosphorus	4	4	4	4	4	3	30	52	58	48	35	33	35	36	32	27	33	26
Parameter Index	Total Nitrogen : Total Phosphorus Ratio	26.8	29.8	40.2	24.4	26.1	43.4	30.3	28.5	22.6	24.5	34.3	49.3	94.0	55.5	29.6	29.3	32.6	30.4
	Chl-a TSI	54.5	50.4	55.9	63.7	65.9	55.8	43.2	40.6	44.5	46.8	37.5	39.7	43.4	26.6	37.3	37.0	26.8	30.3
	SD TSI	58.8	60.0	52.7	49.1	62.7	58.9	60.3	56.0	64.7	68.9	52.7	48.6	56.6	51.3	58.7	53.2	60.6	49.5
	TN TSI	62.7	63.9	56.0	52.2	66.9	62.7	61.4	64.3	69.3	64.7	59.0	58.4	64.6	60.4	56.7	59.3	58.1	56.4
	TN TSI-2	51.6	50.7	38.2	44.2	55.7	42.7	65.5	68.6	74.1	69.1	62.9	62.2	69.0	64.4	60.3	63.2	61.9	60.1
	TP	65.0	63.8	48.1	55.7	70.2	53.7	51.8	55.6	64.6	58.8	47.2	39.8	33.3	39.5	47.7	50.4	47.2	47.0
	TP TSI-2	57.7	58.2	49.0	48.5	61.8	54.8	65.2	70.0	81.5	74.1	59.4	50.1	41.8	49.7	60.1	63.5	59.5	59.2
	(TN TSI + TP TSI) / 2							59.6	62.8	69.3	64.2	56.4	53.5	55.6	54.8	54.9	57.6	55.7	54.5
	Trophic State Index Value	56	54	52	56	64	55	56	53	59	60	50	46	47	43	50	49	49	46
	Condition Assessment	Fair	Fair	Fair	Fair	Poor	Fair	Fair	Fair	Fair	Poor	Fair	Good	Good	Good	Fair	Good	Good	Good
	Trophic State Index Value Without SD	58	58	48	49	67	54	54	52	57	55	48	45	43	35	46	47	43	45
	Condition Assessment	Fair	Fair	Good	Good	Poor	Fair	Fair	Fair	Fair	Fair	Good	Good	Good	Good	Good	Good	Good	Good

Table 6. Trophic State of Canaveral National Seashore (CANA) Surface Water, 1990–2007, based on the means of aggregate data from IRLML02 and IRLV17 (Figure 34). 1 mg/L = 1 ppm; 1 μg/l = 1 ppb.

TROPHIC STATE OF CANA SURFACE WATER AT IRLV17 AND IRLML02 (1990 - 2007)
(0 - 49 = Good, 50 - 59 = Fair, 60 - 100 = Poor)

	Year	1990	1991	1992	1993	1994	1995	1996	1997	1998	1999	2000	2001	2002	2003	2004	2005	2006	2007
Parameter Mean	Chlorophyll-a (μg/L)	7.0	5.7	7.5	6.3	5.0	4.5	7.3	5.4	6.7	7.2	4.4	5.1	5.2	2.3	4.2	4.2	2.3	2.3
	Secchi Depth (m)	1.0	1.1	0.9	0.8	0.8	1.0	1.0	1.1	0.9	0.9	1.2	1.3	1.1	1.2	1.0	1.1	1.0	1.3
	Total Kjeldahl Nitrogen (mg/L)	1.283	1.123	1.115	0.721	0.988	0.956	1.143	1.287	1.590	1.225	0.978	1.026	1.330	1.103	0.930	0.990	0.888	0.830
	NOx (mg/L)					0.025	0.020	0.016	0.013	0.029	0.019	0.009	0.010	0.033	0.033	0.025	0.017		
	Estimated Total Nitrogen (mg/L)	1.283	1.123	1.115	0.721	1.013	0.976	1.159	1.300	1.618	1.243	0.987	1.036	1.364	1.136	0.955	1.007	0.888	0.830
	Total Phosphorus (mg/L)	0.051	0.051	0.062	0.040	0.104	0.044	0.057	0.056	0.072	0.060	0.035	0.032	0.027	0.037	0.039	0.047	0.041	0.036
								Total Number of Observations Used to Calculate Parameter Means											
(n =)	Chlorophyll-a	13	14	14	10	13	16	94	109	107	84	59	57	59	51	43	41	58	41
	Secchi Depth	25	25	24	17	25	26	91	87	107	84	58	57	56	52	44	41	58	41
	Total Kjeldahl Nitrogen	17	17	17	9	17	18	70	101	106	84	59	57	59	52	44	41	58	41
	NOx	0	0	0	0	2	3	79	108	107	84	59	57	58	52	44	30	0	0
	Estimated Total Nitrogen	17	17	17	9	19	21	149	209	213	168	118	114	117	104	88	71	58	41
	Total Phosphorus	17	18	17	9	17	18	62	93	106	84	59	57	59	52	44	41	58	41
	Total Nitrogen: Total Phosphorus Ratio	25.0	21.9	18.0	18.1	9.8	22.3	20.4	23.1	22.4	20.6	28.0	32.2	51.2	31.1	24.4	21.5	21.8	23.2
Parameter Index	Chl-a TSI	44.8	41.8	45.8	43.4	40.1	38.6	45.4	41.0	44.1	45.2	38.0	40.2	40.7	28.7	37.6	37.4	28.8	28.7
	SD TSI	61.3	58.1	62.1	65.0	67.5	60.8	58.7	58.0	61.7	62.2	53.8	53.1	58.0	53.4	59.7	55.9	60.8	52.7
	TN TSI	60.9	58.3	58.2	49.5	56.2	55.5	58.9	61.2	65.5	60.3	55.7	56.7	62.1	58.5	55.1	56.1	53.6	52.3
	TN TSI-2	65.0	62.1	62.0	52.6	59.9	59.1	62.8	65.3	70.0	64.3	59.3	60.4	66.3	62.4	58.6	59.8	57.1	55.6
	TP	54.8	54.9	58.3	50.1	67.9	51.8	56.7	56.5	61.2	57.9	47.9	46.2	42.7	48.5	49.8	53.2	50.6	48.2
	TP TSI-2	69.1	69.1	73.6	63.1	85.7	65.3	71.5	71.1	77.2	73.0	60.3	58.1	53.7	61.1	62.7	67.0	63.7	60.6
	(TN TSI + TP TSI) / 2	60.2	58.4	59.5	50.7	61.4	55.5	59.5	61.0	65.6	60.8	54.3	54.4	57.0	56.5	54.5	56.4	53.8	52.0
	Trophic State Index Value	55	53	56	53	56	52	55	53	57	56	49	50	51	48	51	50	48	44
	Condition Assessment	Fair	Fair	Fair	Fair	Fair	Fair	Fair	Fair	Fair	Fair	Good	Fair	Fair	Fair	Fair	Fair	Good	Good
	Trophic State Index Value Without SD	53	50	53	47	50	47	52	51	55	53	46	49	47	45	46	47	41	40
	Condition Assessment	Fair	Fair	Fair	Good	Fair	Good	Fair	Fair	Fair	Fair	Good	Good	Good	Good	Good	Good	Good	Good

Code "I," which indicates the analytical result was above the laboratory's practical quantification limit. Cleaning the data set and removing all suspect data marked with STORET qualifier codes resulted in too few data for a meaningful analysis.

The use of raw daily data presented a few problems requiring adjustment. First, results with negative values were occasionally reported, and these are often due to irregularities in the calibration methods employed by the analytical laboratory. To avoid losing data that represented low values, negative values for Chl-a, TKN, NOx, and TP were set to zero. In addition, SDD measurements were converted from feet to meters where necessary.

Only Chl-a data that corrected for pheophytin were used in the calculation. Since TN rarely appeared in the data sets, TN was almost always estimated by summing TKN and NO_x. When total NO_x was not available, dissolved NO_x was used in its place. If TKN data were available but neither total nor dissolved NO_x data were available, the TSI was calculated since TKN comprises the majority of TN (Winkler and Ceric, 2006). Although the reported TSI values for 1990–1995 and 2006–2007 must be viewed in context of the above information, they still represent the most complete and accurate TSIs computed to date.

Mean values of raw daily data were obtained for each parameter in the index by year and by station. The means (Chl-a_{mean}, SD_{mean}, TN_{mean}, and TP_{mean}) were used with Equations 1–8 to compute the overall TSI for each year. The final computed TSI value was rounded to the nearest whole number. For an estuarine water body such as Mosquito Lagoon, TSI values between 0–49 are considered good, values between 50–59 are considered fair, and values between 60–100 are considered poor (FDEP, 1996). The following equations are based on Carlson (1977), Hand et.al. (1988), FDEP (1996), and Winkler and Ceric (2006):

TSI = (Chl-a_{TSI} + SD_{TSI} + $NUTR_{TSI}$) / 3 [Eq. 1]

where

Chl-a_{TSI} = 16.8 + 14.4 (ln (Chl-a_{mean})) [Eq. 2]

SD_{TSI} = 60 − 30 (ln (SD_{mean})) [Eq. 3]

If 10 < (TN_{mean} / TP_{mean}) < 30

then nitrogen and phosphorus are co-limiting and

$NUTR_{TSI}$ = ((TN_{TSI} + TP_{TSI}) / 2) *where* [Eq. 4]

TN_{TSI} = 56 + 19.8 (ln (TN_{mean})) [Eq. 5]

TP_{TSI} = [18.6 (ln ((TP_{mean})(1000)))] − 18.4 [Eq. 6]

If $(TN_{mean} / TP_{mean}) < 10$

then nitrogen is limiting and

NUTR$_{TSI}$ = TN$_{TSI-2}$ = 10 [5.96 + 2.15 (ln (TN$_{mean}$ + 0.001))] [Eq. 7]

If $(TN_{mean} / TP_{mean}) > 30$

then phosphorus is limiting and

NUTR$_{TSI}$ = TP$_{TSI-2}$ = 10 [2.36 (ln ((TP$_{mean}$)(1000)) – 2.38] [Eq. 8]

The trophic state of CANA surface water from 1990–2007 is fair to good and the two most recent years of analysis (2006 and 2007) were well within the limit for a good designation (Tables 4, 5, and 6). TN:TP ratios were generally between 10–30 for most years, suggesting that nitrogen and phosphorus may be co-limiting in CANA waters. The only clear instance of nitrogen limitation observed was in 1994 at IRLV17; the effect was strong enough to show nitrogen limitation for the combined TSI calculation of data from both IRLV17 and IRLML02. However, phosphorus limitation was observed many times in the southern Mosquito Lagoon (1992, 1995, 1996, 2000, 2001, 2002, 2003, 2006, and 2007) at IRLML02.

These results are comparable to other studies that described limiting nutrients in this region of the IRL. Badylak and Philips (2004) used two years (1997–1999) of bioassay data, corroborated by water chemistry analysis in their assessment of the entire IRL complex. They reported that "nitrogen was the most frequently limiting nutrient throughout the (IRL), however, there was a greater potential for phosphorus limitation in the north and north-central IRL." For 1999–2003, Kroening (2008) found approximately "96 percent of the computed ratios were 7 or greater, which indicated that phytoplankton growth in Mosquito Lagoon generally" was not limited by the availability of nitrogen. According to FDEP (2010), 2004–2008 showed distinct improvements in water quality and trophic state. Based on 1989–2008 data, nonparametric Kruskall–Wallis analysis indicated a significant ($p<0.05$) difference between the northern and southern areas of Mosquito Lagoon for TN, TP Chl-a, and TSI, but when only the 2004–2008 data are evaluated, the significant differences for Chl-a and TSI disappear (FDEP, 2010a). Although the TSIs computed in this assessment use the FDEP (1996) cutoff limits (<10 for nitrogen limitation and >30 for phosphorus limitation), all of our computed ratios were >7 and thus consistent with Kroening's (2008) findings. Irrespective of the cutoff limit employed, the trend toward P limitation in CANA waters is surprising since the vast majority of estuarine waters are considered nitrogen limited.

With the exceptions of not including SDD as a parameter and not incorporating VCEHL data (1994–2004) and SJRWMD data (1989–2004), the same TSI was applied to the entire Mosquito Lagoon system by Winkler and Ceric in 2006, and they identified the overall water quality in Mosquito Lagoon as good (Winkler and Ceric, 2006; Florida Department of Environmental Protection, 2009). The NEP also evaluated the entire Mosquito Lagoon using an index similar to that computed in this assessment, with the only notable differences being that NEP used dissolved rather than total nitrogen and phosphorus, and they incorporated DO as an additional parameter. Based on their analysis of data collected in 2001 and 2002, they also classified the entire Mosquito Lagoon as "good" (National Estuary Program, 2007). Our findings are also consistent with those of Hand et al. (1988). Based on EPA STORET data collected from 1970 to 1987, Hand et al. (1988) used a similar TSI (including SDD) to assess Mosquito Lagoon surface water and classified the entire Mosquito Lagoon system as "fair to good."

Historically, the water in the northern reach of the park, especially those waters near the surrounding population centers of New Smyrna Beach, Edgewater, and Oak Hill, have been described as of lower quality than water in the undeveloped southern end of the park (Florida Department of Natural Resources, 1991). Recently, however, water north of Haulover Canal and south of Edgewater has been described as being among the best water quality of the whole IRL system (FDEP, 2010a).

The northern part of Mosquito Lagoon (water body identifier [WBID] 2924B) was described as potentially impaired for nutrients due to observed elevations of Chl-a (Paulic et al., 2006). Meanwhile, Winkler and Ceric (2006) found that water quality in the CANA vicinity, specifically near Oak Hill, has been improving due to decreasing concentrations of phosphorus and Chl-a. These findings may be due in part to the decrease in discharge volumes in recent years from publicly owned treatment works.

The findings of the present assessment are consistent with historical and other contemporary findings and therefore suggest that the trophic state of CANA water ranges from fair to good. This "fair to good" trophic state of CANA surface water appears likely to be due to low watershed urbanization and a minimal amount of agricultural discharges and other point sources of pollution to the lagoon (FDEP, 2009). The trophic state of CANA surface water appears to be changing very little from year to year and, based on our analysis of data from 1990–2007 at two stations within the CANA boundary, is remaining very close to a good designation. This simply suggests the water quality of the system is not being degraded and immediately trending toward decreasing light penetration and higher nutrient levels, which in the extreme case, could eventually shift the entire ecosystem to one that is algal based.

Physical and Chemical Properties of Mosquito Lagoon Surface Water
The scientific literature concerning water quality in the IRL system is extensive. However, there are few data available strictly from Mosquito Lagoon and even fewer available solely from the region of the Mosquito Lagoon lying entirely within CANA boundaries. In this assessment where appropriate, sources are referenced that include data from nearby locations considered representative of the CANA region.

One such source is a USGS study by Kroening (2008) that used data collected from 61 locations throughout the Mosquito Lagoon between 1999 and 2003. Many of the 61 locations were north of the CANA boundary in the Mosquito Lagoon Aquatic Preserve (Florida Department of Environmental Protection, 2009). The USGS report documented and quantified "significant spatial and/or seasonal variations in water-quality for pH, coliform bacteria, and concentrations of dissolved oxygen, total nitrogen, total phosphorus, Chl-a, and total suspended solids" (Kroening, 2008). While the USGS report determined that data were limited for pesticides, trace metals, and ground water quality, the water quality data is some of the most recent comprehensive water quality data for the Mosquito Lagoon.

Other studies contributing greatly to this assessment (Provancha et al., 1992; Woodward-Clyde Consultants, 1994d,e; Hall et al., 2001) have focused on the area immediately surrounding KSC in MINWR and include regions of the Banana River and North IRL in addition to Mosquito Lagoon. Since much of the Mosquito Lagoon segment containing CANA overlaps KSC and MINWR waters, these studies are certainly representative of resource conditions at CANA and have been included. Where possible, only the most relevant data collected from sites strictly within park boundaries are reported. However, some of these studies report only average values that often are based in part on sites outside CANA and occasionally in the adjacent North IRL and Banana River. The results of these studies are reported where appropriate.

In 1996, the Water Resources Division of NPS published a report characterizing baseline water quality conditions at CANA (NPS, 1996). The results of the study are used where possible, along with other pertinent data from various regulatory agencies with jurisdiction in CANA's watershed (EPA, FDEP, SJRWMD) to provide a context for the water quality conditions documented in this assessment.

Many of the following sections begin with a bar graph that was generated from 17 yrs of data (1990–2007) collected from the same water quality stations used in the calculation of the TSI (Table 3 and Figure 34). The data from these two stations (IRLML02 and IRLV17) are presented by wet season (June–October) and dry season (November–May) (Rao et al., 1989). As with the TSI computation, suspect data (those marked with STORET qualifier codes H, I, J, K, L, M, N, Q, T, V, Y, and #) were excluded. Given the initial paucity of data for many parameters, the discontinuous nature of collection regimens, and the large amount of suspect data, there are several instances where data are not available. There are also instances where only a single measurement is available to represent a particular parameter at one of the stations for an entire year.

Bathymetry, Morphometry, and Hydrodynamics
Compared to more densely developed areas of the IRL system, Mosquito Lagoon's drainage basin (the total land area draining into the lagoon) covers 42,000 ac (168 km^2). While it is smaller than the entire lagoon system, it is still affected by surface runoff and groundwater input. The Mosquito Lagoon watershed (the drainage basin including the lagoon) is 79,422 ac (327 km^2). The full extent of the drainage basin is located within Brevard and Volusia counties and extends from Ponce de Leon Inlet to the southernmost extent of the Mosquito Lagoon (Provancha et al., 1992; Woodward-Clyde Consultants, 1994c). A detailed description of land use and land cover in the Mosquito Lagoon basin in terms of acreage, square mileage, and percent coverage of the basin can be found in the 2008 Indian River Lagoon Water Quality Report published by FDEP's Division of Environmental Assessment and Regulation.

The entire Mosquito Lagoon covers approximately 59 mi^2 (152.8 km^2) and is dominated by shallow flats less than 4.9 ft (1.5 m) deep (Provancha et al., 1992). The Mosquito Lagoon represents 15.9% of the total IRL area and 10.7% of the total IRL volume (Cohenour, 1974). The volume of the Mosquito Lagoon is estimated to be 2.1 x 10^8 yd^3 (1.6 x 10^8 m^3) (Hall et al., 2001). Cohenour (1974) separated Mosquito Lagoon into four depth classes (Table 7). Each class is described in terms of the percent area and percent volume of the Mosquito Lagoon. These values represent the entire Mosquito Lagoon; however, only the southern two-thirds of Mosquito Lagoon is contained within CANA boundaries (part of ML 2; ML 3-4).

Table 7. Depth classes in Mosquito Lagoon and corresponding areas and volumes.

Mosquito Lagoon Depth, Area, and Volume		
Depth Class (m)	Area (%)	Volume (%)
0 – 0.6	51	19.1
0.6 – 1.2	16.2	18.1
1.2 – 1.8	30.6	57
1.8 – 2.4	2.2	5.7

Water residence time is an important ecological parameter because it dictates the critical nutrient loading limit required to attain or maintain a desired trophic condition. Mosquito Lagoon exhibits distinct residence time differences between the northern and southern regions. The southern part (ML3–4) is flushed more slowly (residence time = 76 days), whereas the northern and central areas (ML1 and ML2) have much shorter residence times (~3.5 and 8.1 day residence times, respectively) (FDEP, 2010a).

Excluding the AIWW that runs most of the length of the lagoon, the Mosquito Lagoon has a natural approximate maximum depth of 7.9 ft (2.4 m) (Cohenhour, 1974). The estimated average depth of Mosquito Lagoon is 3.3 ft (1 m) (Hall et al., 2001). Water levels are somewhat easy to predict as maximum depths occur in late fall and minimal depths occur in the summer. This is due to an estimated "0.2 m difference in hydraulic head between south Mosquito Lagoon and the Atlantic Ocean [that] generates a net long term flux of water out of the lagoon through Ponce de Leon Inlet" (Hall, 2001). However, short-term wind-driven flux may occur over shorter time periods, even days, and that can affect water levels also (Provancha et al., 1992).

Water circulation by tidal flushing and currents is restricted in Mosquito Lagoon due to the morphometric and bathymetric constraints of a long, narrow, shallow, lagoonal estuary that has been separated from its source of ocean water by distance and numerous spoil islands. Consequently, aeolian processes are primarily responsible for water mixing and movement in the Mosquito Lagoon. Hall et al. (2001) reported a net transport of water and material from the lagoon out through Ponce Inlet to the Atlantic Ocean. This transport takes place "on a long term basis," but no timescale was identified.

<u>Sediments</u>
Sediment characteristics are important in determining the quality of both groundwater and surface water. Since Floridan aquifer recharge in the CANA region occurs strictly by infiltration and percolation of precipitation, the nature of groundwater flow through the sediment interface must be understood to protect groundwater resources from point and non-point sources of pollution (McGurk et al., 1989). Nowicki and Nixon (1985) cite the importance of sediments to surface water and the benthic-pelagic coupling and cycling of nutrients that occurs in shallow

estuarine systems such as the Mosquito Lagoon. When considering the relatively small volume of water overlying a sediment interface, these interactions may be potentially more significant in Mosquito Lagoon than typical marine systems (Provancha et al., 1992).

Sediment sampling in 2006–2007 was completed in the CANA region by Florida Tech for the purpose of "defining water quality targets that are protective of seagrass in Mosquito Lagoon" (Trefry et al., 2007). Bottom sediment surveys revealed considerable deposits of fine sediments (clays) that are susceptible to resuspension and that the suspended clays matched those of bottom sediments. The greatest quantities of fine-grained, easily resuspendable sediments were found in and adjacent to the intracoastal waterway north of Haulover Canal and in a 1.16-mi^2 (3-km^2) region south of Haulover in the central part of the lagoon. Mineralogical signatures indicated that deposits north of Haulover Canal are likely allochthonous and of recent terrigenous origin, while the southern deposits are potentially ancient (>7,000 yrs) relict deposits (Trefry et al., 2007).

Salinity

The Mosquito Lagoon is a bar-built, semi-enclosed estuary that is far removed from its ocean water source. Ponce Inlet in New Smyrna Beach is Mosquito Lagoon's only direct connection to the Atlantic Ocean and consequently the only source of ocean water to the lagoon. Semidiurnal tides send ocean water through the inlet twice daily, but that water must first traverse a channel for approximately 5 miles (8 km) before passing under Highway A1A and entering the lagoon at its north end. Approximately 13 miles (21 km) of the upper Mosquito Lagoon are dominated by spoil islands and marshes that interrupt and restrict flow. The excursion distance of ocean water typically extends south of Edgewater and north of Oak Hill. Tidal exchange between the Mosquito Lagoon and the Atlantic Ocean is therefore very limited (Kroening, 2008).

The only other major point of communication with another water body is the Haulover Canal. Built in 1887, Haulover Canal is part of the AIWW and connects Mosquito Lagoon to the brackish north IRL. There are no major streams and relatively few sources of freshwater discharging CANA waters. Among these sources are precipitation, direct surface runoff, submarine groundwater discharge, a single canal draining the community of Oak Hill, and several smaller canals along the western shore of the lagoon (Steward et al., 1994).

Tidal exchange, stormwater runoff, precipitation, and evaporation (a direct function of insolation), are the factors primarily governing salinity in the Mosquito Lagoon. The net effect of these factors on CANA surface water is an average annual salinity that ranges typically between 28–33 ppt with only occasional exceptions (Table 8).

Intra-annual differences in salinity resulting from Atlantic Ocean tides appear to be small compared to observed seasonal variations (Kroening, 2008). The dependence on weather patterns can make salinity highly variable in the Mosquito Lagoon. Average salinity values between 1988–1991 were reported to be relatively constant, averaging 33.5 ppt during the wet season and 32.5 ppt during the dry season (Woodward-Clyde Consultants, 1994e). Data from the early 1990s indicates that salinity in Mosquito Lagoon ranged from a low of 4.5 ppt in 1992 to a high of 37 ppt in 1993 (Hall et al., 2001).

Table 8. Mean seasonal salinity (ppt = ‰) at the Southeast Coast Network (SECN) monitoring station at Canaveral National Seashore 2005–2009.

Year	Season	Salinity (ppt)	(n =)
2005	Summer	30.61	2733
2005	Fall	28.09	3122
2005-2006	Winter	31.36	989
2006	Spring	41.36	1231
2006	Summer	36.29	3568
2007	Spring	36.13	2565
2007	Summer	37.57	3088
2007	Fall	33.13	3668
2007-2008	Winter	33.94	2702
2008	Spring	39.1	4415
2008	Summer	38.67	2812
2008	Fall	33.86	4368
2008-2009	Winter	35.26	2420

As a direct result of its isolation and confinement, Mosquito Lagoon tends to be very saline (Table 8), averaging about 32 ppt (SECN, 2010). Shallow water makes salinity susceptible to weather extremes, especially in the confined southern reach of the lagoon. Water levels in adjacent freshwater marsh systems, however, are typically higher than the brackish Mosquito Lagoon, and salinities rarely exceed 10 ppt (Provancha, 1992).

Given the few sources of freshwater input and the relatively long excursion distance from Ponce Inlet, Mosquito Lagoon is typically more saline than other subbasins of the IRL system. Based on data gathered between 1983–1990, Provancha (1992) reported salinity levels may be increasing. In the southernmost parts of Mosquito Lagoon, high salinity values of 38 ppt were reported in 1973, values >40 ppt were reported in 1991, and values as high as 55 ppt for extended periods of time were reported in 2001 (Mehta and Brooks, 1973; Florida Department of Natural Resources, 1991; Walters et al., 2001). Reports of higher salinity are not uncommon in summer when evapotranspiration can exceed precipitation, especially in the southern end of Mosquito Lagoon where there is no outflow point and very limited freshwater input.

There is some discrepancy in the literature with respect to the spatial heterogeneity of Mosquito Lagoon salinity. Hall et al. (2001) identified a salinity gradient of decreasing concentration from north to south, with the southern end of Mosquito Lagoon being on average 2–3 ppt less than the northern end. However, no statistical difference (p=0.82) in spatial variability of salinity was found by Kroening (2008) between 1999–2003. For most years, there was no statistically significant difference ($p \leq 0.05$) between north and south CANA waters (Figures 35 and 36).

However, where a difference within a particular year or season was observed, most often the differences reflect the findings of Hall et al. (2001) and indicate higher salinity at IRLV17 in northern reaches of CANA water and comparatively lower salinity at IRLML02, south of Haulover Canal.

n =	1990	1991	1992	1993	1994	1995	1996	1997	1998	1999	2000	2001	2002	2003	2004	2005	2006	2007
IRLML02	4	5	4	4	5	4	25	25	25	17	14	12	15	15	13	11	14	10
IRLV17	6	6	8	<3	5	6	22	23	20	12	8	10	10	4	5	6	11	5

Figure 35. Wet season mean salinity (ppt = ‰), 1990–2007, at IRLV17 and IRLML02 (Figure 34).

Figure 36. Dry season mean salinity (ppt = ‰), 1990–2007, at IRLV17 and IRLML02 (Figure 34).

Temperature

Water temperature is a key determinant of an aquatic system's health but is not directly manageable. Extreme highs in water temperature can depress DO levels and accelerate the rate at which sediments become anoxic (Windsor, 1988). Such temperature-induced anoxia can be detrimental to sessile invertebrates and some submerged aquatic vegetation (FDEP, 2009). Average annual water temperatures for CANA surface water are presented in Table 9.

Table 9. Mean seasonal water temperature at the Southeast Coast Network (SECN) monitoring station at Canaveral National Seashore from 2005–2009.

Year	Season	Mean Temperature (^{0}C) Day	Mean Temperature (^{0}C) Night	(n =)
2005	Summer	30.46	30.56	2734
2005	Fall	21.88	21.96	3122
2005-2006	Winter	15.77	15.89	989
2006	Spring	28.77	28.86	1231
2006	Summer	29.74	29.82	3568
2007	Spring	26.53	26.63	2565
2007	Summer	29.71	29.69	3088
2007	Fall	24.17	24.28	3668
2007-2008	Winter	19.98	19.94	2702
2008	Spring	25.77	25.58	4414
2008	Summer	29.65	29.46	2812
2008	Fall	21.53	21.48	4368
2008-2009	Winter	16.79	16.77	2420

Water temperatures at CANA can vary an average of 35.6−37.4°F (2–3°C) over 24 hrs, with an annual range of 59−88°F (15–31°C) (Hall et al., 2001). Interannual variation within the lagoon can be extreme; Provancha (1992) reported temperatures as high as 93°F (34°C). Recent data indicate water temperatures often exceed 84°F (29°C) during the summer months when insolation is most intense. Between 1990–2007 temperatures averaged 78°F (25.5°C), with a high of 94°F (34.4°C) recorded on July 21, 2005. The passage of frontal systems can often cause water temperatures to quickly drop 41−50°F (5–10°C) over five to six days before gradually returning to pre-storm conditions (Hall et al., 2001). Recent data for water temperature at the SECN monitoring site in Table 9 are consistent with data from IRLV17 and IRLML02 (Figures 37 and 38).

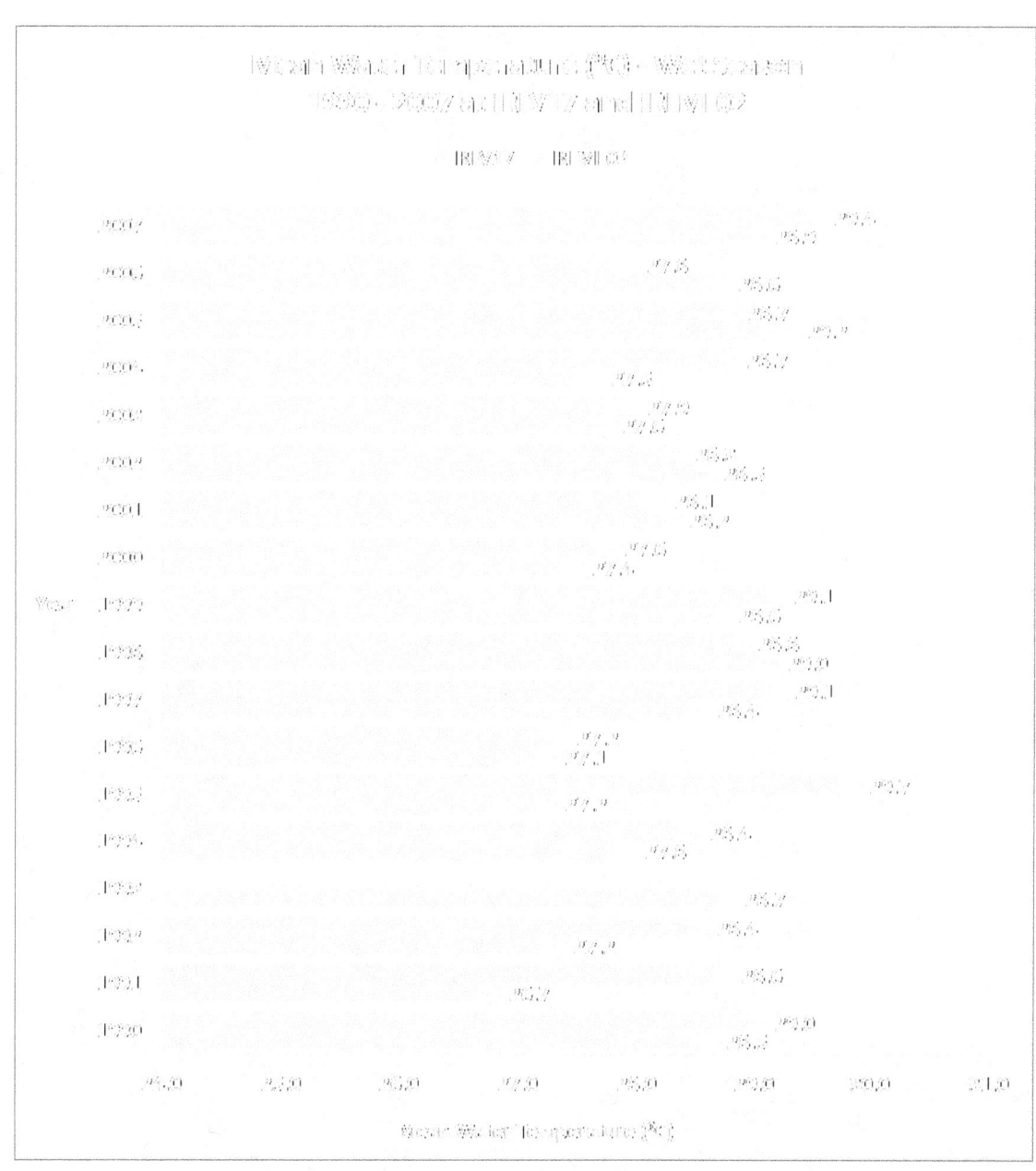

n =	1990	1991	1992	1993	1994	1995	1996	1997	1998	1999	2000	2001	2002	2003	2004	2005	2006	2007
IRLML02	4	5	5	4	5	4	25	25	25	17	14	12	15	15	13	11	14	10
IRLV17	6	6	8	<3	5	6	22	23	20	12	10	10	10	4	5	6	11	5

Figure 37. Wet season mean water temperature (°C), 1990–2007, at IRLV17 and IRLML02 (Figure 34).

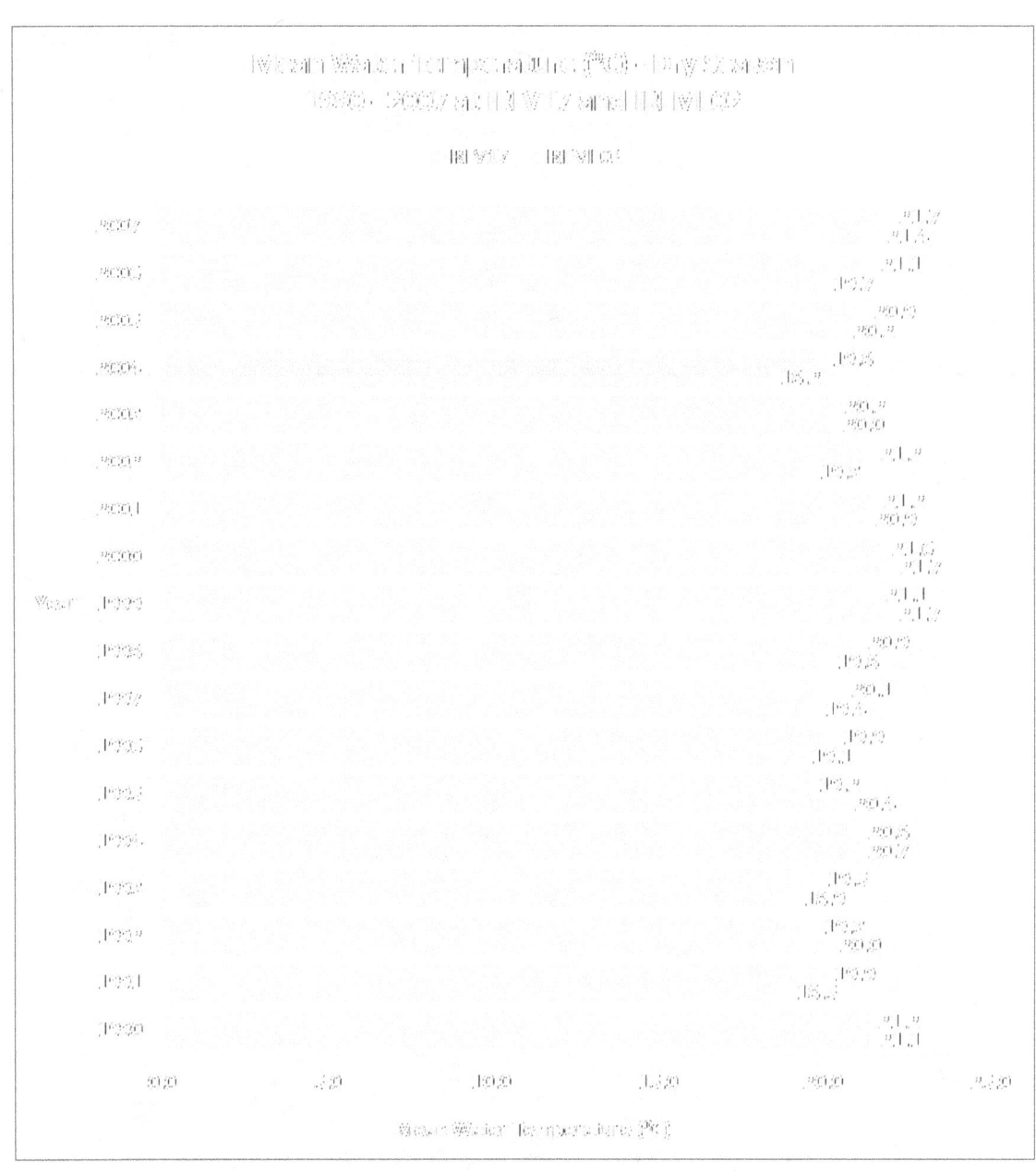

n =	1990	1991	1992	1993	1994	1995	1996	1997	1998	1999	2000	2001	2002	2003	2004	2005	2006	2007
IRLML02	7	7	6	7	7	6	24	33	33	31	21	21	20	21	19	16	19	16
IRLV17	7	8	6	4	8	8	20	24	28	24	14	14	14	11	7	8	13	10

Figure 38. Dry season mean water temperature (°C), 1990–2007, at IRLV17 and IRLML02 (Figure 34).

Dissolved Oxygen

Oxygen's temperature-dependent solubility in water ensures spatial, seasonal, and diurnal dissolved oxygen (DO) fluctuations. FDEP standards for Class II waters state that DO "shall not average less than 5.0 mg/L in a 24-hour period and shall never be less than 4.0 mg/L" and that "normal daily and seasonal fluctuations above these levels shall be maintained (FAC 62-302.530)." Although there are exceptions, DO levels in CANA are typically within FDEP standards.

Average DO values in Mosquito Lagoon were reported to be 6.47 mg/L (6.47 ppm) in 2000 (Sigua et al., 2000). Based on 1983–1990 data, Provancha et al. (1992) reported relatively high average DO values of 7.8 mg/L (7.8 ppm), with typical levels ranging from 5.5–8.5 mg/L (5.5–8.5 ppm). However, values as high as 13.0 mg/L (13 ppm) were recorded for areas with dense submerged aquatic vegetation (Provancha et al., 1992).

Hall et al. (2001) found that between 1991–1993, BOD and chemical oxygen demand (COD) in Mosquito Lagoon were highly variable. BOD ranged from 1.0 mg/L to 78.0 mg/L (78 ppm) with an average of 2.48 mg/L (2.48 ppm), and COD values ranged from 355–9,300 mg/L (355–9300 ppm) with a mean of 1,142 mg/L (1,142 ppm) (Hall et al., 2001). Minimum and maximum values were recorded at the same station at the southern end of Mosquito Lagoon (Hall et al., 2001). Hall et al. also found that extreme lows in DO corresponded to both low pH and a high degree of light attenuation. Light attenuation is a causal factor for this since a decrease in light can lead to a decrease in macrophyte and phytoplankton productivity; the decreased productivity and/or increased respiration are often highly correlated with decreases in pH.

While there has been occasional reporting of DO data from IRLV17 and IRLML02, the longest data set with the most continuous data for DO comes from the SECN monitoring station near the CANA visitor center. Since DO is prone to exhibit wide ranges over short periods of time, this site was selected as a source for assessing DO in CANA surface water as the STORET and SJRWMD data contain many measurements collected only once per day that likely are not representative of actual daily averages.

DO in CANA surface water was assessed by year and season. Seasons were delineated using dates for the vernal and autumnal equinoxes and solstices, which were all assumed to begin and end at midnight on their respective dates. Within each season, average values were calculated for day time (07:00–19:00), night time (19:00–07:00), noon, and midnight to identify specific times of potential concern (Table 10). Although these average values are all above 4.0 mg/L (4 ppm) and suggest DO in the Mosquito Lagoon meets FDEP standards, there are numerous instances of unacceptable DO levels in the data set. The seasonal data indicate very little difference between day and night, indicating biological productivity is less important to the oxygen dynamics than wind mixing or other nonbiological factors. The data indicate a temperature effect, as averages were invariably lower in the summer than the winter.

The SECN data provide a record of 712 days between 2005–2009 when DO measurements were recorded. Twelve days had insufficient data and were excluded from the assessment. Of the remaining 700 days, 155 (22%) days had average daily DO concentrations below 5 mg/L (5 ppm). All instances of low DO were observed between early May and late October from 2005–2008 (data stop at February 9, 2009, and no instances of low DO were observed in 2009).

Table 10. Mean seasonal dissolved oxygen concentrations at the Southeast Coast Network (SECN) monitoring station at Canaveral National Seashore from 2005–2009. 1 mg/L = 1 ppm.

		MEAN SEASONAL DISSOLVED OXYGEN AT THE SECN MONITORING STATION, CANAVERAL NATIONAL SEASHORE (SUMMER 2005 - WINTER 2009)				
Year	Season	Dissolved Oxygen (mg/L)				(n =)
		Day	Night	Noon	Midnight	
2005	Summer	5.34	5.25	4.99	5.34	2383
	Fall	6.87	6.82	6.61	6.74	3122
2005-2006	Winter	6.95	6.89	6.8	6.87	989
2006	Spring	4.23	4.04	4.06	4.22	1015
	Spring	4.68	4.5	4.56	4.21	2565
2007	Summer	4.51	4.35	4.42	4.45	3088
	Fall	5.77	5.65	5.61	5.73	3668
2007-2008	Winter	7.21	7.03	7.09	7.04	2702
	Spring	6.32	5.98	6.29	6.06	4414
2008	Summer	5.57	5.17	5.47	4.84	2812
	Fall	6.2	5.98	6.11	5.88	4368
2008-2009	Winter	7.57	7.47	7.45	7.5	2420

Unfortunately, the data within each year are somewhat discontinuous, and occasionally entire months of data are missing. DO data for the time period of concern (May 1–October 31) are summarized in Table 11 by total number of days per year with average DO <5.0 mg/L (5 ppm) and as a percentage of total DO observations.

The concern for low DO averages in the summer months is further emphasized when unacceptably low DO averages for multiple successive periods are identified. To illustrate the severity of these extended periods of low DO, maximum and minimum recorded daily averages are listed in Table 12. Over the 700 days evaluated for DO in the SECN data set, 3,877 individual observations of DO <4.0 mg/L (<4 ppm) were recorded on 264 days. Data are tabulated in Table 13 as a percentage of all recorded values.

Data indicate low DO concentrations in CANA surface water are a concern in the summer months when water temperatures peak and bacterial decomposition rates and storm water runoff inputs are at a maximum. Although there are discontinuities in the data from year to year, the total percentage of days with average DO <5.0 mg/L (<5 ppm) and the total percentage of instances of DO <4.0 mg/L (<4 ppm) were less in the summer months of 2008 compared to those same months in the previous two years. Even though the data were continuous for 2008, there were fewer multi-day low DO events observed in 2008 (25 days) than in the previous year (98 days). Given the highly variable nature of DO data within the system, several more years of continuous data from this single station should help identify if DO levels are improving.

Table 11. Days with mean dissolved oxygen concentrations <5.0 mg/L (5 ppm) at the Southeast Coast Network (SECN) monitoring station, Canaveral National Seashore, from 2005–2008.

Years	Days with Complete DO Records	Total Days with Mean DO < 5.0 mg/L (n=)	(%)
2005[1]	67	12	18
2006[2]	22	15	68
2007[3]	153	101	66
2008[4]	147	27	18
2005-2008	389	155	40

1 Data not available from 5/1/2005 – 7/24/2005 and 10/4/2005 – 10/31/2005
2 Data not available from 5/1/2006 – 5/26/2006 and 6/17/2006 – 10/31/2006
3 Data not available from 7/24/2007 – 8/26/2007
4 Continuous data from 5/1/2008 – 10/31/2008

pH

pH is a fundamental determinant of many chemical processes in the environment. pH, and to a lesser extent, water temperature, together play a dominant role in determining the concentration of the toxic form of ammonia (NH_3) in water. The pH of water is also a well-known factor in determining the availability of potentially toxic trace metals. In Mosquito Lagoon, for example, Hall et al. (2001) found concentrations of aluminum (Al) and copper (Cu) varied with pH levels. In many cases, relatively high pH can inhibit the release of trace metals from sediment to the overlying water column (Menon, 1979).

The pH in Mosquito Lagoon tends to be slightly alkaline, ranging between 7.9–8.2 when averaged on an annual basis (Table 14). During 1991–1993, Hall et al. (2001) reported an annual average of 8.41 with a range of 7.98–9.04. In a later study using data from 1999–2003, Kroening (2008) reported pH values ranging from 6.7–9.0, with 99% <7.2. Although pH varied seasonally and spatially, the highest pH values were consistently measured in the southern Mosquito Lagoon, approximately 3 miles (4.8 km) south of Haulover Canal, and may be due to more algal productivity in that region (Kroening, 2008). Average seasonal pH values at the SECN monitoring station from 2005–2009 are presented in Table 14.

The natural interannual variability in mean annual pH in Mosquito Lagoon surface water can be seen graphically in Figures 39 and 40. While there is no indication from the data of a trend in pH at either station, it is clear that pH is significantly higher ($p \leq 0.05$) in both the wet and dry seasons in southern CANA surface water (at IRLML02) than in the northern station (at IRLV17).

Table 12. Minimum and maximum mean dissolved oxygen concentrations (mg/L) recorded for successive days at the Southeast Coast Network (SECN) monitoring station, Canaveral National Seashore, from 2005–2008. 1 mg/L = 1 ppm.

\multicolumn{5}{c}{SUCCESSIVE DAYS WITH MEAN DISSOLVED OXYGEN CONCENTRATIONS BELOW 4.0 mg/L AT THE SECN MONITORING STATION, CANAVERAL NATIONAL SEASHORE (July 2005 - October 2008)}
Year	Date Range	Number of Succesive Days	Minimum Mean Daily DO (mg/L)	Maximum Mean Daily DO (mg/L)
2005	8/12 – 8/15	4	3.4	4.7
	9/2 – 9/3	2	4.2	4.9
	10/4 – 10/7	4	2.7	3.1
2006	6/2 – 6/16	15	2.6	4.7
2007	5/2 – 5/6	5	4.3	4.9
	5/17 – 5/19	3	4.3	4.8
	5/29 – 6/2	5	4.6	4.8
	6/6 – 6/28	23	3	4.5
	7/2 – 7/3	2	4.7	4.8
	7/7 – 7/17	11	3.6	4.9
	7/22 – 7/28	7	3.5	4.4
	8/27 – 9/2	7	4.2	4.7
	9/8 – 9/19	12	2.9	4.7
	9/22 – 9/24	3	4.2	4.7
	9/27 – 10/1	5	3.8	4.7
	10/3 – 10/17	15	2.9	4.6
2008	7/8 – 7/9	2	4.6	4.6
	9/5 – 9/6	2	4.6	4.9
	9/8 – 9/12	5	4.4	4.9
	9/15 – 9/23	9	4	4.9
	9/28 – 10/2	5	3.5	4.9
	10/17 – 10/18	2	4.9	4.9

Nutrients

Nutrients are a vital component of a healthy aquatic system and only pose a threat when rising above or falling below critical concentrations. Excessive nutrient levels can cause eutrophication and increase biotic production, possibly causing phytoplankton proliferation and reducing SAV production due to shading effects. Since Mosquito Lagoon is an SAV-based ecosystem, the high nutrient levels eventually could have disastrous ecological effects. External nutrient loading estimates by FDEP (2010) for CANA waters are 1.2 gTN/m^2-yr and 0.12 gTP/m^2-yr for Mosquito Lagoon section 2 as designated by FDEP and 0.76 gTN/m^2-yr and 0.04 gTP/m^2-yr for Mosquito Lagoon sections 3-4. FDEP (2010) also states that these nutrient loadings represent reasonable load limits, and TN and TP concentrations characteristic in 2004–2008 represent

Table 13. Individual occurrences of DO concentrations <4.0 mg/L (4 ppm) at the Southeast Coast Network (SECN) monitoring station, Canaveral National Seashore, from 2005–2008.

Years	Days with Complete DO Records	Total Number of Records	Days with Mean DO < 4.0 mg/L (n=)	Days with Mean DO < 4.0 mg/L (%)	Records with Mean DO < 4.0 mg/L (n=)	Records with Mean DO < 4.0 mg/L (%)
2005[1]	67	3146	44	66	576	18
2006[2]	22	1015	16	73	433	43
2007[3]	153	7489	138	90	2314	31
2008[4]	147	7130	66	45	554	8
2005-2008	389	18780	264	68	3877	21

1 Data not available from 5/1/2005 – 7/24/2005 and 10/4/2005 – 10/31/2005
2 Data not available from 5/1/2006 – 5/26/2006 and 6/17/2006 – 10/31/2006
3 Data not available from 7/24/2007 – 8/26/2007
4 Continuous data from 5/1/2008 – 10/31/2008

reasonable levels for maintaining good water quality. As discussed previously, total nitrogen and total phosphorus are key trophic-state indicator parameters and are used in the FDEP trophic-state index along with Chl-a to evaluate the trophic state trend in Mosquito Lagoon. Based on the analysis of average monthly data from 1989 through 2008 at selected Mosquito Lagoon stations, including CANA, a co-variance between nutrients and Chl-a was indicated, seasonally and over the long term (FDEP, 2010a).

Nutrient concentrations in water bodies in the state of Florida have typically been managed using narrative criteria stated in Chapter 62-302.530 of the Florida Administrative Code (FAC):

> ...in no case shall nutrient concentrations of a body of water be altered so as to cause an imbalance in natural populations of flora or fauna." The criteria also states that "the discharge of nutrients shall continue to be limited as needed to prevent violations of other standards contained in this chapter [Chapter 62-302, FAC]. Man-induced nutrient enrichment (total nitrogen or total phosphorus) shall be considered degradation in relation to the provisions of Sections 62-302.300, 62-302.700, and 62-4.242, F.A.C.

FDEP has been working with the EPA for several years to eliminate exclusive reliance on the narrative criteria and to modify and augment existing criteria with numerical nutrient requirements for Florida waters. Causal variables (nitrogen and phosphorus) and response variables (chlorophyll and transparency) are being evaluated for inclusion in the new regulations (FDEP, 2010b). The FDEP Technical Advisory Committee is gathering public input and assembling requested information for submission to EPA Region IV as part of the process of developing a comprehensive Numeric Nutrient Criteria Development Plan (FDEP, 2010c). Despite reports of good overall water quality, the northern part of Mosquito Lagoon (WBID

Table 14. Mean seasonal pH at the Southeast Coast Network (SECN) monitoring station at Canaveral National Seashore from 2005–2009.

	MEAN SEASONAL pH SECN MONITORING STATION CANAVERAL NATIONAL SEASHORE (SUMMER 2005 - WINTER 2009)		
Year	Season	pH	(n =)
2005	Summer	8.03	2733
2005	Fall	7.96	3122
2005-2006	Winter	8.17	989
2006	Spring	8.04	1231
2006	Summer	7.84	3568
2007	Spring	8.12	2565
2007	Summer	7.98	1786
2007	Fall	8.01	3668
2007-2008	Winter	8.06	2702
2008	Spring	8.01	4414
2008	Summer	8.13	2812
2008	Fall	8.01	4368
2008-2009	Winter	8.16	2420

2924B) was listed as potentially impaired for nutrients based primarily on elevated levels of Chl-a (Paulic et al., 2006). However, general water quality models and trophic-state indices support the assessment that Mosquito Lagoon is not nutrient impaired; the data indicate that it is in the lower mesotrophic category, trending toward oligotrophy. TN:TP ratios indicate N limitation in the northern Mosquito Lagoon, and a gradient of increasing P limitation southward into CANA waters, especially south of Haulover Canal (FDEP, 2010a).

Wastewater treatment plants (WWTP) in the cities of New Smyrna Beach and Edgewater periodically discharge water to the Mosquito Lagoon. The discharge of treated wastewater from both facilities was reduced in the 1990s, and as of 2006, approximately 70% of the discharge from New Smyrna Beach and 80% of the discharge from Edgewater had been routed to re-use distribution systems (Kroening, 2008). At the time of this writing, the City of New Smyrna Beach has increased reuse to 97% while the City of Edgewater has decreased somewhat to 72% (Personal Communication, Dave Hoover, Director of Water Resources, Utilities Commission of New Smyrna Beach, 2010; Personal communication, Dennis Norman, Superintendent, Edgewater Wastewater Treatment, 2010). Current estimates of WWTP external nutrient loading to Mosquito Lagoon were made by FDEP (2010), and the WWTP percentages of TN and TP external loading were 2.6% and 4.4%, respectively, for ML 2 (central Mosquito Lagoon) and 6.5 and 6.6%, respectively, for ML 1 (north Mosquito Lagoon).

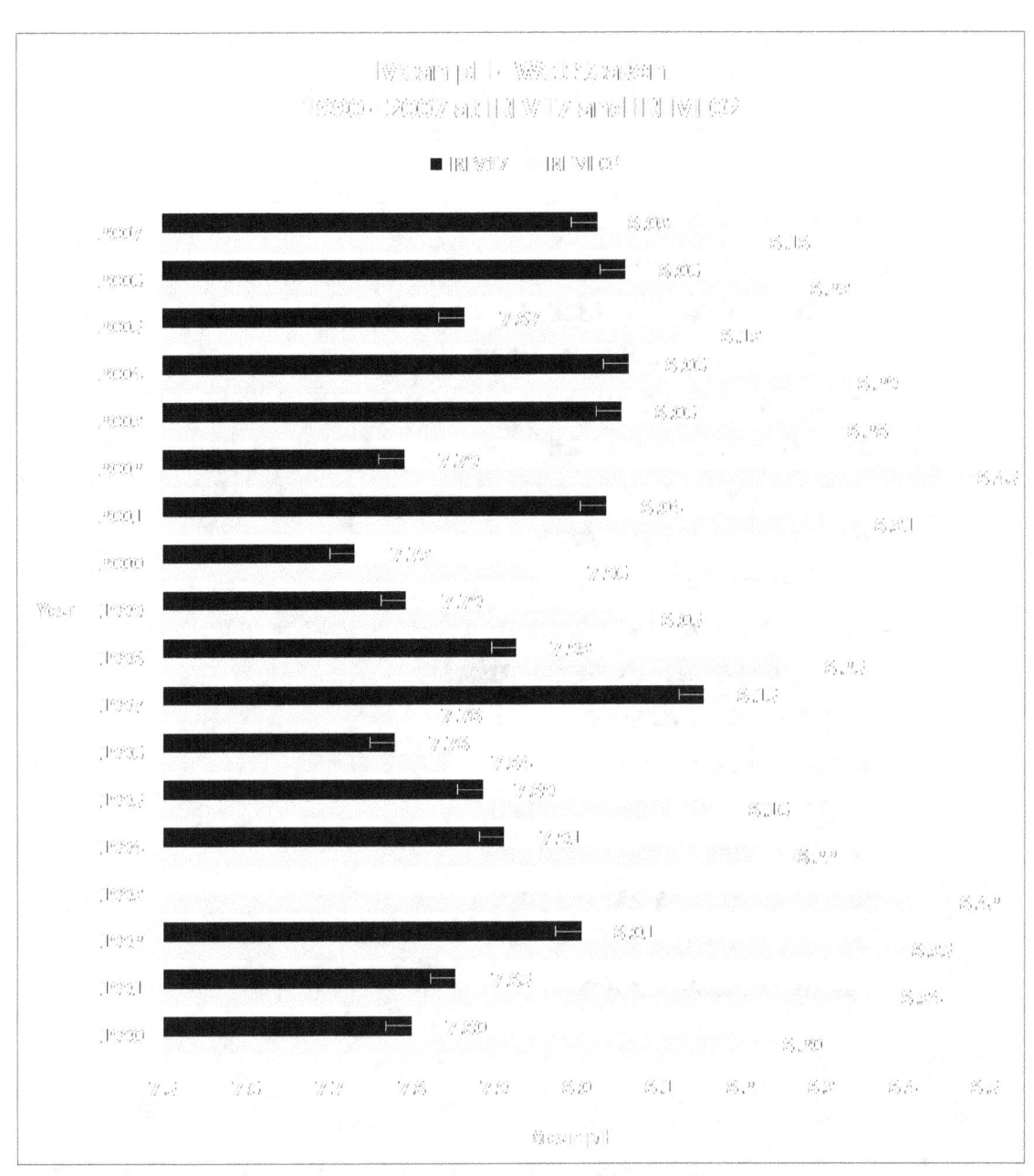

n =	1990	1991	1992	1993	1994	1995	1996	1997	1998	1999	2000	2001	2002	2003	2004	2005	2006	2007
IRLML02	4	5	5	4	5	4	25	20	25	17	14	12	15	15	13	11	14	10
IRLV17	6	6	8	<3	5	6	22	23	20	10	10	10	10	4	5	6	11	5

Figure 39. Wet season mean pH from 1990–2007 at IRLV17 and IRLML02 (Figure 34).

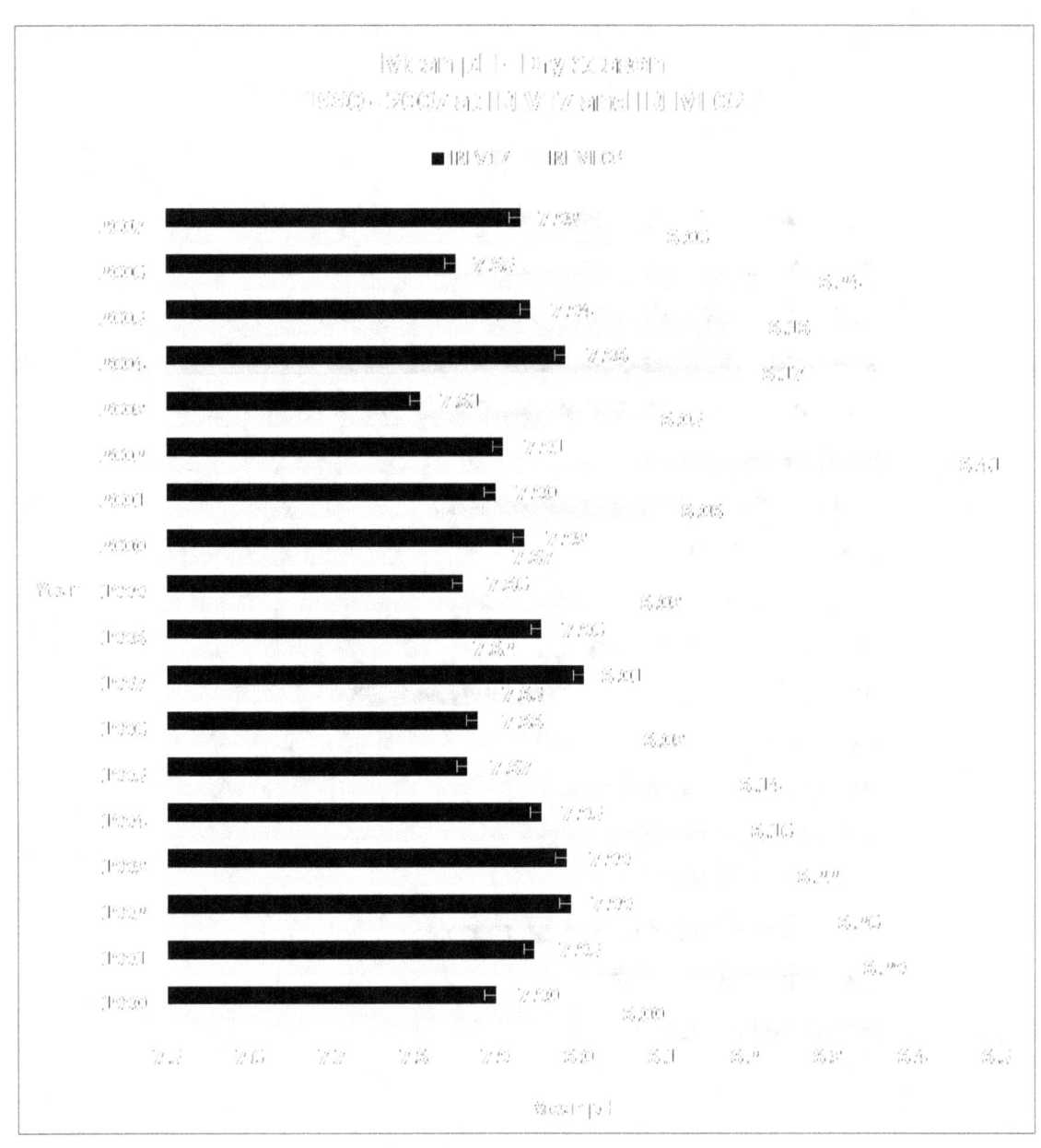

n =	1990	1991	1992	1993	1994	1995	1996	1997	1998	1999	2000	2001	2002	2003	2004	2005	2006	2007
IRLML02	7	7	6	8	7	6	24	28	33	31	21	21	20	21	19	16	19	16
IRLV17	7	8	6	4	7	8	20	24	28	24	14	14	14	11	7	8	13	10

Figure 40. Dry season mean pH from 1990–2007 at IRLV17 and IRLML02 (Figure 34).

Nitrogen

Nitrogen is an essential nutrient required by all plant and animal species. Although nitrogen is generally the limiting nutrient in coastal waters and estuaries, Kroening (2008) suggested phosphorus may be the chief limiting nutrient in Mosquito Lagoon, which is discussed in the trophic state section of this report.

Point sources of nitrogen to the Mosquito Lagoon are potentially numerous, but the most significant sources may be WWTP discharge. Nonpoint sources of nitrogen include on-site treatment and disposal systems (OSTDS) and direct runoff containing organic nitrogen of terrigenous origin, NO_x from agricultural and domestic fertilizer applications, and atmospheric deposition. Preliminary results from an NPS-funded OSTDS loading study on Mosquito Lagoon found that septic tanks are likely less of a nitrogen and phosphorus loading problem than areas that receive regular fertilizer applications (Zarillo et al., 2010).

Important sources of autochthonous nitrogen in Mosquito Lagoon include the direct deposition of plant matter, diazotrophic bacteria, such as those found in the rhizosphere of mangrove communities, and by fish, which directly excrete NH_3 through their gills as a byproduct of protein metabolism. The spatial heterogeneity of nitrogen in Mosquito Lagoon was confirmed by Kroening (2008), who found that all measurements of nitrogen were lowest near the Ponce Inlet and highest at the southern end of the lagoon. Increased concentrations of organic nitrogen and NH_4^+ between July and September (1999–2003) corresponded with periods of elevated total suspended solids and Chl-a concentrations (Kroening, 2008). This suggests seasonal variation related to the resuspension of organic materials from bottom sediments or plant material from algal blooms (Kroening, 2008). NO_x in Mosquito Lagoon sediments from 1991–1993 was 0.33–9.29 mg/kg (0.33–9.29 ppm), with an average of 3.78 mg/kg (3.78 ppm) (Hall et al., 2001).

Based on data collected between October 1988 and December 1991 across Mosquito Lagoon, Woodward-Clyde Consultants (1994e) reported a monthly mean TKN range from 0.62–1.43 mg/L (0.62–1.43 ppm). TKN was higher in the wet season (1.2–1.5 mg/L; 1.2–1.5 ppm) compared to the dry season (0.7–1.0 mg/L; 0.7–1.0 ppm), and overall TKN values were highest at the southern end of the lagoon during wet and dry seasons (Woodward-Clyde Consultants, 1994e). Using data from six water quality stations in CANA gathered between 1991–1993, Hall et al. (2001) reported mean TKN values of 0.84 mg/L (0.84 ppm), with a range of 0.05–3.04 mg/L (0.05–3.04 ppm). The approximate TKN levels at the 16 Mosquito Lagoon sites documented by Kroening (2008) for 1999–2003 ranged from 0.56–38 mg/L (0.56–38 ppm); 90% of reported values were <1.43 mg/L (<1.43 ppm).

From 1991–1993, Hall et al. (2001) found mean values of 0.06 mg/L (0.06 ppm) NO_3, 0.01 mg/L (0.01 ppm) NO_2, and maximum recorded values of 0.31 mg/L (0.31 ppm) NO_3 and 0.02 mg/L (0.02 ppm) NO_2 at their six study sites across Mosquito Lagoon. Kroening (2008) reported results consistent with those results published by Hall et al. (2001) for NO_x concentrations, finding mean values in Mosquito Lagoon between 0.01–2.8 mg/L; 90% of reported values were <0.02 mg/L for 1998–2003.

Figures 41 and 42 present yearly means of TKN from 1990–2007 at IRLV17 and ILRML02 for the dry and wet seasons. Figures 43 and 44 present yearly means of NO_x from 1996–2005 at IRLV17 and IRLML02 for the dry and wet seasons. While interannual variations should be

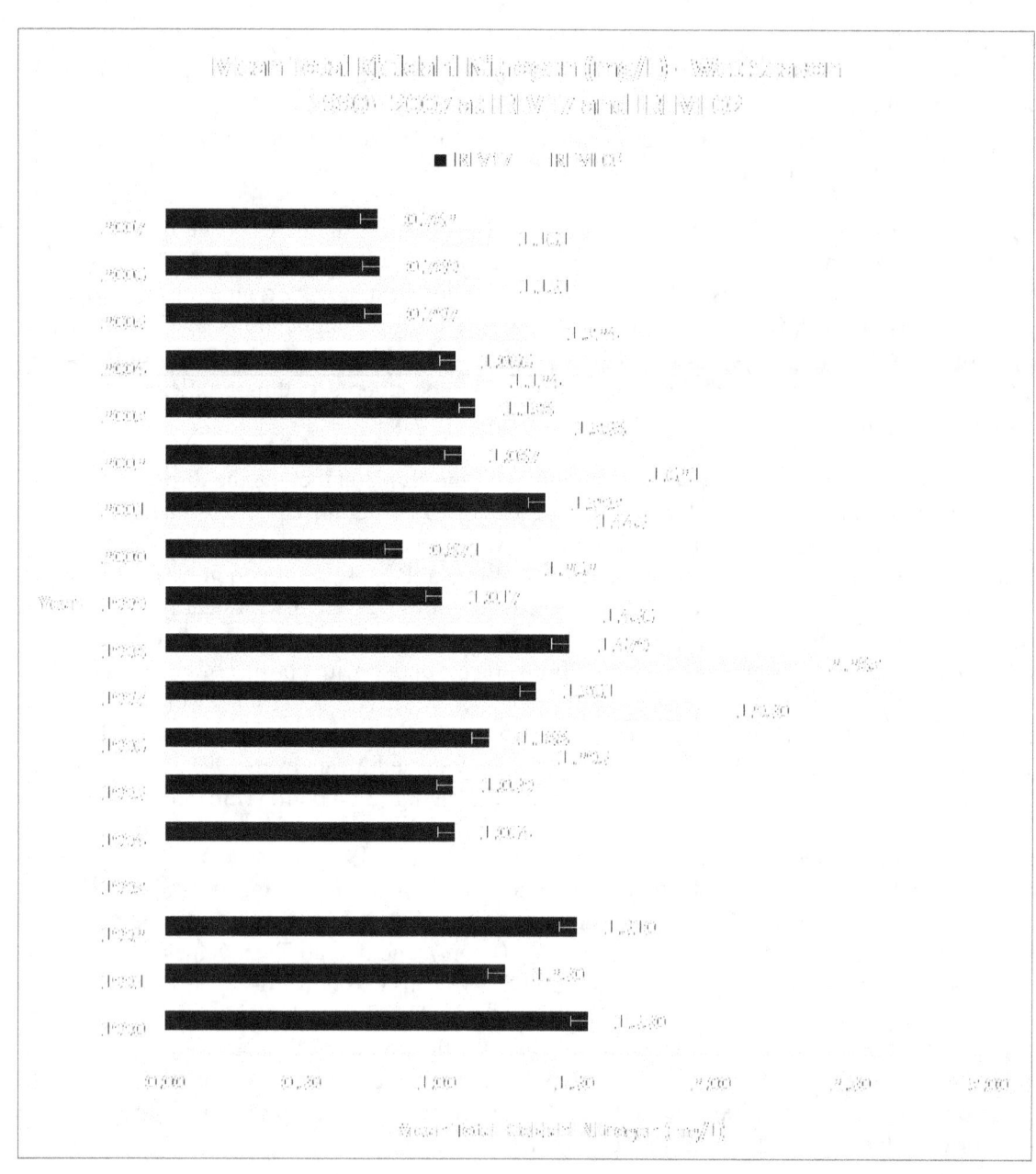

n =	1990	1991	1992	1993	1994	1995	1996	1997	1998	1999	2000	2001	2002	2003	2004	2005	2006	2007
IRLML02	<3	<3	<3	<3	<3	<3	15	24	25	17	14	12	15	15	13	11	14	10
IRLV17	6	6	5	<3	5	7	18	21	19	12	10	10	10	5	5	6	11	5

Figure 41. Wet season mean total Kjedhal nitrogen (mg/L) from 1990–2007 at IRLV17 and IRLML02 (Figure 34). 1 mg/L = 1 ppm.

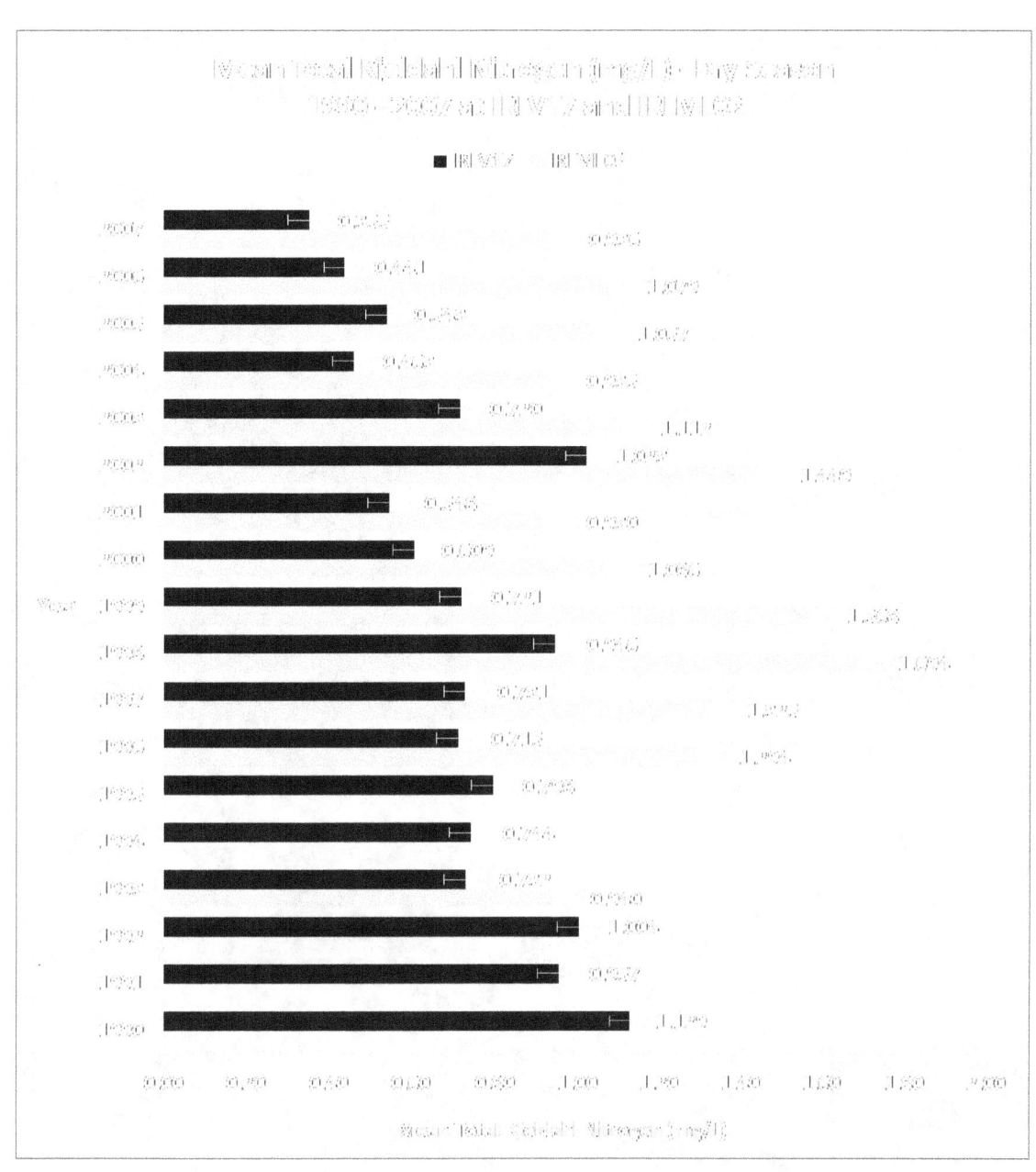

n =	1990	1991	1992	1993	1994	1995	1996	1997	1998	1999	2000	2001	2002	2003	2004	2005	2006	2007
IRLML02	<3	<3	<3	3	<3	<3	22	33	33	31	21	21	20	21	19	16	19	16
IRLV17	7	7	8	5	8	8	15	24	29	24	14	14	14	11	7	8	14	10

Figure 42. Dry season mean total Kjedhal nitrogen (mg/L) from 1990–2007 at IRLV17 and IRLML02 (Figure 34). 1 mg/L = 1 ppm.

n =	1996	1997	1998	1999	2000	2001	2002	2003	2004	2005
IRLML02	20	24	25	17	14	12	15	15	13	11
IRLV17	17	23	20	12	10	10	9	5	5	4

Figure 43. Wet season mean NO_x (mg/L) from 1996–2005 at IRLV17 and IRLML02 (Figure 34). 1 mg/L = 1 ppm.

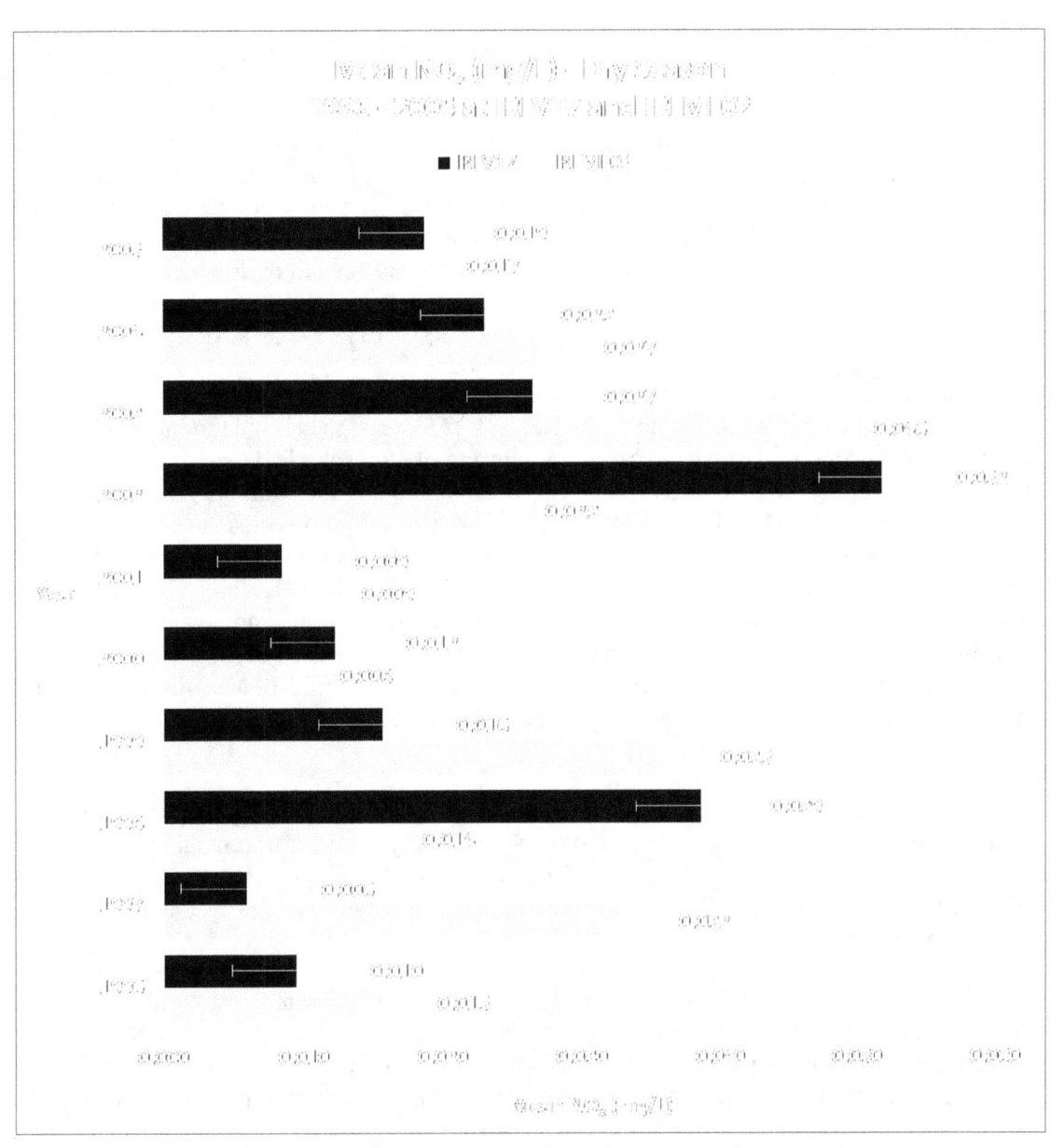

n =	1996	1997	1998	1999	2000	2001	2002	2003	2004	2005
IRLML02	19	33	33	31	21	21	20	21	19	10
IRLV17	23	28	29	24	14	14	14	11	7	5

Figure 44. Dry season mean NO_x (mg/L) from 1996–2005 at IRLV17 and IRLML02 (Figure 34). 1 mg/L = 1 ppm.

expected in a complex estuarine system, it is clear that there is a spatial heterogeneity for TKN between northern and southern CANA water with significantly higher ($p \leq 0.05$) concentrations in the south. NO_x tends to be more homogeneous and the few exceptions of observed significant differences ($p \leq 0.05$) in NO_x concentrations between the south and north do not appear to follow any seasonal or other pattern. The inter-annual variation in NO_x is most likely due to shore effects of the IRLV17 data collection station near the population center of Oak Hill as compared to the open water station at IRLML02. These findings are consistent with the findings of Hall et al. (2001) and Kroening (2008) and do not identify an obvious upward or downward trend for overall TN concentrations in CANA surface water. It is worth noting that there were significant downward trends for TKN in the wet ($\alpha \leq 0.01$) and dry ($\alpha \leq 0.001$) seasons at IRLV17.

The amount of dispersed atmospheric nitrogen deposited by precipitation, aerosols, and gases may be a future concern for CANA surface water as it is forecast to continue to increase throughout North America (Bigelow, 1984). Monitoring of atmospheric deposition in the CANA region is conducted by the SJRWMD (for the past few years) and the National Atmospheric Deposition Program (NADP). The NADP monitoring station (FL 99) is close to CANA, is located on the grounds of the nearby KSC, and is part of the National Trends Network (NTN). Samples have been analyzed for several parameters, including NO_3, NH_4^+, and TIN since 1983 (Table 15). At the time of this writing, 2008 data are the most recent that are available. Increasing trends in the data over the long term are evident (Figures 45, 46, and 47); however, recent years may show a slight downward trend. The phrase "Criteria Not Met" in these figures indicates that the data were not adequate to characterize the summary period.

Phosphorus

Like nitrogen, phosphorus is an essential element necessary for life. While phosphorus is often the limiting nutrient in freshwater systems, estuaries typically have a different chemistry. Redfield ratios (TN:TP) were calculated by Kroening (2008) based on data collected from 1999–2003. Values ranged from 1.1–55.1; approximately 96% of values were ≥ 7 (Kroening, 2008), which he considered the "cutoff value" for P limitation.

The Redfield ratios computed for calculating TSI in the present assessment were all >7. Slightly different criteria were used to determine nutrient limitation by FDEP (1996; 2010). Ratios <10 indicated nitrogen limitation, >30 indicated phosphorus limitation, and ratios between 10–30 indicated co-limitation. The FDEP criteria were used in this nutrient limitation assessment.

Point sources of phosphorus near CANA are, like nitrogen, potentially numerous and may arise from various industrial processes within the watershed. Nonpoint sources of phosphorus near CANA may be allochthonous and include submarine groundwater discharge from OSTDS and direct runoff containing both organic phosphorus of terrigenous origin and inorganic phosphate (PO_4^{-3}) from agricultural and domestic fertilizer applications. Zimmerman et al. (1985) described SRP flux rates in Mosquito Lagoon of $29-50 \times 10^6$ $g/m^2/d$ from submarine groundwater discharge. Autochthonous nonpoint sources of phosphorus typically include direct deposition by plants and animals, atmospheric deposition, and erosion processes. The NADP does not collect PO_4^{-3} deposition data at KSC.

TP shows significant spatial variation within Mosquito Lagoon; phosphorus concentrations were consistently greater in the northern part of the lagoon near Ponce Inlet than at the southern end of

Table 15. Average annual atmospheric deposition of NH_3, NO_3, and TIN in kg/ha from 1983–2008 at National Atmospheric Deposition Program monitoring site FL99 at Kennedy Space Center. 1 kg/ha = 0.9 lbs/ac.

Year	NH_3 (kg/ha)	NO_3 (kg/ha)	TIN (kg/ha)
1983	0.45	5.12	1.51
1984	0.88	5.64	1.96
1985	0.58	6.43	1.91
1986	0.43	5.97	1.68
1987	1.25	9.53	3.13
1988	0.64	6.39	1.94
1989	1.82	9.01	3.45
1990	1.11	9.75	3.07
1991	1.47	9.88	3.37
1992	1.27	11.08	3.49
1993	0.86	6.6	2.16
1994	1.21	10.17	3.24
1995	2.18	12.09	4.43
1996	1.52	10.4	3.53
1997	1.81	15.67	4.95
1998	1.11	8.97	2.89
1999	1.83	13.58	4.49
2000	0.87	6.85	2.22
2001	1.7	11.51	3.92
2002	1.3	9.29	3.11
2003	1.55	9.13	3.27
2004	5.27	13.7	7.19
2005	1.66	9.78	3.5
2006	0.89	6.56	2.17
2007	1.12	8.22	2.73
2008	0.98	8.74	2.73

the lagoon for 1999–2003 (Kroening, 2008). From 1991–1993, TP averaged 0.09 mg/L (0.09 ppm) with a range of 0.02–0.25 mg/L (0.02–0.25 ppm) (Hall et al., 2001). The USGS documented similar but slightly lower values during 1999–2003, reporting a range of <0.04−0.55mg/L (<0.04−0.55 ppm) and 90% of values <0.08 mg/L (<0.08 ppm) (Kroening, 2008). The highest concentrations of TP occurred between April and December and lowest concentrations occurred between January and March (Kroening, 2008). The TP concentration in the southern CANA region (ML 3–4) dropped in 2000 and has remained low for the last 10 yrs (FDEP, 2010a).

Based on data from IRLV17 and IRLML02 in the wet and dry seasons between 1990–2007 (Figure 48 and Figure 49), significantly higher concentrations of TP ($p \leq 0.05$) occasionally occur in the north near the population center of Oak Hill at IRLV17. While there is no significant difference ($p \leq 0.05$) in TP concentrations from north to south, due to the sporadic nature of the

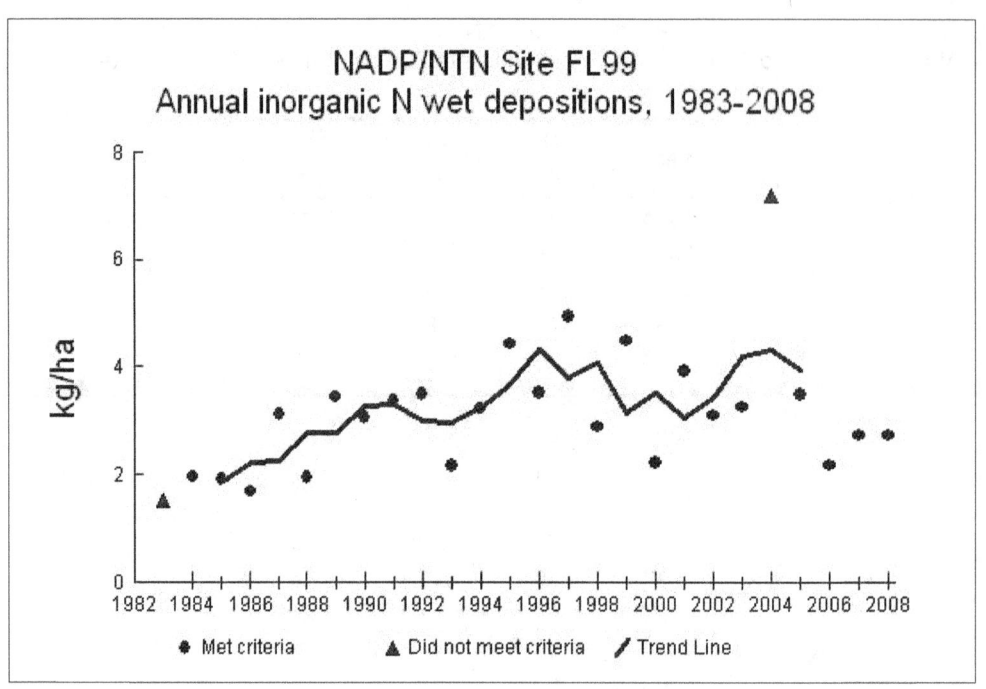

Figure 45. Trend in average annual atmospheric deposition of inorganic nitrogen in kg/ha from 1983–2008 at National Atmospheric Deposition Program monitoring site FL99 at Kennedy Space Center. 1 kg/ha = 0.9 lbs/ac.

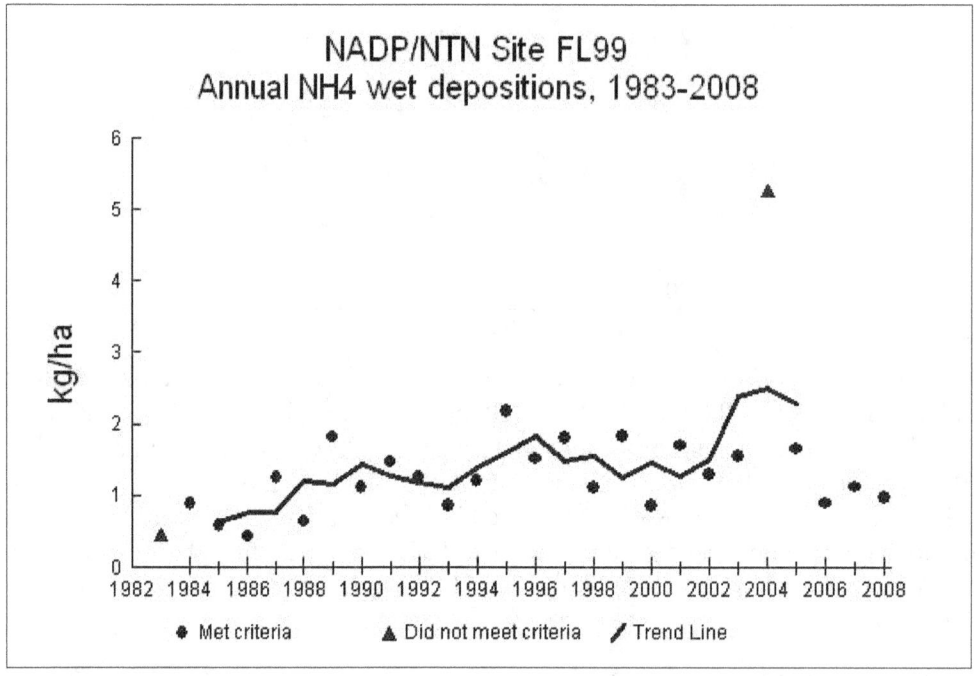

Figure 46. Trend in average annual atmospheric deposition of ammonium (NH_4^+) in kg/ha from 1983–2008 at National Atmospheric Deposition Program monitoring site FL99 at Kennedy Space Center. 1 kg/ha = 0.9 lbs/ac.

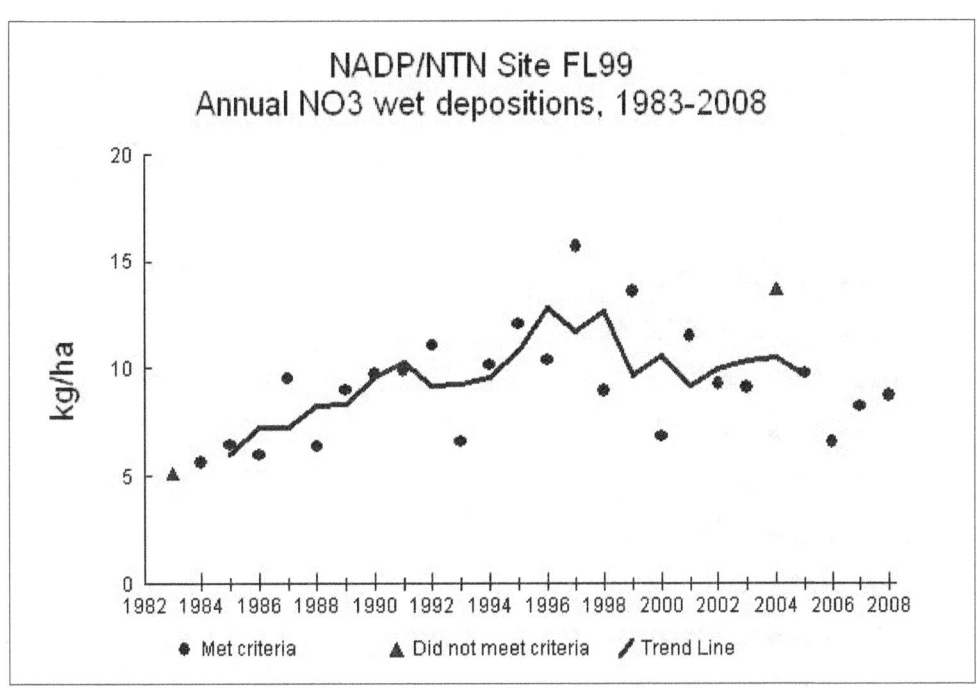

Figure 47. Trend in average annual atmospheric deposition of nitrate (NO_3) in kg/ha from 1983–2008 at NADP monitoring site FL99 at Kennedy Space Center. 1 kg/ha = 0.9 lbs/ac.

collection and the resultant discontinuities in the data from IRLV17 and IRLML02, it is difficult to characterize the apparent anomalies.

Carbon

Few data exist for the total organic carbon (TOC) content in or near the CANA region of Mosquito Lagoon. Hall et al. (2001) reported TOC values between 1991–1993 ranged from 0.24–20.8 mg/L (0.24–20.8 ppm), with an average of 2.63 mg/L (2.63 ppm). TOC data from IRLV17 and IRLML02 are presented for the 1996–2007 wet and dry seasons in Figures 50 and 51. TOC concentrations are significantly greater ($p \leq 0.05$) for both seasons at the southern station, which is in open water (IRLML02), than the nearshore station (IRLV17). Increased bottom resuspension in the southern lagoon from wind mixing in the open water is likely the cause of the difference.

Chlorophyll

Chlorophyll is a photoreceptive molecule occurring in planktonic and benthic organisms and is naturally found in several different varieties, the most common is Chl-a and Chlorophyll-b (Chl-b). In aquatic systems, Chl-b is found mainly in SAV; Chl-a measurements are better for quantitatively estimating the abundance of the plankton community.

The type of chlorophyll found in plankton varies with species, but all types absorb specific wavelengths of light in complementary ways. The structure of the planktonic community across the IRL system can vary from year to year; however, diatoms were the dominant algae by biovolume in Mosquito Lagoon from 1997–1999 (Badylak and Philips, 2004).

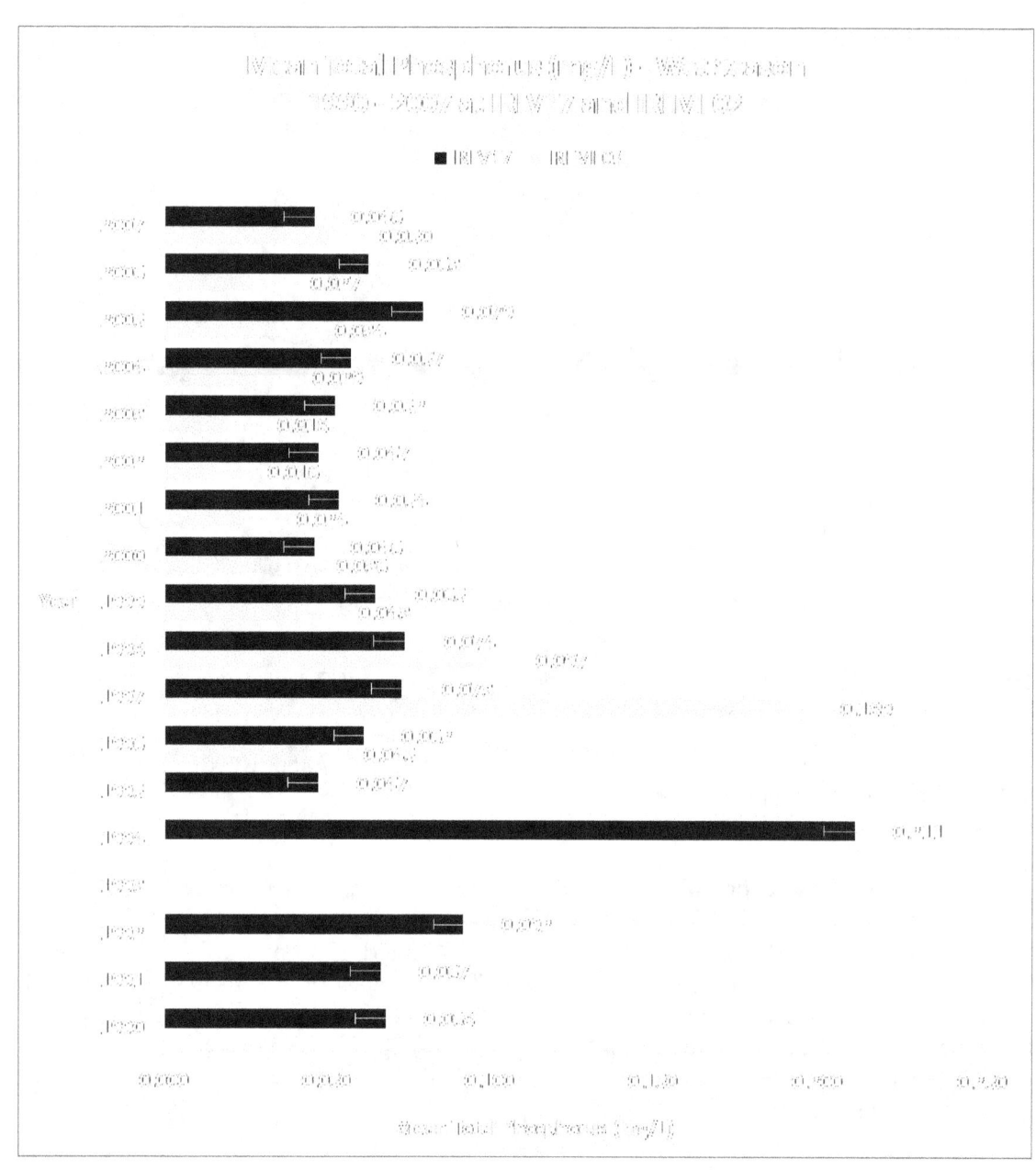

Figure 48. Wet season mean total phosphorus (mg/L) from 1990–2007 at IRLV17 and IRLML02 (Figure 34). 1 mg/L = 1 ppm.

n =	1990	1991	1992	1993	1994	1995	1996	1997	1998	1999	2000	2001	2002	2003	2004	2005	2006	2007
IRLML02	<3	<3	<3	<3	<3	<3	20	24	25	17	14	12	15	15	13	11	14	10
IRLV17	6	6	5	<3	5	7	13	21	19	12	10	10	10	5	5	6	11	5

n =	1990	1991	1992	1993	1994	1995	1996	1997	1998	1999	2000	2001	2002	2003	2004	2005	2006	2007
IRLML02	<3	<3	<3	3	<3	<3	10	29	33	31	21	21	20	21	19	16	19	16
IRLV17	7	8	8	5	8	8	19	20	29	24	14	14	14	11	7	8	14	10

Figure 49. Dry season mean total phosphorus (mg/L) from 1990–2007 at IRLV17 and IRLML02 (Figure 34). 1 mg/L = 1 ppm.

Provancha et al. (1992) reported that Chl-a concentrations in the southern Mosquito Lagoon were "low," indicating primary production in the southern reaches of the lagoon was primarily from SAV. The greatest Chl-a values in Mosquito Lagoon occurred near the major population centers where nutrient loading is greatest. Although the USGS reported no significant ($p=0.86$ spatial heterogeneity of Chl-a in Mosquito Lagoon, peaks in Chl-a and TP occurred in the area between Edgewater and Oak Hill (Woodward- Clyde Consultants, 1994e; Kroening, 2008). Chl-a concentrations ranged from ≤1–902 μg/L (≤1–902 ppb); 90% of values were ≤10 μg/L (≤10 ppb). Chl-a concentrations were highest in the wet season when TP levels were high and the water was warm, the ideal conditions for the growth of phytoplankton (Kroening, 2008).

Chl-a values published in a separate study show similar results for 1991–1993, with an average value of 10.34 μg/L (10.34 ppb) and a range of 2.70−53.40 μg/L (2.70−53.40 ppb) and both extremes occurring in 1992 (Hall et al., 2001). FDEP (2010) reported Chl-a averages for the southern and northern regions of Mosquito Lagoon from data collected between 1989−2008 to be 7.9 ug/L (7.9 ppb) and 5.7 ug/L (5.7 ppb), respectively. Between 2000−2008, Chl-a levels were typically <7 ug/L (<7 ppb), ranging of 4.2−9.9 ug/L (4.2−9.9 ppb) as an annual average and generally indicating a mesotrophic trophic state condition.

Mean yearly Chl-a concentrations in CANA surface water from 1990–2007 at IRLV17 and IRLML02 for the wet and dry seasons are presented in Figures 52 and 53. With the exception of the dry season at IRLML02, there is a significantly decreasing trend in Chl-a concentration in CANA water. The SJRWMD Chl-a data are limited and relatively few instances of significant differences ($p \leq 0.05$) between the two data collection stations were observed. However, it is clear that there is a reversal between seasons, with IRLV17 higher in the wet season and IRLML02 higher in the dry season. The increased nutrient loading from seasonal stormwater runoff from the town of Oak Hill during the wet season may be the cause of the reversal.

Dissolved Solids
The physical and chemical properties of estuaries are equal to those of seawater diluted with pure water (Millero, 1975). Whereas salinity of seawater is a measurement of the total amount of dissolved inorganic components in water, the measurement of total dissolved solids (TDS) quantifies the amount of inorganic salts, organic matter, and all other dissolved materials in water, and is determined by gravimetric means.

A less expensive and more efficient alternative to filtration is the measurement of electrical conductivity, which may be used as a surrogate for the more precise gravimetric method (Thirumalini and Joseph, 2009). However, the relationship between TDS and conductivity is not the same for all natural waters and can be highly variable within a given system (Thirumalini and Joseph, 2009).

Units vary, but conductivity is typically reported as specific conductance in units of conductance (Siemens) per distance (cm). Values have been converted to mS/cm from various other units (μmhos/cm, uS/cm, etc.) to better compare with units in the SECN dataset for specific conductivity, which is in mS/cm (Table 16).

Hall et al. (2001) reported a range of specific conductance measurements for the Mosquito Lagoon from 39.9 mS/cm in 1992 to 59.9 mS/cm in 1993. Total dissolved solids averaged

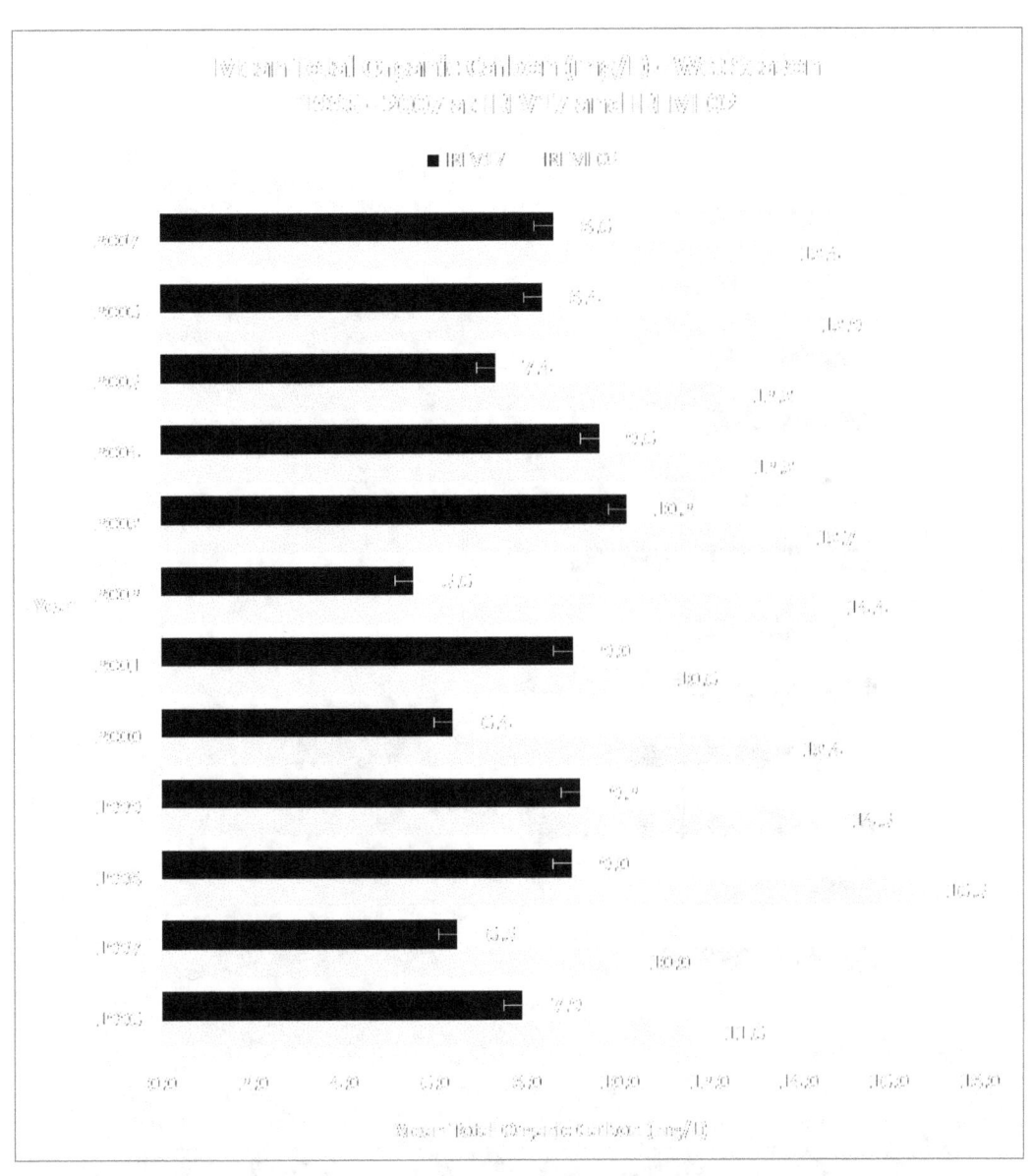

n =	1996	1997	1998	1999	2000	2001	2002	2003	2004	2005	2006	2007
IRLML02	25	24	25	17	14	11	15	15	13	11	14	10
IRLV17	22	23	20	12	10	10	10	5	5	6	11	5

Figure 50. Wet season mean total organic carbon (mg/L) from 1996–2007 at IRLV17 and IRLML02 (Figure 34). 1 mg/L = 1 ppm.

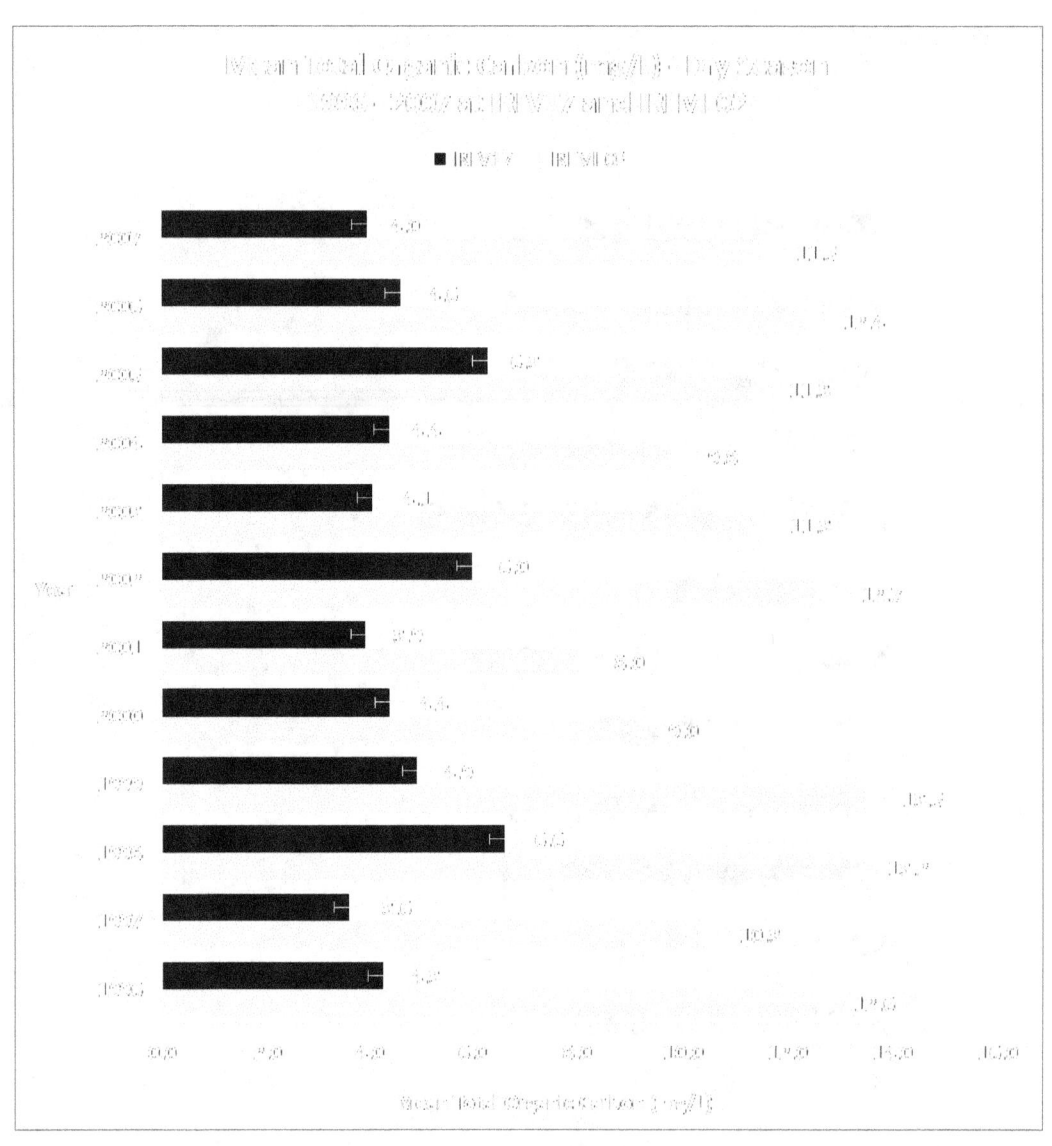

n =	1996	1997	1998	1999	2000	2001	2002	2003	2004	2005	2006	2007
IRLML02	19	27	33	31	21	21	20	21	19	16	19	16
IRLV17	18	28	29	24	14	14	14	11	7	8	14	10

Figure 51. Dry season mean total organic carbon (mg/L) from 1996–2007 at IRLV17 and IRLML02 (Figure 34). 1 mg/L = 1 ppm.

Figure 52. Wet season mean chlorophyll-a (μg/L) from 1990–2007 at IRLV17 and IRLML02 (Figure 34). 1 μg/L = 1 ppb.

Figure 53. Dry season mean chlorphyll-a (µg/L) from 1990–2007 at IRLV17 and IRLML02 (Figure 34). 1 µg/L = 1 ppb.

Table 16. Mean seasonal specific conductivity (mS/cm) at the Southeast Coast Network (SECN) monitoring station at Canaveral National Seashore from 2005–2009.

Year	Season	Mean Specific Conductance (mS/cm)	(n =)
2005	Summer	47.3	2733
	Fall	43.6	3122
2005-2006	Winter	48.1	989
2006	Spring	61.7	1231
	Summer	55	3568
2007	Spring	54.6	2565
	Summer	56.7	3088
	Fall	50.5	3668
2007-2008	Winter	51.6	2702
2008	Spring	58.5	4414
	Summer	58.1	2812
	Fall	51.5	4368
2008-2009	Winter	53.4	2420

32,612 mg/L (33.6‰), ranging from 25,960 mg/L (26‰) in 1991 to 40,230 mg/L (40‰) in 1993 (Hall et al., 2001). Specific conductance and TDS were both comparatively lower at the southern end of Mosquito Lagoon than in the north (Hall et al., 2001).

The dominant dissolved ions in Mosquito Lagoon accounting for its conductivity capacity are calcium, magnesium, sodium, potassium, sulfate, and chloride (Kroening, 2008). The most common anion and cation dissolved in Mosquito Lagoon water is chloride and sodium (Kroening, 2008). USGS reported values for chloride in Mosquito Lagoon ranging from 15,000–23,000 mg/L (15–23‰) and values for sodium ranging from 500–14,000 mg/L (0.5–14‰) (Kroening, 2008). Using data from 1978, Menon et al. (1979) report Ca^{2+} ranges from 325 mg/L (325 ppm) in February to 419 mg/L (419 ppm) in December and Mg^{2+} ranges from 1,086 mg/L (1.086‰) in February to 1,694 mg/L (1.694‰) in July.

From 1991–1993, sulfate (SO_4) throughout Mosquito Lagoon ranged from 2,000–7,140 mg/L, averaging 2,860 mg/L (Hall et al., 2001). Sulfate was found to vary seasonally and spatially in Mosquito Lagoon, reported values ranged from 1,195 –23,000 mg/L, although the maximum value may be in error (Kroening, 2008).

Water Clarity

Clarity is one of the most important water quality parameters since it regulates light attenuation in the water column and, therefore, the overall productivity, diversity, and richness of an aquatic system. The factors determining water clarity are numerous and complex and thus necessitate a variety of approaches. This section assesses the clarity in the CANA region of the Mosquito Lagoon using the following measured parameters: color (PCU), turbidity (NTU), Secchi disk depth (SDD), total dissolved solids (mg/L), and total suspended solids (mg/L). Measurements of color, turbidity, and total suspended solids (TSS) in Mosquito Lagoon in CANA reflect a seasonal pattern that is likely influenced by humic acids leached from adjacent wetlands (Kroening, 2008).

There are many physical factors regulating the clarity of water and light's ability to penetrate. In an IRL-wide study conducted in 2003, 59%–78% of light attenuation was attributed to the presence of tripton (non-algal, suspended, particulate matter) and inorganic solids (Christian and Sheng, 2003). The authors also report tripton concentration was related to wind speed.

Color

The USGS reported water color values for Mosquito Lagoon ranged from <10–175 platinum-cobalt units (PCU), with 90% of those values being <21 PCU (Kroening, 2008). Seasonal coloration is consistent with runoff volume, and the greatest color tends to occur at the end of the wet season between October and December (Kroening, 2008). In Hall et al. (2001), based on a four-year average from 1996 to 2000, Mosquito Lagoon color was reported to range from 5 PCU to 50 PCU. Data from IRLV17 and IRLML02 confirm the findings of higher color in the wet season (Figures 54 and 55).

Turbidity

Turbidity measurements quantify the extent to which light is scattered by particles suspended in the water column. Suspended particles are typically a combination of inorganic and organic materials along with amorphous conglomerations of highly variable size and shape (Trefry et al., 2005). The positive relationship between turbidity, light attenuation, and the health and abundance of seagrass beds is well documented—the more turbidity, the greater the potential for light attenuation (Steward et al., 2003; Morris and Virnstein, 2004; Steward et al., 2005). FDEP (2010), through principal component analysis, found that although chlorophyll is very important, turbidity is the dominant constituent affecting light attenuation in Mosquito lagoon.

Turbidity is commonly quantified in nephelometric turbidity units (NTU) using a nephelometer. While nephelometry is satisfactory for determining how turbid a particular sample is, the use of Secchi disk depth (SDD) to measure turbidity has the advantage of integrating turbidity over depth, where stratification of the water column can result in several layers of variable turbidity. Although SDD is usually strongly correlated with turbidity, it also reflects color and can therefore be an inaccurate measure of turbidity in colored waters.

As with other parameters regulating light attenuation, turbidity usually exhibits seasonality with the lowest clarity in the wet season and the highest in the dry season. Figures 56 and 57 present mean yearly values from 1990–2007 at IRLV17 and IRLML02 for the wet and dry seasons.

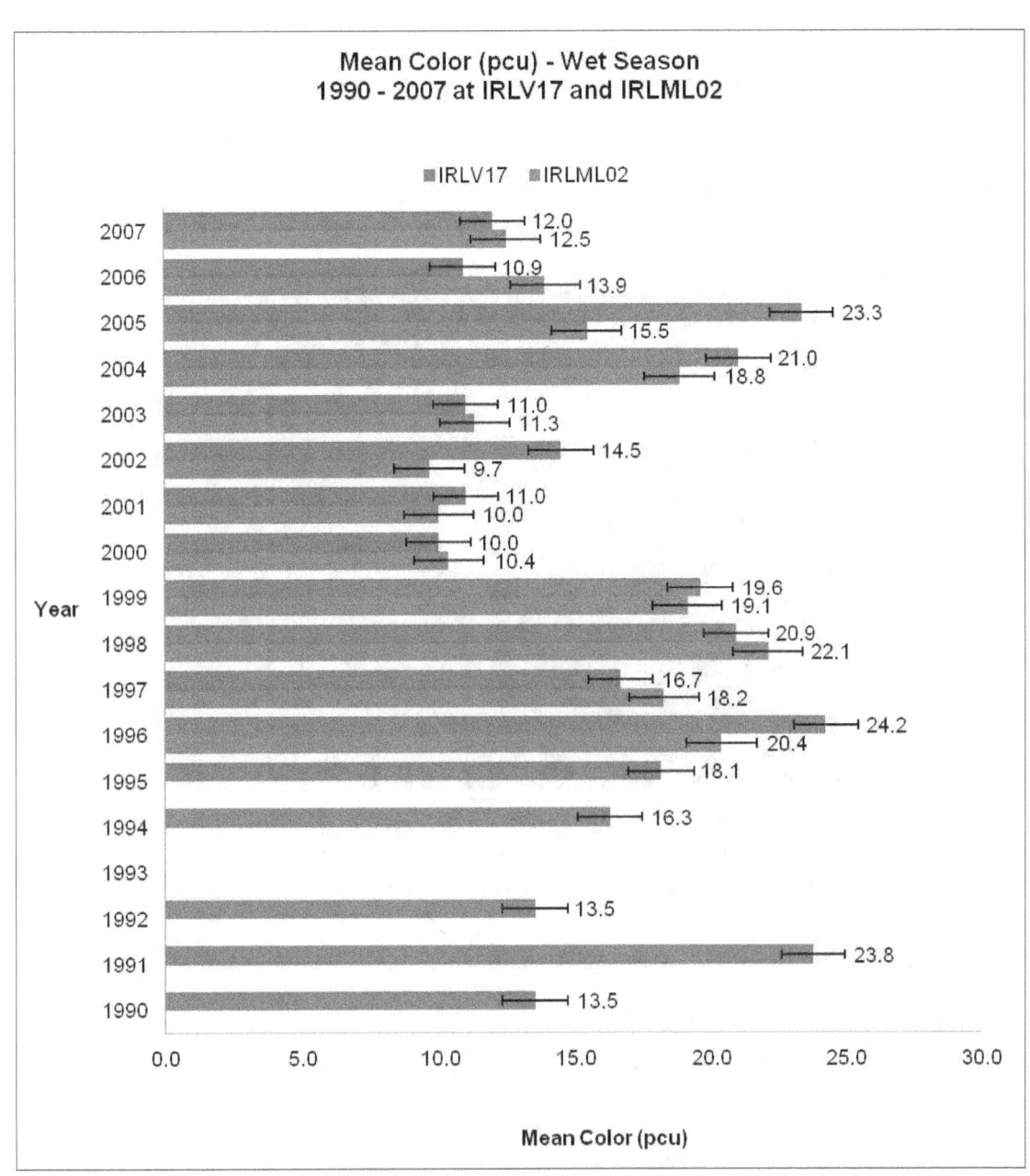

Figure 54. Wet season color (pcu) from 1990–2001 at IRLV17 and IRLML02 (Figure 34).

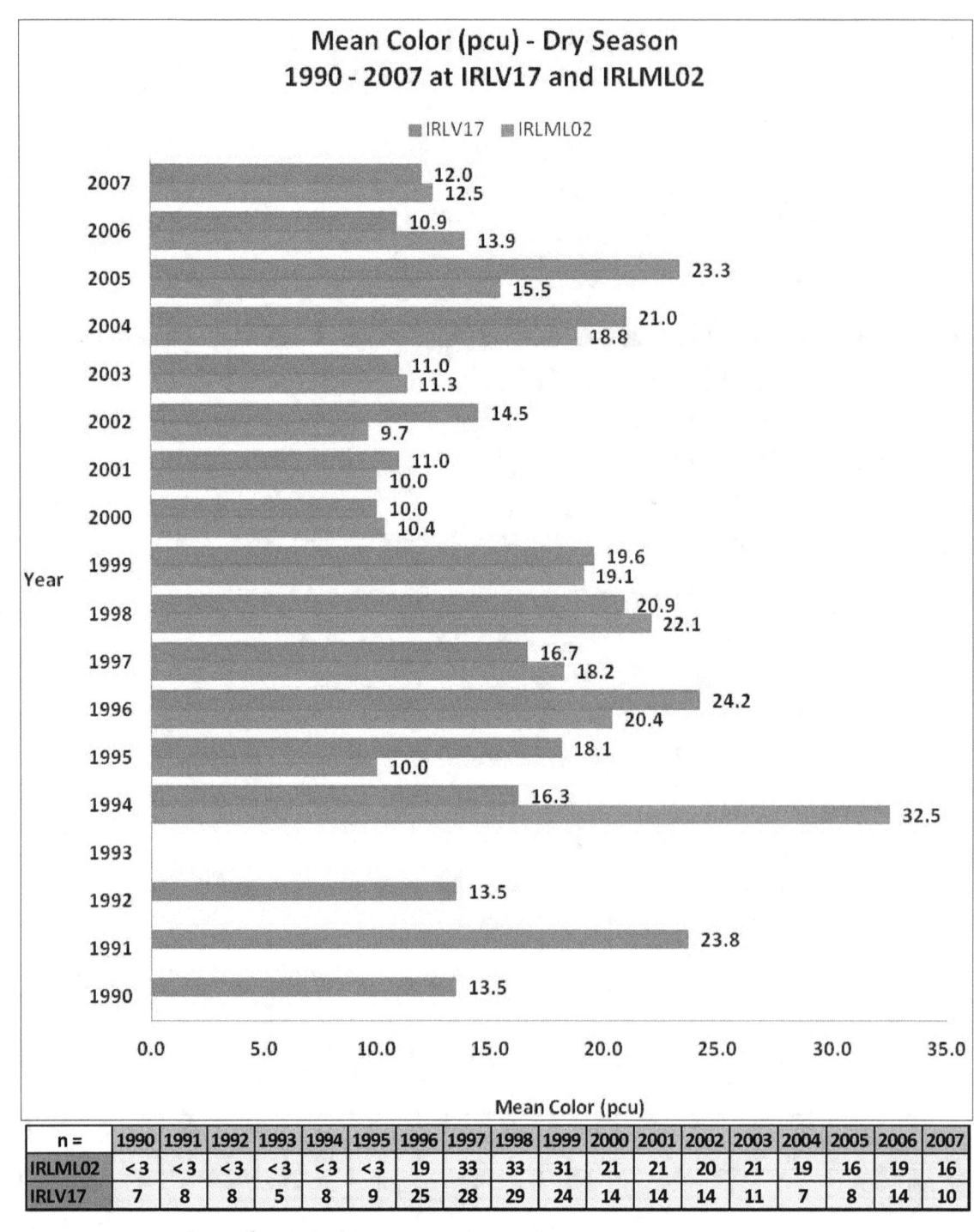

Figure 55. Dry season color (pcu) from 1990–2007 at IRLV17 and IRLML02 (Figure 34).

n =	1990	1991	1992	1993	1994	1995	1996	1997	1998	1999	2000	2001	2002	2003	2004	2005	2006	2007
IRLML02	<3	<3	<3	<3	<3	<3	25	25	25	17	14	12	15	15	13	11	14	10
IRLV17	6	6	6	<3	5	7	20	23	20	12	10	10	10	5	5	6	11	5

Figure 56. Wet season turbidity (NTU) from 1990–2007 at IRLV17 and IRLML02 (Figure 34).

Figure 57. Dry season turbidity (NTU) from 1990–2007 at IRLV17 and IRLML02 (Figure 34).

n =	1990	1991	1992	1993	1994	1995	1996	1997	1998	1999	2000	2001	2002	2003	2004	2005	2006	2007
IRLML02	<3	<3	<3	3	<3	<3	24	33	33	31	21	21	20	21	19	16	19	16
IRLV17	7	8	8	5	8	9	23	24	29	24	14	14	14	11	7	8	14	10

Turbidity in Mosquito Lagoon is also highest near the major population centers of New Smyrna Beach and Edgewater (Woodward-Clyde Consultants, 1994e). As expected, SDD measurements also exhibited lowest values (worst clarity, with ranges of 1.3–4.3 ft [0.4–1.3 m]) in the wet season and highest values (better clarity with ranges of 1.6–4.9 ft [0.5–1.5 m]) during the dry season (Woodward-Clyde Consultants, 1994e). Mean SDD measurements for the period 1990–2007 at IRLV17 and IRLML02 for the wet and dry seasons are presented in Figures 58 and 59.

The 10-year average for turbidity in Mosquito Lagoon was >6 NTU, which is higher than most other areas in the IRL (Steward et al., 2003).

SECN monitoring station data evaluated for this assessment included 27,224 measurements of turbidity, of which 83.7% were <25 NTU, but only 35.2% were ≤6 NTU. The overall median turbidity was approximately 9 NTU (n=1,205). Given the discontinuities in the SECN data set and the consequent variation in cardinality with respect to the wet and dry seasons, overall median and average turbidity values are reported by season in Table 17 and further divided by year and season in Table 18. Median values are approximate, as actual measurements were rounded to the nearest whole number prior to counting.

Table 17. Mean and median seasonal turbidity at the Southeast Coast Network (SECN) monitoring station at Canaveral National Seashore from 2005–2009.

\multicolumn{4}{c}{MEAN AND MEDIAN SEASONAL TURBIDITY SECN MONITORING STATION, CANAVERAL NATIONAL SEASHORE (SUMMER 2005 - WINTER 2009)}
Season	Mean Turbidity (NTU)	Median Turbidity (NTU)	(n =)
Winter	6.2	3	4620
Spring	26.2	7	7268
Summer	24.1	15	5973
Fall	19.9	12	9366

Suspended Solids

Given the importance of light attenuation in regulating the health and abundance of seagrasses (Steward et al., 2003), Florida Tech conducted a study for SJRWMD to 1) quantify the relationship between turbidity and TSS, 2) characterize the components of TSS that attenuate light in the IRL, 3) develop statistical relationships between light attenuation and the key components of TSS, and 4) identify the sources of the TSS material (Trefry et al., 2005).

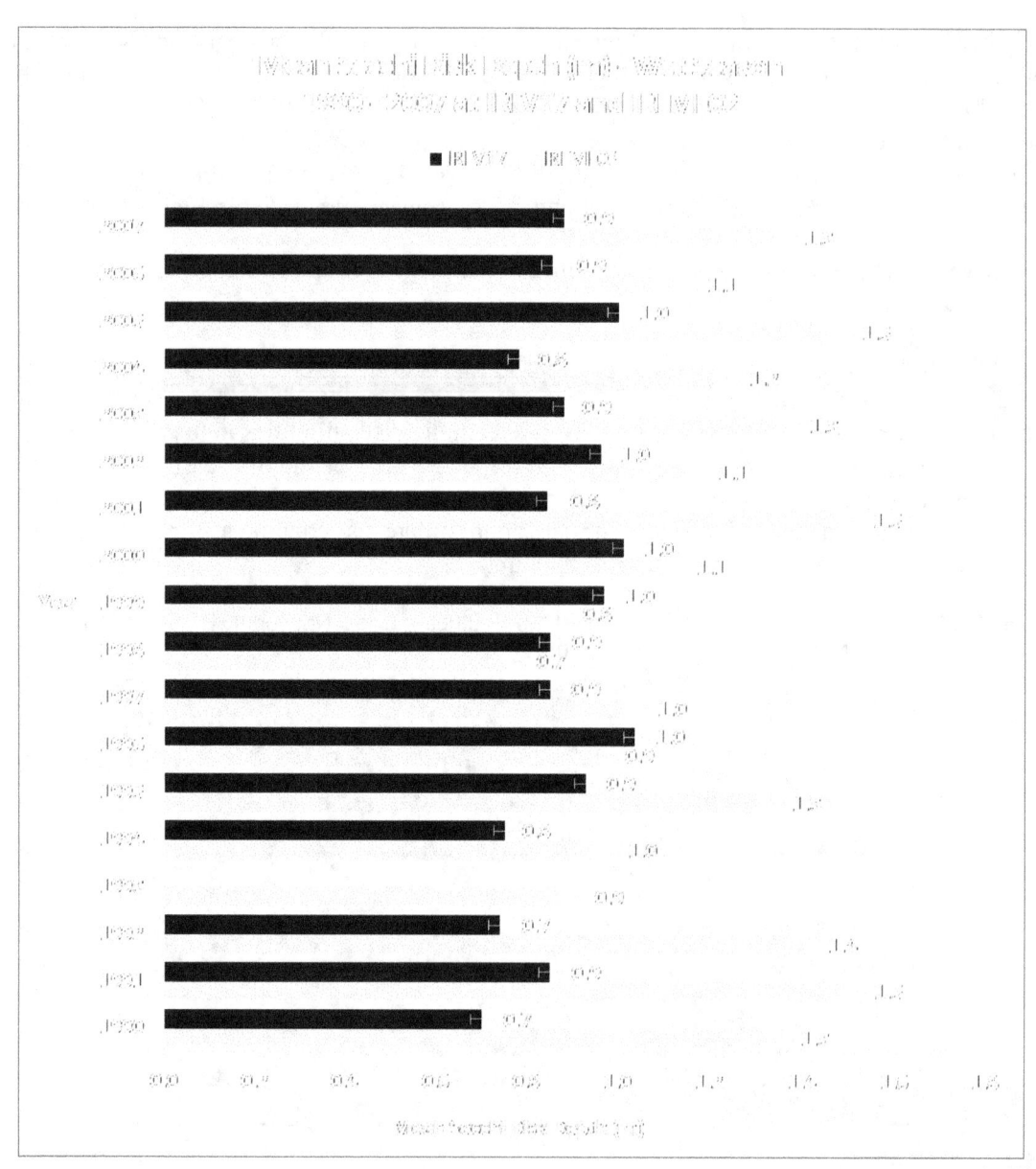

Figure 58. Wet season Secchi disk depth (m) from 1990–2007 at IRLV17 and IRLML02 (Figure 34).

n =	1990	1991	1992	1993	1994	1995	1996	1997	1998	1999	2000	2001	2002	2003	2004	2005	2006	2007
IRLML02	8	7	6	8	7	6	24	33	33	31	21	21	20	21	19	16	19	16
IRLV17	7	7	8	5	8	9	20	11	29	24	14	14	14	11	7	8	14	10

Figure 59. Dry season Secchi disk depth (m) from 1990–2007 at IRLV17 and IRLML02 (Figure 34).

Table 18. Mean and median turbidity by year and season at the Southeast coast Network (SECN) monitoring station at Canaveral National Seashore from 2005–2009.

Year	Season	Mean Turbidity (NTU)	Median Turbidity (NTU)	(n =)
2005	Summer	21	18	1539
	Fall	32.9	14	2556
2006	Spring	116.8	59	995
	Spring	3.4	3	2553
2007	Summer	25.4	11	1654
	Fall	18.3	12	2447
2007-2008	Winter	7.5	4	2694
	Spring	17.4	9	3720
2008	Summer	25	14	2780
	Fall	13	11	4363
2008-2009	Winter	4.3	2	1926

Data were gathered from 2003–2004 at five locations in Mosquito Lagoon, one of which was within CANA in the southern reach of the lagoon near Haulover Canal. In 2007, the same team conducted a similar study in the CANA region of the Mosquito Lagoon. Using data from Trefry (2005), along with data collected in Mosquito Lagoon in 2006–2007, the authors derived the following statistical relationships between TSS concentrations (on glass fiber filters) and field measurements of turbidity and the photosynthetically active radiation attenuation coefficient (K_{PAR}) (Trefry et al., 2007):

$$\textbf{TSS}_{GF} \text{ (as mg/L)} = 1.72 \text{ (Turbidity as NTU)} + 0.81 \quad \text{(Eq. 9)}$$

$$\textbf{TSS}_{GF} \text{ (as mg/L)} = 11.2 \text{ (}K_{PAR}\text{ as m}^{-1}\text{)} - 0.5 \quad \text{(Eq. 10)}$$

$$\textbf{Turbidity} \text{ (as NTU)} = 7.1 \text{ (}K_{PAR}\text{ as m}^{-1}\text{)} - 1.3 \quad \text{(Eq. 11)}$$

The seasonality of TSS (increased amounts present in the wet season and decreased amounts present in the dry season) has been confirmed many times (Hall et al., 2001; Trefry et al., 2005, 2007; Kroening, 2008). Total suspended solids were relatively constant during the dry season and variable in the wet season (Hall et al., 2001).

Total suspended solids were highest near the major population centers of New Smyrna Beach and Edgewater (Woodward-Clyde Consultants, 1994e). Turbidity is less of a problem south of Haulover Canal, but of concern to the north. Data collected in 2006–2007 indicated high turbidity at seven of 16 sample locations in Mosquito lagoon; six of the seven locations were north of Haulover Canal (Trefry et al., 2007).

Hall et al. (2001) also quantified TSS in Mosquito Lagoon using data gathered between 1991–1993. TSS averaged 61.49 mg/L (61 ppm) and ranged from 16.0 mg/L (16 ppm) in 1993 to 350 mg/L (350 ppm) in 1992 (Hall et al., 2001). The same study found that TSS was positively correlated at varying levels of statistical significance with salinity, conductivity, TDS, TKN, NO_x, and concentrations of several trace metals, including aluminum (Al), silica (Si), calcium (Ca), iron (Fe), and sulfate (SO_4) (Hall et al., 2001). Kroening (2008) reported TSS concentrations ranging for the period 1999–2003 from 5–113 mg/L (5–113 ppm), with 90% <61 mg/L (61 ppm) (Kroening, 2008).

The TSS composition is highly variable and reflects a diverse mix of organic and inorganic particulates. Overall, TSS in Mosquito Lagoon was derived from approximately half organic and half inorganic materials. A chief problem causing light attenuation in the IRL was creek runoff containing aluminosilicates (Trefry et al., 2005). Particles were responsible for approximately 95% of light attenuation in the IRL, while aluminosilicates accounted for 67% of light attenuation in Mosquito Lagoon (Trefry et al., 2005; Trefry et al., 2007). Trefry et al. (2007) provide an in-depth chemical analysis of the organic and inorganic constituents of TSS at CANA. Table 19 is based on Trefry et al. (2007) and summarizes the composition of TSS at CANA. Figures 60 and 61 show mean annual TSS data from 1990–2007 at IRLV17 and IRLML02 for the wet and dry seasons.

Table 19. Total suspended solids (TSS) percent composition and origin description in the Canaveral National Seashore (CANA) region of Mosquito Lagoon.

TSS COMPOSITION AND ORGIN IN CANA SURFACE WATER	
TSS Description	TSS %
Terrigenous Origin	18
Produced In Situ	20
Aluminosilicates (clays)	50
Other inorganics such as biogenic exoskeletons and amorphous silicate particulate	12

Contaminants and Pollutants
Little data for organic pesticides and trace elements are available for the Mosquito Lagoon basin. Available pesticide data generally cover compounds not in use from 1990–2002 (Kroening, 2008). The hydrophobicity of these compounds and their tendency to bioaccumulate or partition

into sediments make it unlikely that evidence of historical pesticide use would be found in Mosquito Lagoon water today.

Pesticides
The 2001 Canaveral National Seashore Water Resources Management Plan summarizes the history of pesticide use in the Mosquito Lagoon basin. Chemicals used included diesel fuel (1930s–1980s), DDT (1940s–1960s), and other chlorinated compounds, such as dieldrin and BHC (from the 1940s) (Walters et al., 2001). A study by Florida Tech in the 1970s reported common use of pesticides, such as ethion and malathion in and around Mosquito Lagoon (Lasater, 1974). The use of malathion was discontinued in 1989 in response to new NPS regulations (FDEP, 2009).

The Baseline Water Quality Data Inventory and Analysis (NPS, 1996) lists 13 pesticides detected in CANA waters between 1975–1984, including endosulfan, endosulfan alpha, endosulfan Beta, P-P' DDD, P-P' DDE, lindane, chlordane, DDT, dieldrin, endrin, toxaphene, heptachlor, and heptachlor epoxide. Only 23 observations were conducted for these compounds, and all were below their respective EPA-mandated marine acute criteria (NPS, 1996).

Schmalzer et al. (1992) detected benzo(a)anthrecene, benzo(b)fluoranthene, napthalene, and pyrene in Mosquito Lagoon sediments. In a later study, benzo(a)anthracene, benzo(a)pyrene, chrysene, indeno(1,2,3-cd)pyrene were also detected (Schmalzer et al., 2000). In 2008, Mosquito Lagoon was sampled by USGS and analyzed for 20 pesticides and their common degradants. The only pesticide detected was alpha hexachlorobenzene (1.24 µg/L; 1 ppb). Polychlorinated biphenyls (PCB) were below the reporting limit of 0.1 mg/kg (1 ppm) (Kroening, 2008).

Metals
Chemical equilibrium plays a dominant role in fixing the different phases of metal concentrations *in situ* (Menon et al., 1979). Ionic strength of water, pH, and temperature play as dominant a role in determining the availability of trace metals as the concentrations of the metals and their various coordinating ligands. For example, Mosquito Lagoon's relatively high pH, particularly in winter, inhibits release of trace metals from sediment. Other factors controlling the partitioning of metals between sediment and water include salinity, redox potential, the amount and type of organic material present, particle grain size distributions, biological activity, physical mixing, and temperature (Hall et al., 2001). The primary mechanism for the release of trace metals from estuarine sediments may involve the competition between the trace metal and major cations (Ca^{+2} and Mg^{+2}) for ion-exchangeable sites in sediments (Menon et al., 1979).

Menon et al. (1979) sampled eight sites along the western shore of the southern Mosquito Lagoon five times during 1977. Samples were analyzed for zinc (Zn), manganese (Mn), cadmium (Cd), and copper (Cu); the mechanisms by which they may be released from sediments were evaluated. The concentrations of the metals exhibited seasonal variations in rates of release from sediments. Generally, release was inhibited in winter and promoted in the summer of 1977 (Menon et al., 1979). Mn in water peaked in mid-March at >4 mg/L (>4 ppm) and in sediment, it peaked in early January at <5 mg/L (<5 ppm). Cd peaked in water in June at 0.3 mg/L (0.3 ppm), and in sediment, at 0.5 mg/L (0.5 ppm). Cu peaked in December in water and sediment between 2.5–3.0 mg/L (2.5–3.0 ppm). Zn peaked in January in sediments at 25 mg/L (25 ppm), and in

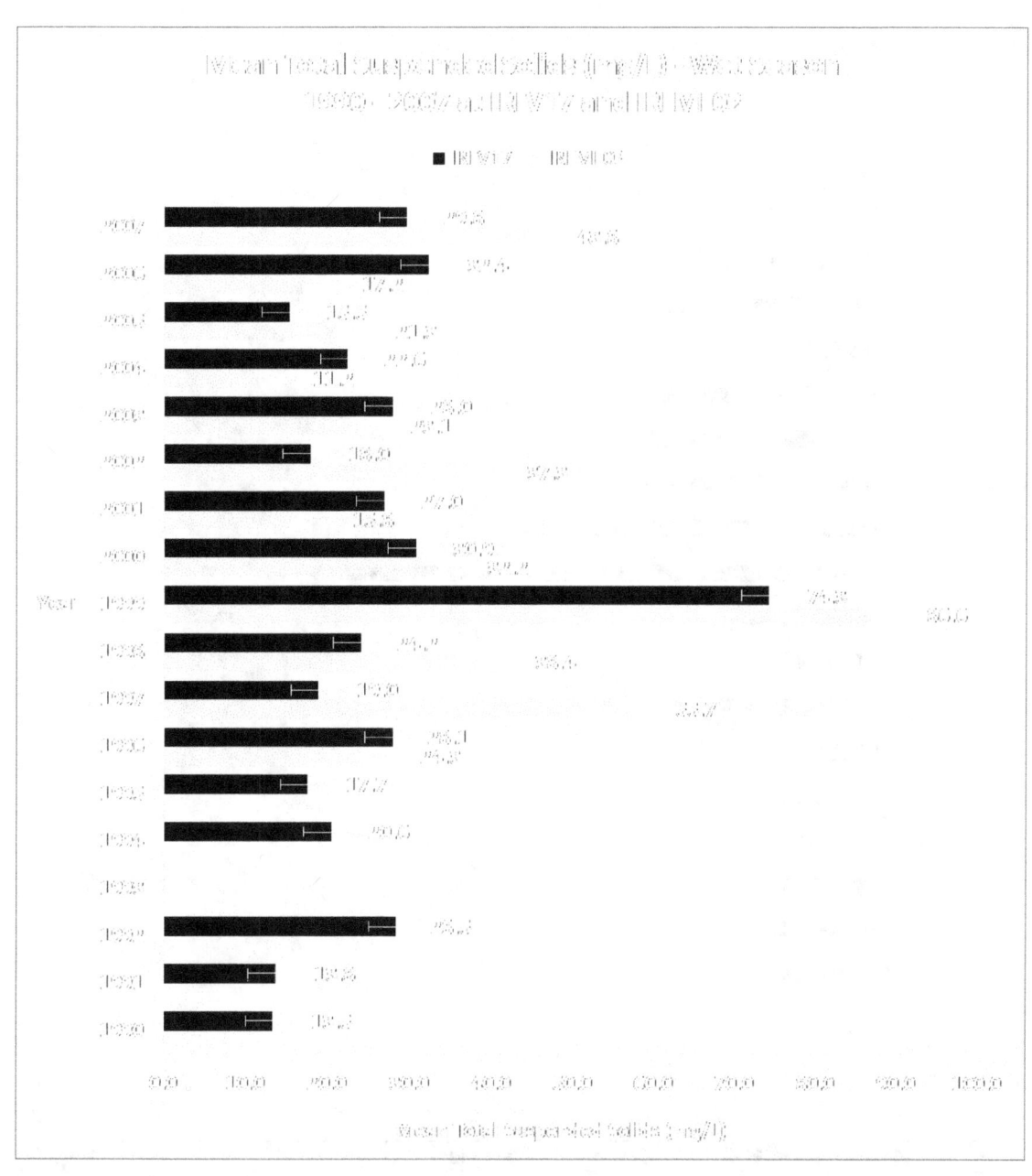

n =	1990	1991	1992	1993	1994	1995	1996	1997	1998	1999	2000	2001	2002	2003	2004	2005	2006	2007
IRLML02	<3	<3	<3	<3	<3	<3	25	25	25	17	14	12	15	15	13	11	14	10
IRLV17	6	6	6	<3	5	7	18	23	20	12	10	10	10	5	5	6	11	5

Figure 60. Wet season total suspended solids (mg/L) from 1990–2007 at IRLV17 and IRLML02 (Figure 34). 1 mg/L = 1 ppm.

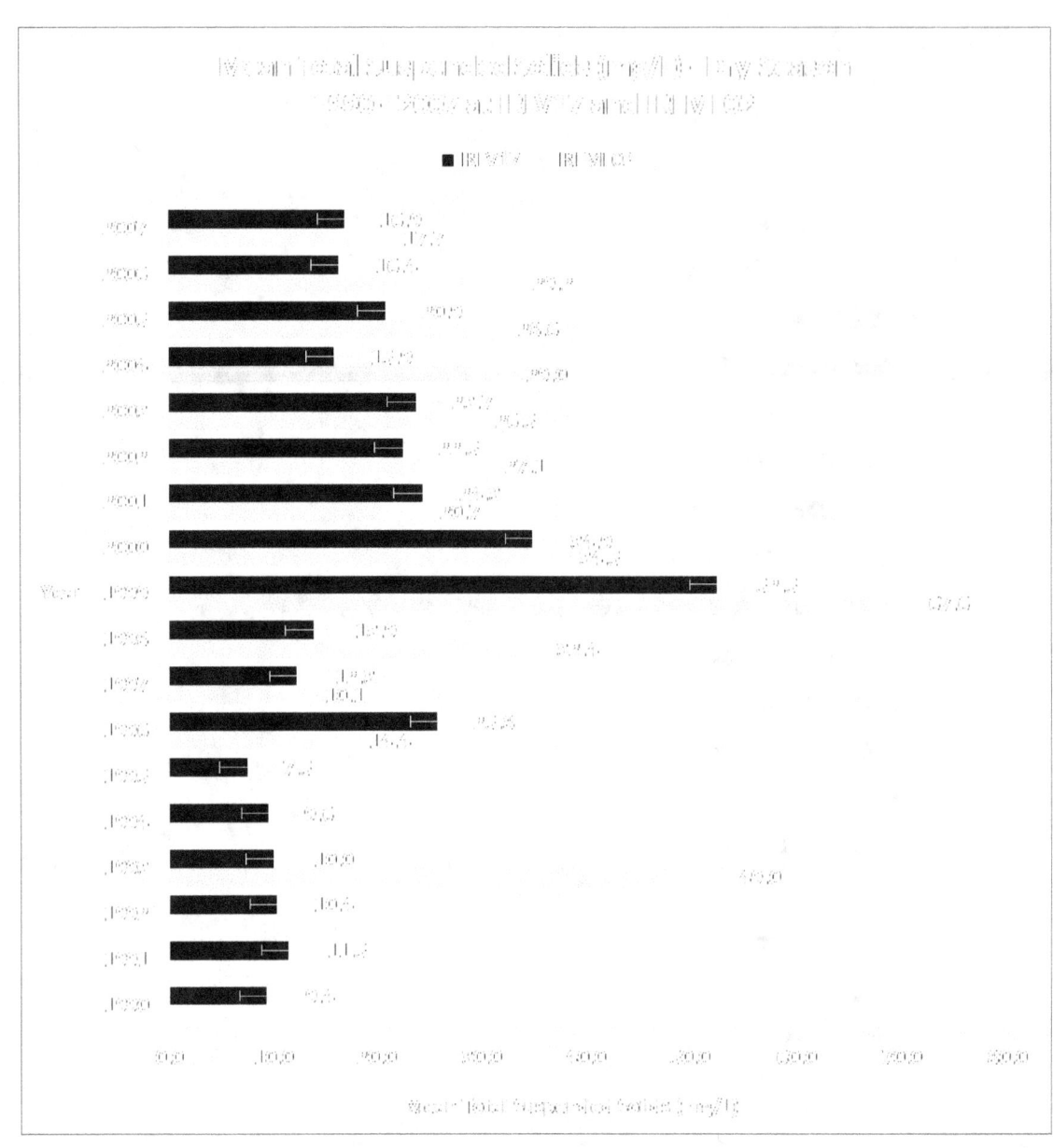

n =	1990	1991	1992	1993	1994	1995	1996	1997	1998	1999	2000	2001	2002	2003	2004	2005	2006	2007
IRLML02	<3	<3	<3	3	<3	<3	24	33	33	31	21	21	14	21	19	16	19	16
IRLV17	7	8	8	5	8	8	25	28	29	24	14	14	10	11	7	8	14	10

Figure 61. Dry season total suspended solids (mg/L) from 1990–2007 at IRLV17 and IRLML02 (Figure 34). 1 mg/L = 1 ppm.

water in August at 25 mg/L (25 ppm). With the exception of Mn, metals had the lowest concentrations in winter and highest in summer (Menon et al., 1979).

Provancha et al. (1992) reported elevated levels of iron (Fe) but described their occurrence as potentially natural. Silver (Ag) was reported to be several orders of magnitude higher than allowed by the state of Florida's Department of Natural Resources and the authors describe Ag, Fe, and aluminum (Al) as being consistently in excess of state-mandated requirements (Provancha et al., 1992).

A detailed account of the sediment sources of trace metals to Mosquito Lagoon water can be found in Schmalzer et al. (2000). In that study, 51 sites were evaluated, 10 of which were within CANA boundaries. The authors analyzed 24 trace metal parameters and reported detecting Al, calcium (Ca), Fe, lead (Pb), magnesium (Mg), potassium (K), sodium (Na), antimony (Sb), and thallium (Tl); that barium (Ba), Cd, chromium (Cr), cobalt (Co), mercury (Hg), vanadium (Vn), and Zn were consistently below detection limits (Schmalzer et al., 2000).

The most recent information available on trace metals in Mosquito Lagoon water comes from USGS. Based on data compiled from eight sites between 1978 and 2002, they report that arsenic (As), Cd, Cr, Cu, nickel (Ni), and Zn were detected periodically in Mosquito Lagoon surface water (Kroening, 2008). Hg, however, was not detected in Mosquito Lagoon surface water (Kroening, 2008).

In 2001, Hall et al. (2001) reported that Ag, Al, Be, B, Cr, Cu, Fe, Ni, Pb, and Zn, as well as several more common cations, had all been detected at least once in Mosquito Lagoon surface water between 1991–1993. Detected concentrations, as reported for these metals (Schmalzer et al., 2000; Hall et al., 2001; Kroening, 2008) and their respective Class II water quality criteria as currently defined in FAC 63.202.500, are summarized in Table 20.

Hydrocarbons
Little data exist in the literature for the hydrocarbon content of Mosquito Lagoon surface water. In 1992, Provancha et al. (1992) reported phenol concentrations consistently in excess of state-mandated criteria; however, these high concentrations were believed to be naturally occurring. Hall et al. (2001) reported average phenol values of 111.4 µg/L (111 ppb), with a range of 43.8–399.0 µg/L (44–399 ppb), for samples collected between 1991–1993. Greases and oils ranged in concentration from 0.52–86.0 mg/L (0.5–86 ppm), with an average value of 3.31 mg/L (3.3 ppm) (Hall et al., 2001).

Microbial Content
Enterococci bacteria are the recommended indicator organism to determine the suitability of marine waters for recreation (EPA, 1986). Various methods of quantifying the coliform content of water complicate an assessment such as this; historically two methods have been commonly employed. They are: the determination of the most probable number (MPN) of coliform and the determination of the number of colony forming units (CFU). Both are typically reported per 100 mL of water but can vary greatly from each other within a single sample. This intra-sample variability is not caused by human error or differing laboratory procedures, but is a consequence of the probabilistic basis for calculating MPN (Gronewold and Wolpert, 2008).

Table 20. Trace metal concentrations in Mosquito Lagoon water from various agencies between 1979–2002 and Class II water quality criteria (FAC 63.202.500). NR = Not Reported. 1 mg/L = 1 ppm; 1 μg/L = 1 ppb.

Metal	Number of Detections	Reported Concentration	Class II Criterion	Units
Ag[†]	53	1.07[*]	≤ 2.3	μg/L
Al[†]	59	0.54[*]	≤ 1.5	mg/L
As[††]	NR	3.6 – 500[**]	≤ 50	μg/L
B[†]	71	2.96[*]	[†††]	mg/L
Be[†]	30	0.2 – 2.2[***]	≤ 0.13	μg/L
Cd[†]	44	1.28[*]	< 8.8	μg/L
Cr[†]	54	0.03[*]	[†††]	mg/L
Cu[†]	14	50[*]	≤ 3.7	μg/L
Fe[†]	44	0.5[*]	≤ 0.3	mg/L
Ni[†]	22	100[*]	≤ 8.3	μg/L
Pb[†]	19	100[*]	≤ 8.5	μg/L
Zn[††]	NR	0 – 310	≤ 86	μg/L

[†] Hall et al., 2001
[††] Kroening, 2008
[†††] Class II Criteria do not exist
[*] Average of all detected concentrations
[**] Range of concentrations detected between 1984–2002
[***] Range of concentrations detected between 1991–1992

With respect to fecal coliform bacteria, the allowable bacteriological content of Class II Florida waters is described in Florida Administrative Code 62.302.530 as follows: "MPN shall not exceed a median value of 14 with not more than 10% of the samples exceeding 43, nor exceed 800 on any one day." Alternatively, EPA (1986) recommends that enterococci counts should not exceed a geometric mean of 35 CFU/100 mL based on at least five samples collected over a 30-day period, or that the count of a single sample should not exceed 158 CFU/100 mL in waters moderately used for recreation.

The Florida Department of Agriculture and Consumer Services (FDACS) classifies water bodies for shellfish harvesting and issues daily status reports of closures and openings. Shellfish harvesting in the southern two-thirds of Mosquito Lagoon from Three Cabbage Island to Pelican Island is classified "Approved" for shellfish harvest, while south of Pelican Island is "Prohibited" (www.floridaaquaculture.com/pdfmaps/80.PDF) (FDACS, 1997). The northern extent of CANA limits in Mosquito Lagoon from Three Cabbage Island to Shipyard Island is generally classified as "Conditionally Approved Zones 1 and 2," (www.floridaaquaculture.com/pdfmaps/82b.PDF) (FDACS, 2000). In 2009, FDACS revised classifications and boundaries for shellfish management and incorporated the National Shellfish Sanitation Program standards.

Conditionally approved zones 1 and 2 may experience closures due to rain events and/or if the threshold for fecal coliform median or geometric mean exceeds 14 MPN/100 ml, and more than 10% exceed 43 MPN/100 ml. (FDACS, 2009). Zone 2 areas are generally in open water and may be closed for shellfish harvesting when the two-day cumulative rainfall at the WWTP in Edgewater exceeds 4.03 in (10.2 cm), while zone 1 along the western shore of the north

Mosquito Lagoon in CANA may close when the two-day cumulative rainfall at the Edgewater WWTP exceeds 1.15 inches (2.9 cm) (Kroening, 2008).

Shellfish harvesting in the small linear areas along the west shore classified as "Conditionally Restricted" require a special permit and controlled purification of harvested shellfish. The National Shellfish Sanitation Program 88/260 standard for restricted areas is that fecal coliform median or geometric mean must not exceed 88 MPN/100 ml, and not more than 10% may exceed 260 MPN/100 ml. (FDACS, 2009).

Because of the changes in regulations, increases in population, and changes in management practices during the last 30 yrs, the historical studies of bacterial concentrations are best used as background information for current studies. A Florida Tech study conducted in the early 1970s reported that one site in Mosquito Lagoon near Max Hoeck Creek had values of 130,000 MPN/100 mL (Lasater, 1974). The author also stated all other samples in the study had values of <8,000 MPN/100 mL (Lasater, 1974). Reasons for larger values are unclear at this time.

The USGS reviewed historical bacteriological data in Mosquito Lagoon from Volusia County Environmental Health Laboratory (VCEHL) and Florida Department of Agriculture and Consumer Services (FDACS). Data collected by VCEHL were excluded from the analysis. Only FDACS data from 1999 through 2003 were pooled and used to identify the occurrence and seasonal variations in coliform levels since those data represent almost 90% of the fecal coliform bacteria observations in lagoon areas that are not restricted (Kroening, 2008). Counts varied seasonally and spatially; 90%were ≥21 MPN/100 mL and they ranged from 1–920 MPN/100 mL (Kroening, 2008). Shellfish closures to prevent fecal coliform contamination due to rain events have occurred in Mosquito Lagoon. On January 22, 2011, "8212 South Volusia Conditionally Approved Zone 1" was closed due to rainfall (FDACS, 2011). Daily status reports for Florida are available at: (http://shellfish.floridaaquaculture.com/seas/seas_statusmap.htm).

Bacteria counts from 1999–2003 were typically greatest from September to October and from December to February and lowest from April to June. Since the period from September to October is approximately the end of the wet season, the higher counts may be attributable to surface runoff (Kroening, 2008). Citing a study conducted in an English estuary and noting that TSS are typically highest when bacterial counts are highest, Kroening (2008) suggests the resuspension of bottom sediments may also be a significant factor in promoting bacterial growth.

Trend Analysis

Irregularities and discontinuities in collection and analysis procedures resulted in a data set that was heteroscedastic and nonparametric. Since the data were not normally distributed, the example of Winkler and Ceric (2006) was followed by using a Mann-Kendall Trend Test, which is appropriate for analyzing data sets with missing data (Winkler and Ceric, 2006). Since the Mann-Kendall test is best suited to the detection of a monotonic trend of a time series with no seasonal cycle, the data were separated by station (IRLV17 and IRLML02) and the dry and wet seasons were analyzed separately. To estimate the magnitude of the trend, Sen's Slope Estimate was applied; it uses a linear model to estimate the true slope of a trend as change per year.

Computations for the Mann-Kendall Trend Test and Sen's Slope Estimate were performed using the method and Microsoft Excel template (MAKESENS) developed by Salmi et al. (2002). Their method tests the null hypothesis of no trend (observations are randomly ordered in time) against the alternative hypothesis of an increasing or decreasing monotonic trend. The significance level computed by this method indicates the probability that the values are from a random distribution and with that same probability, rejecting the null hypothesis of no trend would be in error. Therefore, a significance level 0.001 indicates that a true monotonic trend is 99.9% probable and a significance level 0.1 means that there is a 10% probability that a monotonic trend is occurring or that an error is made when rejecting the null hypothesis of no trend.

Table 21 shows the trend analysis results for 12 water quality parameters measured at IRLV17 and IRLML02. Most parameters are analyzed for 1990–2007 at both stations by season. Data were limited for Chl-a (1996–2007 at IRLML02 and 1990–2007 at IRLV17), TOC (1996–2007 at IRLML02 and IRLV17), and NO_x (1994–2005 at IRLML02 and 1996–2005 at IRLV17). The observed downward trends in Chl-a and TKN are consistent with an improved trophic state.

Table 21. Significance of seasonal trends in 10 key surface water quality parameters from 1990–2007 at IRLML02 and IRLV17 in Mosquito Lagoon (Figure 34).

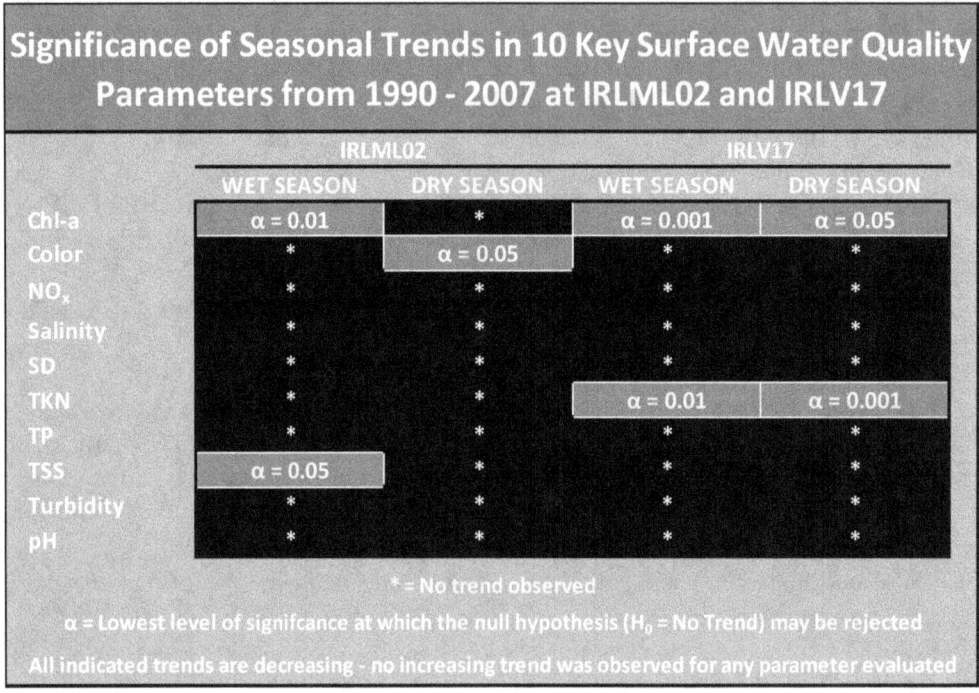

	IRLML02		IRLV17	
	WET SEASON	DRY SEASON	WET SEASON	DRY SEASON
Chl-a	α = 0.01	*	α = 0.001	α = 0.05
Color	*	α = 0.05	*	*
NO_x	*	*	*	*
Salinity	*	*	*	*
SD	*	*	*	*
TKN	*	*	α = 0.01	α = 0.001
TP	*	*	*	*
TSS	α = 0.05	*	*	*
Turbidity	*	*	*	*
pH	*	*	*	*

* = No trend observed
α = Lowest level of signifcance at which the null hypothesis (H_0 = No Trend) may be rejected
All indicated trends are decreasing - no increasing trend was observed for any parameter evaluated

Mosquito Lagoon Hydrological and Water Quality Model
Under a National Park Service contract to Scientific Environmental Applications, Inc. of Melbourne, FL, a three-dimensional hydrological and water quality model was developed to assist CANA in managing estuarine water quality resource of the Mosquito Lagoon. Because of its long residence time, Mosquito Lagoon is sensitive to pollutant loadings from the watershed. Inputs from the watershed have increased due to an almost 200% increase in population adjacent to the lagoon within the past 20 yrs, causing a decline in water quality and in the ecological and biological integrity of the lagoon. The hydrological model is being applied to assess current trends and possible future threats to Mosquito Lagoon water quality.

The hydrological model is based on the EPA-supported Environmental Fluid Dynamics Code/Hydrodynamic and Eutrophication Three-Dimensional Model (EFDC/HEM3D). EFDC/HEM3D includes features and capabilities that make it superior and more applicable to shallow estuarine environments than other models. This multi-parameter finite difference model represents estuarine flow and material transport in three dimensions and has been extensively applied to shallow estuarine environments in Florida and other coastal states. A few examples include the IRL just the south of the Mosquito Lagoon (Zarillo and Surak, 1994); the Loxahatchee River Estuary in South Florida (Zarillo, 2004); Lake Worth, FL (Zarillo, 2003); the lower Savannah River, GA (Tetra Tech, 2005); the Peconic Estuary, Long Island New York (Tetra Tech, 2000); and the German Wadden Sea (Zarillo, 1997).

The kinetic processes included in the HEM3D water quality model have been derived and updated from the Chesapeake Bay three-dimensional water quality model, CE-QUAL-ICM (Cerco and Cole, 1994). A detailed description of the water quality model is provided by Park et al. (1995) and Tetra Tech (2007).

The total number of active water cells in the EFDC grid is 4,200. Cell sizes in the grid range from approximately 40 m x 40 m to approximately 450 m on a side where the model extends over broad wetlands. The finer grid cell sizes were used to resolve the details of tidal drainage as well as the AIW (Figure 62). At the model boundaries measured time series of water level, salinity and temperature are applied to drive the model. Meteorological time series are used to drive the air–sea interaction component of the model.

Measured time series of water quality constituents are alsopresent at the mode l boundaries to drive eutrophication calculations. Table 22 lists the water quality variables calculated by HEM3D.

Table 22. Water Quality variables calculated by the Hydrodynamic and Eutrophication Three-Dimensional Model.

Variables	
(1) cyanobacteria **Bc**	(12) labile particulate organic nitrogen **LPON**
(2) diatom algae **Bd**	(13) dissolved organic nitrogen **DON**
(3) green algae **Bg**	(14) ammonia nitrogen **NH$_4$**
(4) refractory particulate organic carbon **RPOC**	(15) nitrate nitrogen **NO23**
(5) labile particulate organic carbon **LPOC**	(16) particulate biogenic silica **SAP**
(6) dissolved organic carbon **DOC**	(17) dissolved available silica **SDd**
(7) refractory particulate org. phosphorus **RPOP**	(18) chemical oxygen demand **COD**
(8) labile particulate organic phosphorus	(19) dissolved oxygen **DO**
(9) dissolved organic phosphorus **DOP**	(20) total active metal **TAM**
(10) total phosphate **TP**	(21) fecal coliform bacteria **FCB**
(11) refractory particulate organic nitrogen **RPON**	

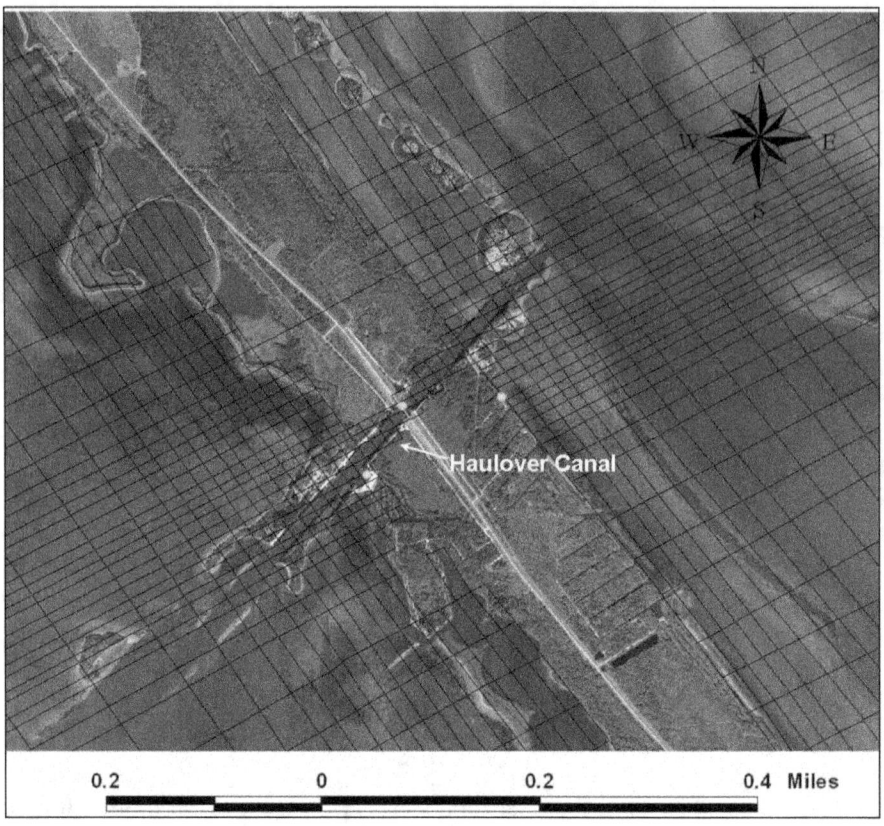

Figure 62. Model grid detail at Haulover Canal connecting the Mosquito Lagoon to the north end of the Indian River Lagoon. Green symbols show the locations of water level or metrological observation stations maintained by SJRWMD.

Comparison between measured and predicted time series of water elevation (Figure 63), salinity, and temperature indicate that the EFDC/HEM3D model application to the Mosquito Lagoon is well calibrated. Within the limits of the availability of measured water quality constituents, the eutrophication portion of the hydrological model is also well calibrated. Figure 64 shows a comparison between measured and predicted values of DO. Measured values of water quality constituents are available only on a quarterly basis or less, however.

The model application includes a long-term simulation as allowed by available physical forcing and water quality inputs. The goals of the model application include:

- Evaluating the sensitivity of the estuary to changes in tributary inflows, canal discharges, and pollutant loadings;
- Evaluating the effectiveness of load reductions in accordance with management priorities;
- Developing recommendations for practical and feasible restoration actions and plans for management;
- Developing recommendations in the development of pollutant loading limitations; and
- Developing pollution load-reduction goals.

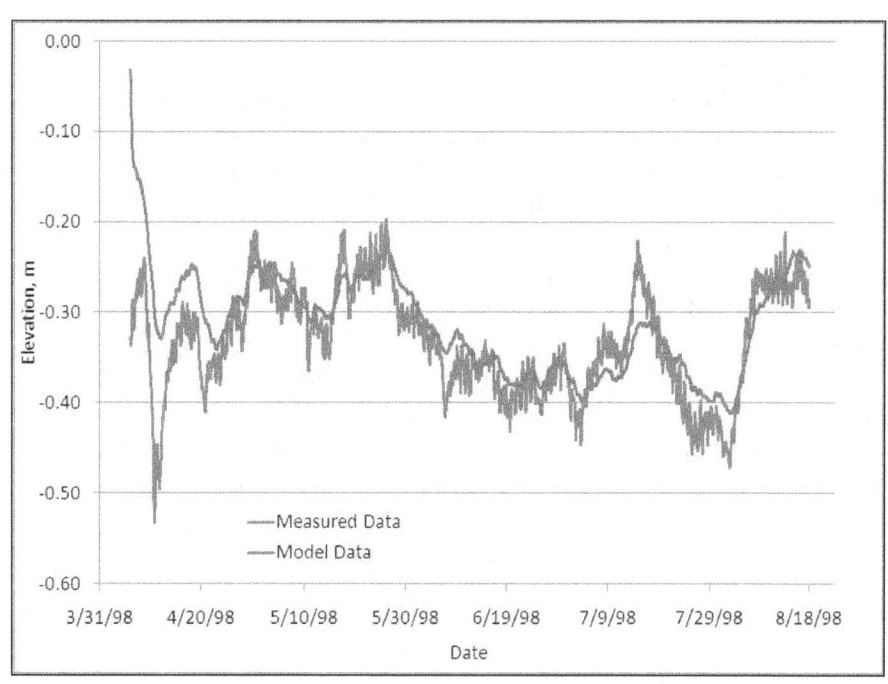

Figure 63. Comparison of measured and modeled water elevation data from the center of Haulover Canal for the 100-day calibration period. Elevation is relative to NAVD88.

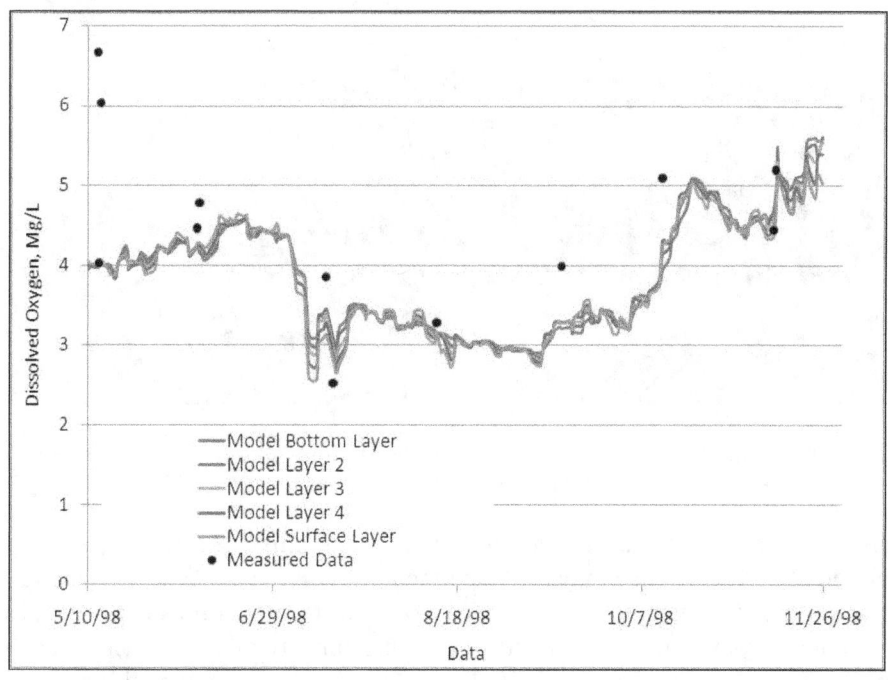

Figure 64. Comparison between predicted and measured dissolved oxygen values at station IRLV11 in the north section of the Mosquito Lagoon.

Biological Resources
Coastal Waters and Beach

The strip of the barrier island that lies between the Atlantic Ocean and the Mosquito Lagoon is subjected to the harsh conditions of storms, limited freshwater water, and extreme temperatures. In some segments of CANA, the barrier island narrows to approximately 100 yards (~91 m) and widens to about 1,100 yards (~1,000 m) in other segments. The subaerial superstructure of the barrier island is formed by the beach and dune system (Figures 65 and 66). Varieties of species live year round, seasonally or migrate through the environs of CANA. The coastline is within the USFWS northern right whale (*Eubalaena glacialis*) critical habitat designated in 1994 (NMFS, 2009). Protected species, such as sea turtles, nest on the upper beach, and beach mice inhabit the dunes. Other species that inhabit or use the surf zone and beach are reptiles, fishes, shore birds, mole crabs (*Emerita talpoida*), ghost crabs (*Ocypode quadrata*), and the coquina clam (*Donax variabilis*). Among the factors that limit or aid in the success of an animal species is the quality and quantity of habitat for cover and reproduction, water, and food.

Figure 65. General features of the barrier island in Canaveral National Seashore; noted are surf zone and dune crest or berm; Mosquito Lagoon in the background (Photo: October 2010).

Natural disasters, such as northeasters and hurricanes, can modify the landscape. Climate change and the likelihood of sea level rise may diminish the total volume of the barrier shoreface, making the island more vulnerable to breaching or overwash. Increased storm events as a result of global warming may increase rainfall and stormwater runoff, which in turn, can affect salinity levels. Pollution, marine debris, and some human activities threaten the health and well being of the natural resources in CANA. Exotic plants and animals can disrupt natural ecological systems.

The conditions of the habitats and specific species found in the coastal ocean and barrier island system are discussed next. The potential impacts of pollution, marine debris, and climate change

Figure 66. General features of the barrier island in Canaveral National Seashore noted are swale, back barrier, and Mosquito Lagoon (Photo: October 2010).

are nonselective threats that can negatively affect multiple resources in the park and are discussed at the end of the Mosquito Lagoon habitat subsection.

Sea Turtles

Five species of sea turtles occur offshore of the Atlantic Ocean, while three species frequently nest on the central Florida coast: loggerhead (*Caretta caretta*), green (*Chelonia mydas*), leatherback (*Dermochelys coriacea*), Kemp's Ridley (*Lepidochelys kempi*), and hawksbill (*Eretmochelys imbricata*). All five species are threatened or endangered (USFWS, 1994). For the past 25 yrs, loggerhead nests outnumber those of the other species in Brevard and Volusia counties and CANA (Meylan et al., 1995; ACOE, 2007; Stiner, 2010a; FWC-FWRI, 2010a). Nest counts of the other species from greatest to smallest are: greens, leatherbacks, Kemp's Ridley, and unknown (FWC-FWRI, 2010a; Stiner, 2010a). The hawksbill and Kemp's Ridley nest infrequently according to Statewide Nesting Totals, 1979–2009 (FWC-FWRI, 2009a, (http://research.myfwc.com/images/articles/11812/statewide_totals_1979_-_2009.pdf)

Figure 67 shows a comparison of loggerhead and green sea turtle nests from 1984–2010. In 26 yrs of nesting data, there were 85,489 loggerhead and 8,983 green nests. Not shown are park nest counts from 1984–2010 for leatherbacks (172), Kemp's Ridley (47), and unknown species (44) (Stiner, 2010a).

Loggerhead, green, and leatherback turtles nest near the base of the dune or on the upper beach from April to September (Antworth et al., 2006). Eggs hatch and hatchlings emerge from the nest when surface–sediment temperatures drop at nightfall. The young turtles migrate toward the light horizon of the ocean, enter the surf, and swim until they are well offshore.

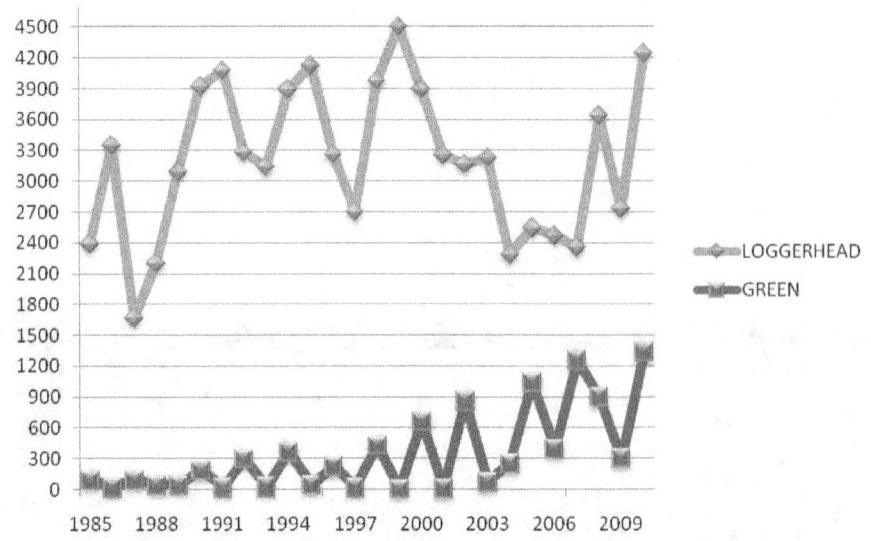

Figure 67. Comparison of loggerhead (*Caretta caretta*) and green (*Chelonia mydas*) sea turtle nest counts in Canaveral National Seashore from 1984–2010 (Stiner, 2010a).

Researchers have collected data and analyzed the annual reproductive process of sea turtles statewide for more than 30 yrs (Meylan et al., 1995; Witherington, 2009; FWC-FWRI, 2010b). Like other local entities, the CANA staff monitors and submits annual nest numbers to FWC-FWRI. Although data collection methods have changed over time, the extensive long-term data sets collected throughout Florida beaches enable scientists to review nesting trends and determine ways to improve nesting success. Witherington et al. (2009) analyzed loggerhead nest counts collected under the Index Nesting Beach Survey program for years 1989 to 2006 and found a declining trend in the nest numbers. Analysis that extended the data set to include data from 2006 to 2010 shows that the long-term downward trend of nest counts may be stabilizing (FWC-FWRI, 2010b). The CANA nesting total in 2010 was 5,621, which was over 1,000 nests more than any previous survey year (1984–2010) (Stiner, 2010a).

Threats to Sea Turtles
Threats to sea turtles in and outside of CANA, as depicted in Figure 68, may include erosion/accretion to the beach, predation by native and exotic species, interference by human activities, diseases, water pollution, and entanglement in debris and/or ingestion of debris. Diseases are discussed under the Mosquito Lagoon section and juvenile turtles.

Physical changes to the beach slope or width may affect nesting success. If the beach, from either natural erosion or human alteration, is too steep for female turtles to reach the upper beach, they may "false crawl" or abandon their attempt to nest. If the beach is extremely narrow, they may deposit their eggs too close to the shore where the eggs can be washed away by high tides. Nests can be inundated during natural storm events, such as northeasters and tropical cyclones (Pike and Stiner, 2007). Accretion of sand over nests can cause the hatchling to use more energy to crawl out of the nest and reduce its chances of reaching the ocean (NMFS-FWS, 2008).

Natural predation is the one of the greatest threats to hatchlings. The longer young turtles stay on the beach, the greater the exposure to nocturnal predators (Barton, 2005; Barton and Roth, 2008). The most common predators are ghost crabs, raccoons (*Procyon lotor*), feral hogs (*Sus scrofa*), foxes (*Urocyon cinereoargenteus* and *Vulpes vulpes*), coyotes (*Canis latrans*), armadillos (*Dasypus novemcinctus*), and red fire ants (*Solenopsis invicta*) (Dodd, 1988; Stancyk, 1982).

Prior to covering nests with cages, depredation by raccoons reached 96% in nesting areas of the southeastern U.S. (NMFS-FWS, 2008). CANA implemented a nest protection program in 1984, placing flat, wire mesh screens over the nests to exclude predators. Over the last 10 yrs, the annual nest depredation rate in CANA has ranged from 5–20% (John Stiner, personal communication, January 7, 2011), and MINWR (2008) reported rates below 10%. Forty-five percent of the nests at Cape Canaveral Air Force Station were depredated by feral hogs before hog control was implemented as reported by Florida Fish and Wildlife Conservation Commission (FWC) unpublished data in MINWR (2008). In the Recovery Plan for the Northwest Atlantic Population of the Loggerhead Sea Turtle (NMFS-FWS, 2008), other predators, such as coyotes, foxes, domestic dogs, and red fire ants, may destroy nests to consume the eggs and/or prey on emerging hatchlings. The researchers of NMFS-FWS (2008) believe that "nest protection activities have substantially reduced loggerhead nest depredations."

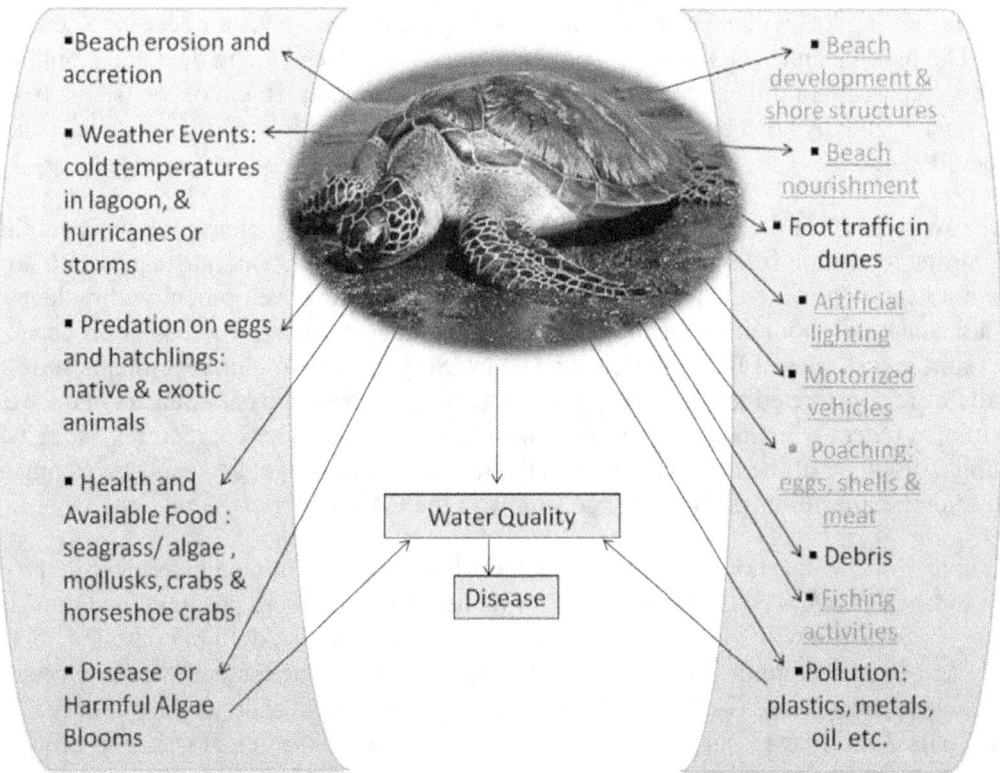

Figure 68. Threats and stressors to sea turtle populations throughout the stages of their life cycle from nesting, hatchling, juveniles, and adults. Black text indicates stressors that are relatively more important in influencing sea turtles using Canaveral National Seashore (CANA) beaches or Mosquito Lagoon. Stressors underlined in blue text are unlikely to occur in CANA.

Witherington and Martin (1996) report artificial light affects the nocturnal behavior of sea turtles in the selection of nesting sites and that light can disorient nesting females and hatchlings on their way to the ocean. The research of Witherington and Martin (1996) recommended reducing light impacts to turtles by removing light in the direction of the beach and using low-level light in the short wavelength range (yellow and red). Many of these recommendations were codified in coastal county light ordinances, including Brevard and Volusia counties, to protect sea turtles. At CANA, light pollution may only occur if the nesting and hatching season overlap with preparation for a launch and/or return of a space vehicle at NASA; this is likely a very limited problem. Few instances of light disorientation occur at CANA, as beaches are unlit and closed to the public at night.

Tire tracks or vehicle ruts left behind from motorized vehicles can cause harm or lead to death for young sea turtles emerging from nests, leaving them exposed to fatigue, desiccation, and predators (EAI, 2008). Hatchlings trapped in tire tracks may move parallel to shore instead of perpendicular and toward the ocean. Off-road vehicle use is limited to turtle nest monitoring and resource assessment and is therefore not considered a major threat.

The integrity of the dune structure can be compromised and lead to dune blow out if the dune vegetation is repeatedly trampled and the sandy surface is exposed to the natural elements. The numerous parking lots with boardwalks and crossovers concentrate visitor access to defined points. The parking areas, boardwalks, and dune crossovers placed along the beach minimize overcrowding and foot traffic to beach access areas. In the middle 16 km of the island, beaches are only accessible by horseback or foot. Currently the impact of foot traffic on dunes is not considered excessive.

The narrow sections of the barrier island and the single dune ridge increase the susceptibility of the shoreline to erosion from natural processes such as northeasters and hurricanes. Sea level rise is also a potential threat to the barrier island. Since there is little development within the park boundaries, natural shore line retreat can occur without major concern for loss of property. North of the park, in the cities of Bethune Beach and New Smyrna Beach, rock revetments and seawalls were constructed to protect development. North of New Smyrna Beach is Ponce de Leon Inlet, a federally maintained inlet stabilized by rock jetties. These structures, along with occasional dredging of the inlet, may impact the regional sand budget and sand bypassing around Ponce Inlet and may limit the littoral sand supply to the CANA barrier island system.

Beach nourishment and shore protection structures have not been implemented within the park to a great extent. CANA is not in the state of Florida beach management program, and thus, it is unlikely either action will come to pass. Offshore sand sources identified in coastal waters of Volusia and Brevard counties are more likely to be used for renourishment in county projects on nearby developed beaches (FDEP, 2007a,b). Mining of these sand sources for use in beach projects outside of the park may have implications to the natural sediment transport processes that could affect erosion and/or accretion of sediments within CANA. Since the dune serves as the backbone of the barrier island and helps to stabilize the beach, CANA is restoring eroded dune areas with sand fencing and native vegetation.

Roots of sea oats, railroad vine, and other dune plants sometimes invade the nest cavity of sea turtles and penetrate incubating eggs (Witherington, 1986). Invasion of the nest cavity by plant roots occurs primarily in nests laid high on the beach at, or landward, of the toe of the dune.

Shellfish and Crabs
Several common species occupy the area between the dune and/or the swash zone, such as the mole crab, ghost crab, and the coquina clam. Mole crabs and the coquina clam are filter feeders that burrow in the sediment of the swash zone. They are a food source for shore birds, fish, and crabs. Mole crab activities, different among males, females, and young, may be affected by hurricanes or events that upset the rhythm, timing of activity, and tide amplitude (Diaz, 1980; Forward et al., 2005). Ghost crabs live in burrows above the high tide line during the day and come out to feed in the swash zone at night. Ghost crabs feed on mole crabs, insects, vegetation, and coquina clams and scavenge organic debris, thus contributing to cycling nutrients within the beach ecosystem (Williams, 1984). The flexible feeding pattern of ghost crabs, their ability to starve for long periods of time, and their position as a top carnivore of filter feeders in a narrow niche may make them a good indicator of a healthy habitat (SCDNR, no date; Wolcott 1978). Ghost crabs and coquina clams are considered abundant and may serve as indicators of beach health (SCDNR, no date; Wolcott 1978). Cobb (2007) summarized data on ghost crab burrow size and density, along with the size of mole crab and coquina clam and their population densities, to observe the before and after effects of beach nourishment on Florida's west coast from 2005 to 2007. As part of the FWC-FWRI research, they also collected and analyzed sediment samples for grain size and organic content (Cobb, 2007). Although tidal range and sediment characteristics differ on Florida's east and west coasts, the study provides information on the relationship of sediment grain size and organic content, as well as the response of the ghost crab, mole crab, and coquina clam to a beach renourishment project.

Harmful threats to filter feeders, coquina clams, and mole crabs may be affected by harmful algal blooms (native and non-native), beach nourishment projects or storm events that cause erosion or accretion, and introduction of non-native species that compete for the same ecological niche. The introduction of non-native marine life is known to have been transported in ship ballasts (FWC-FWRI, 2011).

The long-term effects of these threats are unknown. Naturally occurring events, such as storms or hurricanes that physically alter the beach may have a temporary impact on organisms that have adapted to natural cycles. Climate change and the anticipated corresponding sea level rise could shift the entire coastline and the inhabitants west.

Barrier Island Vegetation: Beach Dune Swale and Ridge System
On the east coast of Central Florida, coastal-strand is the natural plant association of the beach dune, swale, and ridge system; it is composed of grasses, herbs, woody shrubs, and scrub oaks. Soil conditions are poor: plants are normally <5 ft (1.5 m) tall and are salt pruned to nearly a 45° angle by wind-borne salt spray. The common grasses are sea oats (*Uniola paniculata*), beach grass (*Panicum amarum*), salt meadow cordgrass (*Spartina patens*), and saltgrass (*Distichlis spicata*). Other non-woody plants found on the dune are beach tea (*Croton punctatus*), prickly pear cactus (*Opuntia humifusa*), and coastal ragweed (*Ambrosia hispida*). Vines in the dune and ridge system that sometimes reach the toe of the dune are railroad vine (*Ipomoea pes-caprae*), and beach morning glory (*Ipomaea stolonifera*). Woody shrubs and understory trees found on the

dune are saw palmetto (*Serenoa repens*), tough bully (*Sideroxylon tenax*), wax myrtle (*Myrica cerifera*), and subtropical plants such as sea grape (*Coccoloba uvifera*) and snowberry (*Chiococca alba*).

Animals found in the beach dune swale and ridges system are gopher tortoise (*Gopherus polyphemus*), southeastern beach mouse (*Peromyscus polionotus niveiventris*), six-lined racer (*Cnemidophorus sexlineatus*), southern hognose (*Heterodon* sp.), coachwhip (*Masticophis flagellum*), and eastern diamond rattlesnake (*Crotalus adamanteus*). Byrne et al. (2010) recorded 12 reptiles and amphibians at two stations on the barrier island during a study in 2009. The coastal strand plant community, as described above, is habitat for the southeastern beach mouse, which is listed as federally threatened. Beach mice have been found in communities with scrub plants, but they have a preference for palmetto and open sandy areas (Extine, 1980; Extine and Stout, 1987). Historically, beach mice occurred in coastal dunes along 174 mi (280 km) from Ponce Inlet in Volusia County south to Hollywood in Broward County (Stout, 1992). Currently, its range extends from Volusia and Brevard counties, with scattered populations in Indian River and St. Lucie counties (USFWS, 2005). Fairly healthy populations were found in the early 1990s within CANA, MINWR, and Cape Canaveral Air Force Station (CCAFS) (Provancha and Oddy, 1992). A multi-agency survey is being conducted (2010–2011) to determine the presence/absence of the beach mouse throughout CANA, MINWR, KSC, and CCAFS.

The primary threat to populations of southeastern beach mice is habitat loss (USFWS, 2005), which may be the loss of dunes and removal and/or burial of the appropriate vegetative cover (Pries et al., 2009). Coastal construction on beaches and nourishment projects that destroy or fragment habitat occupied by or within the range of beach mice have created isolated populations subject to local extinction. Secondary threats are predation by domesticated cats and dogs, natural predators, and competition with house mice. The cotton mouse distribution overlaps with the southeastern beach mice, and the two may compete for limited resources. Within CANA and the adjacent federally owned lands, the potential for habitat loss and fragmentation from development and urbanization is relatively low. Maintaining healthy dunes, dune vegetation, and open sandy spaces would benefit beach mice populations within the park. Threats to beach and dune habitat are shown in Figure 69.

Shorebirds

Several species of pelagic, migrant, and coastal birds use the inner shelf of east Florida. Bird species observed along the coastal regions of east Florida can be divided into six general guilds (shorebirds, waterfowl, wading birds, seabirds, raptors, and passerines) based on habitat use and the relative amount of time spent in the open oceanic waters of the Atlantic. Regulatory protection of birds is covered under provisions of the USFWS Endangered Species Act, the Migratory Bird Treaty Act, and the Florida Endangered and Threatened Species Act. Some local counties or towns also have ordinances protecting seabirds. Threats to shorebirds are discussed below.

Migratory birds and the occasional pelagic birds are more likely to be observed in fall and winter. Since the 1950s, migratory and seasonal birds have been documented at MINWR during the annual Audubon Christmas Counts organized locally by the Space Coast Audubon Society (SCAS) (SCAS, 2010a). The roseate tern, a Florida threatened species observed in MINWR, is known to nest in the lower Florida Keys, but travels during migration to all parts of the state

Figure 69. Potential threats that can directly or indirectly affect the quantity and quality of beach and dune habitats in Canaveral National Seashore (CANA). Threats in blue are unlikely to occur in CANA (Photo: G. Zarillo, October 2010).

(FWC, 2003; MINWR, 2008). White pelicans (*Pelecanus erythrorhynchos*), brown pelicans (*Pelecanus occidentalis*), osprey (*Pandion haliaetus*), sanderlings (*Calidris alba*), willets (*Tringa semipalmata*), red knots (*Calidris canutus*), ruddy turnstones (*Arenaria interpres*), black-bellied plovers (*Pluvialis squatarola*), piping plovers (rare) (*Charadrius melodus*), laughing gulls (*Leucophaeus atricilla*), ringbilled gulls (*Larus delawarensis*), herring gulls (*Larus smithsonianus*), great black-backed gulls (*Larus marinus*), Caspian terns (*Hydroprogne caspia*), royal terns (*Thalasseus maximus*), Sandwich terns (rare) (*Thalasseus sandvicensis*), common terns (rare) (*Sterna hirundo*), Forster's terns (*Sterna forsteri*), and least terns (*Sternula antillarum*) have been observed in the coastal areas of CANA-MINWR (SCAS, 2010b; MINWR, 2008; PIA, 2008). In the fall, migrating birds of prey, or raptors, including merlins (*Falco columbarius*) and peregrine falcons (*Falco peregrinus*), are seen regularly and may winter at the seashore and the MINWR (SCA, 2010b). Data collected and discussed on birds also relied on information available from Cruickshank (1980), Lee and Cardiff (1993), USFWS (1995), and FWC (2003).

Pelagic seabirds represent a wide range of species that spend much of their time in or over water and can stay far from land for long periods of time. They are rarely seen on the east coast of Florida. Most of these birds have adaptive salt glands that allow them to regulate the salt content in their blood (Ehrlich et al., 1988). Some such as albatrosses (Diomedeidae), frigate birds (Fregatidae), shearwaters (Procellariidae), boobies and gannets (Sulidae), and petrels (Procellariiformes) spend the majority of their life cycle offshore (Ehrlich et al. 1988; PIA, 2008). Information on the population status and movements of pelagic birds is limited, largely due to vast geographical areas, differences among species-specific migration, difficulty in studying bird movement during adverse weather conditions, and a lack of standard methodology (Tasker et al., 1984; Michel and Burkhard, 2007).

Pelicans, gulls, terns, and cormorants (Phalacrocoracidae) are neritic, meaning that they are more common in the coastal waters; they use land for feeding or resting at certain times, although some can be seen with regularity well offshore (Erhlich et al., 1988; Browne et. al., 2004). The east coast of Florida populations of brown pelican are listed as a species of special concern by the state of Florida (FWC, 2004), but they are excluded from the Migratory Bird Treaty Act list.

Mosquito Lagoon
Benthic Macroinvertebrates of the Indian River Lagoon
Results of water quality, sediment chemistry, SAV, and benthic macroinvertebrate samples collected and analyzed in connection with Florida's Inshore Marine Monitoring and Assessment Program (IMAP) conducted from 2000−2004 provide the best information on inshore benthic macroinvertebrates (McRae, 2002; McRae et al., 2003; McRae et al., 2005). IMAP sites sampled in or near Mosquito Lagoon were the Halifax/Mosquito Lagoon (McRae, 2002) and the north IRL (McRae et al., 2003). Results of macroinvertebrate samples collected for IMAP in the third year were not reported (McRae et al., 2005).

In 2002, samples collected from stations in the northern IRL (IRN) varied in the large numbers of particular taxa. For example, one site—IRN200217—contained 1,443 individuals of the tanaidacean *Halmyrapseudes* sp., while site IRN200203 contained large numbers of the ostracod *Parasterope* pollex and the gastropod *Caecum pulchellum* (McRae et al., 2003). In the IRN and statewide, tubificid oligochaetes were the most frequently caught taxa in grab samples collected in 2002. Other taxa commonly found statewide were *Mediomastus* sp., rhynchocoelaean worms, the sabellid polychaetes, *Fabricinuda trilobata*, brittlestars (Ophiuroidea), and the gastropod, *Acteocina canaliculata* (McRae et al., 2003).

Eight taxa (or taxa groups) of macroinvertebrates found in all sites sampled during 2004, including IRL, were *Exogone rolani*, Rhynchocoela, Tubificidae, Cirratulidae, *Mediomastus* sp., Bivalvia, *Podarkeopsis levifuscina*, and *Scoloplos rubrar* (McRae et al., 2005). The most frequently sampled macroinvertebrates in the IRL site according to McRae et al. (2005) were members of the Tubificidae, *Mediomastus* sp., and the gastropods, *Acteocina canaliculata* and *Mitrella lunata*.

In an earlier study by McRae et al. (1998), samples taken from Nassau County to the St. Lucie River were analyzed for water quality, sediment characteristics, and benthic macroinvertebrates. He found that species diversity increased from north to south. Polychaetes were found at all sample sites. The north IRL/Banana River and Mosquito Lagoon shared representatives from gastropods, amphipods, and other unidentified groups (McRae et al., 1998).

Saltwater Wetlands
Saltwater wetlands are protected by state and federal law; they provide shelter for economically and ecologically important species and help stabilize shorelines. Mangroves and salt marshes found in CANA are adapted to the transition zone between subtropical and temperate climates. Mangroves and salt marshes provide important habitat for fish, manatees, amphibians, reptiles, and invertebrates. Mangrove trees are used by birds for nesting, resting, and/or foraging. Primary production from mangroves and salt marshes contribute large amounts of carbon that may be exported from the wetlands to the adjacent waters, supporting extensive detrital pathways that contribute to large amounts of secondary production (Odum et al., 1982).

Mangroves

Mangroves fringe the Mosquito Lagoon, thrive in the interior, and are found on the edges of dikes or ridges within lagoon waters (Figure 70).Three species of mangrove trees—red mangrove (*Rhizophora mangle*), black mangrove (*Avicennia germinans*), and white mangrove (*Laguncularia racemosa*)—live in the salt marsh or tidal swamp. Buttonwood, (*Conocarpus erectus*), sometimes called the fourth mangrove, occurs on higher ground adjacent to the back barrier or on the western edge of the lagoon. Mangroves possess adaptations that allow them to tolerate saline waters and loose, muddy soils with low oxygen content (Odum et al., 1982).

Mangroves tend to dominate the interior wetlands in the southern portion of the IRL, while wetlands in the north, including Mosquito Lagoon, are dominated by herbaceous salt marsh plants and freeze-stunted mangroves (Schmalzer, 1995). Mangroves are tropical species that do not tolerate prolonged freezing temperatures and will periodically die back when freezes occur in Florida (Provancha et al., 1986; Stevens et al., 2006). Black mangroves are more tolerant to low temperatures and may persist when red and white mangroves perish (Markley et al., 1982; McMillan and Sherrod, 1986). Following years of mild winters, the height, distribution, and abundance of mangroves may increase. Long-term predictions of higher global temperatures may accelerate the pattern of mangrove mild winter growth and lead to increased size and distribution of mangroves in the lagoon. Once established, mangroves may out-compete salt marsh plants due to shading effects, as salt marsh grasses do not grow beneath the mangrove canopy (Kangas and Lugo, 1990). Periodic freezes prevent mangroves from taking over saltwater wetlands in Mosquito Lagoon (Provancha et al., 1986).

Figure 70. Canaveral National Seashore (CANA) mangrove coverage in north Mosquito Lagoon (left) is extensive in the interior, on the fringe of the back barrier, and on the lagoon's western edge. Salt marshes in central Mosquito Lagoon (right) lie between ancient Qh beach ridges (Figure 28) and on the back barrier island. Figure 71 shows salt marshes in the south section of the lagoon. CANA boundary is outlined in red.

Climate change experts predict more storm events and the possibility of water level changes. Since mangroves are susceptible to damage from strong winds associated with hurricanes, they could suffer greater loss of limbs and productivity from repeated storms (Milbrandt et al., 2006).

In the lagoon, estimated mangrove landscape coverage dropped from 1,657 ac (671 ha) in 1943 to a low of 655 ac (265 ha) in 2003. The landscape area compatible with the growth of mangroves according to the soil survey data is 3,842 ac (1,555 ha) (Table 23).

Salt Marshes

Salt marshes are comprised of herbaceous, salt tolerant plants capable of living in low oxygen muddy substrates. In Mosquito Lagoon salt marsh communities are categorized by the vegetation association of sand cordgrass (*Spartina bakerii*), black needle rush (*Juncus romarianus*), glasswort (*Salicornia* spp.), saltwort (*Batis maritima*), salt grass (*Distichlis spicata*), sea oxeye daisy (*Borrichia frutescens*), and seashore paspalum (*Paspalum vaginatum*) (Schmalzer, 1995). It is estimated that in 2003 there were 6,998 ac (2,832 ha) of salt marsh in the lagoon (Table 23). Figure 71 shows the distribution of salt marsh in the south section of the lagoon.

Table 23. Land cover classes and size for saltwater wetlands. Acres are estimated for all years using land-use (LU) codes of Duncan et al. (2004) and NPS thematic layers, land use 2003, and soils. See Appendix for a description of land cover classes.

LU Codes	Land Cover Class*	SIZE (acres)			Soils 2003**
		1943*	1990*	2003**	
6120	Mangrove	1,657	1,756	655	3,842
6420	Salt marsh	6,600	4,764	6,998	4,462
6460	Disturbed Estuarine Wetlands	20	219	297	
	Total	8,277	6,739	7,950	8,304

*Land cover classes combined by Duncan et al. (2004).
**Land cover 2003 and soils from National Park Service.

Nearly all of the salt water wetlands have been affected by rotary ditching and construction of impoundments for mosquito control (Montague and Zale, 1989; Rey and Kain 1990; Carlson et al., 1999). When marshes are impounded, a perimeter ditch is dug along the margin of the marsh and the spoil is used to create an earthen dike or berm. Water is then pumped into the impoundment either from the lagoon or from artesian wells to maintain water levels that will prevent mosquitoes from laying eggs on the sediment surface. Impounding greatly alters the topography and physical characteristics of the normal hydroperiods and salinity regimes from hypersaline to freshwater depending on the source of water used to flood the impoundment and rainfall (Provost, 1959).

Plant composition may have been altered by impounding wetlands, as some suggest red mangroves tend to dominate impoundments because they can tolerate higher water levels than black or white mangroves (Schmalzer, 1995; Middleton et al., 2008). Herbaceous marsh plants decline in salt marshes because they are not capable of withstanding constant inundation (Gilmore et al., 1982; Harrington and Harrington, 1982; Rey et al., 1990; Schmalzer, 1995).

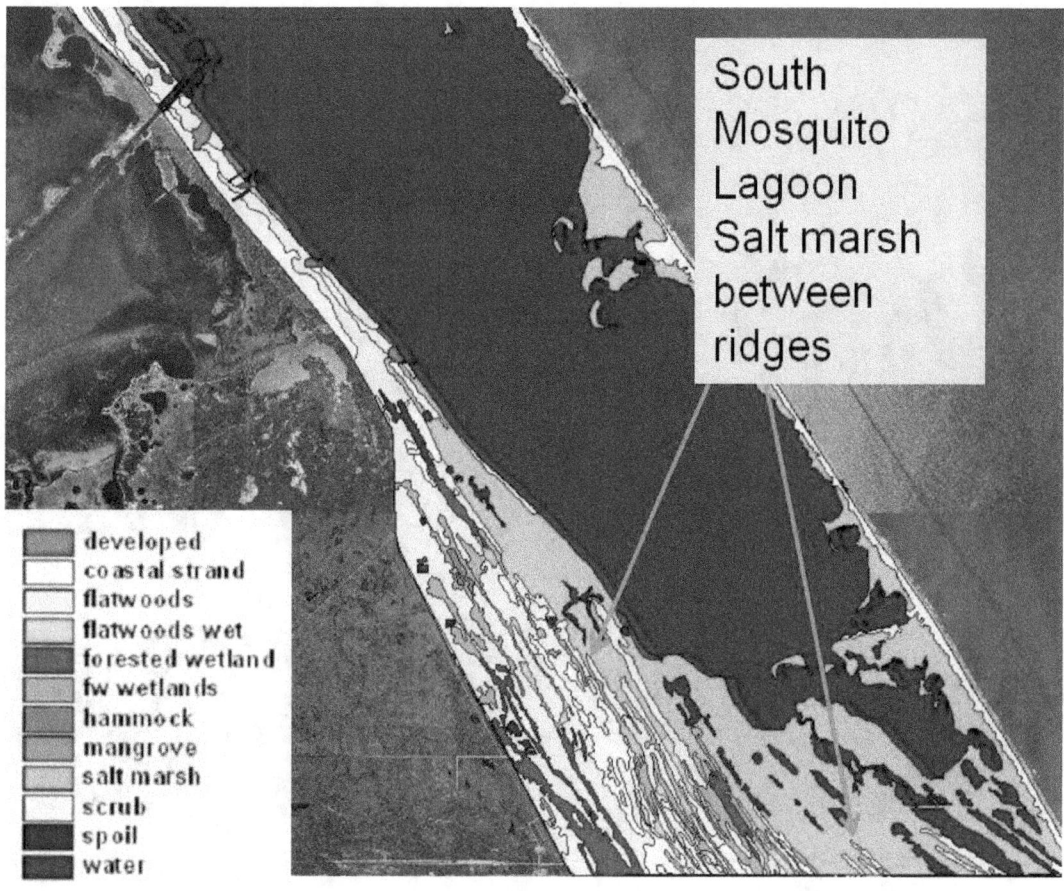

Figure 71. Salt marsh coverage of Canaveral National Seashore (CANA) between Qh ridges as depicted in Figure 28. See Figure 70 for salt marshes in central Mosquito Lagoon and on back barrier. CANA boundary is outlined in red.

The ecological consequences of preventing access to the marsh by transient species that rely on marsh habitat during the early stages of their life history have been severe (Gilmore et al., 1982; Harrington and Harrington, 1982). Declines in the production of important fishery species have led fishery experts to test Rotational Impoundment Management (RIM). In the RIM method, impoundments are reconnected to adjacent waters with culverts and water retention is regulated to coincide with peak mosquito breeding times; fish and invertebrates exchange freely during the rest of the year (Brockmeyer et al., 1997). In some places, earthen dikes are removed and shorelines regraded to allow natural inundation of marsh surfaces (Brockmeyer et al., 1997; Scott Taylor, personal communication 2010). In RIM marshes, the problem of invasion by the exotic Brazilian pepper can be severe and may be due to lower soil salinity (Middleton et al., 2008).

The threats to salt water wetland composition and distribution are changes in salinity, water level, wind damage from storms, climate change, and exotic pest plants. Examples of the different salt water wetland associations are illustrated in Figure 72.

Figure 72. Saltwater wetland plant composition in Canaveral National Seashore. Sand cordgrass (*Spartina bakerii*) is seen in the foreground of images A and C. Glasswort (*Salicornia* spp.) and saltwort (*Batis maritima*) are in center of image D. Live mangroves and dead branches from earlier freezes are seen in the bottom of D. Coverage locations are shown in Figures 70 and 71 (Photos: A and C taken by A. Cox, April 2010 photos B and D taken by G. Zarillo, October 2010).

Submerged Aquatic Vegetation

Submerged Aquatic Vegetation (SAV) is a generic term for plants that live below the waterline. The SAV section includes discussion of seagrasses, macroalgae, and drift algae. Factors considered to influence SAV growth and distribution are water depth, water clarity, the availability of light, the type of substrate, nutrient levels, salinity, temperature, and anthropogenic influences. Aquatic vegetation produces food and provides cover for many aquatic organisms, improves water clarity and quality, and helps stabilize sediments (FWC-FWRI, 2003). Threats to SAV species are invasive species, pollution, weather events, or land alterations that substantially alter salinity, temperature, turbidity, and substrate beyond desirable tolerances.

Programs like the Indian River Lagoon National Estuary (IRLNEP) and the Surface Water Improvement and Management (SWIM) work to maintain and enhance SAV through the Submerged Aquatic Vegetative Initiative (SAVI) established in 1992 (Morris and Tomasko, 1993; SWIM, 2002). One goal set by SWIM of the SAVI was, "to maintain or improve water clarity to a point that submerged aquatic vegetation could increase bottom coverage throughout the Lagoon to a depth of two meters" (SWIM, 2002).

Seagrass Ecology

Four of seven seagrasses documented in the IRL system—shoal grass (*Halodule wrightii*), manatee grass (*Syringodium filiforme*), widgeon grass (*Ruppia maritima*), star grass (*Halophila englemanni*) —and macroalgae (*Caulerpa prolifera*)—are found in Mosquito Lagoon (Provancha et al., 1992; Virnstein, 1999). Seagrasses provide food and cover for many aquatic organisms, improve water clarity, water quality, and stabilize sediments (Dawes, 1981; Zieman, 1982; Virnstein, 1999). Mosquito Lagoon is used as a baseline of SAV coverage due to the lagoon's water quality relative to other subbasins of the IRL system. The presence of KSC, the lack of development, and limited boat access in the southern Mosquito Lagoon provide a refuge for seagrasses and their associated fauna (Provancha and Scheidt, 2000).

Physical dynamics unique to the lagoon that control circulation and water quality may influence SAV species composition and distribution. Mosquito Lagoon is segmented; segments have differential residence times of 2–75 days (Zarillo et al., 2010). In some segments, circulation is wind-driven, and in others, tidal flow through Ponce de Leon Inlet is important. The average depth of 1.5 m is within the ideal depth range for seagrass growth. The amount of groundwater influence is estimated by numerical models but has not been directly measured. It is assumed that the primary freshwater source is rain. Salinity in the lagoon is higher than other segments of the IRL system and may reach >35 ppt (hypersaline) in dry months. There are natural fluctuations of salinity, temperature, and nutrients operate in differential residence times of 2–75 days.

Shoal Grass

Shoal grass is the most widespread and abundant seagrass in the IRL (Littler et al., 2008). It reproduces asexually by an extensive rhizome system (IRLNEP, 1994). Often the first seagrass to colonize disturbed areas and considered a pioneer species, shoal grass has been a dominant seagrass along transects surveyed within the Mosquito Lagoon, ranging from 25–68% coverage (Provancha et al., 1992). From 1983–1996, there were three distinct periods of decrease in coverage; they were not considered a significant trend (Provancha and Scheidt, 2000). During 1995–1996, decreases were associated with increases in widgeon grass and a decrease in salinity.

Surveys conducted by Mondoncea (1983) showed shoal grass areas that dominated depths of up to 0.8 m were displaced by manatee grass. In the mid IRL, shoal grass was found to dominate in water depths <1.3 ft (<0.4 m) before being outcompeted by manatee grass at 1.6 ft (0.5 m) (Virnstein and Carbonara, 1985). A transitional pattern of occupation between shoal grass and manatee grass has also been documented in the southern IRL, with a monoculture of shoal grass in the shallowest waters and mixed beds of both species occurring in water depths up to 5.7–9.0 ft (1.75–2.75 m) (Kenworthy and Fronseca, 1996). The occurrence of both species in the southern IRL suggests they require similar minimum light levels.

Manatee Grass

The Mosquito Lagoon is the northernmost range of manatee grass (IRLNEP, 1994) with a depth range of 1.6–4.9 ft (0.5–1.5 m). Manatee grass (synonym *Cymodocea filiformis*) leaves can reach 17.7 in (45 cm) in length; it is the only seagrass with cylindrical leaves in the lagoon (IRLNEP, 1994; Littler et al., 2008). Asexual and sexual reproduction both occur within the lagoon (IRLNEP, 1994). In the southern IRL, seasonal leaf growth rates are 0.8 in/day (0.2 cm/day) November through December and 0.5 in/day (1.2 cm/day) in July (Fry and Virnstein, 1988). In the northern IRL, maximum biomass of manatee grass occurred in September followed by a rapid decline from October to February (Gilberg and Clark, 1981). In the Gilberg and Clark (1981), study regrowth began in March and increased in April and May, corresponding with an increase in water temperature. Short et al. (1993) found that light, not temperature, was the major controlling factor for seasonal variations in biomass of manatee grass in the southern IRL, and nitrogen was the controlling factor during peak growth periods.

Widgeon Grass
Widgeon grass is the only member of the family Ruppiaceae in Florida. It is similar in appearance to shoal grass, but generally has narrower leaves that taper at the ends and branched stems (IRLNEP, 1994). Widgeon grass readily reproduces sexually, and the rhizome system is not as well developed as in shoal grass. Widgeon grass is more tolerant of lower salinity, is the most temperate seagrass species in the IRL, and occurs in the northeastern United States (IRLNEP, 1994; Walters et al., 2001).

Star Grass
Star grass is a small, delicate perennial species with erect stems rarely longer than 4.7 in (12 cm). It is found in the Mosquito Lagoon, but the extent is unknown (IRLNEP, 1994). Star grass was not reported in the Mosquito Lagoon by Provancha et al. (1992) or Provancha and Scheidt (2000). Star grass is known to occur in depths of 1.0–6.2 ft (0.3–1.9 m) in the IRL; however, it has been reported in depths of 46 ft (14 m) (Woodward-Clyde Consultants, 1994f).

Seagrass Trends
The IRLNEP, SJRWMD, FWRI, NPS, USFWS, MINWR, and NASA have all had an interest in data collection and assessment of SAV in the IRL system (FWC-FWRI, 2003). Historical assessments of seagrass coverage of the IRL system have been completed for years 1943, 1986, 1989, 1992, 1994, 1996, 1999, 2001, 2003, 2005, 2006, 2007, and 2009, and GIS files are available for download from the SJRWMD (ftp://www.sjrwmd.com/disk3/wetlands/ IRL_Seagrass). A summary of SAV data collected and analyzed for Mosquito Lagoon for the 1970s, 1986, and 1992 is provided in Table 24. This table shows a decrease between 1970 and 1986 and an increase in overall SAV coverage by 1992 (Woodward-Clyde Consultants, 1994f).

Table 24. Submerged aquatic vegetation coverage for Mosquito Lagoon for 1970–1974, 1986, and 1992. Total bottom area is 33,131.3 acres (13,410 ha) (Woodward-Clyde Consultants, 1994f).

Year	Total (Acres)
1970*	13,582.82
1986	12,413.92
1992	16,699.41

*1970–1974

Coverage collected in 1986 by Provancha et al. (1992) classifies 61% of the SAV as very dense or within 70%–100% coverage in the lagoon. Fletcher and Fletcher (1995) estimated the available bottom area of the lagoon for seagrass coverage to be 28,321 ac (11,460 ha), and SAV coverage fluctuated from 13,583 ac (5,497 ha) in 1970–1976 to 12,414 ac (5,024 ha) in 1984–

1986 and increased to 16,700 ac (6,758 ha) in 1992. They estimated that seagrass abundance in the IRL system decreased by 11% between 1970 and 1992. The maximum water depth limits of seagrass did not vary more than 15% in the Mosquito Lagoon but decreased as much as 76% in the northern IRL (Fletcher and Fletcher, 1995).

The 2003 statewide seagrass resource management plan created five regional divisions similar to the geographical jurisdictions of the water management districts (FWC-FWRI, 2003). The plan's purpose is to organize and coordinate efforts among 18 federal agencies, state offices, and local governments to assess and report the condition of seagrass resources. The Mosquito Lagoon is within Region 4—the Atlantic Peninsula—and includes the coastal waters of Volusia, Brevard, Indian River, St. Lucie, Martin, and Palm Beach counties and contains about 3%, or 74,456 ac (30,130 ha), of the state's total seagrasses (FWC-FWRI, 2003).

In the FWC-FWRI plan (2003), the status of seagrass information by region is summarized. The highlights of the summary applicable to Mosquito Lagoon are based on changes in coverage between 1943 and 1999 from the IRL SWIM Plan (2002, located at www.sfwmd.gov) and are as follows:

> Lagoon areas containing the largest seagrass coverages are around N. Merritt Island in the federally protected bottomlands of NASA/Kennedy Space Center (North IRL and northern Banana River) and the Canaveral National Seashore (southern Mosquito Lagoon). These areas experienced little change between 1943 and 1999.
>
> Within the SJRWMD portion of the IRL (Mosquito Lagoon, Banana River, North and Central IRL), the current (1999) 61,884 ac [25,040 ha] of seagrass is 63% of the potential 98,274 ac [39,770 ha[of coverage (based on 1.7 m [5.6 ft] depth). The 1943 seagrass coverage was 63,238 ac [25,590 ha]; 64% of the potential acreage.

A more recent study examining seagrass data in the IRL from 1943 to the 1990s calculated a 13% loss in seagrass coverage, with some areas showing a 90% loss (Virnstein et al., 2007). In the Virnstein et al. (2007) study, two out of three locations within the Mosquito Lagoon showed stable seagrass coverage from data spanning 1943−2005. One location in the northern section of Mosquito Lagoon had dramatically lower seagrass coverage from 1992−2005 as compared to coverage of 1943. In Figure 73, the latest percent coverage of seagrass for 2009 is provided. Threats and stressors of SAV are shown in Figure 74.

Macroalgae
Macroalgae occur throughout the IRL and within Mosquito Lagoon, but were not listed in a long-term study of SAV coverage around KSC (Provancha and Scheidt, 2000). The fronds of macroalgae are thin, undivided, and flat, extending 2.4−5.9 in (6−15 cm) long, and typically grow in sand or fine sediments along with seagrasses in depths of up to 49 ft (15 m) (Littler et al., 2008). Green algae (Chlorophyta) bear some resemblance to seagrass because they have a complex morphology consisting of fronds, which resemble seagrass blades, and stolons, which resemble seagrass rhizomes. However, macroalgae lack the conductive tissue of seagrasses, and they also lack the ability to produce "true seeds." Instead, they reproduce through fragmentation or by producing spores like other algae (Littler et al., 1989). Similarities in the morphology of seagrass and macroalgae suggest that they provide the same ecosystem functions as seagrass (i.e., sediment stabilization and nutrient uptake), but their relationship with organisms may not be functionally equivalent (White and Snodgrass, 1988; Kehl, 1990; Raves, 2001).

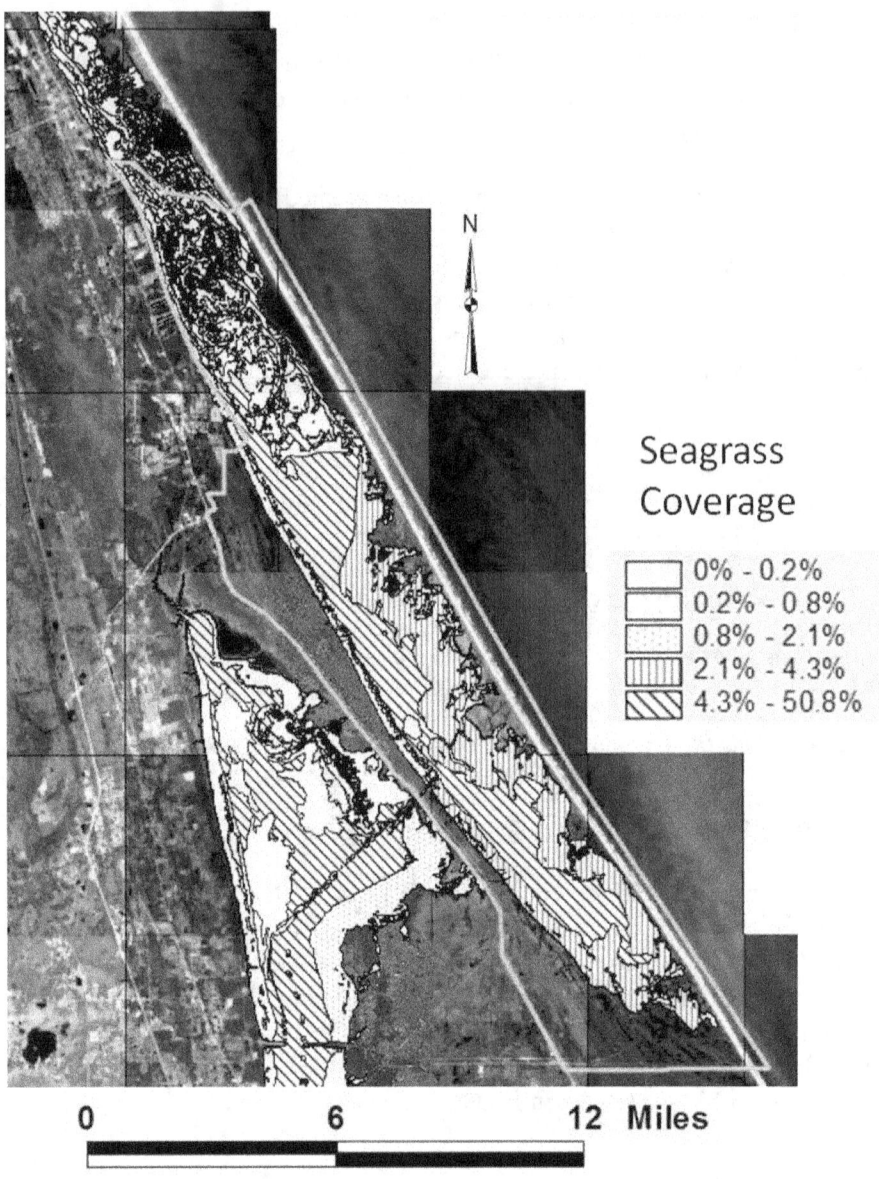

Figure 73. Percent coverage of seagrass in Canaveral National Seashore in 2009 (SJRWMD).

Drift Algae

Drift algae are a habitat comparable to seagrasses for some marine organisms within the IRL (Virnstein and Howard, 1987). A two-year survey of drift macrophytes in the Mosquito Lagoon identified 26 species (Abgrall and Walters, 2003). Red algae *Gracilaria* spp. accounted for 51.7%, followed by fragments of the seagrass *H. wrightii* (23.7%), *Cladophora* sp. (12.5%), *Dasya baillouviana* (7.7%), *Enteromorpha* spp. (1.5%), *Spyridia filamentosa* (1.4%), and 1.5% consisted of *Acanthophora spicifera, Hypnea spinella, Agardhiella subulata,* and *Chondria littoralis*. No correlations of drift algae abundance with wind speed, flow, or temporal patterns were found by Abgrall and Walters (2003).

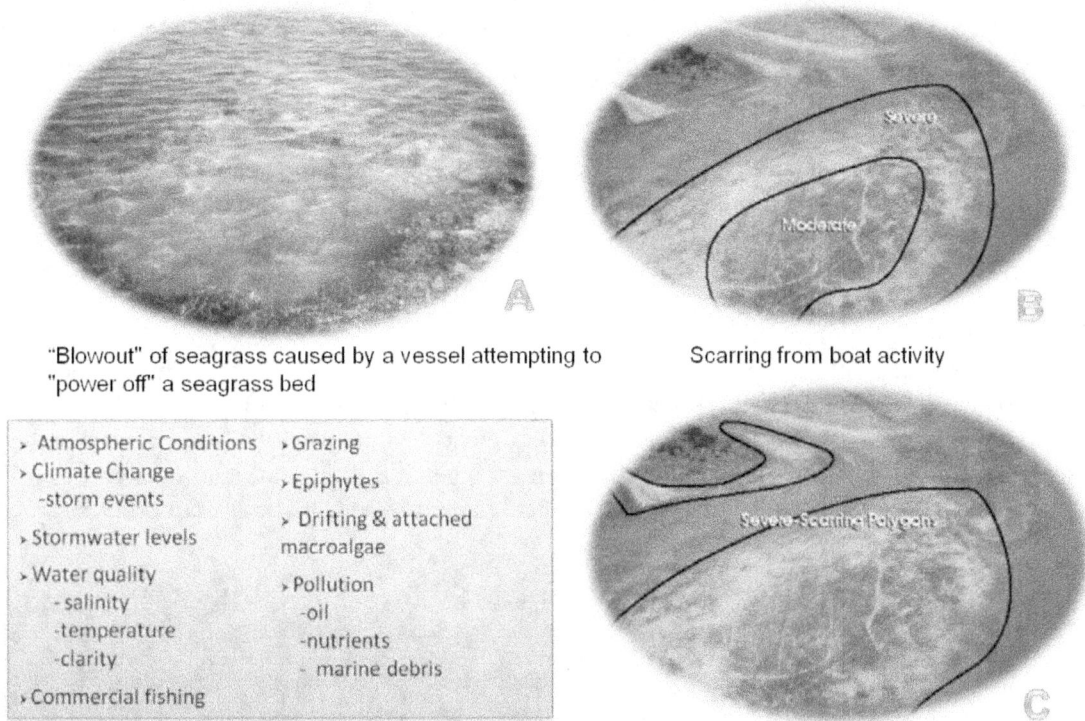

Figure 74. Threats and stressors to seagrasses. Blowout and scaring (seen in A, B, and C) fragment habitat and often kill submerged vegetation (Photos: A from FDEP; B and C from Sargent et al., 1995).

Some researchers believe drift algae coverage can be quite extensive throughout the IRL, but seasonal and spatial trends vary by location (Virnstein and Carbonara, 1985; Reigl et al., 2005). A large-scale acoustic survey conducted April–May 2008 by Nova Southeastern University Oceanographic Center (NSUOC) quantified the abundance and distribution of seasonal drift macroalgae in the IRL from the Sebastian Inlet to the Titusville area, including Banana River northward to the federal Manatee Zone near Cape Canaveral (2009). The NSUOC (2009) survey found drift macroalgae biomass per unit area (1,361 lb/mi^2, 238.3 kg/km^2) was roughly 34% less than reported for the 2005 survey. The mean percent cover of drift macroalgae was significantly greater within the navigation channels (18.3%) than outside (12.2%) and significantly greater in the Indian River (12.9%) than (9.3%) in the Banana River (NSUOC, 2009). The overall predictive accuracy of total SAV was 78.9% (n=246) with SAV limited to ~4 in (~10 cm). The study area did not include Mosquito Lagoon, yet a comparison of results from the Banana River and the southern parts of the IRL is useful since the north segment of IRL is considered to be more similar to Mosquito Lagoon than the other segments of the IRL. A study using the same methodology in CANA may be beneficial to assess the coverage of drift algae and SAV within the size constraints of ~4 in (~10 cm).

Animals of Mosquito Lagoon
All marine mammals are protected under the Marine Mammal Protection Act of 1972 and are under the jurisdiction of NMFS. There are a number of species also protected under the

Endangered Species Act. Federally protected species commonly found on Florida's northeast coast are the northern right whale and the Florida manatee. They are also listed as endangered by the state of Florida (FWC 2009). In addition, the Florida manatee is protected by the Manatee Sanctuary Act of 1978 and also may be protected by local regulations under county manatee management plans. Marine mammals present in the lagoon are Atlantic bottlenose dolphins (*Tursiops truncatus*) and Florida manatee. Each is threatened in varying degrees by boat-related injury or death, marine debris, disease, water quality, and (manatees only) cold temperature. Harmful algal bloom (HAB) events, which are more frequent on the west coast of Florida, can lead to sickness and/or death. Threats and stressors to marine mammals in the lagoon are shown in Figure 75.

Atlantic Bottlenose Dolphin

Atlantic bottlenose dolphins are seen throughout the IRL system and are long-term residents (Provancha et al., 1982; Odell and Asper, 1990; Fick, 1995) that exhibit a high degree of site fidelity (Mazzoil et al., 2008; Murdoch et al., 2008). Nearly 2,000 dolphins were sighted in the Mosquito Lagoon from 2002–2005, with the highest repeated sighting rate, the strongest site fidelity, and a mean range of 13.7 mi (22 km) (Mazzoil et al., 2008). Estimates of dolphin group

Figure 75. Threats and stressors to marine mammals (Photos: A from NOAA Marine Debris Program; B and C from FWRI).

sizes range from 3–15, with a mean of 1.8 in November in Indian River County portions of the IRL (Booth, 1993) and 2.78 in portions of the IRL in Brevard County (Rudin, 1991; Fick, 1995). The time of day or season does not seem to affect dolphin distribution, but group size has been shown to increase as water depth decreases (Fick, 1995), which is supported in previous findings that dolphins concentrate in areas ≤6.6 ft (≤2 m) (Rudin, 1991; Booth, 1993).

Threats to the Atlantic bottlenose populations are primarily anthropogenic in nature and include pollution, accidental take in fishing gear (e.g., gillnets or shrimp trawls), boating activity, and habitat alteration. Durden et al. (2007) assayed mercury and selenium concentrations of liver and muscle tissues from dolphins stranded in the IRL. While they acknowledged the problems of comparing studies, "due to differences in sample age composition," the measured "mean total mercury concentrations in IRL dolphins tended to be slightly higher than in bottlenose dolphins from the Gulf of Mexico and along the coast of South Carolina."

PCBs are linked to immune weakness and susceptibility to the *Morbillivirus* that was implicated in dolphin die-offs in 1987 and 1988 (Bossart et al., 2010). Another concern is lobomycosis, a chronic fungal disease found on the skin of dolphins and humans. Infection rates of lobomycosis was reported ranging from 16.99% in the southern IRL to <1% in the Mosquito Lagoon (Reif et al., 2006). Most recent estimates by Murdoch et al. (2008) do not find infection rates to be increasing.

Harmful algal blooms have been implicated in dolphin mortality events on the west coast of Florida (FWC-FWRI, 2006). In 2007, an HAB event occurred on the east coast of Florida (FWC-FWRI, 2007). Also, toxins produced by phytoplankton can accumulate in fish consumed by dolphins, causing them to suffer a variety of conditions from high levels of these toxins in their tissues that can eventually lead to death.

Florida Manatee
Although manatees have strayed as far north as Rhode Island and as far west as Texas, there are four regional populations in Florida. The Atlantic region consists of counties along the Atlantic coast from Nassau County south to Miami–Dade County (USFWS, 2002). Manatees and other aquatic herbivores eat seagrass found in shallow waters (>3.3 ft, >1 m) of fresh, estuarine, and salt water systems. The IRL is a very important feeding area (Reynolds and Odell, 1991). Manatees are sensitive to cooler water temperature (≤20°C) and exhibit seasonal variation in their distribution (Shane, 1983; Reynolds and Odell, 1991). In the spring and summer, manatees are found throughout the IRL, although greater abundances tend to occur in the Banana River and in the IRL south of Titusville (Leatherman, 1979; Shane, 1983; Provancha and Provancha, 1988). Often the public mistakenly believes manatees use Mosquito Lagoon as a corridor; however, manatees regularly loiter throughout the warmer months on the east side of Mosquito Lagoon along East Channel, Eldora, and the North District ranger station (John Stiner, personal observation, January 7, 2010). To avoid cold water temperatures during the winter, manatees move to warmer waters such as freshwater springs and discharge sites for power plant cooling canals (Shane, 1983; Reynolds and Odell, 1991).

The highest two-day minimum count of manatees from winter synoptic aerial surveys and ground counts was 3,276 manatees in January 2001; the highest count on the east coast of Florida was 1,756 and the highest on the west coast was 1,520, both in 2001 (UFWS, 2002). In

2002, the total count was 1,796. The FWC stated in a press release that the "low count merely reflects the poor visibility during the count, not a dramatic change in the manatee population." Due to the nearly ideal conditions for the 2001 synoptic survey, the results of that survey are considered to be the best available estimate of the current minimum population size of 3,276 (USFWS, 2002). The USFWS (2002) also found the unreliable methods of counting manatees preclude a true census, as they are surveys of visible manatees.

The number one avoidable threat to manatees is boat collisions (24%) (Reynolds and Odell, 1991; USFWS, 2001) followed by entrapment in water control structures (4%). The large volume of boat traffic traveling through the Intracoastal Waterway contributes to manatee mortality and injury. The Intracoastal Waterway at Haulover Canal is a federal slow speed zone. Brevard County has the highest rate of manatee boat-related mortality, and boater noncompliance of speed zones is greater on weekends in the Banana River region of the IRL (Morris and Nodine, 1995). Boating activity is estimated at greater than 46,000 watercraft visits to the park annually, and a large percentage of boats are targeting seagrass areas where manatees feed (Scheidt and Garreau, 2007). Boater activity is concentrated in certain areas of Mosquito Lagoon (Figure 8).

Waterfowl and Wading Birds
Waterfowl
Estuarine waters and impoundments provide important habitat to both resident and wintering waterfowl. Waterfowl numbers on MINWR vary dramatically during the year, with thousands seen during the winter, but only several hundred resident mottled ducks (*Anas fulvigula*) present in the summer. Wintering waterfowl on MINWR of blue-winged teal (*Anas discors*), American widgeon (*Anas americana*), northern pintail (*Anas acuta*), lesser scaup (*Aythya affinis*), redhead (*Aythya americana*), and mergansers (Anatidae) have varied in number. Recent counts have been generally low, and the northern pintail and the lesser scaup are of particular concern. Pintail population numbers from 1978 to 2003 have steadily declined by 93% and may no longer winter at the refuge. A similar decline has been witnessed of the continental lesser scaup since the mid-1980s. The estuarine areas of Banana River, IRL, and Mosquito Lagoon provide the most valuable wintering habitat for scaup on the Atlantic Flyway, harboring up to 62% of the flyway's scaup and 15% of the continental scaup population (MINWR, 2008).

Wading Birds
Wading birds (e.g., egrets and herons (Ardeidae), and ibises (Threskiornithidae) use a broad range of wetland habitat types for foraging, roosting, and nesting. Habitats frequented by wading birds include natural and manmade features – open estuary, natural freshwater wetlands, impoundments, and roadside ditches. Many wading birds use vegetated dredge spoil islands in the IRL as roosting and nesting sites.

Populations of the federally endangered wood stork (*Mycteria americana*) have declined sharply in Florida, from 60,000 in the 1930s to 5,000 pairs with the complete loss of wood stork nesting on MINWR. Two hundred and fifty wood stork nests recorded in 1986 located in mangroves of Banana River and Moore Creek were lost after a severe winter freeze of 1985–1986, when the storks abandoned the freeze-damaged rookery. No successful nesting has occurred in MINWR since 1986, although approximately 250 wood storks currently use the refuge for feeding and roosting.

Threats to Birds
Threats to shorebirds are the result of entanglement and ingestion of debris, loss and fragmentation of habitat, pollution, and the secondary effects of climate change. Humans may interfere with the nesting and feeding behaviors of birds by approaching and startling them while nesting or attempting to nest. Eggs can be accidently crushed, especially when they are camouflaged to resemble the background on the beach where nests may be a slight depression in the sand and shells. Natural feeding behaviors of birds in the wild can be changed by hand feeding or leaving food scraps for them to consume.

In the State of the Bird Report by the North American Bird Conservation Initiative, U.S. Committee contributors present indicators of vulnerability (low, medium, and high) for what may happen to North American bird species by geographic region and habitat due to climate change (NABI, 2010). Seventy-four of 84 species in coastal habitats (beaches, mudflats, and salt marshes) studied received a vulnerability index of medium to high due to an anticipated increase in loss and/or fragmentation of habitat caused by sea level rise and by warming temperatures that may cause species distribution to shift northward, which may alter the timing of migration (NABI, 2010). Habitat loss and/or fragmentation can disrupt reproduction, feeding, and resting behaviors. The threat of habitat loss from sea level rise and breaching of the barrier island is a problem even in undeveloped beaches like those in CANA (resources would be more susceptible to increased stormwater flows). If global warming creates more storms that bring more rainfall, the influx and frequency of freshwater flow can increase stormwater runoff that can change the salinity of coastal waters and carry harmful pollutants to the food chain of estuaries, wetlands, and oceans. If the estuarine wetlands do not keep pace with a potential increase in the rate of sea level rise, wetlands can drown, eventually fragment, and decrease in size and function, resulting in the loss of habitat.

Blue Crab
In a study of blue crab, *Callinectes sapidus* may be confused with *C. similis* and *C. ornatus*, which are also reported in east Central Florida (Norse and Fox-Norse, 1979). Blue crabs can tolerate a wide salinity range from freshwater to hypersaline that occur in coastal waters including bays and estuaries from Nova Scotia to the east coast of South America and the Gulf of Mexico (Guillory et al., 2001; FWC-FWRI, 2009b). Survival and success of blue crabs is dependent on the quality of habitat; areas with large tidal marshes and submerged vegetation are most productive. Adult blue crabs are consumed by sea turtles, wading birds, fishes, dolphins, and raccoons. They are opportunistic omnivores, consuming plant material, shellfish, shrimp, worms, and other animals.

Studies of blue crab began soon after it was identified in 1896 (FWC-FWRI, 2009b), probably because of its importance to commercial and recreational fisheries. Historic landings data have been collected for the east and west coasts of Florida since 1950 (Murphy et al., 2007). FWRI commercial fishery data are available from 1986 to present by county and species (http://research.myfwc.com/features/view_article.asp?id=19224) (FWC-FWRI, 2010c). Commercial landings data collected by NMFS from 1950 to present can be accessed for the Florida east coast and inland waters (Personal communication from the NMFS, 2010b). Neither source parses data specifically for Mosquito Lagoon, and neither NMFS nor FWC-FWRI collect or enumerate recreational harvest data for blue crab. Figure 76 shows annual blue crab landings for Brevard and Volusia counties from 2001–2010. Blue crab data are not available for Mosquito Lagoon; thus it is not possible to estimate blue crab abundance for the lagoon.

Abundance estimates for blue crab in Florida were derived from fisherman survey data and landings data to better understand the species along Florida's east coast and the Gulf of Mexico. In a Florida assessment of blue crab stocks, results from a quantitative model were conflicted for years 2002–2005. Catch-survey results indicating overfishing had not occurred and the stochastic stock reduction analysis results were unclear as to whether the stock was overfished. The low biomass of blue crab was likely not from overfishing nor was it undergoing overfishing during 2002–2005. Low biomass was due to the dry weather conditions that preceded 2002, and was followed by the increased storm activity between 2003–2005 that created a wetter period and the reason for greater landings in 2005. The study also found Florida blue crabs resilient to high fishing rates (Murphy et al., 2007).

During its life cycle, a blue crab may spend time in different salinity regimes. Adults mate in brackish water, and afterward, females migrate to areas of higher salinity to brood and release larvae. As larval development is thought to be impeded in waters <20.1 ppt, larvae return to

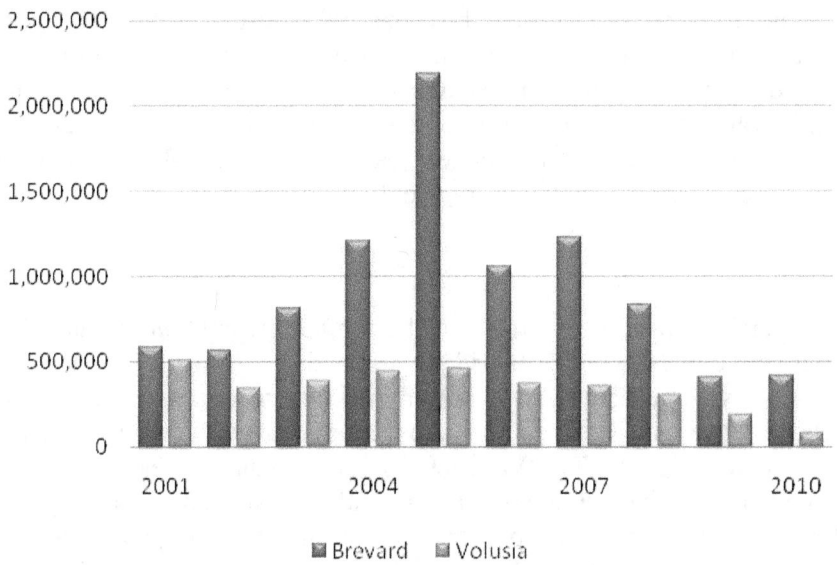

Figure 76. Blue crab landings in Brevard and Volusia counties for 2001–2010 (Personal communication from the NMFS, 2010b).

estuaries where they grow into juveniles, and juveniles move into lower salinity waters (Guillory et al., 2001; Murphy et al., 2007).

A study of young juvenile blue crab diet in the open water of Delaware Bay and salt marshes found that young juveniles fed on zooplankton in the bay, and those in the salt marsh fed on plants (Fantle et al., 1999). Dittel et al. (2006) determined that late-stage juveniles and adults are opportunistic and consume bivalves, mysid shrimp, annelids, and plant material. Juveniles feed on small, young adult oysters, and in tidal marshes they will consume fiddler crabs or marsh periwinkles (Guillory et al., 2001; Walters et al., 2001; Boudreaux et al., 2006). Although blue crabs have been found from freshwater to saline concentrations of 60 ppt, and in water depths from the shallow ocean shore to depths of 968 ft (295 m), post-settlement blue crabs are associated with inshore and nearshore areas. They utilize a range of habitat types including sandy and muddy bottoms to high-density vegetative areas (Murphy et al., 2007).

Potential threats to blue crabs are changes in salinity due to altered hydrology and pollutants, parasites, and disease. There are a variety of parasites, fungus, viruses, and bacteria that can affect the health of blue crabs (Guillory et al., 2001; FWC-FWRI, 2005a). In studies done by FWC-FWRI from 2006 and 2007 in Tampa Bay, FL, 11 different bacterial species, including *Vibrio*, were identified in the hemolymph collected from blue crabs (FWC-FWRI, 2010d).

Females spawn April to October, the optimal salinity ranges for hatchlings is from 23–30 ppt, and larvae rarely survive the first molt in salinities less than 20 ppt (Guillory et al., 2001). Mating occurs in lower salinity and may be year-round, with the greatest frequencies between February and July (Murphy et al., 2007).

Numerical model simulations of the Mosquito Lagoon conducted by Zarillo et al. (2010) found salinity ranged from 20–30 ppt in the central and southern compartments of the lagoon, well within the optimum levels of hatchling success. The central and southern compartments of the lagoon also have the most saltwater wetlands (Figures 70 and 71) and SAV (Figure 73). Water levels over most parts of the lagoon are low, except for water impounded on wetland surfaces. In the northern compartment, salinity concentration is high and near open ocean values.

Protozoa, passed on when crabs cannibalize infected crabs, affect the muscle tissue, turning it white and cotton-like when cooked (FWC-FWRI, 2005a). When an amoeba, *Paramoeba perniciosa*, invades the connective tissues and hemolymph of crabs, the ventral surfaces of infected crabs turn gray in color (Shields, 1997). In high salinity environments, nemertean worms and goose-necked barnacles infect the gills (Guillory et al., 2001; FWC-FWRI, 2005a). In low salinity water, brown leeches (Hirudinea) not thought to be harmful may adhere to the abdomen (FWC-FWRI, 2005a). A widespread fungus, *Lagenidium callinectes*, tolerant of moderately low salinities, can integrate in large numbers of crab eggs, and in some cases, most of the egg clutch can be destroyed by the fungus (Shields, 1997; Guillory et al., 2001).

The sacculinid barnacle is a serious parasite that can prevent a crab from molting; it is sometimes mistaken for an egg mass and may modify sexual characteristics of blue crabs (Guillory et al., 2001; FWC-FWRI, 2005a). Post-mortem study results in 2006 of a fish kill that included blue crabs in Choctawhatchee Bay, FL, is thought to have originated from brevetoxins left in the food web from a red tide (*Karenia brevis*) event that started at west Central Florida in August 2005 and traveled to the Panhandle by fall of 2005. Although no red tide was tested by December of 2005, brevetoxin is considered the primary cause of the fish kills (FWC-FWRI, 2006).

Some crab diseases are associated with heavy metals, pesticides, and industrial and chemical pollution to estuaries (FWC-FWRI, 2005a). Figure 77 depicts the threats to blue crabs.

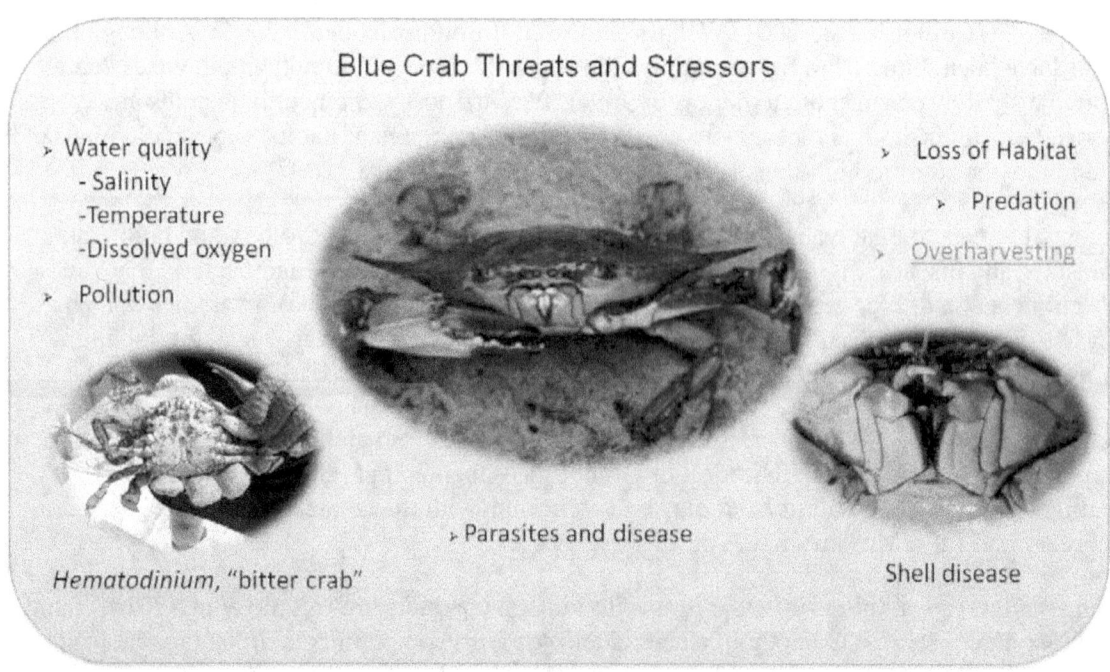

Figure 77. Blue crab threats and stressors. Those unlikely to occur at Canaveral National Seashore are in blue text and underlined (Photos: FWRI).

Horseshoe Crab

Horseshoe crabs (Limulus polyphemus) are not "true crabs," but members of the subphylum Chelicerata and relatives of arachnids, or spiders (Pechenik, 2000). They often are referred to as living fossils because their morphology has remained relatively unchanged for millions of years (Eldredge and Stanley, 1984). The horseshoe crab occurs in the sublittoral zone of estuaries from Maine to the Gulf Coast of Florida and in the Yucatan Peninsula. Genetic analysis shows distinctions between Atlantic Coast and Gulf populations (Gehart, 2007). Horseshoe crabs are found throughout the IRL with the greatest abundance found in the northern IRL, southern Banana River, and southern Mosquito Lagoon (Ehlinger et al., 2003). Adult horseshoe crabs feed mainly on clams and worms. Adults are food for sea turtles, while eggs and larvae provide food for migrating shore birds and fish (EPA, 2003). Additionally, the feeding mechanism of the horseshoe crab aerates the bottom substrate, thereby contributing to the diversity of infaunal community structure (Botton and Ropes 1987, 1989).

Horseshoe crabs reproduce in large numbers along sandy beaches of the Atlantic and Gulf of Mexico (Rudloe, 1980). Previous studies (Rudloe 1980; Shuster 1982; Brockmann 1990) done along the northeast coast of the U.S. and on the Gulf Coast of Florida found spawning patterns related to tidal height, lunar phase, and seasons. These findings differ from those of Ehlinger (2000) who found spawning of the horseshoe crab in the IRL was erratic and random.

The microtidal regime of the Mosquito Lagoon allows reproduction of horseshoe crab throughout the year, including a seasonal increase in early spring unrelated to lunar periods (Smith, 1993; Ehlinger et al., 2003). Gehart (2007) reports that beach morphology and tides may influence spawning in Florida.

Penn and Brockmann (1994) demonstrated that optimal egg development in Florida and Delaware coincided with nest sites located at mid-elevations to avoid desiccation associated with the upper beach and low oxygen concentrations associated with water-saturated sediments of the lower beach. The eggs develop in sediment depths of 5–20 cm over the course of 2–4 weeks, while embryos undergo four non-feeding molts (Rudloe, 1979; Sekiguchi et al., 1982; Sekiguchi, 1988; Brockmann, 1990; Penn and Brockmann, 1994). In the IRL, the presence of larvae in the water column was correlated with changes in water depth after wind events inundated the nests, possibly acting as a cue for larval emergence in place of tidal change (Ehlinger, 2003). After hatching, the larvae emerge, and many stay in shallow water "nurseries" near the spawning beaches (Rudloe, 1979; Shuster 1982). Eventually, juveniles move into deeper water farther offshore and in 9–11 yrs reach sexual maturity and may live another 10 yrs.

Results of extensive studies of horseshoe crabs conducted by Ehlinger (2002) in the IRL and Mosquito Lagoon show that year-round spawning could partially be explained by the cessation of embryonic development of horseshoe crabs in temperatures greater than 95°F (35°C). The optimal temperature and salinity for embryonic and larval development in horseshoe crabs ranges between 30−40 ppt and 86−91°F (30C−33°C) (Ehlinger and Tankersley, 2004). Low densities of larvae found in the IRL may be due to the low numbers of spawning adults in the IRL in comparison to other locations in Florida and Delaware (EPA, 2003).

Status and Trends: Little information is available on population estimates and fishery landings data in Florida, since most research and data collection has concentrated on populations in northeastern states, particularly Delaware Bay. The Atlantic States Marine Fishery Commission (ASMFC) Fishery Management Plan for Horseshoe crabs, completed in 1998 and appended six times hence, set catch limits for the Mid-Atlantic States (Schrading, et al., 1998). Catch limits for licensed marine-life collectors of aquarium and research specimens, who are limited to 100 horseshoe crabs per day, are excluded from the plan. These licensees capture mostly juveniles and are concentrated in South Florida. If the bag limit of marine-life collectors should increase, the ability of the local population to replenish itself could be threatened (Gerhart, 2007). The ASMFC Horseshoe Crab Management Board has noted that the large number of horseshoe crabs harvested in Florida for marine-life uses are not counted under the management plan quota. If the ASMFC decides to include the marine-life fishery in the management plan quota, permitted harvests would likely be reduced.

Some incidental data on horseshoe abundance were reported as by-catch in nets set to assess sea turtle populations in Mosquito Lagoon. During 1978 and 1979, large numbers of horseshoe crabs were caught and in 1994 much smaller amounts were netted, suggesting a dramatic decline of horseshoe crabs in the lagoon over 16 yrs (Provancha, 1998). The decrease in horseshoe crabs may be linked to the reversal in the number of loggerheads and green sea turtles netted in the early 1970s and in the 1990s (Provancha, 2006). In Delaware Bay, the decline has been attributed to human harvest of horseshoe crabs to sell for eel and whelk bait (Botton et al. 1994). In Florida, few eel fishermen are licensed to harvest horseshoe crabs for bait, while more than 22,000 horseshoe crabs were harvested in 2005 for resale to aquariums and as research specimens (Gerhart, 2007). The extent of horseshoe crab harvest within the Mosquito Lagoon is unknown, but truckloads of adult horseshoe crabs have been observed leaving from the IRL (EPA, 2003).

Pharmaceutical-related industries collect the blue, copper-based blood of horseshoe crabs that is used to test bacterial endotoxins of sterile fluids for human medical patients. Companies bleed approximately one-third of the horseshoe crab's blood and return them to the water, where they have a 90% survival rate. Florida did not have a biomedical fishery for horseshoe crabs as of the publication of Gerhart's report in 2007.

Threats to Horseshoe Crabs
- Unpredictable large-scale mortality events; for example, in 1999, about 100,000 adult horseshoe crabs died of unknown cause(s) in the northern IRL and southern Mosquito Lagoon (Scheidt and Lowers, 2000).

- Loss of habitat from degradation; for example, a reduction in beach nesting areas or changes in hydrology caused by mosquito impoundments.

- Repeated harvesting of large numbers of horseshoe crabs in specific areas may affect the abundance of local populations.

Additional research is needed, to determine the cause(s) of horseshoe crab decline within the Mosquito Lagoon. Florida Tech faculty and students have studied the reproductive ecology of horseshoe crabs in the IRL (Ehlinger and Tankersley, 2007) and are continuing their work to identify early settlement habitat of larval and juvenile horseshoe crabs to determine appropriate management strategies that will protect horsecrab populations in Mosquito Lagoon.

Decreases in horseshoe crab abundance and distribution can have ecological consequences. Declines in the red knot, a migratory shore bird, were attributed to insufficient quantities of their primary food source, horseshoe crab eggs (Karpanty et al. 2006). Populations of red knots have declined 75% in the Delaware Bay area (Niles et al., 2009). Threats to horseshoe crabs are depicted in Figure 78.

Oyster Reefs
The oyster reef is a three-dimensional structure that provides habitat for a variety of organisms, is created by many generations of larvae settling onto adult oyster shells (Boudreaux et al., 2006), and is one reason oysters, *Crassostrea virginica* are considered a foundation species and ecosystem engineers (Coen et al., 2007; Stiner and Walters, 2008). Oyster reefs provide the substrate for attachment of sessile organisms as well as refuge and/or foraging sites for mobile organisms (Boudreaux and Walters, 2006c). Oysters influence overall habitat health by filtering suspended fine particulate matter and concentrating heavy metals and bacteria, thus improving the water quality of estuarine ecosystems. There are numerous potential causes for oyster decline including parasites/disease, competition from invasive species, overharvesting, water quality (including HABs), and boating activity. Threats to oyster reefs are shown in Figure 79.

Parasites and disease (e.g., *Perkinsus marinus*/dermo and *Haplosporidium nelson*/MSX), can harm oysters. No evidence of MSX infection was found in monthly samples over a three-year study. The presence of dermo infection, however, was relatively high, averaging ~40% of individuals, but the intensity of infection was low (stage 1) in nearly all months (Arnold et al., 2008).

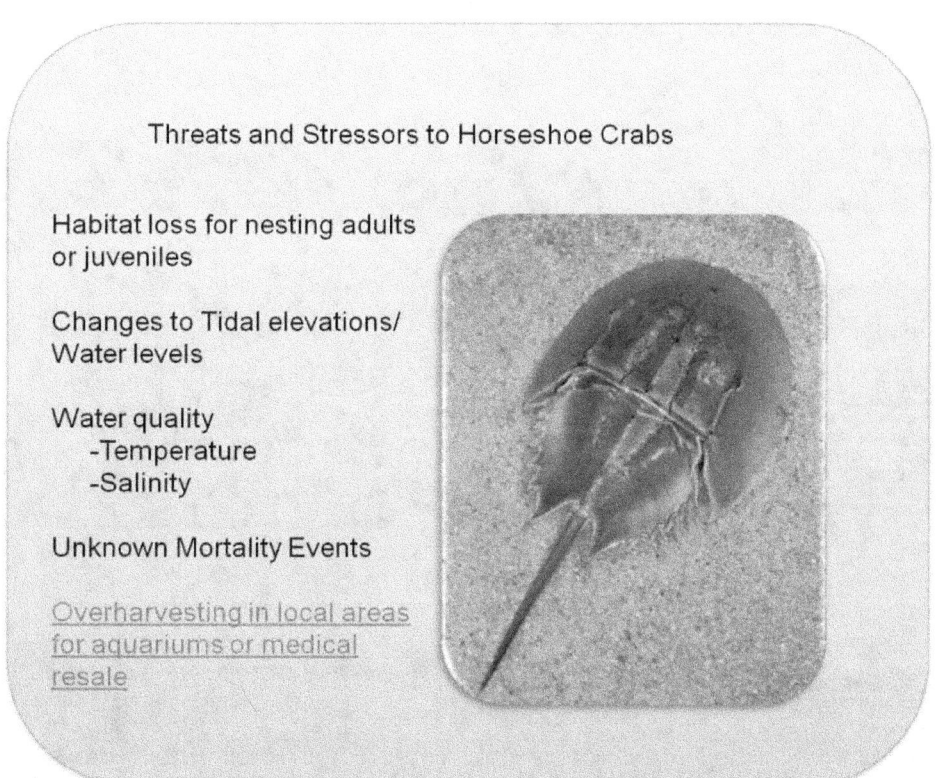

Figure 78. Threats and stressors of horseshoe crabs. Overharvesting for the aquarium trade is more likely to occur in south Florida noted in blue text and underlined. Horseshoe crabs are not collected for medical purpose in Florida. (Photo: http://beachchairscientist.wordpress.com/2008/07/13/hello-world/).

Another threat to oyster reefs is the introduction of non-native species. The bivalve mussel, *Mytella charruana*, was first found in the Mosquito Lagoon in August 2004, and it has rapidly spread within the northern portion of the lagoon (Boudreaux et al., 2006). Another potential non-native competitor is the Asian green mussel, *Perna viridis*, which has been documented in the Mosquito Lagoon. These mussels have devastated oyster reefs in the Tampa Bay area and are continuing to be monitored in the IRL (Boudreaux et al., 2006). Native *Balanus eburneus* and non-native *Balanus amphitrite* barnacles in the Mosquito Lagoon have also been shown to compete for recruitment and growing space (Boudreaux, 2005; Boudreaux and Walters, 2006a,b,c; Boudreaux et al., 2009).

Numerous oyster reefs occur in the northern end of Mosquito Lagoon; however, over the past 50 yrs, a declining trend in the distribution of oyster reefs within CANA has been observed, with a significant increase in the mortality of oysters along the reef margins adjacent to boat channels (Grizzle et al., 2002). This study identified 60 of 400 reefs displayed dead margins from aerial images. Data from the samples show some variability in the trend, but there is a decrease of overall live reef area from 16.2–10 ac (6.6–4.0 ha) and an increase in dead margin area from 0.5–2.8 ac (0.2–1.1 ha).

Much of the recent decline in oysters has been attributed to boating activity (Grizzle et al., 2002; Wall et al., 2005). Florida currently ranks second only to Michigan in the number of registered

Figure 79. Threats and stressors to oyster reefs. (Photos: A from Jonathan Wilker, Purdue University; B and C from Grizzle et al., 2002).

recreational vessels (Wall et al., 2005). From 1998 to 2003, there was a 42.8% increase in the number of recreational vessels registered in Florida (Wall et al., 2005) although the number of registered vessels decreased in years 2007–2009 (see Public Use, Boating section of this report). The development of dead margins on oyster reefs adjacent to heavily trafficked channel areas such as the AIWW is correlated with increased recreational boating activity (Walters et al., 2007). In addition, reefs along the AIWW in the lagoon have migrated away from the channel by as much as 164 ft (50 m) in some locations, and many of the reefs consist of empty shells that may be a meter or more above the highwater line (Wall et al., 2005). Boat wakes are believed to have contributed to an increase in dead margins from the effects of wave transport and the increased vertical accretion of oyster reefs to unsustainable elevations, smothering by suspended sediments of boat wakes, substrate instability induced by excessive sediment transport, and the inhibition of larval settlement due to sediment scour (Grizzle et al., 2002). CANA has been working with University of Central Florida and the Nature Conservancy to restore dead reef margins utilizing newly developed technology. Approximately 40 reefs have been restored since 2007 (Linda Walters, personal communication, January 20, 2011).

Juvenile Sea Turtles

After spending approximately 10 yrs at sea, juvenile sea turtles return to the IRL system. Mosquito Lagoon is a very important nursery area for juvenile green and loggerhead sea turtles (Ehrhart, 1980; Medonca and Ehrhart, 1982; Ehrhart, 1983). Greens feed on seagrass and algae in the lagoon (Medonca, 1983), while loggerheads feed on mollusks and crabs. Netting studies in Mosquito Lagoon have documented numerous loggerhead and green turtles over the past 20 yrs (Provancha, 1998; 2006). The relative abundance of the two species has shifted dramatically; in the late 1970s, nearly 80% of the turtles captured were loggerheads and 20% were greens, while in the late 1990s, only 15% were loggerheads and 85% were greens (Medonca and Ehrhart, 1982; Provancha et al., 1998). Concurrently, there was a significant decrease in the abundance of horseshoe crabs collected in the nets (Provancha, 2006). Whether the relationship between a decrease in prey abundance and a decline in loggerheads is coincidental or causal requires further examination.

Eaton et al. (2008) compiled and reviewed in-water turtle monitoring programs to assess the existing data sets and standardize methods for future monitoring that will gain knowledge of various life stages both spatially and temporally throughout Florida. The goal is for in-water programs to complement Florida's sea turtle nesting surveys (Eaton et al., 2008).

The aerial extent and species composition of SAV may affect the survival of juvenile turtles while in the Mosquito Lagoon. If green turtle consumption of SAV is less than necessary for survival and if the food choices of juvenile loggerheads that require SAV are diminished, the success of these species may be negatively affected.

Juvenile sea turtles in the IRL system have shown signs of a herpes-type virus known as fibropapillomatosis (FP), first observed in the 1930s (Provancha et al., 1998; Fick et al., 2000; Foley et al., 2005). The disease is manifested in the form of tumors that can affect breathing, feeding, and vision, if lesions occur around the eyes (Balazs et al., 1997; Herbst et al., 1999). Foley et al. (2005) examined dead or stranded sea turtles from the coasts of Massachusetts to Texas during 1980 to 1998. Green sea turtles collected from the Atlantic coast with FP were more prevalent inshore than offshore in degraded and polluted, largely shallow coastal waters with low wave energy, supporting the belief that one or more of these factors could serve as an environmental cofactor in the expression of FP (Foley et al., 2005).

Loggerheads are susceptible to cold stunning; turtles may be unable to swim and dive and often float to the surface as a result of rapidly dropping water temperatures (Witherington and Ehrhart, 1989; Morreale et al. 1992). Turtles overwintering inshore are most susceptible if water temperatures drop quickly below 46–50°F (8–10°C), as temperature change is most rapid in shallow water (Conant et al., 2009). The stunning effect was demonstrated during a week-long cold spell in January 2010 when temperatures dropped as low as 39°F (4°C) in Mosquito Lagoon (Stiner, 2010b). Over 2,000 juvenile turtles, primarily greens, stunned by the cold floated to the surface and were retrieved in a massive multi-agency effort and held in rehabilitation facilities until the weather improved (Stiner, 2010b). Across Florida, massive rescues retrieved an estimated 3,000 sea turtles stunned by two cold weather spells in 2010 (FWC-FWRI, 2010e).

Fish

Compared to other regions in Florida, marine and estuarine fishes have not been well studied in waters around CANA. Although there are differences in sampling techniques and experimental designs between past and present fishery studies in the region, historical results can provide important broad-scale benchmark information regarding fishes in CANA waters. Early studies of estuarine fishes in the CANA region of Mosquito Lagoon primarily involved a multi-gear approach (gigs, dip nets, seines, and gill nets) along with fixed station sampling with trawls (Snelson 1976, 1980, 1983). Surveys from 1972–1980 reported 141 species from northern IRL west of Haulover Canal and Mosquito Lagoon. A portion of the sampling occurred during the summer with fixed-station trawls (Mulligan and Snelson, 1983). These efforts involved two fixed stations in a channel or deeper water habitat in southern Mosquito Lagoon during the summers of 1979 and 1980. The survey results indicated that the epibenthic fish community was dominated by a few species. Among the 15 most abundant fish species collected in the Mosquito Lagoon stations, the bay anchovy (*Anchoa mitchilli*) accounted for approximately 85% of the total catch.

Three additional fixed trawl stations were sampled along with the two previous stations in Mosquito Lagoon in the summers of 1991 and 1992 for comparative purposes (Snelson and Johnson, 1995). Similarly, bay anchovy was numerically dominant, often composing over 90% of the trawl catch. A total of 49 fish species was collected during 1991–1992 within the basin. Other numerically dominant species included silver perch (*Bairdiella chrysoura*), pinfish (*Lagodon rhomboides*), spot (*Leiostomus xanthurus*), croaker (*Micropogonias undulatus*), Gulf pipefish (*Syngnathus scovelli*), silver jenny (*Eucinostomus harengulus*), and code goby (*Gobiosoma robustum*). The species assemblages encountered at the two stations were considered relatively similar between 1979–1980 and the 1991–1992. This early survey work also provided detailed life history information on several elasmobranchs with comments on factors that affect their distribution and abundance within the system (Snelson et al., 1988).

Funicelli et al. (1988) assessed the effectiveness of marine sanctuaries when they completed a trammel net survey comparing the "closed to fishing" Banana River Lagoon versus the "open to fishing" Mosquito Lagoon. In this study, the catch rate in the Mosquito Lagoon was over half the rate that was found in the Banana River Lagoon. The study also provided some of the first habitat use information generated from tagging data and some habitat descriptions of the sample areas within each basin.

More recently, Paperno et al. (2001) sampled fishes at 11 year-round fixed stations in Mosquito Lagoon (1993–1997) using 69-ft (21-m) seines and 200-ft (61-m) trawls as part of the Florida Fish and Wildlife Conservation Commission's Fish and Wildlife Research Institute's (FWC-FWRI) Fisheries-Independent Monitoring Program. Paperno et al. (2001) found the fish assemblage was dominated by seagrass-associated species such as rainwater killifish (*Lucania parva*) and pinfish, both common in seagrass habitats of the subbasin. The survey also provided a detailed comparison of spot recruitment (Figure 80) and growth in Mosquito Lagoon/Halifax River and the IRL basins of the greater IRL system (Paperno, 2002). In this study, it was suggested that because environmental conditions are relatively mild and recruitment of spot occurs over a long period compared to more northern estuaries, predation and advective processes may be the driving forces behind successful year classes in this and other estuarine-dependent species that spawn in nearshore waters.

Twenty-two sites including freshwater, estuarine, and marine areas within CANA were sampled by the NPS SECN in July of 2004 (personal communication, C. Wright, NPS, Southeast Coast Network, 2010). The inventory used electrofishing, snorkeling, and seining (10–100-ft [3-30-m] seines nets) and recorded a total of 65 estuarine and freshwater fish species (Johnston et al., 2006).

There is limited information on marine fish populations adjacent to CANA in the Cape Canaveral region (Collins et al., 1989; SEAMAP-SCDNR, 2000; and others). Few data are available even on the recent discoveries of critical nursery habitats for several shark species in nearshore waters adjacent to CANA and the Cape Canaveral region (Adams and Paperno, 2007; Aubrey and Snelson, 2007; Reyier et. al., 2008).

Mosquito impoundments in the IRL have long been recognized as valuable habitats for fish populations (Stevens et al., 2006). Concomitant with the FWC-FWRI's early survey, Klassen (1998) sampled the fish community within an unmanaged impoundment on the eastern shore of Mosquito Lagoon. His study documented the spatial and temporal use of the impoundment by resident and important transient fish species (i.e., spot, ladyfish (*Elops saurus*), and striped mullet (*Mugil cephalus*)), which provided useful data for future restoration efforts planned for the area.

The FWC-FWRI's Fisheries-Independent Monitoring Program's recent expansion into Mosquito Lagoon is the most current and quantitative study of estuarine and marine fish in the region. This three-year study, based on a stratified-random sampling design, was conducted to provide comprehensive distribution and abundance data on fishes in Mosquito Lagoon (Adams and Paperno, 2008; 2009). Sampling was conducted throughout the year, with 20 standardized haul seine samples completed each month. Additionally, exploratory gear testing with other sampling gears (e.g., 600-ft [183-m] haul seines, trammel nets, gillnets, fish traps, and hook and line) was conducted on a quarterly basis to assess the potential to effectively collect additional larger sub-adult and adult fish in the basin. More than 148,200 fish and macroinvertebrates were collected during 2007–2008. Sixty-seven fish species were collected during 2007 and 73 fish species were collected in 2008. The rainwater killifish, bay anchovy, and silversides (*Menidia* spp.) numerically dominated collections in 2007, accounting for approximately 74% of the total catch (Table 25). Similarly in 2008, these three species dominated the catch, along with seasonally abundant spot (Table 26). Spot were abundant throughout the Mosquito Lagoon sampling area during key recruitment periods, with large concentrations of young-of-the-year found in distinct habitats (Figure 81).

Mosquito Lagoon is well known as an important area for many sportfish species, including red drum (*Sciaenops ocellatus*). The recreational red drum fishery in Mosquito Lagoon has attained national recognition (FWC-FWRI, unpublished data; Florida Department of Environmental Protection, 2009). Recent evidence indicates that some adult red drum reside and spawn within the confines of Mosquito Lagoon. Initial evidence included estuarine spawning in the late 1980s via the collection of both ripe/gravid individuals and red drum eggs many kilometers within estuarine waters (Johnson and Funicelli, 1991; Murphy and Taylor, 1991). An intensive two-year ichthyoplankton survey consistently collected red drum larvae up to 56 mi (90 km) away from the nearest ocean inlet from June to October, with average nightly larval densities as high as 11.5/yd^3 (15/100 m^3) of water (Reyier and Shenker, 2007).

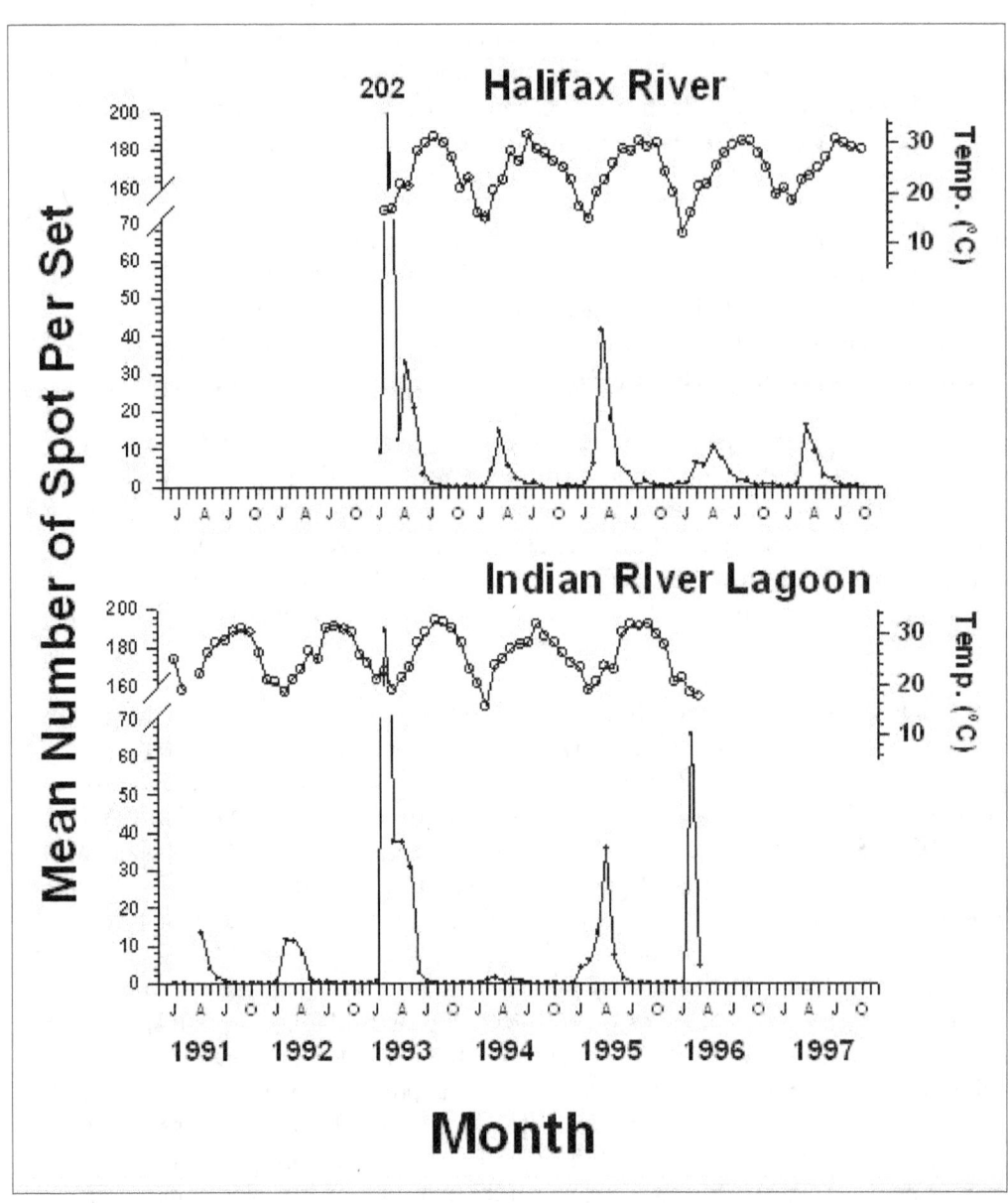

Figure 80. Monthly indices of relative abundance for age-0 spot (*Leiostomus xanthurus*) and mean temperature from the Halifax River (1993–1997) and IRL (1991–1996) (Paperno, 2002).

Conventional mark–recapture tagging suggest that some mature fish are year-round estuarine residents as opposed to transient seasonal migrants from offshore waters (Stevens and Sulak, 2001; Tremain et al., 2004). A key question is whether estuarine spawning is the prevailing local strategy, or one adopted by a small proportion of mature red drum in the basin. The most recent red drum study in Mosquito Lagoon involved autonomous acoustic telemetry to resolve the seasonal and daily movement patterns of this sportfish species (Reyier et al., 2010). The majority of acoustically tagged red drum exhibited strong site fidelity from winter through early summer, with movement rates increasing significantly during fall spawning months (Figure 82). While some fish migrated to the nearest ocean inlet during the spawning period, the majority remained within the lagoon year-round, suggesting that estuarine reproduction, an activity uncommon or poorly documented elsewhere, is the dominant life history strategy within the Mosquito Lagoon basin (Reyier et al., 2010). Tag recapture data from this study suggest high fishing pressure on large breeding adult red drum data in Mosquito Lagoon, with a 41% recapture rate in 50 months.

Aerial and boat ramp surveys in the area indicate watercraft use within CANA estuarine waters has increased. Increases in watercraft use, predominately related to fishing, suggest greater fishing pressure or fishing effort within the area in recent years. Recreational anglers, the largest user group encountered during the boat ramp survey, primarily targeted red drum and spotted sea trout (*Cynoscion nebulosus*) within CANA waters (Scheidt and Garreau, 2007: Reyier et al., 2011). The authors concluded that the increase in watercraft use will have a direct negative influence on the natural resources in Mosquito Lagoon managed by CANA and MINWR.

Harmful algal blooms have occurred in nearshore coastal waters near CANA, resulting in fish kills (FWC-FWRI, unpublished data). Whereas the long-term impacts of these HABs are unknown, recent research in the surf zone off Cape Canaveral also suggests that brevetoxins produced by HABs in the area can cause sub-lethal effects in sharks and potentially other marine biota (Nam et al., 2010). Results from free-ranging lemon sharks (*Negaprion brevirostris*) in nearshore Cape Canaveral waters indicate that brevetoxins may cause significant negative changes in brain neurochemistry (Nam et al., 2010). The specific ecological and physiological impacts of HABs and the additive effects of multiple stressors on lemon sharks and other marine fish species in the region require additional study.

Recently observed increases in watercraft use, related habitat perturbations, increased human population within the region, and suggested increases in fishing pressure within CANA waters infer potentially increased negative anthropogenic influences on estuarine fish communities within the Mosquito Lagoon basin. Additional stressors and historical habitat- and water quality-related changes (e.g., loss of oyster habitat, seagrass degradation, presence of HABs) outlined in this assessment report also work to influence overall community structure. Fundamental differences in experimental designs of past and present fisheries studies preclude rigorous statistical comparisons and contrasts of historical and current fish communities within CANA. However, comparisons of current measures of community structure (Adams and Paperno, 2008; 2009) with historical fisheries studies within Mosquito Lagoon (Snelson and Johnson, 1995; Paperno et al., 2001) and in adjacent IRL basins (Tremain and Adams, 1995) suggest relatively stable fish communities in the system within recent time. Recent management measures within Mosquito Lagoon (e.g., reconnection of salt marsh systems to lagoon waters, pole-and-troll zones/no-motor zones, and continued control of shoreline development) will likely have direct positive effects on CANA fish communities, and research regarding these potential effects is ongoing.

Table 25. Catch statistics for 10 dominant taxa in Mosquito Lagoon in 2007. Fish were collected in 240 70-ft (21.3-m) seine samples during stratified-random sampling. Percent (%) is the percent of the total catch represented by that taxon; percent occurrence (% Occur) is the percentage of samples in which the taxon was collected; SE is the standard error of the mean; CV is the coefficient of variation of the mean. Taxa are ranked in order of decreasing mean density (Adams and Paperno, 2008).

Species	Number		% Occur	Density Estimate (animals/100m^2)				Standard Length (mm)			
	No.	%		Mean	S.E.	CV	Max	Mean	S.E.	Min	Max
Lucania parva	25,302	37.1	67.1	75.30	26.03	535.47	5,836.43	23	0.03	7	42
Anchoa mitchilli	12,887	18.9	38.3	38.35	9.52	384.38	1,232.86	33	0.08	19	64
Menidia spp.	12,629	18.5	71.7	37.59	6.55	269.92	907.14	43	0.11	12	81
Floridichthys carpio	4,119	6.0	42.9	12.26	2.47	311.83	255.00	32	0.17	9	65
Microgobius gulosus	1,649	2.4	47.5	4.91	1.55	489.51	330.71	30	0.21	9	64
Eucinostomus spp.	1,492	2.2	37.1	4.44	0.91	317.46	111.43	27	0.17	10	44
Lagodon rhomboids	1,288	1.9	51.7	3.83	0.57	230.54	58.57	53	0.77	14	154
Anchoa hepsetus	1,016	1.5	10.8	3.02	1.09	558.82	176.43	34	0.22	20	75
Leiostomus xanthurus	866	1.3	20.8	2.58	0.78	469.09	140.00	26	0.47	10	184
Cyprinodon variegatus	802	1.2	16.3	2.39	0.97	628.92	175.00	29	0.31	12	45
Subtotal	62,050	91.0								7	184
Total	68,288	100.0		203.24	28.85	219.89	5,845.71			2	442

Table 26. Catch statistics for 10 dominant taxa in Mosquito Lagoon in 2008. Fish were collected in 240 70-ft (21.3-m) seine samples during stratified-random sampling. Percent (%) is the percent of the total catch represented by that taxon; percent occurrence (% Occur) is the percentage of samples in which that taxon was collected; SE is the standard error of the mean; CV is the coefficient of variation of the mean. Taxa are ranked in order of decreasing mean density (Adams and Paperno, 2009).

Species	Number		% Occur	Density Estimate (animals/100m²)				Standard Length (mm)			
	No.	%		Mean	S.E.	CV	Max	Mean	S.E.	Min	Max
Lucania parva	27,937	35.1	65.8	83.15	10.13	188.69	914.29	25	0.03	12	40
Anchoa mitchilli	12,311	15.5	32.5	36.64	10.57	446.85	1,850.00	35	0.07	19	68
Leiostomus xanthurus	8,050	10.1	26.7	23.96	7.76	502.10	1,356.43	25	0.10	12	138
Menidia spp.	7,618	9.6	61.3	22.67	4.83	329.78	908.57	43	0.12	12	79
Lagodon rhomboides	6,497	8.2	66.7	19.34	3.19	255.32	412.14	41	0.26	12	183
Cyprinodon variegatus	2,419	3.0	20.8	7.20	2.92	628.26	480.00	27	0.14	7	46
Floridichthys carpio	2,145	2.7	37.1	6.38	1.78	432.67	229.29	32	0.23	10	64
Microgobius gulosus	1,729	2.2	50.4	5.15	1.00	301.92	130.71	28	0.18	8	59
Anchoa hepsetus	1,298	1.6	12.5	3.86	1.32	528.28	210.71	39	0.22	21	63
Eucinostomus spp.	893	1.1	37.9	2.66	0.58	340.58	105.71	27	0.23	10	39
Subtotal	70,896	89.1	.	.	.	.	.	.	.	7	183
Total	79,557	100.0	.	236.78	20.10	131.51	2,280.71	.	.	3	480

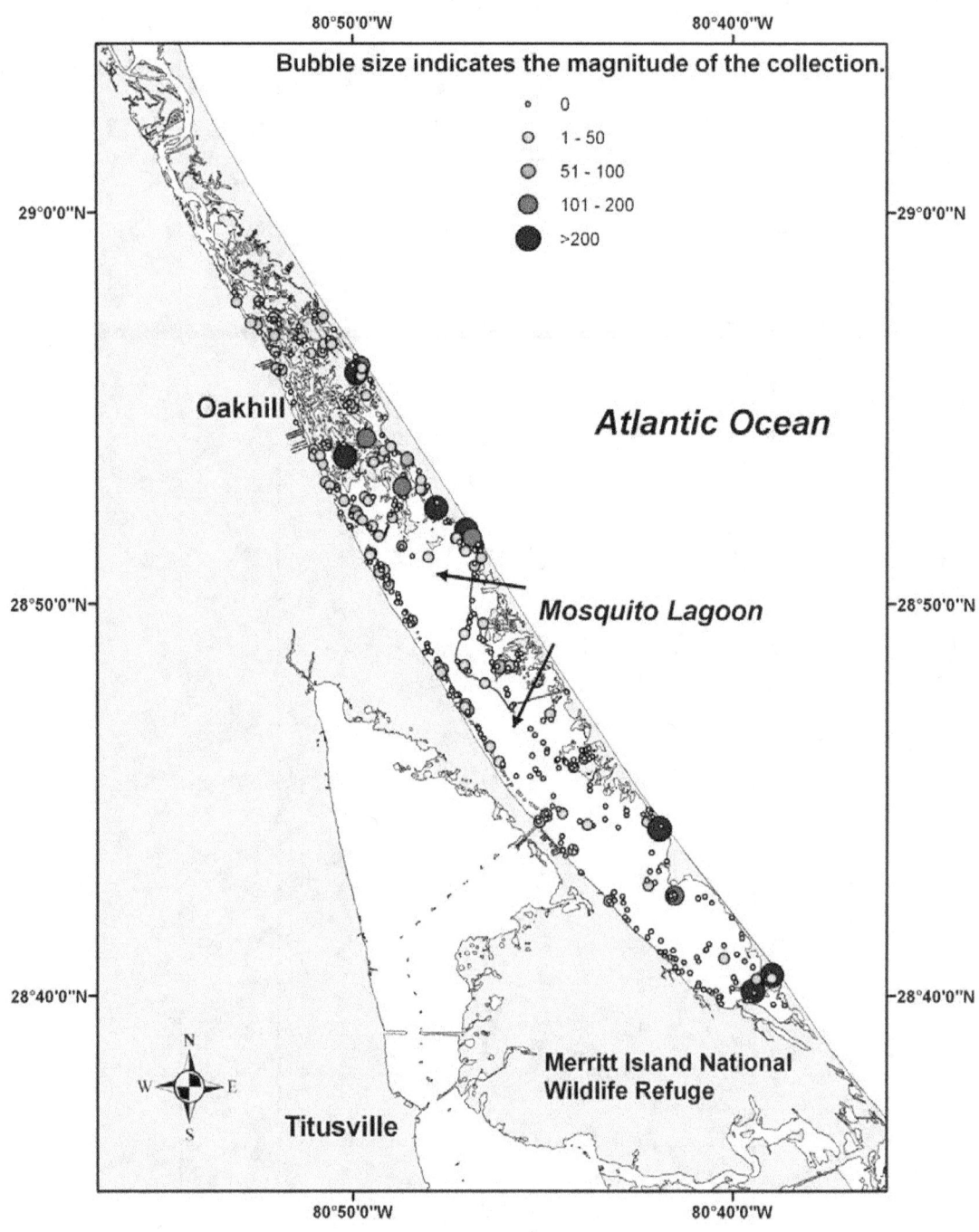

Figure 81. Distribution and abundance of spot (*Leiostomus xanthurus*) in Mosquito Lagoon from FWC-FWRI's Fisheries-Independent Monitoring Program during 2007–2008. Bubbles represent the number of fish collected. Red lines indicate current pole-and-troll zones (Adams and Paperno, In prep.).

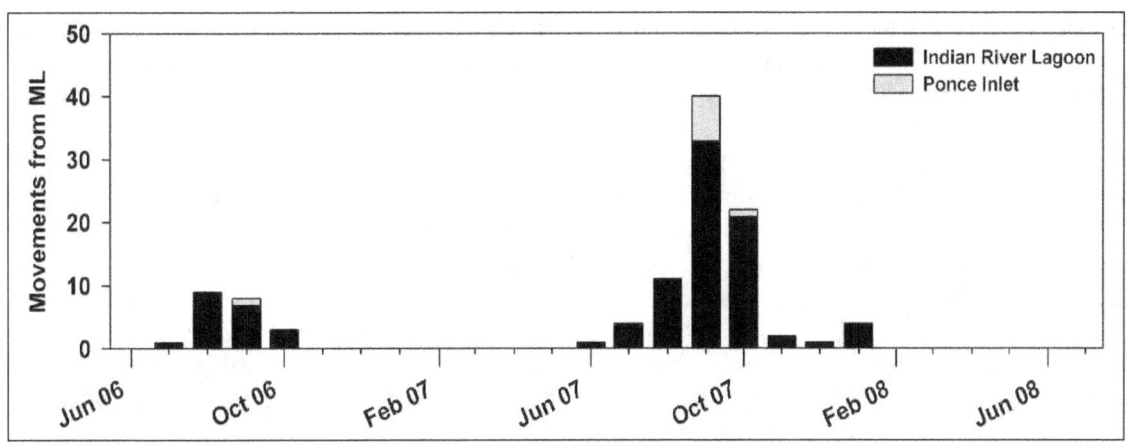

Figure 82. Number and timing of adult red drum (*Sciaenops ocellatus*) movements out of Mosquito Lagoon (ML) to Ponce Inlet or the northern Indian River Lagoon (Reyier et al., 2011).

Contaminants in Fish
Periodic broad-scale testing of contaminants, including metals, PCBs, and pesticides, in selected fish from estuarine waters of the southeastern U.S. was conducted via the EMAP and IMAP programs (Hyland et al., 1996; 1998; FWC-FWRI, 2002; 2005b). Limited periodic testing of overall contaminants in spot, Atlantic croaker, blue crab, and penaeid shrimp in the southeastern U.S. suggests analytes were below U.S. Food and Drug Administration action levels related to human consumption (EPA, 2001). PCBs and flame retardants (PBDEs, HBCDs and TBBPA) were examined in sharks and other fish species from the Indian River Lagoon and adjacent waters (Johnson-Restrepo et al., 2005, 2008). Limited information exists regarding contaminants in fish tissue for estuarine species of Mosquito Lagoon. There have been exploratory analyses of total mercury in marine fishes (e.g., tunas, mackerels, grouper–snapper complex, dolphinfish) collected in offshore waters of Volusia County and Brevard County, adjacent to CANA (Adams et al., 2003; Adams and McMichael, 2007; Adams 2004; 2010). Given the sampling designs of these large-scale studies and highly migratory nature of these species, it was not possible to determine spatial variation in total mercury with a specific focus on CANA. Additionally, limited mercury results are available for juvenile bull sharks (*Carcharhinus leucas*) from the IRL system that includes the Mosquito Lagoon basin as well as the Banana River Lagoon and IRL proper (Adams and McMichael, 1999). Mean total mercury concentration reported for bull sharks (dorsal muscle) was 0.77 ppm, which was similar to concentrations of total mercury found in juveniles of this species from limited sampling elsewhere in Florida (Adams et al., 2003). Examination of mercury in fish from the Indian River Lagoon found elevated mercury could cause quantifiable pathological and biochemical changes that may directly influence the health of spotted seatrout (Adams et al., 2010).

Threats to the Animals of Mosquito Lagoon
Climate Change
The effects of climate change could cause primary producers (algal, plankton, and other plants) in the marine ecosystem to shift in distribution and abundance (IPPC, 2007), and in turn affect predator–prey relationships (Conant et al., 2009). It is likely that storm activity will cause increasingly greater amounts of rainfall, and the stormwater runoff will carry pollutants to receiving water bodies. Increased stormwater levels may impact the composition and distribution

of plant communities, such as fresh and saltwater wetlands. CANA recently received funding for FY12 to create a climate change sensitive model to understand larval oyster dynamics in Mosquito Lagoon (UCF, 2010).

Threats from Marine Debris
The threat of trash, litter, and/or debris in the marine environment is a worldwide problem that negatively affects wildlife, habitat, and use of waterways (FWC-FWRI, 2010f; NOAA, 2009). For the purpose of illustration, a striking example is the Laysan albatross (*Phoebastria immutabilis*), found on the Midway atoll, where plastics consisted of 40–50% of the intestinal tract content of dead adult and young (USFWS, 2003). Brown and white pelicans are still vulnerable to death and disfigurement resulting from entanglement in monofilament line (http://myfwc.com/WILDLIFEHABITATS/BirdSpecies_AmWhitePelican.htm) (FWC-FWRI, 2003; IBRRC, 2001). Nearly all birds, marine mammals, and sea turtles suffer injury or death from entanglement in marine debris.

Threats from Pollution
Pesticides, hydrocarbons, pathogens–coliform bacteria and viruses, and other contaminants are the main pollutants present in the aquatic environment (Gilliom and others, 2006). The danger lies not in the effects of a single pollutant, but the effects of bioaccumulation or the cocktail effect in the environment, concentration in the food chain, and effects to wildlife and humans. Pollutants are implicated in weakened immune responses (e.g., dolphins infected with mobile virus and contaminated with PCBs). Public health notices provide guidelines for human consumption of fish (FDOH, 2009). The third annual coastal assessment for the southeastern U.S. lists mercury, PCBs, and dioxin as the pollutants responsible for fish advisories in 2003 (EPA, 2008).

Florida Department of Agriculture and Consumer Services (FDACS) issues shellfish harvesting advisories in response to HABs and/or unsafe concentrations of harmful algae. Hard clam and oyster harvesting was periodically closed in the IRL for HABs in 2002, 2007, and 2009. In 2009, Florida experienced *Pyrodinium bahamense* blooms on both coasts; the IRL bloom lasted from early June to late November (maximum count of 2.4 million cells/L) (International Council for the Exploration of the Sea, 2010). Toxins produced from red tide events can kill fish, sea birds, turtles, and marine mammals (Abbott, 2008). FWC-FWRI maintains HAB status maps and reports at (http://research.myfwc.com/features/category_main.asp?id=2309).

The National Marine Fisheries Service (NMFS) Southeast Fisheries Science Center is the base for the Southeast United States Marine Mammal Stranding Program and works with other agencies to provide tissues from stranded marine mammals to for contaminant studies. Marine mammals bioaccumulate environmental toxins in various tissues and are excellent indicators (http://www.sefsc.noaa.gov/marinemammalstrandingsprog.jsp). Tissues from bottlenose dolphins stranded in the IRL were tested by Durden et al. (2007) for mercury and selenium, which are believed to bioaccumulate and therefore correlate with the age and length. The mean sample concentrations were greater for IRL dolphins than those for Texas, the west coast of Florida, and Gulf of Mexico (Durden et al., 2007).

The FDEP updated section 303 (d) water quality assessment of Mosquito Lagoon for use by aquatic and human life and submitted the update for EPA approval (EPA, 2009). The EPA recognized that Mosquito Lagoon is not achieving Florida state water quality standards. As a result, Mosquito Lagoon is considered water quality limited, primarily due to high mercury levels in fish and low levels of DO. In partial fulfillment of improving impaired water quality, the FDEP agreed to develop total daily maximum loads (TMDL) for mercury and DO. The EPA agreed with the FDEP to delist fecal coliform as a parameter of concern from the Mosquito Lagoon, as tests results for coliform over the past 7.5 yrs have been below 43 CFU.

The Sea Turtle Stranding and Salvage Network, operating since 1980, performs a similar service as its mammal counterpart to track dead or debilitated turtles and report data to partner groups and agencies. FWC-FWRI examines certain carcasses collected by FWRI staff for gross or detailed necropsy (http://research.myfwc.com/features/view_article.asp?id=2122). There are currently no data available to quantify indirect effects from both point and non-point source pollution (e.g., upland runoff, direct sewage discharge) on sea turtles (Conant et al., 2009). Sea turtles exposed to petroleum products may suffer inflammatory dermatitis, ventilatory disturbance, salt gland dysfunction or failure, red blood cell disturbances, immune response, and digestive disorders as shown from physiological experiments (Conant et al., 2009). HAB events are a suspected link to loggerhead mortality during four red tide events where "

> ...turtles washed ashore alive during red tide events displayed symptoms that were consistent with acute brevitoxicosis (e.g., uncoordinated and lethargic but otherwise robust and healthy in appearance) and completely recovered within days of being removed from the area of the red tide (NMFS-FWS, 2008).

Eight turtles, including one loggerhead, found dead during the four events had 10–330 ng/gram (ppb) of brevitoxin in liver tissue (NMFS-FWS, 2008).

Following the Exxon Valdez oil spill, the federal government organized stakeholders in committees by region to plan for similar events should they occur. The north and eastern Central Florida boundary includes CANA. In the area contingency plan prepared by the U.S. Coast Guard (USCG) north and eastern Central Florida Area Committee, the prediction of a spill occurring off the tip of Cape Canaveral with a south wind may contaminate beaches on NASA property or CANA (USCG, 2006). NPS considered CANA among 10 national parks that could have been affected by the Gulf oil spill and created a plan to conduct baseline assessments of the key resources in CANA; the trigger point was the spill reaching the Dry Tortugas, which fortunately did not occur (John Stiner, personal communication, January 20, 2011; NPS, 2010a).

Terrestrial Freshwater Systems
The diversity and composition of the natural plant communities of terrestrial freshwater systems within CANA reflect the soils and the underlying geologic structure of the Anastasia Formation that are topographically expressed in the dune and swale or ridge features. Surface water and groundwater movement in and among these geologic features can determine plant species composition and viability. Brackish–saline water is abundant in Mosquito Lagoon and back barrier marshes where mangroves and marsh grass wetlands of salt-tolerant species thrive. Freshwater is more limited and restricted by rainfall, groundwater withdrawal from the system for potable water, and changes to natural hydrology (i.e., Haulover Canal, mosquito ditching, and stormwater canals). Wildfires induced by lightning and later by Native Americans helped maintain healthy natural communities in Florida.

The major anthropogenic changes of fire suppression, alterations to surface and groundwater quality and quantity, and interruption in the natural hydrology from roads, drainage structures, and/or the introduction of exotic pest plants and animals has disrupted the historic natural communities. CANA and MINWR plan to restore and maintain the natural landscape and to date have, in portions of CANA and in the joint management area, worked to restore the natural hydrology, conduct prescribed fire burns, remove and treat exotics, and plant native plants (NPS, 2006).

Florida Natural Areas Inventory (FNAI) (www.fnai.org) manages extensive data sets of natural community landscapes, invasives, and wildlife in Florida. Florida Natural Areas Inventory and the Florida Department of Natural Resources (FNAI-FDNR) prepared the 1990 Guide to the Natural Communities of Florida. FNAI-FDNR's identifies the natural plant communities of Florida, the plants and animals indigenous to the natural plant communities, example sites, and global and state ranking of rarity (FNAI-FDNR, 1990). FNAI released a new edition in 2010 (FNAI, 2010). A large number of plant species can be found in the range of different freshwater wetland communities present in CANA.

Animals of Terrestrial Freshwater Wetlands
CANA and MINWR have initiated assessment and monitoring projects for wildlife that inhabit the freshwater wetlands within the jurisdiction of NASA, CANA, and MINWR. In an ongoing long-term amphibian and reptile monitoring study, Rich Seigel of Towson University has shown that more than 50% of the amphibians and reptiles in CANA are associated with the freshwater swales of the dune/swale system or roadside ditches (Seigel and Pike, 2003; Seigel and Crabill, 2006). Seigel believes in the 20 yrs he has studied herps throughout KSC, freshwater sources are key ecological niches to preserving the herpetological biodiversity of CANA (Seigel and Pike, 2003). Presently, Seigel is in the second year of a two-year study to identify the importance of specific swales to biodiversity at CANA (John Stiner, personal communication, January 7, 2011). Byrne et al. (2010) is also in the midst of a multi-year inventory of herps for NPS in CANA and has identified 72 species of amphibians and reptiles. FNAI species are listed within each wetland community type.

Literature research on natural communities and freshwater wetlands within CANA and the use of GIS compatible data were analyzed to determine the historical land coverage of wetlands—primarily freshwater transitional and embedded wetlands associated with pine flatwoods. Subcategories of wetlands found from literature research and site visits are wet flatwoods, hammocks, forested wetlands, freshwater marsh, cabbage palm, and disturbed wetlands. The distribution of wetlands was quantified for all community types using aerial images, soils data, and 2003 land-use cover from NPS. Findings from synthesized GIS data were compared with land coverage as coded in GIS 1943 and 1990 land cover data layers created for the report (Duncan et al., 2004).

In the land-use coverage of Duncan et al. (2004), category code 4100, "Flatwoods," included scrubby, mesic, and hydric flatwoods with longleaf, slash or pond pine, palmetto prairie, and sand pine. The wet flatwoods were separated from the mesic flatwoods in GIS according to the soils appropriated for wet flatwoods by the U.S. Soil Conservation Service soil surveys of Brevard and Volusia counties (USDA, 1975 and 1980). The optimal extent of freshwater wetland types was estimated by identification of hydric soils, existing wetland coverage, the condition of the wetlands, and water sources. Potential threats to wetland types and the fauna likely to inhabit them are evaluated and discussed based on evidence from Florida Natural Areas Inventory (FNAI-FDNR, 1990; 2010) ecological community information, soil surveys (USDA, 1974; 1980: NPS, 2010b), and water quality and quantity data.

Plant Communities

Plant communities in the dune and swale topography are determined by the complex soil patterns and different habitats that occur with small changes in elevation (Duncan et al., 2004). The driest habitats, scrub, and sand hill occur on well-drained soils at higher elevations. Palmetto prairie, scrubby, and mesic pine flatwoods grow on the moderately drained soils. Wet pine flatwoods exist on poorly drained soils, and freshwater wetlands occupy the lower elevations where water stands for longer periods (Table 27).

The dune and swale topography consists of a series of long, narrow, moderately-drained sand ridges separated by poorly-drained troughs or swales that were former shoreline ridges (noted as scrub ridges on Figure 83). The scrub ridges are nearly parallel to the present shoreline where elevation ranges from sea level to 20 ft (6.1 m) on top of the dune ridges (USDA, 1980). The freshwater wetlands on CANA are embedded in the swales and transition between the dune and swale topography (Figure 83). Based on NRCS soils, freshwater wetland communities, LC 6100 forested wetlands, and LC 6400 freshwater marsh occupy approximately 1,355 ac (548 ha) (Table 27), or 7%, of the approximately 20,000 ac (8,094 ha) of the terrestrial communities on CANA (Table 28). Terrestrial communities exclude the estuary, waterways and the Atlantic Ocean. The wet flatwoods in Table 27 were separated from the flatwoods category of Duncan et al. (2004) to determine an estimated extent of wet flatwoods on CANA. The wet flatwoods were estimated using the soil and vegetation descriptions from the NPS GIS soil data and Brevard County and Volusia County Soil Surveys (USDA, 1974 and 1980) (Table 28). There may be more wetlands than shown in Table 27 due to the designation of land-use codes.

The wet flatwoods are on ancient marine terraces, such as the exposed coquina (Figure 84). Surface water moves slowly off these broad terraces into poorly drained swales or depressions where the water table is near the surface during the summer rainy season (USDA, 1980).

Differences in parent soil material occur between soils formed in deposits over limestone and those formed in sand. Species composition and habitat types are influenced by soil types (Schmalzer et al., 2001). On higher elevations, such as old dune ridges that consist of sandy soils, rainfall is filtered and percolates to recharge groundwater; in lower elevation pine flatwoods and in swales, the underlying soils have humic hardpans that restrict infiltration (Schmalzer and Hensley, 2001).

The wetland plant communities of CANA include wet flatwoods, hammocks, forested wetlands, freshwater marsh, and disturbed freshwater wetlands (Table 28). Table 27 shows wetland community designations described by FNAI-FDNR (1990) and land cover classes in Duncan et al. (2004). The land cover classes in Duncan et al. (2004) were produced in GIS from a larger database using photo interpretation and modeling (Duncan et al., 1997). General community descriptions are taken from Abrahamson and Hartnett (1990) and FNAI-FDNR (1990). NPS soils data were used to project historic land-use coverage and to estimate the maximum potential areas for community descriptions based on compatible soils types (Tables 19 and 20).

Table 27. Land-cover classes, descriptions, and size. Acres are estimated for all years using land-use (LU) codes of Duncan et al. (2004) and NPS thematic layers, land use 2003, and soils. A description of land cover classes is in the Appendix.

LU Codes	Land Cover Class*	Size (acres)			Soils 2003**
		1943*	1990*	2003**	
1000	Urban/development	154	236	209	57
2000	Agriculture	264	165	157	
3200	Coastal strand	1,008	1,096	1,337	381
4100	Flatwoods	4,166	1,872	4,075	6,865***
4200	Scrub	2,194	2,853	1,467	1,645
4300	Hammocks	1,253	2,613	2,777	
4400	Disturbed uplands	2	647	494	
5100	Waterways	16	902	112	
5400	Estuarine	30,741	30,857	30,328	30,916
5710	Ocean	7,500	7,500	7,547	7,021
6100	Forested wetlands	255	934	305	445
6104	Prairie hammock				128
6120	Mangrove	1657	1,756	655	3,842
6250	Hydric pine flatwoods				530
6400	Freshwater Marsh	1,324	494	378	910
6420	Salt marsh	6,600	4,764	6,998	4,462
6460	Disturbed Estuarine Wetlands	20	219	297	
6470	Disturbed Freshwater Wetlands	53	10	596	
7100	Sand/barren land	421	253	68	
7400	Spoil	208	651		532
8000	Invasive/exotic		34	332	
	Total	57,835	57,856	58,132	57,732

*Land-cover classes combined by Duncan et al. (2004).
**Land cover 2003 and soils from National Park Service.
***Wet pinewoods (530 acres) included in overall acreage for pinewoods.

Table 28. Land-cover classes and acreage of freshwater wetland communities estimated for 1943, 1990, 2003, and soils for 2003. LU = land-use.

LU Codes	Land Cover Class*	Size (acres)			Soils 2003**
		1943*	1990*	2003**	
6104	Prairie Hammocks				128
6110	Wet flatwoods*				530
6100	Forested wetlands	255	934	305	445
6400	Freshwater Marsh	1324	494	378	910
6470	Disturbed Freshwater Wetlands	53	10	596	
	Total	1631	1437	1279	2013

*Land-cover classes from Duncan et al. (2004).
**Land cover 2003 and soils from National Park Service.

<u>Vegetation of Wet Pine Flatwoods</u>
Historically, the most extensive community in Florida and the habitat most influenced by man is the pine flatwoods (Abrahamson and Hartnett, 1990). The wet or hydric flatwoods is

characterized by low elevation, flat topography, and poorly-drained sandy soils with an organic horizon (Myers, 1990). The soils are typically 2–3 ft (0.6–0.9 m) deep sands over an organic hardpan or clay layer and are largely impervious to water (USDA, 1974). Early accounts describe flatwoods as open canopy pinewoods with a sparse canopy of pine and maintained by frequent fire (Laessle, 1942; Abrahamson and Hartnett, 1990).

In Table 28, 530 ac (215 ha) of wet flatwoods occur on the lower elevations of the ridges in the transition areas bordering the wetlands in the swales (Duncan et al., 2004). Wet pine woods with a sparse canopy or with few pines are interspersed with grassy sloughs, ponds, and swamps, and the water movement is gradual from the low sandy ridges to the natural drainage ways.

Canopy structure ranges from scattered pines to a mixture of pine and cabbage palms to cabbage palm prairies that border the intermittent ponds, with cabbage palms sometimes growing in the wet sloughs. The soil associations (Basinger sand, Pineda fine sand, Placid fine sand depressional, Pompano fine sand, and St. Johns sand) for pine-dominated flatwoods are poorly drained, weakly cemented sandy layers, underlain by sand or loam. Wet pine woods are interspersed with grassy sloughs, ponds, and swamps. Water movement is gradual from the low, sandy ridges to the natural drainage ways of these features. Pine-dominated flatwoods may be flooded for several days following heavy rains. The cabbage palm flatwoods tend to occur on soils underlain by limestone or shell beds (USDA, 1974).

The wet flatwoods categories may be referred to as low pine flatwoods, pond pine flatwoods, cabbage palm/pine savannah, and flatwoods, based on the canopy species. Typical canopy plants include south Florida slash pine (*Pinus elliottii* var. *densa*), long-leaf pine (*Pinus palustris*), pond pine (*Pinus serotina*), and cabbage palms (*Sabal palmetto*) and may include sweet bay magnolia (*Magnolia virginiana*) or other hardwoods. In the wetter areas, small stands of pond pine compose the canopy. Subcanopy and understory woody vegetation (shrubs) include wax myrtle (*Myrica cerifera*), gallberry (*Ilex glabra*), titi (*Cyrilla racemosa*), saw palmetto (*Serenoa repens*), Carolina willow (*Salix caroliniana*), and other wetland shrubs. Groundcover includes spike rush (*Eleocharis* spp.), beak rush (*Rhynchospora* spp.), sedges (*Carex* spp. *Cyperus* spp. etc.), grasses (*Andropogon* spp., *Aristida* spp., other grasses), and pitcher plants (*Saracinia* spp.).

Although the wet flatwoods are characterized by a relatively open canopy of scattered pine trees or cabbage palms, the understory shrub and groundcover layers may differ depending on substrate, fire frequency, and hydrology. The understory may be dense, shrubby, and sparse herbaceous ground cover or sparse with dense ground cover of hydrophytic herbs and shrubs (FNAI-FDNR, 1990). For example, the understory in pine–cabbage palm and cabbage palm flatwoods may be dominated by saw palmetto and woody shrubs that tolerate a wide range of flooding and drought. Understory of the thinly scattered slash pine canopy is pineland three-awn (*Aristida stricta*), and wetland herbaceous species inhabit the groundcover.

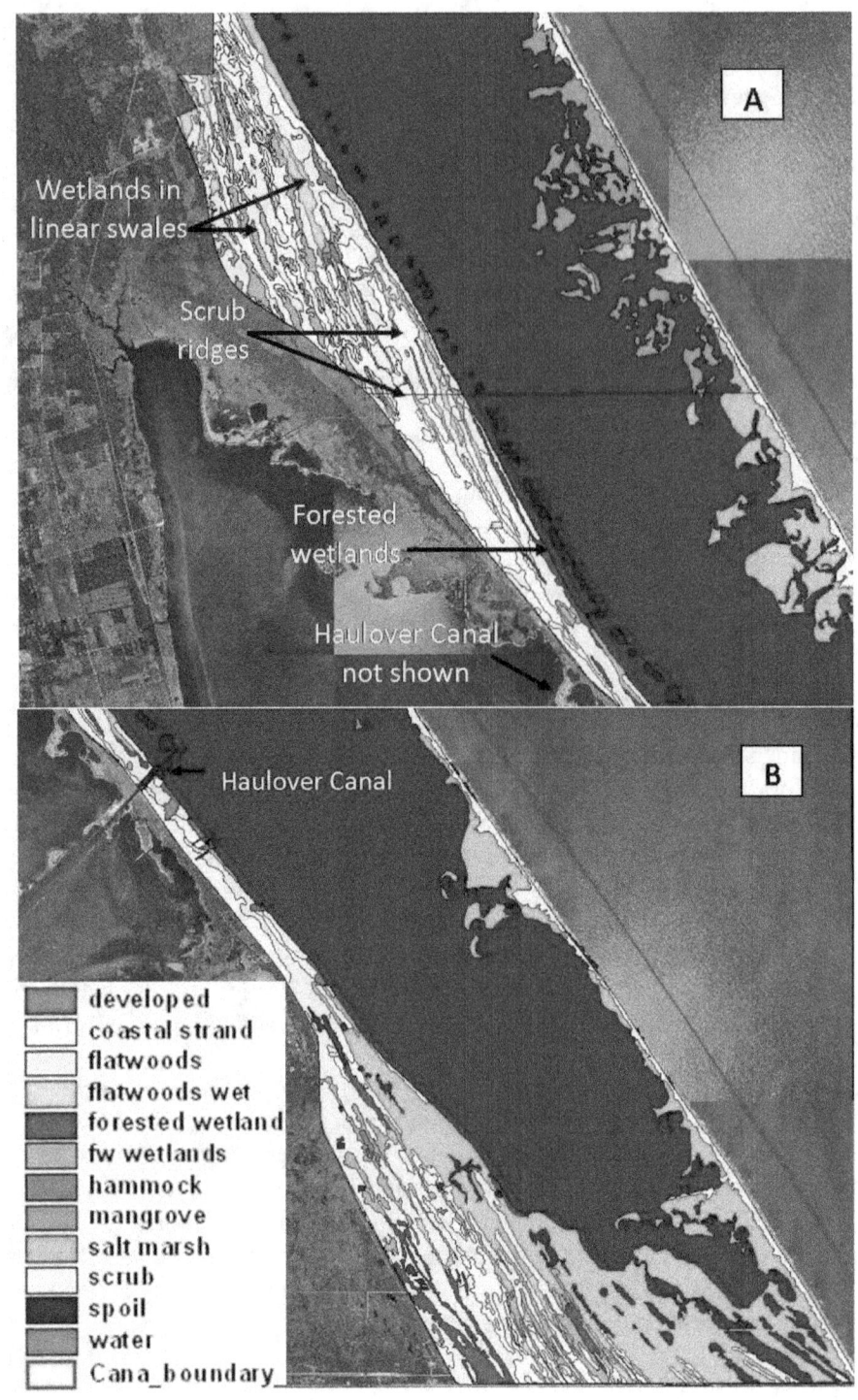

Figure 83. Natural plant communites of Canaveral National Seashore north and south. Panel A shows scrub ridges and wetlands on the north section. Panel B shows native plant communites from Haulover Canal and south.

Figure 84. Exposed coquina ledge south of Haulover Canal. Vegetation cover is disturbed cabbage palm (*Sabal palmetto*). Photo taken March 2010.

Fire is an important factor in wet flatwoods. Natural fires started by lightning probably occurred every 3–10 yrs and maintained the habitat in a stable and arrested climax association (Abrahamson and Hartnett, 1990: FNAI-FDNR, 1990). Human modifications—roads, ditches, and canals—disrupted the stability of the vast areas of pine flatwoods and associated depressional wetlands. Human disruption of the natural fire frequency will change the plant community structure and species composition. Figures 85 and 86 are examples of fire-suppressed flatwoods; tree density is greater than optimal, and all understory layers are overgrown. The flatwoods in Figure 86 show evidence of recent fire, although the burn interval, most likely, was much longer than the natural cycle and the natural hydro period was extended. The pine recruitment occurred during years with no fire in the drier habitats (Figure 85) and on swale edges (Figure 86), and returning prescribed fire to the hydric flatwoods caused high pine mortality (Menges and Marks, 2008).

Fire reduces competition from hardwoods, recycles nutrients, reduces fuel buildup, and creates soil conditions for seedling germination. Many pine flatwood species are adapted to and are maintained by frequent fires (Abrahamson and Hartnett, 1990). Without fire, some of these species will decline and species more adapted to long fire return intervals will replace them (Abrahamson and Hartnett, 1990).

Habitat Requirements of Wet Flatwoods
Wet pine flatwoods at CANA are estimated to cover 530 ac (215 ha) (Table 28), which vary from open canopies with a grassy understory to more closed slash pine canopies with oak and woody shrub understory. The open, wet flatwoods occur at the northwest corner of Mosquito Lagoon and in fewer sites on the western side of the lagoon, north of Haulover Canal, where the lower swales between the ridges are wide and the deeper marshes retain more water. Wetter areas in the central portion of the western side of Mosquito Lagoon north and south of Haulover Canal are characterized by saw palmetto dominating the understory along the linear swales. Woody shrubs and slash pine trees are colonizing some of the wet pine flatwoods in areas where the hydrology has been altered with canals and ditches from previous agricultural activity.

Figure 85. Overgrown pine flatwoods and scrubby flatwoods are a result of fire suppression. Photo taken April 15, 2010 from SR 3, Kennedy Parkway.

Altered hydrology, coupled with the lack of fire for long periods, allowed flatwoods to become more mesic, with oaks reaching canopy size.

In recent years, prescribed burns, fuels thinning, and pile burning have been used to manage the habitats; however, more fire is needed to maintain wet flatwoods and its associated species. Fuel reduction and a decrease in growth of woody understory species is necessary in the appropriate season and frequency to maintain wet habitats. Prescribed fire goals are to reduce hazardous fuels and to promote ecosystem sustainability (NPS, 2006). Wildfires are managed for resource values, life, and property. Naturally ignited and human-ignited wildland fires are appropriate management tools that allow fire to perform its natural role in the environment (NPS, 2006).

Wildlife of the Wet Flatwoods
Typical animals in pinewood understory and ground cover include oak toads, cricket frogs, chorus frogs, black racers, yellow rat snakes, diamondback rattlesnakes, and pygmy rattlesnakes. Red-shouldered hawks and bobwhite birds are commonly observed. Mammals of the flatwoods include opossum, cottontail rabbit, cotton rat, cotton mouse, raccoon, striped skunk, bobcat, and white-tailed deer (FNAI-FDNR, 1990).

Transitional and Embedded Wetlands
Freshwater Marsh
The 910 ac (368 ha) of freshwater marsh category includes freshwater marshes, wet prairie, inland ponds and sloughs, and emergent aquatic vegetation (Table 28). The marshes are

Figure 86. Swale margin (background) with a high density of pines and pine mortality from prescribed fire. Pines colonized during a long period of infrequent fire and decreased hydrology. Photo taken March 2010 from trail east of Kennedy Parkway.

characterized as herbaceous or shrubby wetland in a relatively large or irregular basin (FNAI-FDNR, 1990). The majority of marshes at CANA are more similar in shape to broad shallow channels of freshwater sloughs without flowing water. The vegetation is composed of herbaceous reeds, grasses, broad-leaved species, and wetland woody shrubs. An example of a wet prairie embedded in a swale of pine flatwoods is shown in Figure 87.

Marshes exist in interdunal, grassy swales that lie between former dune ridges (Figure 88) and are seasonally flooded (MINWR, 2008). Species structure is primarily herbaceous and graminoid species that may be divided into zones based on water depth and substrate. A mixture of grasses may grow on the shallow perimeter and monocultures of various herbaceous species grow in deeper organic depressions and areas of open water. Species composition is dependent on soils, accumulated organic materials and drainage patterns.

In the northern portion of the park in Volusia County and on the western side of Mosquito Lagoon, the soils of linear marshes are the Pompano–Placid complex, nearly level poorly-drained soils in flatwood depressions. Some areas with the Pompano–Placid complex may also be forested with mixed hardwoods. In summer and fall, water is less than 6 inches above the soil surface and is frequently covered with 10 inches of water during the wet season (USDA, 1980).

Figure 87. An example of a wet prairie embedded in a swale with adjacent pine flatwoods. Photo taken April 15, 2010 in north section of CANA.

Vegetation of Freshwater Marsh
Plant species in the freshwater marshes include marsh pink, sand cordgrass, sawgrass (*Cladium jamaicense*), broom sedge (*Andropogon* spp.), and other species of grasses, sedges, and rushes. Plants in the deeper areas with open water may include fragrant water lily (*Nymphaea odorata*), large emergent herbs, and floating aquatic plants. Wet prairie species include spikerush (*Eleocharis and Rhynchospora* spp.), and maidencane (*Panicum hemitomon*), and spike rush (*Rhynchospora* spp.). Shrubs that colonize the perimeters include coastal plain willow (*Salix caroliniana*), buttonbush (*Cephalanthus occidentalis*), and elderberry (*Sambucus caroliniana*). The largest areas of freshwater marsh occur on other soil types in the portion of CANA that is north of Haulover Canal. An example can be seen east of the main park entrance in Figure 89.

The larger freshwater marshes in the park are in good condition, as shown in Figure 90. Some marshes are invaded by willow and red maple (*Acer rubrum*) along the extensive edges due to a prolonged absence of fire (NPS, 2010b). Many of the smaller, shallow marshes have converted to willow thickets, as observed along the roadsides that cross from east to west through the linear marshes. Feral hogs are a serious threat to wetlands and the amphibian habitat. They destroy the vegetation of freshwater marshes and substrate as they root in the moist organic soil horizon for food. Their activity increases during droughts (Seigel and Pike, 2003; MINWR, 2008).

Figure 88. Freshwater marsh embedded in swale. Wet flatwoods in the dune–swale transition marked on photo. Photo taken April 15, 2010.

Habitat Requirements of Freshwater Marsh

In marshes, ground fires from lightning strikes occur every 1–5 yrs, normally in late spring when the surface is dry. Grasses, such as sawgrass, and herbs in freshwater marshes, may carry wildfire over water. In extreme droughts when the peat dries out, devastating muck fires may consume the soil lowering the ground surface and creating more open water. Where fire is infrequent, thickets of woody shrub buttonbush and coastal plain willow may colonize the water edges (FNAI-FDNR, 1990).

Fire or removal of woody vegetation is required to return the marshes to open grassy areas. Roads and ditches that cut through these linear wetlands stop the natural drainage patterns and unfavorably change the species composition. Natural drainage or hydration should be restored to improve the quality of the wetlands; otherwise, it is likely that the succession will continue from shrub to trees, as has occurred in CANA (Figure 91).

Wildlife of Freshwater Marsh

The linear wetland marshes are important habitat for reptiles, including American alligator (*Alligator mississippiensis*), Florida redbelly turtle (*Pseudemys nelsoni*), and Florida banded water snake (*Nerodia fasciata pictiventris*); amphibians, including two-toed amphiuma (*Amphiuma means*), lesser siren (*Siren intermedia*), greater siren (*Siren lacertina*), southern cricket frog (*Acris gryllus*), leopard frog (*Rana sphenocephala*) (Figure 92), and pig frog (*Rana grylio*); and for birds that feed on them (Seigel and Pike, 2003; Seigel and Crabill, 2006; Byrne et al., 2010; FNAI, 2010). Birds that use the marshes include great blue heron (*Ardea herodias*), great egret (*Ardea alba*), snowy egret (*Egretta thula*), little blue heron (*Egretta caerulea*), tricolored heron (*Egretta tricolor*), green heron (*Butorides virescens*), bald eagle (*Haliaeetus*

Figure 89. Expanse of sawgrass marsh bordered by pockets of mixed hardwoods in the northern portion of Canaveral National Seashore. Photo taken March 2010 from Kennedy Parkway.

Figure 90. Freshwater marsh in good condition located in the northern portion of Canaveral National Seashore embedded in swale. Photo taken April 15, 2010.

Figure 91. Freshwater marsh displacement by shrub and mixed hardwood succeession in a shallow swale in the northern portion of Canaveral National Seashore. Photo taken April 15, 2010.

leucocephalus), northern harrier (*Circus cyaneus*), purple gallinule (*Porphyrio martinica*), and Florida sandhill crane (*Grus canadensis pratensis*) (FNAI-FDNR, 1990, FNAI, 2010).

Forested Wetland or Hydric Hammocks

The freshwater forested wetlands or hydric hammocks occupy 445 ac (180 ha) at CANA (Table 27; Figure 93). The term hammock generally refers to a closed canopy forest surrounded or embedded in another vegetation type (Davis, 1943) and may be misleading unless the hydric is applied. Wetland forests occur on loamy subsoil over hard limestone of low marine terraces. The soil complex is nearly level, with poorly drained sandy soils and loam below (USDA, 1974).

Considerable organic material occurs in the sand substrate, which is generally saturated. The soils are inundated for short periods following heavy rains. The normal hydroperiod is approximately 60 days/yr. Hydric hammocks rarely burn because of the saturated soils and the sparse herbaceous ground cover (FNAI-FDNR, 1990). Hydric hammocks may have been grassy swales, but altered hydrology and fire exclusion provided conditions favorable for hardwood colonization (MINW 2008). The largest of three hydric hammocks, at 240 ac (97 ha), occurs in the southern portion of CANA in long, linear depressions adjacent to flatwoods. A small area with a drainage ditch can be seen just outside the park entrance on the southern boundary. Few forested wetlands exist in the northern portion of CANA in Volusia County and near the northern boundary of Brevard County; most have been cleared and planted with citrus while the abandoned citrus groves are now cabbage palms (USDA, 1980).

Figure 92. Leopard frog (*Rana sphenocephala*).

Figure 93. Forested wetland or hydric hammock on north section of Canaveral National Seashore. Disturbance from road cut shown in Figure 94.

The hydric hammock canopy is characterized as a well-developed hardwood and cabbage palm forest, and the understory may be variable (FNAI-FDNR, 1990). The structure of these closed canopy forests may have an open, sparse understory or be multilayered, with a canopy, sub-canopy, understory, and sparse groundcover. The canopy may vary and may include live oak (*Quercus virginiana*), laurel oak (*Q. laurifolia*), red maple, other hardwoods, and cabbage palm. The mid-story or sub-canopy trees include southern red cedar (*Juniperus silicicola*), redbay (*Persea borbonia*), southern magnolia (*Magnolia grandiflora* and *M. virginiana*), hackberry (*Celtis laevigata*), and pignut hickory (*Carya glabra*). Understory small trees and shrubs may include tropical species such as nakedwood (*Myrsianthes fragrans*), marlberry (*Ardisia escallonioides*), stoppers (*Eugenia* spp.), and yaupon holly (*Ilex vomitoria*) (FNAI-FDNR, 1990; Schmalzer et al., 2002). The sparse groundcover is typically ferns (*Thelypteris* spp., *Woodwardia* spp.), vines (*Smilax* spp.), a few grasses (e.g., *Panicum hemitomon*) and shade tolerant wetland herbs (FNAI-FDNR, 1990). Several species of rare orchids, bromeliads (*Tillandsia* spp.), and epiphytic ferns may be observed growing on the limbs of the canopy trees, particularly on large live oaks http://www.nps.gov/cana/naturescience/ upload/Forests.pdf.

Roads and drainage near the large hydric hammocks have impacted this smaller habitat at CANA (Figure 94). Excavation of adjacent flatwoods between two linear hydric hammocks and a former citrus grove, along with roads and ditches have affected the hydrology (Figure 95). Ditches along the edge of the road contain water, but as the habitat becomes more mesic, other portions of the hydric hammocks were dry and are being colonized by cabbage palms (Figure 96).

Habitat Requirements of Forested Wetlands
Restoration of the hydrology to saturate soils for longer periods may prevent further colonization by mesic species such as cabbage palms and live oaks. Removal and restoration of the abandoned citrus groves will benefit the hydric hammock and adjacent flatwoods communities

Wildlife of Forested Wetlands
Animals of the hydric hammocks include cricket frog, pig frogs, leopard frogs, tree frogs (*Hyla* sp.), and cottonmouth (*Agkistrodon piscivorus*), and pygmy rattlesnakes (*Sistrurus miliarius*). Mammals include woodrats (*Neotoma* sp.), rice rats (*Oryzomys palustris*), cotton mice (*Peromyscus gossypinus*), raccoons (*Procyon lotor*), and bobcats (*Lynx rufus*). Birds that use or live in these hammocks are pileated woodpeckers (*Dryocopus pileatus*), screech owls (*Megascops* sp.), barred owls (*Strix varia*), and great horned owls (*Bubo virginianus*).

Prairie Hammocks – Cabbage Palm Hammocks
Hammocks, also known as prairie hammocks or cabbage palm hammocks, occupy 128 ac (52 ha) at CANA. Prairie hammocks occur on slight elevation changes in flat terrain. They are a cluster of tall cabbage palms and live oaks in the middle and on the borders of wet prairie or marsh communities (Figure 97). Saw palmettos may ring the perimeter of the clusters of hammocks in wet areas. Generally, the understory is open although tropical species may be present (FNAI-FDNR, 1990).

Prairie hammocks are normally on flat substrates with sand over marl or limestone (FNAI-FDNR, 1990). During high water, they may flood but are rarely under water more than several weeks. At CANA, prairie hammocks are frequently along the edges of impoundments on more or

Figure 94. Forested wetlands (hydric hammock) were dry. As the habitat becomes more mesic, it will be colonized by cabbage palms (*Sabal palmetto*) (Figure 96). An access road interrupts the natural linear feature of the forest. Marked on photo are water-filled ruts in the lowest elevation (swale) and the ridge crest. Photo from the interior of north section of Canaveral National Seashore.

Figure 95. Forested wetland that previously grew citrus is now disturbed. Located in the north section of Canaveral National Seashore. Photo taken April 15, 2010.

Figure 96. Forested wetland (hydric hammock) was dry and being colonized by cabbage palms (*Sabal palmetto*) as the habitat becomes more mesic. Located in the north section of Canaveral National Seashore. Photo taken April 15, 2010.

less saturated soils. Drainage dries out the soils and the vegetation changes toward mesic oak/palm hammock (MINWR, 2008).

The canopy is dominated by cabbage palms and live oak, laurel oak, and magnolia; water oak may be included in the canopy or understory. Shrubs found in prairie hammocks are wax myrtle, coastal plain willow, and elderberry. Tropical species that may occur include stoppers, marlberry, and pigeon plum (*Cocoloba diversifolia*). Herbaceous species include grape vine (*Vitis* spp.), poison ivy (*Toxicodendron radicans*), orchids, and wildflowers.

Drier sites may occasionally burn with light ground fires, but diverse hammocks rarely burn (Figure 98). Hammocks with thick shrub layers can be severely damaged by canopy fires. Prairie hammocks may grade into hydric hammocks or shell mounds.

Prairie hammocks have been affected by hydrological alterations and invasive exotic pest plants. To keep desirable plants in good condition, the hydrology needs to be maintained. In some locations, hogs damage the soil surface and the management of feral hogs and removal of pest plants is an ongoing endeavor by CANA and MINWR. In the 2008 management plan, MINWR's approach to land management established goals and objectives for exotic plant and feral hog removal. Removal and eradication of exotics were prioritized for melaleuca (*Melaleuca quinquenervia*) and Brazilian pepper (*Schinus terebinthifolius*) treatment has begun in disturbed locations (MINWR, 2008; John Stiner, personal communication, January 7, 2011).

Wildlife of Prairie Hammocks
Prairie hammocks are excellent wildlife habitat for small mammals and reptiles. Birds, such as warblers and hawks, use the shrubs and trees for food and resting (Barkazi, 2006). Animals

Figure 97. Example of a prairie hammock with a small creek in center. Brazilian pepper (*Schinus terebinthifolius*) visible in understory.

Figure 98. Prairie hammock with fire scars on the cabbage palms (*Sabal palmetto*). Ditch in the foreground runs parallel to road. Shrub wetlands in the background are on transition edge of hammock.

include box turtle (*Terrapene carolina*), southeastern five-lined skink (*Eumeces inexpectatus*), black racer (*Coluber constrictor*), and shrews (*Blarina* spp.) and rodents (*Peromyscus* spp).

Disturbed Wetlands

Disturbed wetlands include freshwater marshes and forested wetlands as well as prairie hammocks and wet flatwoods. Based on the NPS 2003 Land Cover data, 596 ac (241 ha) of CANA are disturbed wetlands. The primary causes of disturbance are drainage, soil disturbance, and invasion by non-native plants and animals (Figure 99). In 2006, 17 Category I and II plants were management concerns, invading wetlands, uplands, and disturbed sites (FLEPPC, 2005 at http://www.fleppc.org/list/list.htm MINWR, 2008).

Figure 99. Soil disturbance on the perimeter of a freshwater marsh caused by rooting feral hogs and colonization by invasive species.

Trends

A comparison of the data for CANA using land-use data, soils data, and Duncan et al. (2004) showed similarities in the number of acres for upland and wetland communities (Table 27), and, in a few instances (flatwoods, scrub, and hammock), large differences in acreages. Some of the differences are due to the grouping of land-use categories. Use of the GIS soil layer to compare with land cover data from 1943, 1990, and 2003 results in an overestimate of pine flatwood acres because habitat disturbed by agriculture, silviculture, and invasion of exotic species is not included in any soil layers.

The size in acreage of freshwater wetland communities is changing over time. The results of the analysis using the four GIS layers and preliminary field reconnaissance to ground-truth wetland conditions indicate that wetlands are diminishing and being replaced by upland conditions. Wet flatwoods between the wetlands and the upland flatwoods and scrub are being constricted as the perimeters are colonized by upland species because of drainage and past agriculture practices. Upland or mesic hammocks have increased over time from an estimated 1,253 ac to 2,777 ac (507 ha to 1,124 ha) based on comparisons of Duncan et al. (2004) and NPS 2003 land use.

The 128 ac (52 ha) of wetland prairie hammocks (Tables 19 and 20) in the soil data may have been included in the larger acreages for hammocks in Duncan et al. (2004) and also the NPS 2003 land cover GIS layer. Field observations show the size of mesic and hydric hammocks expanding as cabbage palms are expanding downhill into the freshwater marsh and uphill into the flatwoods, forming wide bands of hammocks. Cabbage palms are also colonizing disturbed areas that were previously citrus or other agriculture lands.

Freshwater marshes show decreases from 1,324 ac (536 ha) in 1943 to 494 ac (200 ha) in 1990 in the Duncan et al. (2004) study. The 2003 GIS data show fewer acres (378 ac; 153 ha)) of freshwater marsh on CANA. If 596 ac (241 ha) of disturbed freshwater marsh (Tables 19 and 20) are added to 378 ac (153 ha) of freshwater marsh, the total of potential freshwater marsh is 974 ac (394 ha). The soil data indicate 910 ac (368 ha) of freshwater marsh in Tables 19 and 20, which is consistent with the previous studies. Field observations confirm the presence of disturbed marsh as predominantly linear systems and small isolated herbaceous wetlands that are being colonized by willows and woody shrubs. CANA and MINWR are working to remove woody shrubs from marshes to restore marshes, particularly in the joint-managed area (MINWR 2008, John Stiner, personal communication, January 7, 2011).

Acreages for forested wetlands varied by almost 700 ac (283 ha) between 1943 and 1990, although all are less than 1,000 ac (405 ha) (Table 27) or less than 5% of the 19,796 ac (8,011 ha) of CANA terrestrial communities. The trend in the forested wetlands shows an increase from 1943 to 1990, yet the land-use data of 2003 show only 305 ac (123 ha) at CANA and the soils data indicate 445 ac (180 ha). Discrepancies may be accounted for by the change in species composition in hydric and mesic closed-canopy forests because of drainage and lack of fire over a long time. Drainage in the canals and ditches through the wet sites provide drier conditions for mesic species to colonize. Additionally, the upland hammocks appear to be increasing in size becoming more mesic in nature with overlapping species composition (Table 27). Although hammocks do not burn often, fire will move through these closed-canopy forests during drought years. Evidence of fire is apparent in many of the upland and forested wetlands.

Geographic Information System

Organization of GIS Resources

National Park Service Geographical Information System (GIS) datasets, along with all other types of data held by the NPS, can be accessed through the Integrated Resource Management Aplications (IRMA) Portal at https://irma.nps.gov/App/Portal/Home. Currently, full access to data is limited to NPS users accessing the site from the NPS domain network. A limited number of records are available to partners and the general public. In addition to geospatial data, reports, publications, articles, and gray literature related to NPS holdings are available from IRMA. The Tools tab on the home page leads the user to information and tools on how to manage and apply NPS data.

The GIS coverages for CANA were obtained from NPS and other federal and state resources. Table 29 lists the thematic GIS coverage for CANA and the source of the data. The GIS thematic coverage of most concern for the CANA Natural Resources Inventory are found in the Air and Climate, Geology and Soils, Water, and Landscapes categories. A large amount of GIS coverages from other federal and state sources were assembled for this project. New vegetation GIS themes were developed as part of this project; the wetlands vegetation GIS coverage was developed especially for this project (Table 29). All of the GIS themes assembled for this project include metadata files so the user can identify the data sources and geographic coordinate system when combining the various themes into a working project in ArcView or ArcGIS. This report and the geospatial data are available in IRMA at: https://irma.nps.gov/App/Portal/Home.

Table 29. Thematic GIS coverages for the Canaveral National Seashore.

Theme Type	File Name	Originator/ Agency	Coordinate System	File Availability
Digital Imagery	*.sid	NPS	UTM	IRMA
Digital Imagery	*.sid	USGS	UTM/FL St Pl	FDEP
Digital Imagery	*.sid	FDOT	UTM	FDOT
State Geological Map	Geology_Stratigraphy	FGS	Albers	FDEP
Digital Geologic Map	canamafa_gdb.*	NPS	UTM	IRMA
Landcover	Landcover2003	NPS-CANA	UTM	CANA
Soils	Cana_soils_bounds	NPS	UTM	IRMA
Vegetation		FIT/NPS	UTM	FIT/CANA
Wetlands/seagrass	Wetlands_Brevard Wetlands_Volusia	SJRWMD	UTM	SJRWMD
Water/hydrography	Wq_station.*	EPA/SJRWMD	UTM	IRMA/EPA STORET
Shoreline Changes	Shorelines.*	USGS	UTM	USGS
Shoreline Changes	*.DWG	FDEP	FL St. Plane	FDEP

Digital Imagery and Maps

Baseline data for CANA includes recent aerial imagery and indexes that show imagery coverage with respect to USGS 7.5 minute quadrangle maps. Metadata is provided for the maps and images in the form of Extensible Markup Language (xml) files, which adhere to the Federal Geographic Data Committee (FGDC) Content Standard for Digital Geospatial Metadata. It is important to examine these files to determine the source, data, and projection of the aerial images and maps. The aerial imagery provided in IRMA, like many other GIS layers related to CANA, is in the Universal Transverse Mercator Projection (UTM) on the North American Datum of 1983 (NAD83). The geographic extent of the images is equivalent to a quarter-quadrangle, thus the term digital orthographic quarter quadrangle (DOQQ) is used to describe the images.

Other sets of aerial orthographic images that cover the CANA region were obtained from FDOT and FDEP. The FDOT images have a resolution of approximately 1 ft (0.3 m), and the FDEP images include the USGS DOQQ images taken between 1995 and 2004 with a resolution of 3.3 ft (1 m). All of the digital imagery is available in the Mr SID format that includes layers of data (pyramid layers), allowing for rapid viewing and manipulation of these large image files. The images found on the FDEP Map Server (http://data.labins.org) are also available in the Florida State Plane and Albers projections.

Thematic coverage in the form of vector-based map themes includes information derived from the USGS 7.5 minute quadrangle maps of the area. This information is used to locate park boundaries relative to features such as streams and roads. However, the resolution of detail is low compared to the original USGS maps.

Water
This data set contains small-scale, base GIS data layers compiled by the NPS service-wide Inventory and Monitoring Program and Water Resources Division for use in a Baseline Water Quality Data Inventory and Analysis Report that was prepared for the park. The report presents the results of surface water quality data retrievals for the park from six of the United States EPA's national databases: (1) Storage and Retrieval (STORET) water quality database management system, (2) River Reach File (RF3) Hydrography, (3) Industrial Facilities Discharges, (4) Drinking Water Supplies, (5) Water Gages, and (6) Water Impoundments. The small-scale GIS data layers were used to prepare the maps included in a summary report (NPS, 2005) that depicts the locations of water quality monitoring stations, industrial discharges, drinking intakes, water gages, and water impoundments. The data layers included in the maps and this dataset vary depending on availability, but generally include roads, hydrography, political boundaries, USGS 7.5 minute quadrangle outlines, hydrologic units, trails, and others as appropriate. The scales of each layer vary depending on the data source but are generally 1:100,000. Much of the data included in the EPA's STORET was derived from the lagoon-wide monitoring program conducted by SJRWMD between 1997–2004.

Landcover
The 2003 land cover map is an update of the 2000 land cover map, with refined categorization, an increased extent, and the delineation of new landscape features identified with high-resolution imagery acquired during December 2003 and site-specific ground knowledge. The classification scheme is partly derived from the Florida Land Use, Cover and Forms Classification System (FLUCFCS), with site specific descriptions of class composition from Duncan et al. (2004). A spreadsheet (lc03_class_syst.xls) relates lc03 classes to FLUCFCS, the USGS classification codes, and the National Vegetation Classification System. Source data includes land cover interpretation from SJRWMD, plannimetrics from Space Gateway Support, and LIDAR data (for height profiles), which exists as shapes and grids.

The 2003 land cover map describes the type and extent of anthropogenic and natural features in sufficient detail to be ecologically meaningful and may be used to support natural resource management efforts on a landscape scale. Land cover classes consider species composition and structure. Additional queries of cover type classes may be required to identify specific habitats of interest. The land cover map may not identify features (e.g., wetlands) at a scale suitable for jurisdictional delineation or may not mitigate assessments. The recommended scale for on-screen viewing and hardcopy production is 1:12,000 or smaller.

The 2003 land cover map consists of 26,350 polygons and identifies features generally equal to or less than a minimum area of 1.2 ac (0.5 ha) and a minimum width of 98 ft (30 m). Edge delineation for gross land cover types (e.g., water/land, herbaceous/woody, vegetation/anthropogenic) is generally less than 16 ft (5 m). Delineation within ecotones where the transition between cover types is more gradual (e.g., wetland scrub/upland scrub) is generally within 98 ft (30 m).

Soils

The metadata description of the soils GIS coverage within CANA is minimal. The thematic inventory was developed largely from the NRCS soils survey conducted in 2006 and Brevard and Volusia County Soil Surveys of 1974 and 1977. The GIS thematic coverage of soil types within CANA appears to have been developed by a cooperative agreement between the NPS and NRCS. According to the metadata file included with the soils map, the horizontal datum is North American 1983 within the UTM Zone17N projection. The map units are in meters to match most of the other GIS coverage for CANA.

Terrestrial Vegetation

At the beginning of this project, there was no comprehensive inventory of terrestrial vegetation systems within CANA, although some information on wetland vegetation is available in the wetland thematic GIS coverage available from SJRWMD. An inventory was developed largely from the NRCS soils survey (2003, 2006), Brevard and Volusia County Soil Surveys (1974 and 1977), aerial imagery, and a series of site visits for ground-truthing. The results of the inventory are included in the section on terrestrial vegetation of this report.

Vegetation themes that have been developed to depict CANA's freshwater wetland communities include pine flatwoods and associated transitional wetlands embedded in the dune and swale topography. When combined, these communities occupy almost 2,000 ac (809 ha) for about 3.4% of the approximately 58,000 ac (23,470 ha) in CANA. These freshwater wetlands of the ridge and swale topography consist of a series of long, narrow, moderately drained sand ridges separated by poorly drained troughs or swales that are former shoreline ridges. The ridges are nearly parallel to the present shoreline, with elevation ranges from sea level to above 20 ft (6.1 m) on the top of dune ridges. The wet flatwoods in this section were thematically separated from the mesic flatwoods, using the descriptions from the NRCS Soil Survey (2006) and Brevard and Volusia County Soil Surveys (1974 and 1977).

Seagrasses

The GIS dataset contains the Mosquito Lagoon Aquatic Preserve (MLAP) in the state of Florida, which was originally obtained from the Aquatic Preserves dataset maintained by the Office of Coastal and Aquatic Managed Areas. The existing shapefile of the MLAP boundary in the state of Florida was modified to include only the MLAP of the IRL. The inclusion of the IRL Aquatic Preserve boundaries was done by selecting the MLAP from a dataset containing the IRL Aquatic Preserves boundaries and exporting the data as a separate shapefile. The original data is provided "as is." Users of the seagrass dataset may contact the Indian River Lagoon Aquatic Preserve's FDEP at 3300 Lewis Street, Ft. Pierce, FL 34981 for more information.

Digital Geological Map
In the digital geologic map of CANA and vicinity, Florida is composed of GIS data layers that include ArcMap 9.2 layer (.LYR) files, two ancillary GIS tables, a Windows Help File along with ancillary map text, figures and tables, an FGDC metadata record, and a 9.2 ArcMap (.MXD) map document that serves as a project file to display the digital map in 9.2 ArcGIS. The data were completed as a component of the Geologic Resource Evaluation (GRE) program, an NPS Inventory and Monitoring (I&M) program that is administered by the NPS Geologic Resources Division. Detailed information concerning the sources used and their contribution the GRE product are listed in the Source Citation sections of the metadata record that is associated with the digital map. The development of the digital map is described in Parkinson and Schaub (2007). A further discussion of geological features within the CANA boundaries is provided in the Geological Resources section of this report.

Assessment of Threats and Stressors

CANA is located within a two-hour drive from some of Florida's most populous counties—Orange, Seminole, Volusia, and Brevard—that experienced population growth between 15% and 24% from 2000–2008. According to the origins of boat registrations (Sidman et al., 2007) residents of these counties also contribute to concentrated boating activity in the IRL system and in Mosquito Lagoon. Florida ranks first in the nation in boating activity, with more than one million registered recreational boats (FDEP, 2009). The growth in population is concomitant with increased development in east Central Florida and is demonstrated in the number of medium- and high-density residential and open land-use changes in the Edgewater–New Smyrna Beach area. The small city of Oak Hill is in the process of updating the city comprehensive plan, and it is likely to reflect the growth pressures of the last 10 yrs.

Water quality in the lagoon is important and affects the health and well being of other natural resources in the park. In the early 1990s, CANA water quality was described as generally good, but at the time, an elevation in turbidity, color, TSS, and Chl-a, especially near population centers, was documented (Woodward-Clyde Consultants, 1994d,e). At the time, the authors suggested elevated nitrogen levels, bacterial contamination, and trace metal contamination may be the main threats to the IRL system. The sources of contamination come from point and nonpoint sources and include stormwater runoff, overflow from sewage treatment systems unable to handle the volume of sewage, commercial and industrial releases, septic tank leachate, and fertilizer and pesticide applications.

FDEP (2010) states that nutrient loadings of TN and TP concentrations characteristic during 2004–2008 represent reasonable levels for maintaining good water quality. According to FDEP (2010), general water quality models support their assessment that Mosquito Lagoon is not nutrient impaired and is nitrogen limited in the northern Mosquito Lagoon. There is an increasing gradient of phosphorous limitation in CANA waters, especially south of Haulover Canal (FDEP, 2010a).

Wastewater treatment plants (WWTP) in the cities of New Smyrna Beach and Edgewater periodically discharge water to the Mosquito Lagoon. New Smyrna Beach increased reuse of treated waste water to 97%, whereas the City of Edgewater has decreased reuse somewhat to 72% (Personal Communication, Dave Hoover, Director of Water Resources, Utilities Commission of New Smyrna Beach, 2010; Personal communication, Dennis Norman, Superintendent, Edgewater Wastewater Treatment, 2010). Phosphorus (P) from sources such as septic tank leachate and residential fertilizer applications can move through the coarse, saturated, sandy soils in the watershed. Since Mosquito Lagoon is P limited, even small additions can be detrimental and may increase biotic production.

Nutrient levels may vary seasonally and spatially in the IRL system and within the confines of Mosquito Lagoon. Estimates of WWTP external nutrient loading to Mosquito Lagoon made by FDEP (2010) of Total N and Total P were 2.6% and 4.4% for ML 2 (central Mosquito Lagoon) and 6.5% and 6.6% for ML 1 (north Mosquito Lagoon). Increases in NH_4 and NO_3 nutrients were evident from analysis of 1983–2004 data; however, between 2004 and 2008, these nutrients declined slightly.

Occasionally, higher concentrations of TP (1970–2007) may be found near Oak Hill, north of the lagoon. More often than not, there is no significant difference ($p \leq 0.05$) in TP concentrations from north to south, due to the sporadic nature of data collection and the gaps in available data from stations IRLV17 and IRLML02. It is difficult to characterize the apparent anomalies with any certainty.

Kroenig (2008) found that pesticide monitoring in the lagoon has likely focused on the wrong compounds. The majority of the pesticide data in the literature for CANA concerns chemical agents that generally have not been in use since the 1990s, and only five compounds used as recently as 2004. Additionally, given the typically hydrophobic nature of pesticide compounds, it is unlikely that historical use presents a serious threat to water quality, as the compounds would likely have partitioned into the sediment. Weed killers and pesticides, 2,4-D dichlorprop, endosulfan, lindane, and methoxychlor have been used in the basin between 1990 and 2004, and monitoring efforts of these compounds should be a priority for resource managers.

The threats and stressors of the diverse natural systems and inhabitants of the coastal ocean, beach, and lagoon in CANA are commonly loss of habitat, degradation of the habitat, disease, and parasites that may be accelerated by degradation of the environment, and the impaired health of target species. The introduction of non-native plants and animals has further damaged the habitat. The potential threat of climate change may accentuate the threats to habitats and species.

The threats and stressors to the resources of CANA waters are related to the pressures exerted by anthropogenic alterations to the environment. The data summaries of the most significant threats to water quality and the natural terrestrial and aquatic communities are provided in Table 30. In Table 31, threats and stressors are listed for each category of resource along with status of the threat and knowledge of the threat/stressor.

Table 30. Summaries of data and sources of significant threats and stressors of Canaveral National Seashore (CANA) resources.

GEOLOGICAL RESOURCE SUMMARY

METRIC	CONDITION / DESCRIPTION	DATA SUMMARIES / SELECTED REFERENCES
Shoreline and barrier island stability	Historically Stable or accreting	USGS,2005, Schaub, 2002, Soloman et al., 2007
	The ocean shoreline along CANA has been historically stable or accreting in most areas according to the long-term analysis by the USGS. This 150-year period has included about 1 ft of sea level rise. However, the potential response of the CANA ocean shoreline and integrity of the barrier island superstructure has not been considered with respect to the potential for accelerated sea level rise. More frequent surveys at least on an annual basis are required to track the condition of the shoreline and sedimentary environments linked to shoreline position	Figure 31. Historical shorelines from 1851–2000 are marked with a colored line. Black: 1999-2000, brown: 1967-1980, blue: 1923-1930, yellow: 1851-1884 (Morton and Miller, 2005).
Marsh Substrate Area	Long-term trends unknown	(SJRWMS GIS Land-use Coverage 1973, 1995, 2000, 2004)
	Development of wetlands depends on the availability of stable substrates of sandy, silt and clay mixtures. Vegetated flats can maintain surface area and expand with rising sea level as long as adequate sediment supply is available. The potential acceleration of sea level rise could cause estuarine wetlands to fragment and decrease in area. No effort has been made to map both vegetated and unvegetated intertidal surfaces on the ML over time. A simple comparison of salt marsh and mangrove wetlands shows an increase in area. However, this does not necessarily indicate expansion of sediment substrate available for wetlands. Historical and ongoing accounting from aerial imagery is required.	<table><tr><th>Wetland Type</th><th>1995 (Acres)</th><th>2004 (Acres)</th><th>Change</th></tr><tr><td>Salt Marsh</td><td>3589.6</td><td>38.32</td><td>7.10%</td></tr><tr><td>Mangrove</td><td>470.15</td><td>513.04</td><td>9.10%</td></tr></table>

Table 30. Summaries of data and sources of significant threats and stressors of Canaveral National Seashore (CANA) resources (continued).

GEOLOGICAL RESOURCE SUMMARY

METRIC	CONDITION / DESCRIPTION	DATA SUMMARIES / SELECTED REFERENCES
Quality of Groundwater Aquifers	Unknown– few monitoring wells Groundwater interaction with the surface waters of the Mosquito Lagoon has not been investigated on a regional basis. In addition, groundwater quality of the surficial and Floridan Aquifers has not been extensively investigated within CANA. Only in recent years has the potential for surficial aquifer pollution from septic tanks been considered. Groundwater monitoring occupied by the SJRWMD includes virtually no wells within CANA.	Data from Toth 1987; Belanger et al., 1997; Cable et al. 2004; Pandit et al., 2010. Figure 32. Groundwater limits bounding Mosquito Lagoon (SJRWMD GIS data).

Table 30. Summaries of data and sources of significant threats and stressors of Canaveral National Seashore (CANA) resources (continued).

METRIC	CONDITION / DESCRIPTION	MOSQUITO LAGOON SURFACE WATER RESOURCE DATA SUMMARY / DATA SUMMARIES / SELECTED REFERENCES
Dissolved Oxygen	Poor. Does not meet FDEP Class II criteria for surface water. Days with complete DO records at the SECN monitoring station (wet season) from 2005–2008, showed 68% of DO measurements were <4.0 mg/L and 40% of the days DO averaged <5.0 mg/L.	FAC 62-302.530; Provancha et al., 1992; Sigua et al., 2000; Hall et al., 2001

NUMBER AND PERCENT OF DAYS WITH MEAN DISSOLVED OXYGEN LESS THAN 5.0 mg/L AT THE SECN MONITORING STATION, CANAVERAL NATIONAL SEASHORE
(JULY 2005 – OCTOBER 2008)

Years	Days with Complete DO Records	Total Days with Mean DO < 5.0 mg/L (n=)	(%)
2005[1]	67	12	18
2006[2]	22	15	68
2007[3]	153	101	66
2008[4]	147	27	18
2005–2008	389	155	40

1. Data not available from 5/1/2005 – 7/24/2005 and 10/4/2005 – 10/31/2005
2. Data not available from 5/1/2006 – 5/26/2006 and 6/17/2006 – 10/31/2006
3. Data not available from 7/4/2007 – 8/25/2007
4. Continuous data from 5/1/2008 – 10/31/2008

OCCURRENCE OF DISSOLVED OXYGEN CONCENTRATIONS LESS THAN 4.0 mg/L AT THE SECN MONITORING STATION, CANAVERAL NATIONAL SEASHORE (MAY 2005 – OCTOBER 2008)

Years	Days with Complete DO Records	Total Number of Records	Days with Mean DO < 4.0 mg/L (n=)	(%)	Records with Mean DO < 4.0 mg/L (n=)	(%)
2005[1]	67	3146	44	66	576	18
2006[2]	22	1015	16	73	433	43
2007[3]	153	7489	138	90	2314	31
2008[4]	147	7130	66	45	554	8
2005–2008	389	18780	264	68	3877	21

1. Data not available from 5/1/2005 – 7/24/2005 and 10/4/2005 – 10/31/2005
2. Data not available from 5/1/2006 – 5/26/2006 and 6/17/2006 – 10/31/2006
3. Data not available from 7/23/2007 – 8/26/2007
4. Continuous data from 5/1/2008 – 10/31/2008

Table 30. Summaries of data and sources of significant threats and stressors of Canaveral National Seashore (CANA) resources (continued).

MOSQUITO LAGOON SURFACE WATER RESOURCE DATA SUMMARY

METRIC	CONDITION/ DESCRIPTION	DATA SUMMARIES / SELECTED REFERENCES
Trophic State	Fair to Good	Carlson, 1977; Hand et al., 1988; FDEP, 1996; Winkler and Ceric, 2006; FDEP, 2010a
		The trophic state of CANA surface water, based on Chl-a, SD, TP, and TN (1990–2007) is fair to good. Data results from 2006 and 2007 were within the allowable designation of good (TSI = 0 - 49).

TROPHIC STATE OF CANA SURFACE WATER AT IRLV17 AND IRLML02 (1990 - 2007)
(0 - 49 Good, 50-59 Fair, 60-100 Poor)

Parameter Means	1990	1991	1992	1993	1994	1995	1996	1997	1998	1999	2000	2001	2002	2003	2004	2005	2006	2007
Chlorophyll-a (µg/L)	7.0	5.7	7.5	6.3	5.0	4.5	7.3	5.4	6.7	7.2	4.4	5.1	5.2	2.3	4.2	4.2	2.3	2.3
Secchi Depth (m)	1.0	1.1	0.9	0.6	0.8	1.0	1.0	1.1	0.9	0.9	1.2	1.3	1.3	1.2	1.0	1.1	1.0	1.3
Total Kjeldahl Nitrogen (mg/L)	1.283	1.123	1.115	0.721	0.988	0.956	1.143	1.287	1.590	1.225	0.976	1.026	1.330	1.103	0.930	0.990	1.0	0.830
NOx (mg/L)					0.025	0.020	0.016	0.013	0.029	0.019	0.009	0.010	0.073	0.088	0.025	0.017		
Estimated Total Nitrogen (mg/L)	1.283	1.123	1.115	0.721	1.013	0.976	1.159	1.300	1.618	1.243	0.987	1.035	1.364	1.136	0.955	1.007	0.898	0.830
Total Phosphorus (mg/L)	0.052	0.051	0.062	0.040	0.104	0.044	0.057	0.056	0.072	0.060	0.035	0.032	0.027	0.037	0.035	0.047	0.041	0.086

Total Number of Phosphorus Used to Calculate Parameter Means

	1990	1991	1992	1993	1994	1995	1996	1997	1998	1999	2000	2001	2002	2003	2004	2005	2006	2007
Chlorophyll-a	13	14	14	10	13	16	94	109	107	84	59	57	59	51	43	41	52	41
Secchi Depth	25	25	24	17	25	25	91	87	107	84	58	57	56	52	44	41	58	41
Total Kjeldahl Nitrogen	17	17	17	9	17	18	70	103	106	84	59	57	59	52	44	41	58	41
NOx	0	0	0	0	2	3	79	108	107	84	59	57	58	52	44	30	0	0
Estimated Total Nitrogen	17	17	17	9	19	21	149	209	213	168	118	114	117	104	88	71	58	41
Total Phosphorus	17	17	17	9	18	18	82	93	106	84	59	57	59	52	44	41	58	41
Total Nitrogen : Total Phosphorus Ratio	25.0	21.9	18.0	18.1	9.8	25.3	20.4	23.1	22.3	20.5	28.0	32.3	52.2	31.1	24.4	25.5	25.8	23.0

Parameter Index Value	1990	1991	1992	1993	1994	1995	1996	1997	1998	1999	2000	2001	2002	2003	2004	2005	2006	2007
Chl-a TSI	44.0	41.8	45.8	43.4	40.1	38.6	45.4	41.0	44.1	45.2	38.0	40.2	40.7	28.7	37.6	37.4	25.8	28.7
SD TSI	61.3	58.1	62.1	65.0	67.5	60.8	58.7	58.0	61.7	62.2	53.8	53.1	58.0	53.4	59.7	55.3	60.8	52.7
TN TSI	60.8	58.3	58.2	49.5	56.2	53.5	58.9	58.9	65.5	60.3	55.7	56.7	62.1	58.5	55.1	56.1	53.6	52.3
TN TSI-2	65.0	62.1	62.0	52.6	59.9	59.1	62.8	65.3	70.0	64.3	59.3	60.4	65.3	62.4	58.6	59.3	57.1	55.6
TP	54.3	54.9	58.3	50.1	67.9	51.8	56.7	56.5	63.2	57.9	47.9	46.2	42.7	48.5	49.8	53.2	50.6	48.2
TP TSI-2	69.1	69.1	73.4	63.1	85.7	65.3	71.5	71.3	77.2	73.0	60.3	58.1	53.7	61.1	63.7	67.0	63.7	50.6
(TN TSI + TP TSI) / 2	60.2	58.4	59.5	50.7	61.4	55.5	59.5	61.0	65.6	60.8	54.3	54.4	57.0	57.0	54.5	56.4	53.8	52.0
Trophic State Index Value	55	53	53	47	50	47	55	55	57	56	49	49	51	46	47	48	44	44
Carlson Assessment	Fair	Fair	Fair	Fair	Fair	Fair	Fair	Fair	Fair	Fair	Fair	Fair	Fair	Good	Good	Fair	Good	Good
Trophic State Index Value Without SD	53	56	53	47	50	47	52	52	54	53	48	48	49	45	45	47	41	40
Condition Assessment	Fair	Fair	Fair	Good	Fair	Good	Fair	Fair	Fair	Fair	Good	Good	Good	Good	Good	Good	Good	Good

Table 30. Summaries of data and sources of significant threats and stressors of Canaveral National Seashore (CANA) resources (continued).

MOSQUITO LAGOON SURFACE WATER RESOURCE DATA SUMMARY

METRIC	CONDITION / DESCRIPTION	DATA SUMMARIES / SELECTED REFERENCES
Nitrogen	Fair to Good No significant temporal trend in NOx was observed at either IRLV17 or IRLML02 from 1996–2005.	Hall et al., 2001; Kroenig, 2008; FDEP, 2010a; Zarillo and Belanger, 2010 Mean NO_x (mg/L) - Wet Season, 1996 - 2005 at IRLV17 and IRLML02 Combined: 2005: 0.017; 2004: 0.029; 2003: 0.024; 2002: 0.035; 2001: 0.012; 2000: 0.008; 1999: 0.003; 1998: 0.036; 1997: 0.004; 1996: 0.017 Mean NO_x (mg/L) - Dry Season, 1996 - 2005 at IRLV17 and IRLML02: 2005: 0.018; 2004: 0.025; 2003: 0.036; 2002: 0.037; 2001: 0.009; 2000: 0.010; 1999: 0.026; 1998: 0.026; 1997: 0.019; 1996: 0.012

Table 30. Summaries of data and sources of significant threats and stressors of Canaveral National Seashore (CANA) resources (continued).

MOSQUITO LAGOON SURFACE WATER RESOURCE DATA SUMMARY

METRIC	CONDITION / DESCRIPTION	DATA SUMMARIES / SELECTED REFERENCES
Nitrogen TKN	Fair to Good TKN decreased in the wet ($\alpha \leq 0.01$) and dry ($\alpha \leq 0.001$) seasons at IRLV17 from 1990–2007. No significant trend in TKN ($\alpha \leq 0.05$) was observed at IRLML02 for either season during the same period.	Hall et al., 2001; Kroenig, 2008; FDEP, 2010a; Zarillo and Belanger, 2010 **Mean Total Kjeldahl Nitrogen (mg/L) - Wet Season 1990 - 2007 at IRLV17 and IRLML02 Combined** 1990: 1.550; 1991: 1.250; 1992: 1.510; 1993: —; 1994: 1.064; 1995: 1.059; 1996: 1.242; 1997: 1.655; 1998: 1.881; 1999: 1.236; 2000: 1.066; 2001: 1.419; 2002: 1.354; 2003: 1.248; 2004: 1.095; 2005: 1.060; 2006: 0.970; 2007: 0.972 **Mean Total Kjeldahl Nitrogen (mg/L) - Dry Season 1990 - 2007 at IRLV17 and IRLML02** 1990: 1.129; 1991: 0.957; 1992: 1.004; 1993: 0.836; 1994: 0.744; 1995: 0.798; 1996: 1.004; 1997: 1.026; 1998: 1.320; 1999: 1.145; 2000: 0.847; 2001: 0.739; 2002: 1.236; 2003: 0.916; 2004: 0.699; 2005: 0.800; 2006: 0.760; 2007: 0.645

Table 30. Summaries of data and sources of significant threats and stressors of Canaveral National Seashore (CANA) resources (continued).

	MOSQUITO LAGOON SURFACE WATER RESOURCE DATA SUMMARY	
METRIC	CONDITION / DESCRIPTION	DATA SUMMARIES / SELECTED REFERENCES
Phosphorus	Fair to Good No significant trend ($\alpha \leq 0.05$) in TP was observed at either IRLV17 or IRLML02 for either season between 1990–2007.	Zimmerman et al., 1985; FDEP, 1996; Kroenig, 2008; FEDP, 2010a **Mean Total Phosphorus (mg/L) - Wet Season** 1990 - 2007 at IRLV17 and IRLML02 Combined 2007: 0.048 2006: 0.045 2005: 0.057 2004: 0.043 2003: 0.035 2002: 0.031 2001: 0.039 2000: 0.041 1999: 0.054 1998: 0.086 1997: 0.131 1996: 0.053 1995: 0.047 1994: 0.211 1993: — 1992: 0.092 1991: 0.067 1990: 0.068 **Mean Total Phosphorus (mg/L) - Dry Season** 1990 - 2007 at IRLV17 and IRLML02 2007: 0.030 2006: 0.039 2005: 0.045 2004: 0.042 2003: 0.050 2002: 0.027 2001: 0.031 2000: 0.032 1999: 0.064 1998: 0.051 1997: 0.044 1996: 0.057 1995: 0.047 1994: 0.062 1993: 0.041 1992: 0.064 1991: 0.045 1990: 0.041

Table 30. Summaries of data and sources of significant threats and stressors of Canaveral National Seashore (CANA) resources (continued).

MOSQUITO LAGOON SURFACE WATER RESOURCE DATA SUMMARY

METRIC	CONDITION / DESCRIPTION	DATA SUMMARIES / SELECTED REFERENCES
Chlorophyll-a	Good	Provancha, 1992; Badylak and Philips, 2004; Hall et al., 2001; Kroening, 2008
	From 1990–2007, there was a significant decrease in chlorophyll-a concentration at IRLV17 in the wet ($\alpha \leq 0.001$) and dry ($\alpha \leq 0.05$) seasons and at IRLML02 in the wet ($\alpha \leq 0.01$) season only.	Mean Chlorophyll-a (µg/L) - Wet Season, 1990 - 2007 at IRLV17 and IRLML02 Combined: 2007: 3.7; 2006: 2.7; 2005: 5.8; 2004: 7.0; 2003: 4.7; 2002: 5.7; 2001: 6.9; 2000: 6.0; 1999: 8.8; 1998: 8.7; 1997: 8.3; 1996: 9.6; 1995: 7.2; 1994: 7.7; 1993: 10.1; 1992: 12.5; 1991: 8.7; 1990: 11.4. Mean Chlorophyll-a (µg/L) - Dry Season, 1990 - 2007 at IRLV17 and IRLML02: 2007: 1.4; 2006: 2.1; 2005: 3.1; 2004: 2.4; 2003: 1.4; 2002: 4.5; 2001: 3.9; 2000: 3.3; 1999: 6.2; 1998: 5.2; 1997: 3.1; 1996: 5.1; 1995: 2.5; 1994: 3.4; 1993: 2.6; 1992: 3.8; 1991: 3.4; 1990: 3.2.

Table 30. Summaries of data and sources of significant threats and stressors of Canaveral National Seashore (CANA) resources (continued).

METRIC	CONDITION / DESCRIPTION	MOSQUITO LAGOON SURFACE WATER RESOURCE DATA SUMMARY	
		DATA SUMMARIES / SELECTED REFERENCES	
	Fair to Good	Woodward-Clyde Associates, 1994	
Secchi Disk	No significant temporal trend ($\alpha \leq 0.05$) in SD was observed at either IRLV17 or IRLML02 for either season from 1990–2007.	Mean Secchi Disk Depth (m) - Wet Season 1990 - 2007 at IRLV17 and IRLML02 Combined	Mean Secchi Disk Depth (m) - Dry Season 1990 - 2007 at IRLV17 and IRLML02

Table 30. Summaries of data and sources of significant threats and stressors of Canaveral National Seashore (CANA) resources (continued).

METRIC	CONDITION / DESCRIPTION	MOSQUITO LAGOON SURFACE WATER RESOURCE DATA SUMMARY DATA SUMMARIES / SELECTED REFERENCES
Turbidity	Fair to Good No significant temporal trend ($\alpha \leq 0.05$) in turbidity was observed at either IRLV17 or IRLML02 for either season during 1990 to 2007.	Woodward-Clyde Associate, 1994; Steward et al., 2003 Mean Turbidity (NTU) - Wet Season 1990 - 2007 at IRLV17 and IRLML02 Combined 2007: 3.3, 2006: 7.2, 2005: 6.8, 2004: 5.3, 2003: 6.9, 2002: 8.0, 2001: 4.8, 2000: 4.6, 1999: 7.9, 1998: 9.2, 1997: 11.2, 1996: 9.0, 1995: 5.9, 1994: 9.0, 1992: 8.0, 1991: 6.2, 1990: 10.0 Mean Turbidity (NTU) - Dry Season 1990 - 2007 at IRLV17 and IRLML02 2007: 3.4, 2006: 6.1, 2005: 6.9, 2004: 7.6, 2003: 5.8, 2002: 6.9, 2001: 5.2, 2000: 2.6, 1999: 9.9, 1998: 8.8, 1997: 4.9, 1996: 6.3, 1995: 3.3, 1994: 4.3, 1993: 6.6, 1992: 4.6, 1991: 4.7, 1990: 5.2

Table 30. Summaries of data and sources of significant threats and stressors of Canaveral National Seashore (CANA) resources (continued).

MOSQUITO LAGOON SURFACE WATER RESOURCE DATA SUMMARY

METRIC	CONDITION / DESCRIPTION	DATA SUMMARIES / SELECTED REFERENCES
Total Suspended Solids	Fair to Good	Hall et al., 2001; Steward et al., 2003; Trefry et al., 2005; 2007; Kroening, 2008
	Fair to Good with the exception of a significant decrease ($\alpha \leq 0.05$) at IRLML02 in the wet season, no significant trend ($\alpha \leq 0.05$) in TSS was observed at IRLML02 in the dry season or at IRLV17 for either season between 1990–2007.	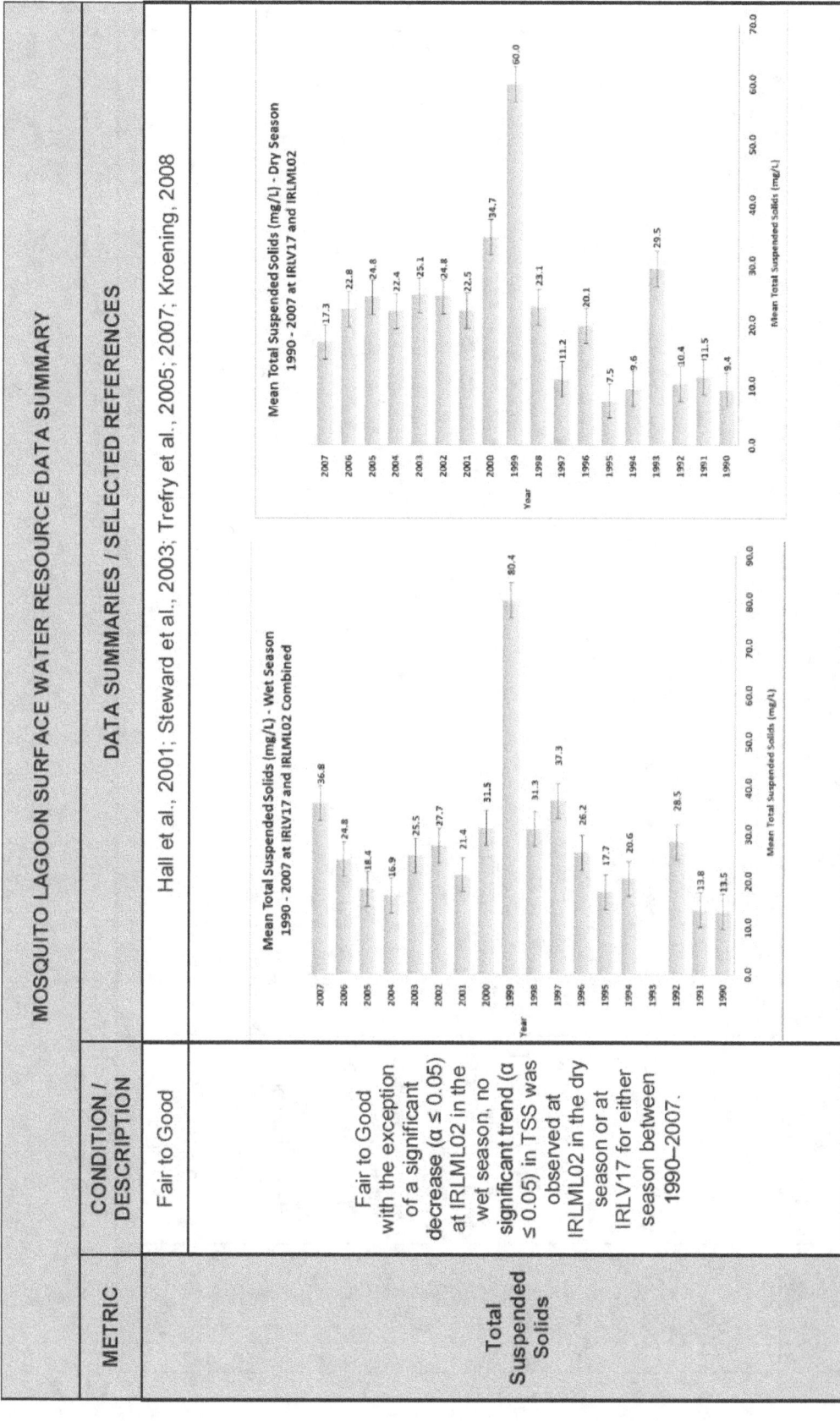

Table 30. Summaries of data and sources of significant threats and stressors of Canaveral National Seashore (CANA) resources (continued).

MOSQUITO LAGOON SURFACE WATER RESOURCE DATA SUMMARY

METRIC	CONDITION / DESCRIPTION	DATA SUMMARIES / SELECTED REFERENCES
Salinity	Fair Although there is no significant seasonal temporal trend, salinity levels of ($\alpha \leq 0.05$) was observed between 1990–2007. Salinity may occasionally reach levels stressful for aquatic life (see salinity section of this assessment).	Mehta and Brooks, 1973; Provancha, 1992; Hall et al., 2001; Walters et al., 2001; Kroening, 2008 **Mean Salinity (ppt) - Wet Season 1990 - 2007 at IRLV17 and IRLML02 Combined** 2007: 38.8; 2006: 36.0; 2005: 28.7; 2004: 29.1; 2003: 26.9; 2002: 31.9; 2001: 36.2; 2000: 40; 1999: 34.9; 1998: 30.9; 1997: 33.1; 1996: 22.2; 1995: 26.9; 1994: 30.6; 1993: 32.3; 1992: 30.1; 1991: 28.8; 1990: 35.8 **Mean Salinity (ppt) - Dry Season 1990 - 2007 at IRLV17 and IRLML02** 2007: 35.3; 2006: 33.0; 2005: 28.0; 2004: 31.9; 2003: 29.7; 2002: 31.2; 2001: 33.9; 2000: 35.9; 1999: 32.4; 1998: 26.4; 1997: 30.1; 1996: 24.7; 1995: 29.5; 1994: 31.9; 1993: 30.9; 1992: 31.3; 1991: 33.9; 1990: 33.7

Table 30. Summaries of data and sources of significant threats and stressors of Canaveral National Seashore resources (continued).

SUMMARY OF BIOTA DATA FOR COASTAL DUNES AND BEACHES, AND MOSQUITO LAGOON		
Metric	CONDITION	REFERENCES
Status of Coastal Strand Plant Community & Loss of Habitat or Damage to Habitat Coverage in CANA	**FAIR-GOOD** Visitor access to boat launches and dune crossovers via the main road help manage vehicle traffic and minimize visitor foot impacts. While the plants or native weedy species are fairly well known, the aerial extent and specific location of these are unknown. Abundance of non-native animals is unknown. Damage done by non-native animals is known to occur but is not monitored throughout	Plant communities and associations are estimated for MINWNR and known non-native plant and animal species (MINWR, 2008).
Status of Saltwater Wetlands & Loss of Habitat or Damage to Habitat Coverage in CANA	**FAIR-GOOD** While the plants or native weedy species are fairly well known, the aerial extent and specific location of these are unknown. Abundance of non-native animals is unknown. Damage done by non-native animals is known to occur but is not monitored throughout (feral hogs).	Table 23. Land cover classes and size for saltwater wetlands. Acres are estimated for all years using land-use codes of Duncan et al. (2004) and NPS land use 2003 and soil layers. For a description of land cover classes (see Appendix). | LU Codes*	Land Cover Class	SIZE (acres)			
---	---	---	---	---	---
		1943*	1990*	2003**	Soils 2003***
6120	Mangrove	1,657	1,756	655	3,842
6420	Saltmarsh	6,600	4,764	6,998	4,462
6460	Disturbed Estuarine Wetlands	20	219	297	
	Total	8,277	6,739	7,950	8,304	 *Land cover classes combined by Duncan et al. (2004). ** Land cover 2003 and soils from National Park Service. ***Wet pinewoods (530 acres) included in overall acreage for pinewoods Plant communities and associations are estimated for MINWR, and known non-native plant and animal species, MINWR, 2008

Table 30. Summaries of data and sources of significant threats and stressors of Canaveral National Seashore resources (continued).

SUMMARY OF BIOTA DATA FOR COASTAL DUNES AND BEACHES, AND MOSQUITO LAGOON

Metric	CONDITION	REFERENCES
Land-use Cover Change	**CAUTION** The land cover map may not identify features (e.g., salt wetlands) at a scale suitable for jurisdictional delineation or mitigate assessments. The 2003 land cover map consists of 26,350 polygons and identifies features generally equal to or less than a minimum area of 1.2 ac (0.5 ha) and a minimum width of 98 ft (30 m).	Duncan et al. (2004) NPS GIS Digital Files U.S. Soil Conservation Service for Brevard and Volusia Counties (1975 & 1977).
Sea Turtles Nesting	**GOOD / CAUTION** Nesting data, historic and recent, are available, and ongoing monitoring continues to develop the ability to observe trends and improve resource management. **EXISTING** Erosion and Accretion of Nests. Nests can be inundated during natural storm events, such as northeasters and tropical cyclones. Accretions of sand in large amounts over nests can cause the hatchling to use more energy to crawl out of the nest and reduce its chances of reaching the ocean.	Figure 67. Comparison of loggerhead (*Caretta caretta*) and green (*Chelonia mydas*) sea turtle nest counts in Canaveral National Seashore from 1984–2010 (Stiner, 2010a). (http://research.myfwc.com/images/articles/11812/statewide totals 1979 - 2009.pdf) (FWC-FWRI, 2009b) Meylan et al., 1995; Witherington, 2009; FWC-FWRI, 2010a; Stiner, 2010a Pike and Stiner, 2007; NMFS-FWS, 2008

Table 30. Summaries of data and sources of significant threats and stressors of Canaveral National Seashore resources (continued).

SUMMARY OF BIOTA DATA FOR COASTAL DUNES AND BEACHES, AND MOSQUITO LAGOON

METRIC	CONDITION	REFERENCES
Sea Turtle Hatchlings and Adults	**FAIR** Sea Turtle Hatchling Predators The most common predators are ghost crabs, raccoons, feral hogs, foxes, coyotes, armadillos, and red fire ants. Canaveral National Seashore has 30 yrs of data, providing a good estimate of annual nest depredation by raccoons and other mesopredators. "Nest protection activities have substantially reduced loggerhead nest depredations" between 5–20%. Threats: Disease-Juvenile sea turtles in the IRL system have shown signs of a herpes-type virus known as Fibropapillomatosis (FP), first observed in the 1930s. Cold stunning. Trapped in fishing nets more so during commercial fishing, sickness or death from HABs, boat injury/death, entanglement in marine debris or ingestion thereof, effects of climate change are believed to affect food supply.	Presence/ Threats: Dodd, 1988; Stancyk, 1982; Provancha et al., 1998; Fick et al., 2000; Foley et al., 2005; Barton, 2005; Barton and Roth, 2008; NMFS-FWS, 2008; MINWR, 2008; John Stiner, personal communication, January 7, 2011. Cold stunning- Witherington and Ehrhart, 1989; Morreale et al., 1992
Shellfish (*Donax* sp.), Mole Crabs, Ghost Crabs, and Blue Crabs	*Ghost crabs and coquina clams are considered abundant and may serve as indicators of beach health.* Blue crabs –Abundance: One way to gage the abundance of blue crabs is from commercial fishery landing data. Fishery landings are not population counts, as fishing activities change over time. Population numbers are unknown. In the 1930s and 1940s, statewide, blue crab landings were about 4.5–7.0 million. From 2001–201, landing from Brevard and Volusia counties have ranged from under 500,000 to >2 million.	SCDNR, no date; Wolcott 1978; Murphy et al., 2007 Figure 76. Blue crab landings Brevard and Volusia Counties for 2001–2010 (Personal communication from the NMFS, 2010b).

Table 30. Summaries of data and sources of significant threats and stressors of Canaveral National Seashore resources (continued).

SUMMARY OF BIOTA DATA FOR COASTAL DUNES AND BEACHES, AND MOSQUITO LAGOON

Metric	CONDITION	REFERENCES
Horseshoe Crabs	Abundance: Unknown. No landing data. Horseshoe crabs are not collected for the medical industry in Florida. Incidental data on horseshoe abundance reported as by-catch in nets set to assess sea turtle populations in Mosquito Lagoon. From 1978–1979, large numbers of horseshoe crabs were caught (Provancha, 1998) and in 1994, much smaller amounts were netted of (0-4) horseshoe crabs per 957 yd^2 (800 m^2) (Provancha, 1998), suggesting a dramatic decline of *Limulus* in the lagoon over 15–16 yrs. Threats: Unpredictable large-scale mortality events; for example in 1999, about 100,000 adult horseshoe crabs died of unknown cause(s) in the northern IRL and southern Mosquito Lagoon. Loss of habitat from degradation brought about by reduction in beach nesting area or changes in hydrology caused by mosquito impoundments. Repeated harvesting of large number of horseshoe crabs in specific areas (south Florida) for aquarium resale may affect the abundance of local populations.	Provancha, 1998; Scheidt and Lowers 2000; Ehlinger et al., 2003; Ehlinger and Tankersley, 2004; Gerhart, 2007
Benthic Macroinvertebrates	UNKNOWN Taxa (or taxa groups) of marcoinvertebrates found in IRL were *Exogone rolani*, Rhynchocoela, Tubificidae, Cirratulidae, *Mediomastus* sp., Bivalvia, *Podarkeopsis levifuscina*, and *Scoloplos rubrar*. Gastropods, *Acteocina canaliculata* and *Mitrella lunata*.	McRae et al., 1998; McRae et al., 2003; McRae et al., 2005

Table 30. Summaries of data and sources of significant threats and stressors of Canaveral National Seashore resources (continued).

SUMMARY OF BIOTA DATA FOR COASTAL DUNES AND BEACHES, AND MOSQUITO LAGOON

Metric	CONDITION	REFERENCES
Oyster Reef	Abundance: Numerous oyster reefs occur in the northern end of Mosquito Lagoon; however, over the past 50 yrs, a declining trend in the distribution of oyster reefs within CANA has been observed with a significant increase in the mortality of oysters along the reef margins adjacent to boat channels. Since 1943, the percent of reef dead margins in the park increased from 0.3% to 27.6% in 2000, with oyster mortality ranging from less than 10% to nearly 100% of total reef area. Threats: Water quality: Larval Supply and resettlement: Disease/Parasites: The presence of *Perkinsus marinus* or dermo infection, however, was relatively high (averaging ~40% of individuals), but the intensity of infection was low (stage 1) in nearly all months (Arnold et al., 2008). Non-native species- bivalve mussel (*Mytella charruana*) found in the lagoon in 2004 has rapidly spread within the northern portion of the lagoon. Another potential non-native competitor is the Asian green mussel, *Perna viridis*. Harmful algal blooms; Boat wakes; Overharvesting:	Figure 79. Threats and stressors to oyster reefs. (Source of Photos: A-Jonathan Wilker, Purdue University, and B and C Grizzle et al., 2002.) Abundance and Threats: Grizzle et al., 2002: Boudreaux et al., 2006; Arnold et al., 2008 Importance: Coen et al., 2007; Stiner and Walters, 2008
Birds	Shorebirds: Present in habitats of CANA and MINWR area (shorebirds, waterfowl, wading birds, seabirds, raptors, and passerines) Wintering waterfowl on MINWR of blue-winged teal, American widgeon, northern pintail, lesser scaup, redhead, and mergansers have varied in number. Recent counts are generally low, and the northern pintail and the lesser scaup are of particular concern. Wading birds (e.g., egrets, herons, and ibises) use a broad range of wetland habitat types for foraging, roosting, and nesting. Many wading birds will use vegetated dredge spoil islands in the IRL to roost and nest. Federally endangered wood stork (*Mycteria americana*)—no nests since 1986. Population estimates for some species, abundance unknown	Cruickshank, 1980; Lee and Cardiff, 1993; USFWS, 1995; FWC, 2003; MINWR, 2003:2008; PIA, 2008; SCAS, 2010a,b

Table 30. Summaries of data and sources of significant threats and stressors of Canaveral National Seashore resources (continued).

DATA SUMMARY OF BIOTA FOR MOSQUITO LAGOON

METRIC	CONDITION	REFERENCES
Fishes	**FAIR-GOOD** Lagoon diversity: Fish sampling programs 1972-1980, 1983, reported 141 species. Among the 15 most abundant fish species collected in these Mosquito Lagoon stations, the bay anchovy, *Anchoa mitchilli*, accounted for approximately 85% of the total catch. 1991-92: Fixed trawl stations sampled in Mosquito Lagoon with 49 fish species caught and bay anchovy numerically dominant, again, often composing over 90% of the trawl catch. Additional numerically dominant species collected included silver perch, *Bairdiella chrysoura*, pinfish, *Lagodon rhomboides*, spot, *Leiostomus xanthurus*, croaker, *Micropogonias undulatus*, Gulf pipefish, *Syngnathus scovelli*, silver jenny, *Eucinostomus harengulus*, and code goby, *Gobiosoma robustum*. 1993-97: Sampling in lagoon dominated by seagrass-associated species such as rainwater killifish, *Lucania parva* and pinfish. 2004: Samples yielded 65 estuarine and freshwater fish species. 2007-2008: Of the 148,200 fish and macroinvertebrates collected, there were 67 fish species/taxa in 2007 and 73 fish species/taxa in 2008. The rainwater killifish, bay anchovy, and silversides, *Menidia* spp. accounted for 74% of the total catch in 2007 and 2008; the three species dominated the catch, plus the seasonally abundant spot. **Threats:** Overfishing, reduction in habitat, and pollution	**Figure 81.** Distribution and abundance of spot, *Leiostomus xanthurus*, in Mosquito Lagoon from FWC-FWRI's Fisheries-Independent Monitoring Program sampling during 2007 and 2008. Bubbles refer to number of fish collected. Red lines indicate current "Pole and Troll" zones within the basin. (Figure from Adams and Paperno, In prep.). Snelson 1976; 1980, 1983 Studies (1972-80); Mulligan and Snelson, 1983; Snelson et al., 1989; Paperno et al., 2001; Johnston, et al., 2006 **Figure 82.** Number and timing of adult red drum, *Sciaenops ocellatus*, movements out of Mosquito Lagoon to Ponce Inlet or the northern IRL proper (Figure from Reyier et al., 2011).

Table 30. Summaries of data and sources of significant threats and stressors of Canaveral National Seashore resources (continued).

DATA SUMMARY OF BIOTA FOR MOSQUITO LAGOON

Metric	CONDITION	REFERENCES
SAV-Seagrass Drift Algae, and Macroalgae	FAIR-GOOD Known SAV Shoal Grass (*Halodule wrightii*), Manatee Grass (*Syringodium filiforme*), Widgeon Grass (*Ruppia maritima*), Star grass (*Halophila englemanni*), and Macroalgae (*Caulerpa prolifera*) occur in Mosquito Lagoon. GIS seagrass coverage of the IRL system available for years 1943, 1986, 1989, 1992, 1994, 1996, 1999, 2001, 2003, 2005, 2006, 2007, and 2009. Drift macrophytes: The red algae *Gracilaria* spp. accounted for 51.7%, followed by fragments of the seagrass shoal grass (23.7%), *Cladophora* sp. (12.5%), *Dasya baillouviana* (7.7%), *Enteromorpha* spp. (1.5%), *Spyridia filamentosa* (1.4%), and 1.5% consisted of *Acanthophora spicifera*, *Hypnea spinella*, *Agardhiella subulata*, and *Chondria littoralis*. Threats: Scarring and turbidity from boat propellers.	Figure 73. Percent coverage of seagrass for 2009 is provided (source SJRWMD). Provancha et al., 1992; Virnstein, 1999 SJRWMD (ftp://www.sjrwmd.com/disk3/wetlands/IRL_Seagrass) Abgrall and Walters, 2003

Table 30. Summaries of data and sources of significant threats and stressors of Canaveral National Seashore resources (continued).

METRIC	DATA SUMMARY OF BIOTA FOR MOSQUITO LAGOON	
	CONDITION	REFERENCES
Marine Mammals	**FAIR-GOOD** Dolphins: Atlantic bottlenose dolphins are throughout the IRL system and are considered long-term residents. Nearly 2,000 dolphins were sighted in the Mosquito Lagoon during 2002–2005. **CAUTION** Manatees: Results of 2001 survey are the best available estimate of the current minimum population size (3,276).	Figure 75. Threats and stressors to marine mammals. (Photos: A-NOAA Marine Debris Program, B- and C-FWRI). Dolphins-Abundance: Provancha et al., 1982; Odell and Asper, 1990; Fick, 1995 Mazzoil et al., 2008 Disease: Reif et al., 2006, Murdoch et al., 2008 Manatees-Abundance: USFWS, 2002 Distribution: Leatherman, 1979; Shane, 1983; Provancha and Provancha, 1988 Boat Injury or death: Reynolds and Odell, 1991; USFWS, 2001
Harmful Algal Blooms	**UNKNOWN** Fall 2007: Harmful algal bloom caused by the red tide dinoflagellate, *Karenia brevis*. The dinoflagellate was trapped in cooler waters under warm, less dense surface water. *K. brevis* decreased oxygen concentrations, which resulted in the mortality of benthic organisms and can also sicken or kill manatee and sea turtles.	*Karenia brevis* counts, October 6–12, 2007 (from Zarillo et al., 2009 FWC-FWRI www.floridamarine.org).

Table 30. Summaries of data and sources of significant threats and stressors of Canaveral National Seashore resources (continued).

SUMMARY OF DATA FOR FRESHWATER RESOURCES

METRIC	CONDITION	THREATS	RECOMMENDATIONS	REFERENCES
Anthropogenic Land Use	GOOD / CAUTION Recent low-intensity application of prescribed fire is now being conducted to ameliorate the effects of previous fire suppression over many years	Alteration to surface and groundwater quality and quantity Interruption in natural hydrology by roads, drainage structures Introduction of exotic pest plants and animals Previous agricultural practices.	Continue prescribed fire; increase intensity and frequency and alternate season of burn.	MINWR, 2008; NPS, 2006
Land-use Cover Change	CAUTION The land cover map may not identify features (e.g., wetlands) at a scale suitable for jurisdictional delineation or mitigate assessments. The 2003 land cover map consists of 26,350 polygons and identifies features generally equal to or less than a minimum area of 0.5 ha and a minimum width of 30 m.	Underestimating the land cover acreage of wetlands on site. Misidentification and simplification of land cover classes that may lead to degradation of existing habitats. Habitat alteration and fragmentation	Provide additional studies to determine more exact land cover classes. Implement comprehensive mapping using ground-truth studies.	Duncan et al. (2004) NPS GIS Files U.S. Soil Conservation Service for Brevard and Volusia Counties (1975 & 1980).
Wet Pine Flatwoods	GOOD / CAUTION Periodic thinning of pine flatwoods provides enhanced nesting habitat for bald eagles. Control of exotic, invasive, and nuisance species.	Fire suppression over long intervals decreases species richness, changes the composition and increases pine density. Pines and cabbage palms are invading the wet flatwoods impacted by lowered water table.	Increase frequency and intensity of prescribed fires. Restore hydrology to pine flatwoods. Continue invasive and nuisance species control.	MINWR, 2008; NPS, 2006 USDA, 1974

Table 30. Summaries of data and sources of significant threats and stressors of Canaveral National Seashore resources (continued).

SUMMARY OF DATA FOR FRESHWATER RESOURCES

METRIC	CONDITION	THREATS	RECOMMENDATIONS	REFERENCES
Freshwater Marsh	GOOD / CAUTION Shrubs and trees are invading the perimeters of some marshes due to prolonged absence of fire. Many of the smaller, shallow marshes have converted to willow thickets in the absence of fire. Roads and ditches that cut through these linear wetlands stop the natural drainage patterns and unfavorably change the species composition.	Absent or infrequent fire encourages woody species encroachment. Some areas have changed to forested wetlands from fire exclusion and hydrological alteration. Roads and ditches cut through linear wetlands in the interdunal swales, impeding natural water flow.	Continue prescribed burning program including spring and summer burns to select for grasses and herbaceous species. Restore hydrology by removing roads and trails across linear wetland swales. Place culverts or concrete "water crossings" to restore hydrology.	FNAI-FDNR, 1990; FNAI, 2010; MINWR, 2008; NPS, 2010b
Forested Wetlands	CAUTION Roads and drainage in the vicinity of the large hydric hammocks have impacted the habitat. Habitat is becoming more mesic due to altered hydrology, ditches, and previous agriculture practices in adjacent uplands. Species composition is changing because of altered hydrology and fires that burn infrequently into forested wetlands	Roads and ditches cut through forested wetlands. Changes to mesic conditions and subsequent loss of species diversity. Colonization by cabbage palms as habitat dries out. Invasive species colonizing mesic communities.	Restore the hydrology by removing ditches, placing culverts under roads, or using rock "water crossings" across roads. Prevent prescribed fire from entering forested wetlands in drought and extreme drought years.	FNAI-FDNR, 1990; FNAI, 2010; MINWR, 2008; USDA 1980

Table 30. Summaries of data and sources of significant threats and stressors of Canaveral National Seashore resources (continued).

SUMMARY OF DATA FOR FRESHWATER RESOURCES

METRIC	CONDITION	THREATS	RECOMMENDATIONS	REFERENCES
Prairie Hammocks	CAUTION Altered hydrology is changing the community on limestone substrate on the borders of wetlands to a more mesic community. The small size of the hammocks makes them more vulnerable to invasive non-native species.	Changes in species composition due to altered hydrology. Invasive non-native plant species colonizing smaller hammocks. Feral hogs damage the soil surface on community perimeter.	Restore hydrology by removing ditches and roads. Eradicate invasive plant species. Remove feral hog populations.	FNAI-FDNR, 1990; FNAI, 2010; MINWR, 2008
Disturbed wetlands	CAUTION Invasive species colonize disturbed wetlands, especially in areas of soil disturbance.	Expansion of invasive species within disturbed wetlands to ecotones with undisturbed native habitat. Loss of native species and biological diversity.	Continue eradication efforts for invasive species.	NPS, 2006.
Invasive and Exotic Plants	CAUTION Invasive species have displaced many native species in upland and wetland plant communities.	Expansion of invasive species on the perimeters of native habitat and areas of soil disturbance. Introduction of invasive species on management equipment used in prescribed fire, road maintenance, and other management activities.	Continue eradication efforts for invasive species. Clean resource management equipment before and after usage.	MINWR, 2008; FLEPPC, 2010
Status of Rare Plant Populations	GOOD Federally threatened or endangered species regularly occur as well as species listed by the state of Florida as either threatened, endangered, of special concern, or commercially exploited.	Decline in populations and potential extinction due to loss of habitat; loss of biological diversity; invasion of exotic, nuisance, and invasive species; disturbance due to resource development and other human activities; impacts of pollution and water quality degradation; and impacts of sea level rise and global warming.	Implement monitoring methodology for baseline and continuing studies. Conduct resource management activities, controlled burning, exotic removal, etc., that will maintain native communities in optimal condition, thus benefitting the listed species.	MINWR, 2008; FNAI, 2010;

Table 30. Summaries of data and sources of significant threats and stressors of Canaveral National Seashore resources (continued).

SUMMARY OF DATA FOR FRESHWATER RESOURCES

METRIC	CONDITION	THREATS	RECOMMENDATIONS	REFERENCES
Terrestrial Invasive Fauna	CAUTION Invasive fauna includes feral animals and free-roaming pets.	Feral animals, free-roaming pets may increase due to adjacent urbanization and increased demand for public-use activities.	Implement removal and eradication programs.	MINWR, 2008
Birds (Frequency of Occurrence)	CAUTION migratory birds resident birds	Impoundment of estuarine wetlands (salt marsh and mangrove swamp). Increased disturbance to nesting and roosting habitat.	Reconnect impoundments and restore natural flow and biological interchange. Reduce disturbance to wetlands, and native upland habitat	FNAI-FDNR, 1990; FNAI, 2010; MINWR, 2008
Birds Population Trends	CAUTION Important habitat exists for a wide variety of bird species. Information is available for Merritt Island National Wildlife Refuge.	Fire suppression in appropriate plant communities Invasive species colonization.	Conduct bird surveys for common and listed bird species; monitor populations. Manage habitats for species diversity.	FNAI-FDNR, 1990; FNAI, 2010; MINWR, 2008
Mammals: Other Population Trends	CAUTION Important habitat exists for the southeastern beach mouse. Information is available for MINWR and CANA.	Fire suppression in appropriate plant communities Invasive species colonization.	Conduct mammal surveys; monitor populations. Manage habitats for species diversity	FNAI-FDNR, 1990; FNAI, 2010; MINWR, 2008
Plant Species Richness	CAUTION Plant species richness is higher in undisturbed wetlands.	Fragmentation of existing native plant communities. Degradation of existing native plant communities due to inconsistent management.	Maintain habitat health through prescribed burning in communities that require fire. Maintain habitats free of invasive species.	FNAI-FDNR, 1990; FNAI, 2010; MINWR, 2008
Water Quality in Wetlands	CAUTION Information is available for Merritt Island National Wildlife Refuge.	Point and non-point pollution from past citrus agricultural practices.	Conduct water quality testing in wetlands adjacent to previous agriculture. Cleanup contaminated areas.	

Table 31. Canaveral National Seashore threats and stressors matrix.

THREATS AND STRESSORS TO THE SURFACE WATER OF MOSQUITO LAGOON			
THREAT / STRESSOR		EXTENT OF PROBLEM	KNOWLEDGE BASE
Dissolved Oxygen		EXISTING	POOR
Salinity		POTENTIAL	GOOD
Water Clarity	Secchi Disk	OK	GOOD
	Turbidity	OK	GOOD
	Chlorophyll-a	OK	FAIR
	Total Suspended Solids	POTENTIAL	FAIR
Nutrient Enrichment	Surface Water Runoff	POTENTIAL	POOR
	Submarine Groundwater Discharge	POTENTIAL	POOR
	Atmospheric Deposition	POTENTIAL	POOR
Contaminants	Metals	UNKNOWN	POOR
	Pesticides	UNKNOWN	POOR
	Hydrocarbons	UNKNOWN	POOR
	Fecal Coliform Bacteria	POTENTIAL	POOR

Table 31. Canaveral National Seashore threats and stressors matrix (continued).

THREATS AND STRESSORS TO GEOLOGICAL FEATURES			
THREAT / STRESSOR		EXTENT OF PROBLEM	KNOWLEDGE BASE
Barrier Island Superstructure	Shoreline Erosion and/or Accretion	EXISTING	FAIR
	New Inlets	POTENTIAL	POOR
	Storms	EXISTING	FAIR
	Climate Change/Sea Level Rise	POTENTIAL	POOR
Beaches and Dunes	Erosion	POTENTIAL	FAIR
	Storms	EXISTING	FAIR
	Vehicular Traffic	NONE	GOOD
	Marine Debris	EXISTING	FAIR
	Climate Change/Sea Level	POTENTIAL	POOR
	Marine Debris	EXISTING	GOOD
	Climate Change/Sea Level Rise	POTENTIAL	POOR
Surficial Aquifer	Nutrients	POTENTIAL	POOR
	Contaminants	POTENTIAL	POOR
Floridian Aquifer	High Chlorinity	POTENTIAL	POOR
	Contaminants	POTENTIAL	POOR

Table 31. Canaveral National Seashore threats and stressors matrix (continued).

THREATS AND STRESSORS TO THE BIOTIA OF CANAVERAL NATIONAL SEASHORE			
THREAT / STRESSOR		EXTENT OF PROBLEM	KNOWLEDGE BASE
Coastal Strand Plant Community and Loss of Habitat or Damage to Habitat	Status of Plant Community Coverage	EXISTING	FAIR
	Shoreline erosion and/or accretion	EXISTING	GOOD
	Coastal Construction	NONE	GOOD
	Invasion of non-native species	EXISTING	POOR-FAIR
	Foot traffic and dune cuts (may occur in limited areas)	POTENTIAL	GOOD
	Climate Change	POTENTIAL	POOR-FAIR
	Storm Events	EXISTING	GOOD
Sea Turtles	Habitat-Nesting Beach	NONE	GOOD
	Predators	EXISTING	GOOD
	Diseases (tumors)	EXISTING	FAIR
	Harmful Algae Blooms	EXISTING	FAIR
	Marine Debris	EXISTING	GOOD
	Pollution	EXISTING-POTENTIAL	FAIR
	Beach Renourishment	NONE	GOOD
	Boating injury or death	EXISTING	GOOD
	Weather (cold stunning) and Climate Change	EXISTING-POTENTIAL	POOR-FAIR
	Commercial fishing offshore	EXISTING	GOOD
Marine Mammals	Unpredicted mortality events	EXISTING	POOR
	Climate Change	POTENTIAL	FAIR
	Pollution	EXISTING-POTENTIAL	FAIR
	Diseases	EXISTING	POOR-FAIR
	Boating injury or death	EXISTING	GOOD
	Commercial fishing offshore	EXISTING	FAIR-GOOD
	Harmful Algae Blooms	EXISTING	FAIR
	Marine Debris	EXISTING	GOOD

Table 31. Canaveral National Seashore threats and stressors matrix (continued).

THREATS AND STRESSORS TO THE BIOTIA OF CANAVERAL NATIONAL SEASHORE			
	THREAT / STRESSOR	EXTENT OF PROBLEM	KNOWLEDGE BASE
Shellfish (*Donax* sp.), Mole Crabs, Ghost Crabs, and Blue Crabs	Storm Events-Climate Change	EXISTING	POOR-FAIR
	Pollution	UNKNOWN	POOR
	Harmful Algae Blooms	EXISTING	POOR-FAIR
	Exotic animals that displace natives or consume resources	EXISTING-POTENTIAL	POOR
	Overharvesting (county landings) Blue Crabs	UNKOWN	POOR
Birds of Coastal Beaches and Dunes	Storm Events-Climate Change	EXISTING-POTENTIAL	FAIR-GOOD
	Pollution	EXISTING-POTENTIAL	POOR-FAIR
	Harmful Algae Blooms	EXISTING	POOR-FAIR
	Marine Debris	EXISTING	GOOD
	Habitat quality - Coastal strand	UNKNOWN	POOR
	Exotic animals that displace natives or consume resources	EXISTING	FAIR-GOOD
Beach Mice	Storm Events - Climate Change	EXISTING-POTENTIAL	POOR-FAIR
	Pollution	EXISTING-POTENTIAL	POOR-FAIR
	Habitat quality - Coastal strand	EXISTING	FAIR
	Marine Debris	UNKOWN	POOR
	Exotic animals that displace natives or consume resources	EXISTING	FAIR
Saltwater Wetlands and Loss of Habitat or Damage to Habitat	Exotic plants	EXISTING	FAIR
	Shoreline erosion and/accretion	EXISTING	FAIR
	Habitat quality-Salt water wetlands	EXISTING	FAIR-GOOD
	Alteration of Hydrology	EXISTING	FAIR-GOOD
	Climate Change	POTENTIAL	FAIR
	Storm Events	EXISTING	GOOD
	Nesting places in rookeries, on spoil islands, and sandy pockets	EXISTING - POTENTIAL	POOR
Birds of Saltwater and Freshwater Wetlands	Predators	EXISTING	GOOD
	Diseases	EXISTING	POOR-FAIR
	Harmful Algae Blooms	EXISTING	FAIR
	Marine Debris	EXISTING	GOOD
	Pollution	EXISTING - POTENTIAL	POOR-FAIR
	Exotic birds/non-native animals that displace natives or consume resources	EXISTING	FAIR
	Climate Change	POTENTIAL	FAIR-GOOD
	Fishing/hunting	EXISTING	POOR-FAIR

Table 31. Canaveral National Seashore threats and stressors matrix (continued).

| THREATS AND STRESSORS TO THE BIOTIA OF CANAVERAL NATIONAL SEASHORE ||||
THREAT / STRESSOR		EXTENT OF PROBLEM	KNOWLEDGE BASE
Oyster Reefs	Harmful Algae Blooms	EXISTING	POOR-FAIR
	Exotic species that displace natives or consume resources	EXISTING-POTENTIAL	POOR-FAIR
	Climate Change	POTENTIAL	FAIR
	Boat damage to reef systems and potential overharvesting	EXISTING	GOOD
	Storm Events	EXISTING	FAIR
	Pollution	POTENTIAL	POOR-FAIR
Reptiles (juvenile sea turtles, snakes, amphibians)	Harmful Algae Blooms	EXISTING	FAIR-GOOD
	Boating injury or death (especially sea turtles)	EXISTING	GOOD
	Marine Debris	EXISTING	GOOD
	Climate Change	POTENTIAL	POOR-FAIR
	Exotic species that displace natives or consume resources	EXISTING	POOR-FAIR
	Storm Events	EXISTING	POOR-FAIR
	Climate Change	POTENTIAL	POOR-FAIR
Benthic Macro-invertebrates	Exotic species that displace natives or consume resources	POTENTIAL	POOR
	Pollution	EXISTING	POOR
	Harmful Algae Blooms	EXISTING	POOR-FAIR
	Harmful Algae Blooms	EXISTING	POOR-FAIR
	Decrease in species diversity	EXISTING	POOR-FAIR
	Invasion of non-native species	EXISTING	FAIR
	Change in habitat due to altered hydrology	EXISTING	GOOD
	Habitat degradation due to animal damage (i.e., feral hogs)	EXISTING	FAIR-GOOD
	Storm Events/Climate Change	EXISTING	POOR-FAIR
	Habitat degradation due to insufficient seasonal and frequent prescribed fire	EXISTING	FAIR-GOOD
Wildlife and Listed Species	Storm Events/Climate Change	EXISTING	POOR-FAIR
	Fishing/hunting	EXISTING	POOR-FAIR
	Exotic animal that displace natives or consume resources	EXISTING	POOR-FAIR
	Habitat degradation due to altered hydrology	EXISTING	FAIR-GOOD

Conclusions and Recommendations

The majority of factors that threaten to impair CANA waters and terrestrial ecosystems are due to the pressures exerted by an increasing population in the vicinity of CANA and the associated increase in development. As demonstrated by increases in medium and high density residential land use and changes in open land use in the Edgewater-New Smyrna Beach area. Thus, the increasing human population in the Mosquito Lagoon watershed is of particular concern as contaminant loads from increased development and land-use changes may present a serious threat to water quality, especially in the northern Mosquito Lagoon region near population centers. An additional threat not directly related to local development is climate change that may alter weather patterns, water and air temperature, and the rate of sea level rise.

In terms of the physical and geological setting, climate change and natural variability are the greatest threats and stressors to these resources. Since the magnitude of climate change is uncertain, it is recommended that the NPS establish well-defined baselines from which to evaluate this threat. Specifically, the NPS should re-evaluate trends and variability of water levels and shoreline position on an annual basis in a convenient format so that the analysis can be extended year by year with limited effort.

Increased development in the Mosquito Lagoon watershed particularly north of CANA negatively impacts water quality by increasing pollution from point and nonpoint sources. Trophic state analysis of CANA surface waters using 1990-2007 data indicates that the trophic state is stable and the water quality has remained in the fair/good range, with the last two years of data analysis (2006; 2007) falling well within the allowable limit for a good designation. N and P were generally co-limiting, however P limitation occurred many times in the southern Mosquito Lagoon. This is in contrast to most of the IRL and the vast majority of estuaries in the U.S. Although the water quality of the CANA section of Mosquito Lagoon has remained good, threats from sources such as storm water runoff, OSTDS, and POTW's still need to be recognized and minimized when possible. Although the surface water hydrology in Mosquito Lagoon is fairly well understood, the role of submarine groundwater discharge to the lagoon has been largely ignored. Groundwater seepage can affect the receiving water quality. Advective sediment water exchange processes, induced by submarine groundwater discharge, are often critical components of coastal nutrient. However, very little groundwater quantity or quality data have been collected in Mosquito Lagoon.

An unexpected increase in nutrient enrichment could affect the healthy SAV, primarily the areas of seagrass in the central and southern parts of the Mosquito Lagoon and saltwater wetlands. SAV and saltwater wetlands in CANA are in good condition. Freshwater wetlands have been disturbed by road cuts, invasive exotic plants, and alterations to the local hydrology. Park staff members are cooperating with MINWR to remedy the impacts to wetlands in CANA. Results of monitoring amphibians and reptiles in CANA have recognized the diversity of species that inhabit the swales of freshwater wetlands and their susceptibility to changes in habitat.

Boating activity and fishing has been a part of the Mosquito Lagoon's history, but has intensified in recent years. Boating activity on the water body impacts populations of fish, shellfish, marine mammals, and SAV. Watercraft activities are probably one of the greatest sources of negative impacts to the park's natural resources.

Ongoing biological monitoring programs conducted by CANA, MINWR, CAFS, FWC-FWRI and NASA in the park and local environs have established baseline knowledge for several species, the salt water wetlands and the terrestrial ecology. Hopefully programs, such as the in-water sea turtle monitoring and nest counts, amphibian and reptile monitoring, fish sampling, horseshoe crab, oyster reef research, and the MINWR land management plan will continue. Additional research in the park to establish a baseline understanding of the status of other key species for example, blue crabs and clams should be considered. Plant community field surveys in CANA should be considered to develop to inventory freshwater wetlands and saltwater wetlands and ground truth aerial imagery.

This report is based on an extensive review of data. However, the knowledge base is incomplete in many areas (Table 31). For instance, a few of the knowledge gaps that cut across biotic categories include the potential effects of climate change, storms, pollution loading, and invasion of non-native species. It is recommended that the NPS consider expanding their monitoring and modeling efforts to account for these gaps. A useful tool would be to use this report as a basis for an annual state-of-the-park update that addresses key issues of concern. The major issues that should be addressed include trends and variability in surface water and groundwater quality, ocean shoreline position, and important biological resources, such as submerged aquatic vegetation, sea turtles, recreationally important species, and invasive species.

It is further recommended that CANA establish a central digital database that includes files of raw datasets, GIS thematic coverages, and a digital reference library. The database should be updated on a continuing basis. This process can begin with the GIS files assembled for this project.

Literature Cited

Abbott, J. 2008. Florida Red Tide Monitoring and Reporting. Florida Fish and Wildlife Conservation Commission, Fish and Wildlife Research Institute, St. Petersburg, FL. http://www.dep.state.fl.us/coastal/WaterMonitoringCouncil/files/meetings/2008/09-24/Florida_Red_Tide_Monitoring.pdf (accessed 22 January 2011).

Abgrall, M. J. and Walters, L.J., 2003. Temporal diversity and abundance of drift macrophytes and associated organisms in Mosquito Lagoon, Volusia County, Florida. *Fla. Sci.* 66 (2), 113-127.

Abrahamson, W.G. and D.C. Hartnett. 1990. Pine flatwoods and dry prairies. Pages 103-149. *in* Myers, R.L. and J.J. Ewel, eds. Ecosystems of Florida. University of Central Florida Press, Orlando, FL.

Adams, D.H., C. Sonne, N. Basu, R. Dietz, D-H. Nam, P.S. Leifsson, and A.L. Jensen. 2010. Mercury contamination in spotted seatrout, *Cynoscion nebulosus*: an assessment of liver, kidney, blood, and nervous system health. Science of the Total Environment 408:5808-5816.

Adams, D. H. 2004. Total mercury levels in tunas from offshore waters of the Florida Atlantic coast. Marine Pollution Bulletin 49:659-663.

Adams, D. H. 2010. Consistently low mercury concentrations in dolphinfish, *Coryphaena hippurus*, an oceanic pelagic predator. *Environmental Research* 109:697-701.

Adams, D.H, and R.H. McMichael, Jr. 1999. Mercury Levels in Four Species of Sharks from the Atlantic Coast of Florida; *Fishery Bulletin* 97: 372-379.

Adams, D. H., R. H., Jr., McMichael, and G. H. Henderson. 2003. Mercury levels in marine and estuarine fishes of Florida: 1989-2001. FWC-FWRI, Florida Marine Research Institute Technical Report TR-9. 2nd ed. rev. 57 pp.

Adams, D. H., and McMichael, R. H., Jr. 2007. Mercury in king mackerel, *Scomberomorus cavalla*, and Spanish mackerel, *S. maculatus*, from waters of the south-eastern USA: regional and historical trends. Marine and Freshwater Research 58:187-193.

Adams, D. H., and R. Paperno. 2007. Preliminary assessment of a nearshore nursery ground for the scalloped hammerhead off the Atlantic coast of Florida. Pages 65-174 in McCandless C.T., Kohler N.E., Pratt H.L.J., editors. Shark nursery grounds of the Gulf of Mexico and the east coast waters of the United States. American Fisheries Society, Symposium 50, Bethesda, MD. http://afsbooks.org/54050P (accessed 14 May 2012).

Adams, D. H., and R. Paperno. 2008. Mosquito Lagoon Fisheries Monitoring. Annual report, January-December, 2007. Florida Fish and Wildlife Conservation Commission, Fish and Wildlife Research Institute, St. Petersburg, FL Report No. F2652-07-A1.

Adams, D. H., and R. Paperno. 2009. Mosquito Lagoon Fisheries Monitoring. Annual report, January-December, 2008. Florida Fish and Wildlife Conservation Commission, Fish and Wildlife Research Institute, St. Petersburg, FL Report No. F2652-07-A2.

Antworth, R. L., G. A. Pike, and J. C. Stiner. 2006. Nesting ecology, current status, and conservation of sea turtles on an uninhabited beach in Florida, USA. Biological Conservation 130:10-15.

Arnold, W.S., M.L. Parker, and S.P. Stephenson. 2008. Oyster Monitoring in the Northern Estuaries. Report to the South Florida Water Management District in Fulfillment of Grant Number:CP040614. Florida Fish and Wildlife Research Institute, St. Petersburg, Florida 33701.

Aubrey, C., and F. Snelson, Jr. 2007. Early life history of the spinner shark in a Florida nursery. *In* Shark nursery grounds of the Gulf of Mexico and the east coast waters of the United States. McCandless, C. T., N. E. Kohler, and H. L. Pratt, Jr., editors. Symposium 50. The American Fisheries Society. 402 p.

Badylak, S., and E. J. Philips. 2004. Spatial and temporal patterns of phytoplankton composition in a subtropical coastal lagoon, the Indian River Lagoon, Florida, USA. *Journal of Plankton Research* 26(10):1229-1247.

Barber A. L. 2007. Restoration of Intertidal Oyster Reefs Affected by Intense Recreational Boating Activity in Mosquito Lagoon, FL. Master Thesis, University of Central Florida, Orlando, FL.

Barton, B.T. 2005. Cascading effects of predator removal on the ecology of sea turtle nesting beaches. Masters Thesis, University of Central Florida, Orlando, FL. 48 pp.

Barton, B.T. and J.D. Roth. 2008. Implications of intraguild predation for sea turtle nest protection. *Biological Conservation* Volume 141, Issue 8, August 2008, pp. 2139-2145.

Belanger, T. V., H. H. Heck, and M. S. Andrews. 1997. Groundwater Flow Characteristics of the Mosquito Lagoon, FL. Final Report, Project Number: CANA-N-027.000. Submitted to the Water Resources Division, National Park Service.

Bigelow, D. S. 1984. Instruction Manual NADP/NTN Site selection and installation. NADP Manual 1984-01, National Atmospheric Deposition Program, Program Coordinator's Office, Colorado State University, Fort Collins, CO 80523.

Booth, K. 1993. Spatial distribution, group composition and habitat utilization of the Atlantic bottlenose dolphin (*Tursiops tuncatus*) in the Indian River Lagoon, Indian River County, Florida. Masters Thesis, Florida Institute of Technology, Melbourne, FL 52 pp.

Bossart, G. D., J. S. Reif, A. M. Schaefer, J. Goldstein, P. A. Fair, and J. T. Saliki. 2010. Morbillivirus infection in free-ranging Atlantic bottlenose dolphins (*Tursiops truncatus*) from the Southeastern United States: Seroepidemiologic and pathologic evidence of subclinical infection. *Veterinary Microbiology* Vol. 143, Issues 2-4, 14, 160-166 pp.

Boudreaux, M. L. 2005. Native and invasive sessile competitors of the eastern oyster, *Crassostrea virginica*, in Mosquito Lagoon, Florida. M.S. Thesis, University of Central Florida, Orlando, Florida, 104. pp.

Boudreaux, M. L., and L. Walters. 2006a. *Mytella charruana* (Bivalvia: Mytilidae): a new, invasive bivalve in Mosquito Lagoon, Florida. *The Nautilus* 120:34-36.

Boudreaux, M. L., and L. Walters. 2006b. *Mytella charruana* along the Atlantic coast of Florida: A successful invasion? *Journal of Shellfish Research* 25(2):713.

Boudreaux, M.L., and L. Walters. 2006c. Spatial competition between oysters and barnacles in a Florida estuary. *Journal of Shellfish Research* 25(2):713.

Boudreaux, M. L., J. L. Stiner, and L. Walters. 2006. Biodiversity of sessile and motile macrofauna on intertidal oyster reefs in Mosquito Lagoon, Florida. *Journal of Shellfish Research* 25:1079-1089.

Boudreaux, M. L., Walters, L. J. and D. Rittschof. 2009. Interactions between native barnacles, non-native barnacles, and the eastern oyster *Crassostrea virginica*. *Bull. Mar. Sci.* 84: 43-57.

Byrne, M. W., L. E. Elston, B. D. Smrekar, B. A. Blankley, and P. A. Bazemore. 2010. Summary of amphibian community monitoring at Canaveral National Seashore, 2009. Natural Resource Data Series NPS/SECN/NRDS—2010/098. National Park Service, Fort Collins, Colorado.

Cable, J. E., W. C Burnett, J. P. Chanton, D. R. Corbett, and P. H. Cable. 1997. Field evaluation of seepage meters in the coastal marine environment. Estuarine, *Coastal and Shelf Science* 45:367-375.

Cable, J. E., J. B. Martin, P. W. Swarzenski, M. Lindenburg, and J. Steward. 2004. Advection within shallow pore waters of a coastal lagoon, Ground Water, 42, 1011–1020, doi:10.1111/j.1745-6584.2004.tb02640.x.

Carlson, R. E. 1977. A trophic state index for lakes. *Limnology and Oceanography*. 22: 361-368.

Carlson, D.B., P.D. O'Bryan, and J.R. Rey. 1999. Florida's salt marsh management issues: 1991-98. *Journal of the American Mosquito Control Association* 152:186-193.

Cerco, C. F., and T. Cole. 1994: Three-dimensional eutrophication model of Chesapeake Bay. *J. Environ. Eng.* 119, 1006-1025.

Christian, D. and Y.P. Sheng. 2003. Relative influence of various water quality parameters on light attenuation in Indian River Lagoon: *Estuarine Coastal and Shelf Science* 57:961-971.

Cobb, J. 2007. Monitoring the Effects of Beach Nourishment - Data and Graphs Data collected for the beach nourishment monitoring project, by the Molluscan Fisheries at the Fish and Wildlife Research Institute: October 2005 – July 2007. http://research.myfwc.com/features/view_article.asp?id=33028 (accessed 22 November 2010).

Cohenour, B. 1974. Statistical study of total surface area and total volume of the lagoonal system of east Florida coast. (Mosquito Lagoon and Indian River) from 28-52-N to 27-10-N. Florida Institute of Technology, Melbourne, FL.

Collins, M. R., D. J. Schmidt, C. W. Waltz, and J. L. Pickney. 1989. Age and growth of king mackerel, *Scomberomorus cavalla*, from the Atlantic coast of the United States. *Fishery Bulletin* 87(1):49-61.

Conant, T. A., P. H. Dutton, T. Eguchi, S. P. Epperly, C. C. Fahy, M. H. Godfrey, S. L. MacPherson, E. E. Possardt, B. A. Schroeder, J. A. Seminoff, M .L. Snover, C. M. Upite, and B.E. Witherington. 2009. Loggerhead sea turtle (*Caretta caretta*) 2009 status review under the U.S. Endangered Species Act. Report of the Loggerhead Biological Review Team to the National Marine Fisheries Service, August 2009. 222 pages.

Diaz, Humberto. 1980. The Mole Crab *Emerita talpoida*: A Case of Changing Life History Pattern. Ecological Monographs 50:437–456.

Duncan, B. W., V. L. Larson, and P. A. Schmalzer. 2004. Historic and recent landscape change in the North Indian River Lagoon watershed, Florida. *Natural Areas Journal* 24, 198–215.

Durden, W. N., M. K. Megan, D. H. Adams, and E.D. Stolen. 2007. Mercury and selenium concentrations in stranded bottlenose dolphins from the Indian River Lagoon System, Florida. *Bulletin of Marine Science* 81(1): 37–54, 2007.

Ehlinger, G.S., R.A. Tankersley, and M.B. Bush. 2003. Spatial and temporal patterns of spawning and larval hatching by the horseshoe crab *Limulus polyphemus* in a microtidal coastal lagoon. *Estuaries* 26: 631-640.

Ehlinger, G.S. and R.A. Tankersley. 2004. Survival and development of horseshoe crab (*Limulus polyphemus*) embryos and larvae in hypersaline conditions. *Biol. Bull.* 206:87-94.

Ehlinger, G. S., and R. A. Tankersley. 2007. Reproductive ecology of the American horseshoe crab *Limulus polyphemus* in the Indian River Lagoon: An overview. *Florida Scientist* 70:449-463.

Federal Register. June 3, 1994. 50 CFR Part 226 [Docket No. 930363-4145, I.D. 012793B] ACTION: Final rule Designated Critical Habitat; Northern Right Whale. National Marine

Fisheries Service (NMFS), National Oceanic and Atmospheric Administration (NOAA), Commerce. http://www.nmfs.noaa.gov/pr/pdfs/fr/fr59-28805.pdf (accessed March 2009).

Fick, K. J. 1995. An investigation of the abundance, group size, and activities of the Atlantic bottlenose dolphin (TE Montague 1821) in the Indian River, Brevard County, Florida. Masters Thesis, Florida Institute of Technology, Melbourne, FL. 98 pp.

Fick, K. J., A. E. Redlow, A. M. Foley, and K. E. Singel. 2000. The occurrence of fibropapillomatosis in stranded green turtles in Florida, 1980-1998. p. 236-237. *in*: Proceedings of the 19th Annual Symposium on Sea Turtle Biology and Conservation. U.S. Department of Commerce., NOAA Technical Memo. NMFS-SEFSC-443.

Florida Department of Agriculture & Consumer Services Division of Aquaculture (FDACS). 1997. Shellfish Harvesting Area Classification Map #80 (Effective: December 28, 1997) Body A (#80) Shellfish Harvesting Area in Brevard County. www.floridaaquaculture.com/pdfmaps/80.PDF (accessed 20 January 2011).

Florida Department of Agriculture & Consumer Services Division of Aquaculture (FDACS). 2000. Shellfish Harvesting Area Classification Map #82B (Effective: August 9, 2000). South Volusia (#82) Shellfish Harvesting Area in Volusia County Map 82b. www.floridaaquaculture.com/pdfmaps/82b.PDF (accessed 20 January 2011).

Florida Department of Agriculture & Consumer Services Division of Aquaculture (FDACS). 2009. Shellfish Harvesting Area Classification Boundaries and Management Plans Revised December 28, 2009. Shellfish Environmental Assessment Section, Tallahassee, FL.

Florida Department of Environmental Protection (FDEP). 1996. 1996 Water-Quality Assessment for the State of Florida, Section 305(b) Main Report. Paulic M., J. Hand, and L. Lord, Eds. Bureau of Water Resources Protection, Division of Water Facilities, Florida Department of Environmental Protection. Tallahassee, FL. http://www.seminole.wateratlas.usf.edu/upload/documents/1996_305b.pdf

Florida Department of Environmental Protection (FDEP). 2007. Critically eroded beaches in Florida. Florida Department of Environmental Protection Bureau of Beaches and Coastal Systems Division of Water Resource Management Department of Environmental Protection. Update June. Tallahassee, FL.

Florida Department of Environmental Protection (FDEP). 2008. Water Quality Assessment Report: Indian River Lagoon. Division of Environmental Assessment and Restoration, Tallahassee, FL.

Florida Department of Environmental Protection (FDEP). 2009. Mosquito Lagoon Aquatic Preserve Management Plan: August 2009 - July 2019. Mosquito Lagoon Aquatic Preserve. Cocoa, FL. Florida Department of Environmental Protection, Coastal and Aquatic Managed Areas. Tallahassee, FL.

Florida Department of Environmental Protection (FDEP), 2010a. March 31, 2010. Estuarine and Coastal Waters Nutrient Criteria Workshop. Ft. Pierce, FL.

Florida Department of Environmental Protection (FDEP). 2010b. Development of Numeric Nutrient Criteria for Florida Waters. http://www.dep.state.fl.us/water/wqssp/nutrients/index.htm (accessed 20 April 2010)

Florida Department of Environmental Protection (FDEP). 2010c. Volume 2, Public Meeting, Technical Advisory Committee, Numeric Nutrient Criteria, April 7, 2010, Florida State University, Tallahassee, FL 32308 http://www.dep.state.fl.us/water/wqssp/nutrients/docs/nutrient_tac_transcript_040710_aftern oon.pdf (accessed 20 April 2010)

Florida Department of Motor Vehicles (FLDMV). 2010. Facts and Figures 2008-2010. Tallahassee, FL. http://www.flhsmv.gov/dmv/vslfacts.html (accessed 7 October 2010).

Florida Fish and Wildlife Conservation Commission (FWC). 2002. Brevard County Manatee Protection Zones. http://myfwc.com/WILDLIFEHABITATS/Manatee_protectionzones.htm (accessed 30 November 2010).

Florida Fish and Wildlife Conservation Commission (FWC). 2003. January 6. Florida's breeding bird atlas: A collaborative study of Florida's birdlife. http://www.myfwc.com/bba/ (accessed 23 November 2010.

Florida Fish and Wildlife Conservation Commission-Florida Wildlife Research Institute (FWC-FWRI). 2003. Conserving Florida's Seagrass Resources: Developing a Coordinated Statewide Management Program. St. Petersburg, FL.

Florida Fish and Wildlife Conservation Commission-Florida Wildlife Research Institute (FWC-FWRI). 2005a. Sea Stats, Blue Crab.

Florida Fish and Wildlife Conservation Commission-Fish and Wildlife Research Institute (FWC-FWRI). 2005b. Florida's Inshore Marine Monitoring and Assessment Program (IMAP) Annual Report, Year Six. IMAP Annual Report 2004. FWRI File Code: F2248-99-A5. 89 pp.

Florida Fish and Wildlife Conservation Commission-Florida Wildlife Research Institute (FWC-FWRI). 2006. Summary of Choctawhatchee Bay Aquatic Animal Mortalities (Updated April 20, 2006). http://research.myfwc.com/features/view_article.asp?id=26721 (accessed 25 November 2010).

Florida Fish and Wildlife Conservation Commission-Florida Wildlife Research Institute (FWC-FWRI). 2009a. Statewide Nesting Totals 1979 – 2009. http://research.myfwc.com/images/articles/11812/statewide_totals_1979_-_2009.pdf (accessed 25 November 2010).

Florida Fish and Wildlife Conservation Commission-Florida Wildlife Research Institute (FWC-FWRI). 2009b. Florida's Inshore and Nearshore Species: 2008 Status and Trends Report. Blue Crab (Callinectes sapidus). pp. 226-231. http://research.myfwc.com/features/view_article.asp?id=30223 (accessed 25 November 2010).

Florida Fish and Wildlife Conservation Commission-Florida Wildlife Research Institute (FWC-FWRI). 2010a. Index Nesting Beach Survey Totals (1989-2010). http://research.myfwc.com/features/view_article.asp?id=10690 (accessed 24 November 2010).

Florida Fish and Wildlife Conservation Commission-Florida Wildlife Research Institute (FWC-FWRI). 2010b. A Good Nesting Season for Loggerheads in 2010 Does Not Reverse a Recent Declining Trend. http://research.myfwc.com/features/view_article.asp?id=27537 (accessed 23 November 2010).

Florida Fish and Wildlife Conservation Commission-Florida Wildlife Research Institute (FWC-FWRI). 2010c. Commercial Fisheries Landings in Florida. http://research.myfwc.com/features/view_article.asp?id=19224 (accessed 25 November 2010).

Florida Fish and Wildlife Conservation Commission-Florida Wildlife Research Institute (FWC-FWRI). 2010d. Health Assessment of Blue Crab in Tampa Bay: A project to study blue crab health in Tampa Bay from August 2006 through August 2007. (accessed 28 November 2010).

Florida Fish and Wildlife Conservation Commission-Florida Wildlife Research Institute (FWC-FWRI). 2010e. January 2010 Statewide Sea Turtle Cold-Stunning Event. http://research.myfwc.com/features/view_article.asp?id=34303 (accessed 17 January 2011).

Florida Fish and Wildlife Conservation Commission-Florida Wildlife Research Institute (FWC-FWRI). 2010f. Descriptions of Manatee Death Categories. http://research.myfwc.com/features/view_article.asp?id=6780 (accessed 17 January 2011).

Florida Fish and Wildlife Conservation Commission-Florida Wildlife Research Institute (FWC-FWRI). 2011. Ballast Water and the Transport of Harmful Algae. http://research.myfwc.com/features/view_article.asp?id=23967 (accessed 22 January 2011).

Florida Natural Areas Inventory and Florida Department of Natural Resources (FNAI-FDNR). 1990. Guide to the natural communities of Florida. Florida Natural Areas Inventory and Florida Department of Natural Resources, Tallahassee, Florida. Available at: http://www.fnai.org/PDF/Natural_Communities_Guide.pdf

Florida Natural Areas Inventory (FNAI). 2010. Guide to the natural communities of Florida: 2010 edition. Florida Natural Areas Inventory, Tallahassee, FL.

Florida Oceans and Coastal Council (FOCC). Revised June 2009. The effects of climate change on Florida's ocean and coastal resources. A special report to the Florida Energy and Climate Commission and the people of Florida. Tallahassee, FL. 34 pp.

Forward R.B., Diaz H. and J. H. Cohen. 2005. The tidal rhythm in activity of the mole crab *Emerita talpoida*. Journal of the Marine Biological Association of the United Kingdom. Vol. 85, Issue 04, pp. 895-901. DOI 10.1017/S0025315405011860.

Funicelli, N.A., D.R. Johnson, and D.A. Meineke. 1988. Assessment of the effectiveness of an existing fish sanctuary within the Kennedy Space Center. Special Purpose Report to the Marine Fisheries Commission of Florida. 54 p.

Gilliom and others, 2006. The Quality of Our Nation's Waters—Pesticides in the Nation's Streams and Ground Water, 1992–2001: U.S. Geological Survey Circular 1291,172 p.

Grizzle, R. E., J. R. Adams, and L. J. Walters. 2002. Historical changes in intertidal oyster (*Crassostrea virginica*) reefs in a Florida lagoon potentially related to boating activities. *Journal of Shellfish Research* 21(2):749-756.

Gronewold, A. D., and R. L. Wolpert. 2008. Modeling the relationship between most probable number (MPN) and colony-forming unit (CFU) estimates of fecal coliform concentration. *Water Research* 42(13):3327-3334.

Guillory V., H. Perry, P. Steele, T. Wagner, W. Keithly, B. Pelligrin, J. Petterson, T. Floyd, B. Buckson, L. Hartman, E. Holder, and C. Moss. 2001. The Blue Crab Fishery of the Gulf of Mexico, U.S. A Regional Management Plan. Gulf States Marine Fisheries Commission, Ocean Springs, MS.

Hall, C. R., J. A. Provancha, D. M. Oddy, R. L. Lowers, and J. D. Drese. 2001. Canaveral National Seashore Water Quality and Aquatic Resource Inventory. NASA Technical Memorandum 2001-210261. Dynamac Corporation, Kennedy Space Center, FL, USA.

Hand, J., V. Tauxe, M. Friedemann. 1988. Middle East Coast Basin Technical Report: An Appendix of the 305(b) Water Quality Assessment for the State of Florida. Standards and Monitoring Section, Bureau of Surface Water Management, Division of Water Management, Department of Environmental Regulation. Standards and Monitoring Technical Report # 113.

Hayes, M. O. 1979. Barrier island morphology as a function of wave and tide regime. In: Leatherman, S. P. ed., Barrier islands from the Gulf of St. Lawrence to the Gulf of Mexico. New York, NY: Academic Press. Pp 1–29.

Hannah, G. V. 1965. Chronology of work stoppages and related events - KSC/NASA/AFETR – through 1965. NASA. October 1965.

Hyland, J. L., T. J. Herrlinger, T. R. Snoots, A. H. Ringwood, R. F. Van Dolah, C. T. Hackney, G. A. Nelson, J. S. Rosen, and S. A. Kokkinakis. 1996. Environmental quality of estuaries of the Carolinian Province: 1994. Annual statistical summary for the 1994 EMAP-Estuaries Demonstration Project in the Carolinian Province. NOAA Technical Memorandum NOS ORCA 97. NOAA/NOS, Office of Ocean Resources Conservation and Assessment, Silver Spring, MD. 102 p.

Hyland, J.L., L. Balthis, C.T. Hackney, G. McRae, A.H. Ringwood, T.R. Snoots, R.F. Van Dolah, and T.L. Wade. 1998. Environmental quality of estuaries of the Carolinian Province: 1995. Annual statistical summary for the 1995 EMAP Estuaries Demonstration Project in the Carolinian Province. NOAA Technical Memorandum NOS ORCA 123 NOAA/NOS, Office of Ocean Resources Conservation and Assessment, Silver Spring, MD. 143 p.

Johnson, D. R. and N. A. Funicelli. 1991. Spawning of the red drum in Mosquito Lagoon, east-central Florida. *Estuaries* 14, 74-79.

Johnson-Restrepo, B, K. Kannan, R. Addink, and D.H. Adams. 2005. Polybrominated diphenyl ethers (PBDEs) and polychlorinated biphenyls (PCBs) in a marine foodweb of coastal Florida. Environmental Science and Technology 39:8243-8250.

Johnson-Restrepo, B, D.H. Adams and K. Kannan. 2008. Tetrabromobisphenol A (TBBPA) and hexabromocyclododecanes (HBCDs) in tissues of humans, dolphins, and sharks from the United States. Chemosphere 70(11):1935-1944.

Johnston, C. E., M. Castro, L. Casten, A. Henderson, and A. Kennon. 2006. Fish inventories at Southeast Coast Network Parks. Report to the Southeast Coast Network, National Park Service. 20 p.

Kroening, S. E. 2008. Assessment of Water-Quality Monitoring and a Proposed Water-Quality Monitoring Network for the Mosquito Lagoon Basin, East-Central Florida: U.S. Geological Survey Scientific Investigations Report 2007-5238, 53 p.

Lasater, J. A. 1974. A study of lagoonal and estuarine processes in the area of Merritt Island encompassing Kennedy Space Center. Florida Institute of Technology, Melbourne, FL, USA.

Lichtler, W. F. 1960. Geology and Groundwater Resources of Martin County, Florida. Florida Geological Survey: Report of investigations: 23:149.

McBride, R. A. 1987. Tidal inlet history, morphology, and stability, eastern coast of Florida, USA. In: N. Kraus, ed. Coastal Sediments '87, American Society of Civil Engineers, New York, NY: 2:1592-1607.

McBride, R. A., and T. F. Moslow. 1991. Origin, evolution, and distribution of shoreface sand ridges, Atlantic inner shelf, U.S.A. *Mar. Geol.* 97:57–85.

McGurk, B., P. Bond, and D. Mehan. 1989. Hydrogeologic and lithologic characteristics of the surficial sediments in Volusia County, Florida. St. Johns River Water Management District Technical Publication SJ 89-7.

McMichael, R. H., Jr., R. Paperno, B. J. McLaughlin, and M. E. Mitchell. 1995. Florida's marine fisheries-independent monitoring program: A long-term ecological dataset. *Bulletin of Marine Science* 57(1):282-5.

McRae, G. 2002. Florida's Inshore Marine Monitoring and Assessment Program (IMAP) Year 3 Annual Report, July 1, 2002. EPA Assistance ID NO. C R 827240-01-0. Florida Fish and Wildlife Conservation Commission, Florida Marine Research Institute, St. Petersburg, FL.

McRae, G., M. Julian, and H. Brown. 2003. Florida's Inshore Marine Monitoring and Assessment Program (IMAP) Annual Report, September 30, 2003.Year Four. EPA Assistance ID NO. C R 827240-01-0. Florida Fish and Wildlife Conservation Commission, Florida Marine Research Institute, St. Petersburg, FL.

McRae, G., M. Julian, and H. Brown. 2005. Florida Fish and Wildlife Conservation Commission-Florida Wildlife Research Institute (FWC-FWRI). Florida's Inshore Marine Monitoring and Assessment Program (IMAP) Annual Report, September 30, 2005. Year Six, EPA Assistance ID NO. C R 827240-01-0. Florida Fish and Wildlife Conservation Commission, Florida Marine Research Institute, St. Petersburg, FL.

Mehta, A. J., H. K. Brooks. 1973. Mosquito Lagoon Barrier Beach Study. *Shore and Beach* 41(2):26-34.

Menon, M. P., G. S. Ghuman, C. O. Emeh. 1979. Trace element release from estuarine sediments of South Mosquito Lagoon near Kennedy Space Center. *Water, Air, and Soil Pollution* 12:295-306.

Meisburger, E. F., and M. E. Field. 1975. Geomorphology, shallow structure, and sediments of the Florida Inner Continental Shelf, Cape Canaveral to Georgia Technical Memorandum No. 54 U. S. Army Corp of Engineers Coastal Engineering Research Center (CERC).

Meisburger, E. F., and M. E. Field. 1976. Neogene sediments of Atlantic inner continental shelf off northeastern Florida. *American Association of Petroleum Geologists Bulletin* 60(11):2019–2037.

Merritt Island National Wildlife Refuge (MINWR). 2008. Comprehensive Conservation Plan Merritt Island National Wildlife Refuge, Brevard and Volusia Counties, Florida. Submitted by Ron Hight. U.S. Department of the Interior, Fish and Wildlife Service, Southeast Region.

Millero, F. J. 1975. Marine chemistry in the coastal environment. Pages 25-55 *in* American Chemical Society.

Morris, J., and B. Nodine. 1995. Boating activity, boat speed regulation and manatee protection in Brevard County, Florida. *Bulletin of Marine Science* 57(1): 283-285.

Murdoch, M. E., J. S. Reif, M. Mazzoil, S. D. McCulloch, P. A. Fair, and G. D. Bossart. 2008. Lobomycosis in Bottlenose Dolphins (*Tursiops truncates*) from the Indian River Lagoon, Florida: Estimation of prevalence, temporal trends, and spatial distribution. *EcoHealth*

Murphy, M. D., A. L. McMillen-Jackson, and B. Mahmoudi. 2007. A stock assessment for blue crab, *Callinectes sapidus*, in Florida waters. Florida Fish and Wildlife Conservation Commission Fish and Wildlife Research Institute, St. Petersburg, FL.

Murphy, M. D., and R. G. Taylor. 1991. Direct validation of ages determined for adult red drums from otolith sections. *Trans. Am. Fish Soc.* 120(2):267-9.

Nam, D. H., D. H. Adams, L. J. Flewelling, and N. Basu. 2010. Neurochemical alterations in lemon shark, *Negaprion brevirostris*, brains in association with brevetoxin exposure. *Aquatic Toxicology* 99:351-359.

National Estuary Program. 2007. Southeast National Estuary Program Condition, Indian River Lagoon. National Estuary Program. (CCR, Chapter 4, 212-222). http://www.epa.gov/owow/oceans/nepccr/index.html (accessed 20 December 2007).

National Marine Fisheries Service (NMFS). 2009. North Atlantic Right Whale (*Eubalaena glacialis*): Western Atlantic Stock. NOAA Fisheries Office of Protected Species. http://www.nmfs.noaa.gov/pr/pdfs/sars/ao2009whnr-w.pdf (accessed 24 November 2010).

National Marine Fisheries Service (NMFS). 2010a. Species & Critical Habitats. Personal communication from the National Marine Fisheries Service, Fisheries Statistics Division, Silver Spring, MD. http://www.nmfs.noaa.gov/pr/species/criticalhabitat.htm (accessed 19 October 2010).

National Marine Fisheries Service (NMFS). 2010b. Commercial Fisheries Landings. http://www.st.nmfs.noaa.gov/st1/commercial/index.html (accessed 24 November 2010).

National Marine Fisheries Service and U.S. Fish and Wildlife Service (NMFS-FWS). 2008. Recovery Plan for the Northwest Atlantic Population of the Loggerhead Sea Turtle (*Caretta caretta*), Second Revision. National Marine Fisheries Service, Silver Spring, MD.

National Park Service (NPS). 1996. Baseline water quality data inventory and analysis: Canaveral National Seashore. Water Resources Division, Technical Report. NPS/NRWRD/NRTR-96/85, Washington, DC.

National Park Service (NPS). 2005. Canaveral National Seashore Public Use Reporting and Counting Instructions. http://www.nature.nps.gov/stats/CountingInstructions/CANACI2005.pdf (accessed 9/24/2010).

National Park Service (NPS). 2006. Draft Canaveral National Seashore Fire Management Plan. National Park Service DOI. Canaveral National Seashore, Titusville, FL.

DeVivo, J. C., C. J. Wright, M. W. Byrne, E. DiDonato, and T. Curtis. 2008. Vital Signs Monitoring in the Southeast Coast Inventory and Monitoring Network. Natural Resource Report NPS/SECN/NRR-2008/061. National Park Service, Fort Collins, Colorado.

National Park Service (NPS). 2010a. Oil Spill Response. http://www.nps.gov/archive/features/oilspillresponse/FactSheets/NPS_OilSpillResponse_Web.pdf (accessed 22 January 2011).

National Park Service (NPS) 2010b. Canaveral National Seashore http://www.nps.gov/cana/naturescience/index.htm (accessed 29 January 2011).

National Park Service - Social Science Division (NPS-SSD). 2010a. 5 Year Annual Recreation Visits Report 1976 -1980 and 2005 -2009. Public Use Statistics Office. Social Science Division NPS. Fort Collins, CO. http://www.nature.nps.gov/stats/ (accessed 24 September 2010).

National Park Service - Social Science Division (NPS-SSD). 2010b. Canaveral NS Traffic Count Report 1991 - 2009. Public Use Statistics Office. Social Science Division NPS. Fort Collins, CO. (http://www.nature.nps.gov/stats/) (accessed 7 October 2010).

National Park Service - Social Science Division (NPS-SSD). 2010c. Forecast for 2010 and 2011. http://www.nature.nps.gov/stats/forecasts/forecast1011.pdf (accessed 25 September 2010).

Neumann, C. J., B. R. Jarvinen, C. J. McAdie, and J. D. Elms. 1993. Tropical Cyclones of the North Atlantic Ocean, 1871-1992. Prepared by the National Climatic Data Center. Asheville, NC in cooperation with the NHC, Coral Gables, FL. 193 p.

NOAA Center for Operational Oceanographic Products and Services (NOAA-CO-OPS): http://tidesandcurrents.noaa.gov (accessed 2 December 2010).

Nocita, B. W., L. W. Papetti, A. E. Grosz, and K. M. Campbell. 1991. Sand, gravel and heavy - mineral resource potential of Holocene sediments offshore of Florida, Cape Canaveral to the Georgia Border: Phase I: Florida Geological Survey, Open File Report 39, 29 p.

Norse, E. A., and V. Fox-Norse. 1979. Geographical ecology and evolutionary relationships in *Callinectes* spp. (Brachyura: Portunidae). Pages 1–9 in H.M. Perry and W.A. Engel, eds. Proceedings of the blue crab symposium, October 18-19, 1979. Gulf States Marine Fisheries Commission, Ocean Springs.

Nova Southeastern University Oceanographic Center (NSUOC). 2009. Final Report: Mapping the Distribution and Abundance of Macroalgae in the Indian River Lagoon Contract #SK49513. April 1, 2009. Nova Southeastern University Oceanographic Center, Dania Beach, FL.

Odell, D.K. and E.D. Asper 1990. Distribution and movements of freeze-branded bottlenose dolphins in the Indian and Banana Rivers, Florida. Pages 515-540 *in*: S. Leatherwood and R. Reeves, (eds.) The bottlenose dolphin. Academic Press, San Diego, CA.

Odum, H.T. 1982. Role of wetland ecosystems in the landscape of Florida. In Proceedings of the International Scientific Workshop on Freshwater Ecosystem Dynamics in Wetlands and

Shallow Water Bodies, sponsored by the Scientific Committee on Problems of the Environment, of the United Nations Environment Programme, held in Moscow, USSR, 1982. Vol. 2, pp. 33-72.

Pandit, A., H. Heck., and A. Ali. 2010. Nutrient loading in the Indian River Lagoon from groundwater. Third International Perspective on Current and Future State of Water Resources and the Environment. Chennai, India.

Paperno, R., K. J. Mille, and E. Kadison. 2001. Patterns in species composition of fish and selected invertebrate assemblages in estuarine subregions near Ponce de Leon Inlet, Florida. *Estuary Coastal Shelf Science* 52(1):117-30.

Paperno R. 2002. Age-0 spot (Leiostomus xanthurus) from two estuaries along central Florida's East Coast: comparisons of the timing of recruitment, seasonal changes in abundance, and rates of growth and mortality. *Florida Scientist* 65, 85-99.

Park, K., A. Y. Kuo, J. Shen, and J. M. Hamrick. 1995. A three-dimensional hydrodynamic-eutrophication model (HEM3D): description of water quality and sediment processes submodels. The College of William and Mary, Virginia Institute of Marine Science. Special Report 327.

Parker, S. 2008. Canaveral National Seashore Historic Resource Study. National Park Service, Cultural Resources Division, Southeast Regional Office, Atlanta, GA.

Parkinson, R. W., and R. Schwab. 2007. Geologic Map of Canaveral National Seashore 1:24,000 Scale 7.5 Minute Series Quadrangles. Prepared for: Geologic Resource Evaluation Program National Park Service Denver, Colorado.

Paulic, M., G. Xueqing, J. Auilo, J. M. Sawistoski, B. Bess, and E. Pluchino. 2006. Water Quality Status Report, Indian River Lagoon. (pp. 25-145). Tallahassee: Florida Department of Environmental Protection, Division of Water Resource Management.

Pelican Island Audubon (PIA). 2008. Merritt Island National Wildlife Field Trip Bird List Jan. 5, 2008. Compiled by Juanita & Richard Baker, Susan Boyd, and Rick Lucas. http://www.pelicanislandaudubon.org/minwr_bird_list_080105.html (accessed 24 November 2010).

Pike, D. A. and J. C. Stiner. 2007. Sea turtle species vary in their susceptibility to tropical cyclones. *Oecologia* 153:471–478.

Provancha, J. 2006. Annual report for sea turtle netting in Mosquito Lagoon: Reference Florida Permit #114, NMFS Permit #1450. 13 January 2006, 11 pp.

Provancha, J. A., and M. J. Provancha. 1988. Long-term trends in abundance and distribution of manatees (*Trichechus manatus*) in the Northern Banana River, Brevard County, Florida. *Marine Mammal Science* 4(4):323-338.

Provancha, J. A., M. J. Mota, R. H. Lowers, D. M. Scheidt, and M. A. Corsello. 1998. Relative abundance and distribution of marine turtles inhabiting Mosquito Lagoon, Florida, USA. *in*: S. P. Epperly and J. Braun (Compilers). Proceedings of the Seventeenth Annual Sea Turtle Symposium. NOAA Technical Memorandum NMFS-SEFSC-415. pp. 78-79.

Provancha, J. A., C. R. Hall, and D. M. Oddy. 1992. Mosquito Lagoon Environmental Resources Inventory. NASA Technical Memorandum 107548, 121 pp. The Bionetics Corporation, Kennedy Space Center, FL, USA.

Provost, M.W. 2000. Mosquito Control Handbook: Faunal Zones of Florida. Florida Cooperative Extension Service, Institute of Food and Agricultural Sciences, University of Florida. Document ENY-700-2-1.

Pyzoha, J. E., T. J. Callahan, G. E. Sun, C. C. Trettin, and M. Masato. 2008. A conceptual hydrologic model for a forested Carolina bay depressional wetland on the Coastal Plain of South Carolina, USA. Hydrological Processes. 22 (14): 2689-2698.

Reif, J. S., M. M. Peden-Adams, T. A. Romano, C. D. Rice, P. A. Fair, and G. D. Bossart. 2009. Immune dysfunction in Atlantic Bottlenose Dolphins (*Tursiops truncatus*) with *Lobomycosis*. *Medical Mycology* 47(2):125-135.

Reynolds, J.E., III., and D. K. Odell. 1991. Manatees and Dugongs. Facts on File, New York, NY, 192 pp.

Reyier, E. A., D. H. Adams, and R. H. Lowers. 2008. First evidence of a high density nursery ground for the lemon shark, *Negaprion brevirostris*, near Cape Canaveral, Florida. *Florida Scientist* 71(2):134-48.

Reyier, E. A., R. H. Lowers, D. M. Scheidt and D. H. Adams. 2011. Movement patterns of adult red drum, *Sciaenops ocellatus*, in shallow Florida lagoons as inferred through autonomous acoustic telemetry. Environmental Biology of Fishes. In press. DOI 10.1007/s10641-010-9745-3.

Reyier, E.A. and J.M. Shenker. 2007. Ichthyoplankton community structure in a shallow subtropical estuary of the Florida Atlantic coast. *Bull. Mar. Sci.* 80:267-293.

Schaub, R. 2002. Coastal Change along the Merritt Island - Cape Canaveral Barrier Island Complex, Dynamac Corporation, Kennedy Space Center, FL. 2002. Third Biennial Mosquito Lagoon Conference of the U.S. Department of the Interior Fish and Wildlife Service Merritt Island National Wildlife Refuge and the National Park Service Canaveral National Seashore. August 6th and 7th, 2002. Titusville, FL.

Schaub, R., D. M. Scheidt, C. M. Garreau, and C. R. Hall. 2009. Quantitative assessment of seagrass scarring in the southeastern Mosquito Lagoon and Northern Indian River of Brevard and Volusia Counties, Florida. Submitted to U.S. Fish and Wildlife Service Contract No. GS10F0237R, Dynamac Corporation.

Scheidt, D. M., and C. M. Garreau. 2007. Identification of watercraft use patterns in Canaveral National Seashore. PMIS project # 1021131, activity # CANA-00049.

Scheidt, D. M., K. G. Holloway-Adkins, R. H. Lowers, M. Epstein, and D. Whitmore. 2002a. A 1991 Creel and Aerial Survey of the Mosquito Lagoon: The Quondam Study. Third Biennial Mosquito Lagoon Conference of the U.S. Department of the Interior Fish and Wildlife Service Merritt Island National Wildlife Refuge and the National Park Service Canaveral National Seashore. August 6th and 7th, 2002. Titusville, FL.

Scheidt, D. M., M. L. Legare, and M. Epstein. 2002b. Resource Use Characterization Study of Mosquito Lagoon within the Boundaries of the Merritt Island National Wildlife Refuge: Part 1- Preliminary Results from the Aerial Surveys. Third Biennial Mosquito Lagoon Conference of the U.S. Department of the Interior Fish and Wildlife Service Merritt Island National Wildlife Refuge and the National Park Service Canaveral National Seashore. August 6th and 7th, 2002. Titusville, FL.

Schmalzer, P. A., C. R. Hinkle, and C. Ross. 1985. NAS 1.26:197620, NASA-CR-197620 -A brief overview of plant communities and the status of selected plant species at John F. Kennedy Space Center, Florida. Kennedy Space Center, FL.

Schmalzer, P. A., and C. R. Hinkle. 1990. Geology, geohydrology, and soils of Kennedy Space Center: A Review. NASA Technical Memorandum 103813. The Bionetics Corporation, Kennedy Space Center, FL.

Schmalzer, P. A., M. A. Hensley, M. Mota, C.R. Hall, and C. A. Dunlevy. 2000. Soil, Groundwater, Surface Water, and Sediments of Kennedy Space Center Florida: Background Chemical and Physical Characteristics. NASA Technical Memorandum 2000-208583. Dynamac Corporation, Kennedy Space Center, FL.

Schmalzer, P. A., and T. E. Foster. 2005. Flora and threatened and endangered plants of Canaveral National Seashore. Final report to National Park Service. Dynamic Corporation, Kennedy Space Center, Florida.

Scott, T. M. 2001. The Geologic Map of Florida, Florida Geologic Survey Open File Report 80. 28pp.

Shane, S. H. 1983. Abundance, distribution, and movements of manatees (*Trichechus manatus*) in Brevard County, Florida. *Bulletin of Marine Science* 33(1): 1-9.

Sidman, C., T. Fik, R. Swett, B. Sargent, J. Fletcher, S. Fann, D. Fann, and A. Coffin. 2007. A Recreational Boating Characterization for Brevard County.

Siegel, R. A., and D. A. Pike. 2003. Continued studies on amphibians and reptiles of the Kennedy Space Center, Merritt Island National Wildlife Refuge and Canaveral National Seashore, September 2003. Annual Report. Department of Biological Sciences, Towson University, Towson, MD.

Seigel, R. A., and T. Crabill. 2006. Continued Studies on Amphibians and Reptiles of the Kennedy Space Center, Merritt Island National Wildlife Refuge and Canaveral National Seashore Annual Report. December 2006. Department of Biological Sciences Towson University, Towson, MD.

Sigua, G. C., and J. S. Steward. 2000. Water quality monitoring and biological integrity assessment in the Indian River Lagoon, Florida: Status, Trends and Loadings (1988-1994) *Environmental Management* 25:199-209.

Smith, N.P. 1993. Tidal and wind-driven transport between Indian River and Mosquito Lagoon. *Florida Scientist* 50, pp. 49-61.

Snelson F.F., Jr. and S.E. Williams. 1981. Notes on the occurrence, distribution, and biology of elasmobranch fishes in the Indian River Lagoon System, Florida. *Estuaries* 4, pp. 110-120.

Snelson F.F., Jr., S.E. Williams-Hooper, T. H. Schmid. 1988. Reproductive and ecology of the Atlantic stingray, *Dasyatis sabina*, in Florida coastal lagoons. *Copeia*, 3, pp. 729-739.

Snelson, F. F., Jr., S. E. Williams-Hooper, and T.H. Schmid. 1989. Biology of the bluntnose stingray, *Dasyatis sayi*, in Florida coastal lagoons. *Bulletin Marine Science* 45(1), pp.15-25.

Snelson, F.F. Jr., and M.R. Johnson. 1995. Epibenthic fish diversity in Mosquito Lagoon: A decade of relative stability. *Bulletin of Marine Science* 57(1), pp. 284-285.

Solomon, S., D. Qin, M. Manning, Z. Chen, M. Marquis, K. B. Averyt, M. Tignor, and H. L. Miller (eds.). Contribution of Working Group I to the Fourth Assessment Report of the Intergovernmental Panel on Climate Change. 2007. Cambridge University Press, Cambridge, United Kingdom and New York, NY.

Space Coast Audubon Society (SCAS). 2010a. Christmas Bird Counts. http://www.spacecoastaudubon.org/counts.html (accessed 23 November 2010).

Space Coast Audubon Society (SCAS). 2010b. Birding Hotspots. http://www.spacecoastaudubon.org/ (accessed 23 November 2010).

Steward, J. S., R. Virnstein, D. Haunert, and F. Lund. 1994. Surface water improvement and management (SWIM) plan for the Indian River Lagoon: Palatka, FL, St. Johns River Water Management District, and West Palm Beach, South Florida Water Management District.

Steward, J., R. Brockmeyer, P. Gostel, P. Sime, and A. J. Van. 2003. Indian River Lagoon surfacewater and management *(SWIM)* plan. March 2002 update. Palatka, & Miami, FL. St. Johns River Water Management District, & South Florida Water Management District.

Steward, J. S., R. W. Virnstein, L. J. Morris, and E. F. Lowe. 2005. Setting seagrass depth, coverage, and light targets for the Indian River Lagoon system, Florida. *Estuaries* 28:923-935.

Stiner, J. L., and L. J. Walters. 2006. Impacts of oyster reef architecture on species diversity and predation. *Journal of Shellfish Research* 25(2):778.

Stiner, J. L., and L. J. Walters. 2008. Effects of recreational boating on oyster reef architecture and species interactions. *Florida Scientist* 71(1):31-44.

Stiner, J. L. 2010a. Sea Turtle Nest Count Data (1985-2010). Unpublished. Canaveral National Seashore, Titusville, FL.

Stiner, J. L. 2010b. Canaveral National Seashore: Over 2000 Endangered Sea Turtles Rescued. InsideNPS. National Park Service (NPS) Intranet.

St. Johns River Water Management District (SJRWMD). 2009. Indian River Lagoon NEP 2009-2010 Workplan. IRLNEP, Palm Bay, FL. http://www.sjrwmd.com/itsyourlagoon/pdfs/2009-2010_IRL_NEP_Work_Plan.pdf (accessed 2 April 2010).

St. Johns River Water Management District (SJRWMD) and South Florida Water Management District (SFWMD). 1987. Indian River Lagoon Joint Reconnaissance Report. Submitted to Department of Environmental Regulation and OCRM/NOAA. Contract No. CM-137.

St. Johns River Water Management District (SJRWMD). 2008. Indian River Lagoon Comprehensive Conservation and Management Plan Update 2008. Indian River Lagoon National Estuary Program (IRL NEP) SJRWMD, Palm Bay FL.

Szell, G. P. 1993. Aquifer characteristics in the St. Johns River Water Management District, Florida. SJRWMD Technical Publication SJ93-1. 500p.

Tetra Tech. 2000. Three-Dimensional Hydrodynamic and Water Quality Model of Peconic Estuary, Final Report to the Peconic Bay National Estuary Program.

Tetra Tech. 2005. Development of the Hydrodynamic and Water Quality Models for the Savannah Harbor Expansion Project. Final Report prepared for USACE – Savannah District. 101p.

Tetra Tech. 2007. The Environmental Fluid Dynamics Code Theory and Computation Volume1: Hydrodynamics and Mass Transport. 61p.

Toth, D. J. 1987. Hydrogeology: Indian River Lagoon Joint Reconnaissance Report. St. Johns River Water Management District, South Florida Water Management District. Contract No. CM-137.

Trefry, J. H., D. W. Woodall, and R. P. Trocine. 2005. Types and sources of suspended matter blocking light required for seagrass in the Indian River Lagoon. Final Report to the St. Johns Water Management District for Contract SG463AA. Florida Institute of Technology, Melbourne, FL, USA.

Trefry, J. H., R. P. Trocine, and D. W. Woodall. 2007. Turbidity constituents, sources and effects on light attenuation in Mosquito Lagoon. Final Report to the St. Johns Water Management District for Contract SJ47512. Florida Institute of Technology, Melbourne, FL.

Tremain, D.M. and D.H. Adams. 1995. Seasonal variations in species diversity, abundance, and composition of fish communities in the northern Indian River Lagoon, Florida. Bulletin of Marine Science, 57, 171-192.

Tremain, D.M, W. Harnden, and D.H. Adams. 2004. Multidirectional movements of sportfish species between an estuarine no-take zone and surrounding waters of the Indian River Lagoon, Florida. *Fishery Bulletin* 102, 533-544.

University of Central Florida (UCF). 2010. Create Climate-Change Sensitive Model to Understand Larval Hydrodynamics of Imperiled Oysters (2010-2012). Research at UCF, Orlando FL. https://argis.research.ucf.edu/index.cfm?fuseaction=detail.view_proposal_detail&rec_id=1051274&rec_type=research (accessed 17 January 2011).

U.S. Department of Agriculture (USDA). 1974. Soil Survey of Brevard County, Florida (Soil Survey Staff 1974). U.S. Department of Agriculture Soil Conservation Service.

U.S. Department of Agriculture (USDA), Soil Conservation Service. 1980. National Cooperative Soil Survey. Soil Survey of Volusia County, Florida. U.S. Department of Agriculture Soil Conservation Service in cooperation with the University of Florida Institute of Food and Agricultural Sciences. 205 p.

U. S. Army Corps of Engineers-Jacksonville District (ACOE). 1975. Duval County Beaches, Florida general design memorandum: Jacksonville. Department of the Army, Jacksonville District, Corps of Engineers, Jacksonville, FL.

U. S. Army Corps of Engineer-Jacksonville District (ACOE). 1990a. Duval County, Florida shore protection project reevaluation study: Jacksonville, Department of the Army, Jacksonville District, Corps of Engineers, 56 pp.

U. S. Army Corps of Engineer-Jacksonville District (ACOE). 1990b. St. Johns County, Florida beach erosion control project: Special report, St. Augustine Beach nourishment: Jacksonville, Department of the Army, Jacksonville District, Corps of Engineers, 58 pp.

U. S. Army Corps of Engineer-Jacksonville District (ACOE). 1998. St. Johns County, Florida shore protection project: General reevaluation report with final environmental assessment: Jacksonville, Department of the Army, Jacksonville District, Corps of Engineers, 81 pp.

U.S. Army Corp of Engineers (ACOE). 2007. FL Shore Protection and Sea Turtle Management System-Volusia County Loggerhead Nesting for Canaveral National Seashore 1979-2005. http://el.erdc.usace.army.mil/flshore/data.cfm?County=Volusia&Location=Canaveral%20National%20Seashore (accessed 17 November 2010).

U. S. Coast Guard (USCG). 2006. Area Contingency Plan for Northeast and Eastern Central Florida. August 2006 Revision Northeast and Eastern Central Florida Area Planning Committee. Jacksonville, FL. http://ocean.floridamarine.org/ACP/jaxacp/index.html (accessed 3 December 2010).

U.S. Environmental Protection Agency (EPA). 1986. Ambient water quality criteria for bacteria – 1986. Washington, D.C., Report Number440/5-84-002.

U.S. Environmental Protection Agency (EPA). 2001. National Coastal Condition Report. Chapter 4. Southeast Coastal Condition. EPA-620/R-01/005. p 95.

U.S. Environmental Protection Agency (EPA) 2003. Horseshoe crabs: living fossils in peril? *in*: Information about Estuaries and Near Coastal Waters, Coastlines April 2003, Issue 13.2.

U.S. Environmental Protection Agency (EPA). 2008. National Coastal Condition Report III Chapter 4: Southeast Coast Coastal Condition Part 2 of 2. pp.115–130. U.S. Environmental Protection Agency, Office of Research and Development and Office of Water, Washington, D.C.

U.S. Environmental Protection Agency (EPA). 2010. Indian River Lagoon National Estuary Program Fiscal Year 2009 – 2010 Workbook. The Indian River Lagoon National Estuary Program, 525 Community College Blvd. SE, Palm Bay, FL 32909.

U.S. Fish and Wildlife Service (USFWS). 2001. Florida Manatee Recovery Plan, *Trichechus manatus latirostris*, Third Revision. U.S. Fish and Wildlife Service. Atlanta, Georgia. 144 pp. + appendices.

U.S. Fish and Wildlife Service (USFWS). 2008. Southeastern Beach Mouse (*Peromyscus polionotus niveiventris*) 5 Year Review: Summary and Evaluation. USFWS Jacksonville Ecological Services Field Office, Southeast Region, Jacksonville, FL.

U.S. Geological Survey (USGS). 2005. Open File Report, 2005-1326. The national assessment of shoreline change: A GIS Compilation of Vector Shorelines and Associated Shoreline Changes for the U.S. Southeast Atlantic Coast, http://pubs.usgs.gov/of/20005/1326

Utilities Commission of New Smyrna Beach. 2010. Wastewater. http://www.ucnsb.net/water/wastewater.aspx (accessed 20 February 2010).

Walters, L., A. Roman, J. Stiner, and D. Weeks. 2001. Water Resources Plan, National Seashore. U.S. http://www.nature.nps.gov/water/management_plans/cana_final_screen.pdf (accessed 8 June 2007).

Walters, L., P. Sacks, L. Wall, J. Grevert, D. LeJeune, S. Fischer, and A. Simpson. 2003. Declining intertidal oyster reefs in Florida: Direct and indirect impacts of boat wakes. *Journal of Shellfish Research* 22(1):359-60.

Walters, L., E. Hoffman, and C. Calestani. 2007. Tracking M*ytella charruana*: A New Invasive Bivalve in the Indian River Lagoon System.

Walters, L. J., P. E. Sacks, M. Y. Bobo, D. L. Richardson, and L. D. Coen. 2007. Impact of hurricanes and boat wakes on intertidal oyster reefs in the Indian River Lagoon: Reef profiles and disease prevalence. *Florida Scientist* 70:506-521.

Wall, L. M., L. J. Walters, R. E. Grizzle, and P. E. Sacks. 2005. Recreational boating activity and its impact on the recruitment and survival of the oyster *Crassostrea virginica* on intertidal reefs in Mosquito Lagoon, Florida. *Journal of Shellfish Research* 24: 965-973.

Williams, A. B. 1984. Shrimps, lobsters, and crabs of the Atlantic coast of the eastern United States, Maine to Florida. Smithsonian Institution Press, Washington, DC. 550 pp.

Windsor, J. W. 1988. A Review of Water Quality and Sediment Chemistry with an Historical Perspective. Unpublished.

Winkler, S., and A. Ceric. 2006. 2004 status and trends in water quality at selected sites in the St. Johns River Water Management District. Technical publication no. SJ2006-6, pp. 50-54. Palatka, FL. St. Johns River Water Management District.

Witherington, B. E., and R. E. Martin. 1996. Understanding, assessing, and resolving light-pollution problems on sea turtle nesting beaches. Florida Marine Research Institute Technical Report TR-2.73p.

Witherington, B. E., P. Kubilis, B. Brost, and A. Meylan. 2009. Decreasing annual nest counts in a globally important loggerhead sea turtle population. *Ecological Applications* 19 (1), 2009, pp. 30–54. The Ecological Society of America.

Woodward-Clyde Consultants. 1994a. Uses of the Indian River Lagoon. Indian River Lagoon National Estuary Program Project Number 92F274C.

Woodward-Clyde Consultants. 1994b. Status and Trends Summary of the Indian River Lagoon. Indian River Lagoon National Estuary Program Project Number 92F274C.

Woodward-Clyde Consultants. 1994c. Physical Features of the Indian River Lagoon. Indian River Lagoon National Estuary Program Project Number 92F274C.

Woodward-Clyde Consultants. 1994d. Loadings Assessment of the Indian River Lagoon. Indian River Lagoon National Estuary Program Project Number 92F274C.

Woodward-Clyde Consultants. 1994e. Preliminary Water and Sediment Quality Assessment of the Indian River Lagoon. National Estuary Program Project 92F274C. National Estuary Program, Melbourne, FL.

Woodward-Clyde Consultants. 1994f. Historical Imagery Inventory and Seagrass Assessment, Indian River Lagoon. National Estuary Program Project 92F274C. National Estuary Program, Melbourne, FL.

Wright, L. D., and D. Short. 1984. Morphodynamic Visibility of Surfzones and Beaches a Synthesis. Marine Geology. Volume 56. *Elevsier Science*, B.V., Amsterdam, The Netherlands, 93-118 pp.

Zarillo, G. A. 1997. Three-Dimensional Modeling of Circulation and Flushing in the German Wadden Sea, GKSS Research Center, Geesthacth, Germany. 45p.

Zarillo, G. A. 2003. Salinity Distribution and Flow Management Studies: A Three Dimensional Model of the Lake Worth Lagoon, FL, South Florida Water Management District, 70p.

Zarillo, G. A. 2004. Final Report: EFDC/HEM3D Hydrodynamic and Water Quality Model of the Loxahatchee River and Estuary. Prepared for: Tetra Tech, Inc., Tallahassee, FL.

Zarillo, G.A. and J., Bishop. 2009. Sub-Bottom Seismic Survey Report: Offshore Sand Borrow Site Assessment St. Johns County, FL. PBS&J, Inc., Coastal & Waterways Division, Tampa, FL.

Zarillo, G. A. and T. S. Bacchus. 1992. Application of Seismic Methods to Sand Source Studies for Beach Nourishment. *in:* Handbook of Geophysical Exploration at ASEA. CRC Press. Boca Raton, FL. pp. 241-258.

Zarillo, G. A. and C. R. Surak. 1994. Indian River Lagoon/Turkey Creek Hydrodynamics and Salinity Model. Final Report to the St. Johns River Water Management District. 145pp.

Zarillo, G. A., T. V., Belanger, K. A. Zarillo, J. Rosario-Llantin, and D. McGinnis. 2010. (*In review*) The Development of a Hydrologic Model of Mosquito Lagoon in Canaveral National Seashore Contract No. N5180070017. Natural Resource Report. National Park Service, Fort Collins, Colorado.

Zarillo, G. A., Zarillo, K.A., Reidenauer, J.A., Reyier, E. A., Shinskey, T., Barkaszi, M.J., Shenker, J.M., Verdugo, M., and N. Hodges, 2009. Final Biological Characterization and Numerical Wave Model Analysis within Borrow Sites Offshore of Florida's Northeast Coast Report-Volume I: Main Text 286 pp. + Volume II: Appendices A-D 448 pp. Contract No. 1435-01-05-CT-39075-M05PC00005 MMS Study 2008-060.

Zieman, J. C. 1982. Food webs in tropical seagrass systems. Report of a Workshop Held at the West Indies Laboratory, St. Croix, U.S. Virgin Islands. May 1982. UNESCO Reports in *Marine Science*. Paris 23: 80-86.

Zimmerman, C. F., J. R. Montgomery, and P. R. Carlson. 1985. Variability of dissolved reactive phosphate flux rates in nearshore estuarine sediments: Effects of Groundwater Flow. *Estuaries* 8(2B):228-236.

Appendix. Land Cover Class Descriptions and Soil Types

Table A1. Land cover classes and descriptions from Duncan et al. (2004).

LU Codes	Landcover Class	Description
1000	Urban/Development	Commercial, industrial, residential, and transportation.
2000	Agriculture/Rangeland	Crops, groves, improved and unimproved pasture, rangeland, and conifer plantations.
3200	Coastal Strand	Herbaceous, coastal dunes vegetation dominated by sea oats and shrub coastal strand vegetation with saw palmetto, sea grape, and
4100	Flatwoods	Scrubby, mesic, and hydric flatwoods with longleaf, slash, or pond pine. Includes palmetto prairie with a saw palmetto-herb layer but no
4200	Scrub	Xeric oak shrub vegetation with no or minimal pine canopy.
4300	Hammocks	Temperate and tropical hardwoods, mixed hardwood-conifer, pine-mesic oak, and cabbage palm forests.
4400	Disturbed Uplands	Wax myrtle, mixed and other hardwoods, oak-hickory-pine, shrub and brush, and dead trees on upland sites.
5100	Waterways/Reservoirs	Streams, drainage canals, lakes, reservoirs, and open water in freshwater marshes.
5400	Estuarine Water	Water of the lagoon and salt-water ponds in salt marsh.
5710	Ocean	Atlantic Ocean
6100	Forested Wetlands	Wetland hardwoods, cypress swamps, dwarf cypress, southern red cedar, bottomland swamps, and mixed wetland forests.
6120	Mangrove	Black, white, and red mangroves with halophytes and salt marsh grasses.
6104	Prairie Hammocks - Palm Hammocks	Tall cluster of cabbage palms and live oaks in the middle of and on the borders of wet prairie and marsh communities.
6250	Hydric Pine flatwoods	Forest with a sparse to moderate canopy of Slash pine. The under-story is grasses, wiregrass, forbs, and at times with sparse saw
6400	Freshwater Marsh	Freshwater marsh, wet prairie, inland ponds and sloughs, and emergent aquatic vegetation.
6420	Salt Marsh	Salt marsh and tidal flats including halophytes, saltgrass, sand cordgrass, and black rush.
6460	Disturbed Estuarine Wetlands	Estuarine shrubs, wax myrtle, groundsel, and Brazilian pepper, in former salt marsh.
6470	Disturbed Freshwater Wetlands	Disturbed freshwater marshes, wet prairies, and wetland shrubs.
7100	Sand/Barren Land	Shorelines, beaches, and other sand.
7400	Spoil	Borrow and fill, spoil, dikes, and other disturbed areas.
8000	Invasive/Exotic	Brazilian pepper, Australian pine, and Melaleuca.

Table A2. Land cover classes and soil types associated with the habitat based on categories described by Duncan et al. (2004) and descriptions in soil surveys (USDA 1974, 1977).

LU Codes	Row Labels	Sum of CALCACRES
1000	**Urban/Developed**	**57**
	Canaveral-Urban land complex	57
3200	**Coastal strand**	**381**
	Beaches	381
4100	**Flatwoods**	**6,865**
	Astatula fine sand, 0 to 8 percent slopes	313
	Canaveral sand, 0 to 5 percent slopes	644
	Canaveral-Anclote complex, gently undulating	41
	Candler fine sand	131
	Cocoa sand	342
	Cocoa sand, 0 to 5 percent slopes	48
	Daytona sand, 0 to 5 percent slopes	332
	Immokalee sand	1,846
	Myakka fine sand	162
	Orsino fine sand	67
	Palm Beach sand	556
	Palm Beach sand, 2 to 8 percent slopes	874
	Palm Beach-Paola association, 2 to 8 percent slopes	70
	Paola fine sand, 0 to 5 percent slopes	593
	Paola fine sand, 0 to 8 percent slopes	451
	Pomello sand	280
	Quartzipsamments, smoothed	9
	Tavares fine sand	32
	Tavares fine sand, 0 to 5 percent slopes	21
	Wabasso fine sand	44
	Paola Fine Sand	9
4200	**Scrub**	**1,645**
	Myakka sand	1,645
5400	**Estuarine**	**30,916**
	Water	15,383
5710	Waters of the Atlantic Ocean	15,533
6100	**Forested wetland**	**445**
	Anclote sand	109
	Copeland-Bradenton-Wabasso complex, limestone substratum	283
	Delray sand, occasionally flooded	17
	Riviera sand	36
	St. Johns sand	17
6104	**Hammock (hydric- prairie)**	**128**
	Bulow sand, 0 to 5 percent slopes	59
	Myakka variant fine sand	51
	Tuscawilla fine sand	3
	Wabasso sand	15
6120	**Mangrove**	**3,842**
	Hydraquents	3,842

Table A2. Land cover classes and soil types associated with the habitat based on categories described by Duncan et al. (2004) and descriptions in soil surveys (USDA 1974, 1977) (continued).

LU Codes	Row Labels	Sum of CALCACRES
6250	**Flatwoods wet**	**530**
	Basinger sand	124
	Pineda fine sand	27
	Placid fine sand, depressional	87
	Pompano fine sand	275
6400	**Freshwater marsh**	**910**
	Anclote sand, depressional	30
	Anclote sand, frequently flooded	307
	Basinger sand, depressional	24
	Pompano sand	14
	Pompano-Placid complex	527
	St. Johns sand, depressional	9
6420	**Salt marsh**	**4,462**
	Bessie muck, tidal	4
	Turnbull and Riomar soils, tidal	4,110
	Turnbull muck	348
	Spoil	**532**
7400	Arents, moderately wet	133
	Turnbull variant sand	398
	Grand Total	**57,733**

The Department of the Interior protects and manages the nation's natural resources and cultural heritage; provides scientific and other information about those resources; and honors its special responsibilities to American Indians, Alaska Natives, and affiliated Island Communities.

NPS 639/114663, June 2012